Empire, State, and Society

Titles of Related Interest from Wiley-Blackwell

Early Modern England 1485–1714: A Narrative History
Second Edition
Robert Bucholz & Newton Key

Sources and Debates in English History: 1485–1714
Second Edition
Edited by Newton Key & Robert Bucholz

Imperial Island: A History of Britain and Its Empire, 1660–1837
Paul Kléber Monod

A History of Modern Britain: 1714 to the Present
Ellis Wasson

Sources and Debates in Modern British History: 1714 to the Present
Edited by Ellis Wasson

Empire, State, and Society

Britain Since 1830

Jamie L. Bronstein and Andrew T. Harris

WILEY-BLACKWELL

A John Wiley & Sons, Ltd., Publication

Blackwell Publishing was acquired by John Wiley & Sons in February 2007. Blackwell's publishing program has been merged with Wiley's global Scientific, Technical, and Medical business to form Wiley-Blackwell.

Registered Office
John Wiley & Sons Ltd, The Atrium, Southern Gate, Chichester, West Sussex, PO19 8SQ, UK

Editorial Offices
350 Main Street, Malden, MA 02148-5020, USA
9600 Garsington Road, Oxford, OX4 2DQ, UK
The Atrium, Southern Gate, Chichester, West Sussex, PO19 8SQ, UK

For details of our global editorial offices, for customer services, and for information about how to apply for permission to reuse the copyright material in this book please see our website at www.wiley.com/wiley-blackwell.

Library of Congress Cataloging-in-Publication Data
Bronstein, Jamie L., 1968–
    Empire, state, and society : Britain since 1830 / Jamie L. Bronstein and Andrew T. Harris. – 1st ed.
        p. cm.
    Includes index.
    ISBN 978-1-4051-8181-5 (cloth) – ISBN 978-1-4051-8180-8 (pbk.)   1. Great Britain–History–19th century.   2. Great Britain–History–20th century.   I. Harris, Andrew T. (Andrew Todd), 1968-   II. Title.
    DA530.B75 2012
    941.08–dc23
                                                                                                2011033730

A catalogue record for this book is available from the British Library.

Set in 11/13pt Dante by Aptara Inc., New Delhi, India

Printed in Singapore by Ho Printing Singapore Pte Ltd

First Impression   2012

Contents

List of Illustrations

Figures

Maps

Acknowledgments

Both authors wish to acknowledge and express gratitude to Peter Stansky, who guided us through the pleasures of modern British historiography in graduate school. Tessa Harvey and her colleagues at Wiley-Blackwell proved adept, constructive and flexible editors. The three anonymous reviewers of the final manuscript corrected many mistakes, and we take responsibility for any that remain.

Andrew Harris thanks his students at Bridgewater State University for their curiosity and excitement about that other England new to them, for many wonderful conversations, and for the opportunity to think through some of the ideas incorporated here. His colleagues in the history department and the university offered stimulating and supportive collegiality, especially Ann Brunjes, who has been close friend, colleague, co-teacher and conscience. Howard London and Dana Mohler-Faria supported work on this project while the author undertook administrative positions in their respective offices, and Ron Pitt has been friend and mentor extraordinaire. Bob Woods first showed how historical study could be rigorous, exacting and fulfilling as a temperament as well as a discipline. Deepest gratitude goes to Ted and Gilda Harris, and to Laurie and Eli, without whose love and support such an undertaking would have been impossible.

Jamie Bronstein would like to thank colleagues and friends who made helpful suggestions or read chapters of the manuscript, including Ken Hammond, Chad Martin, Andrew Muldoon, Dawn Rafferty, and Mark Walker. She would also like to thank the students in her classes at New Mexico State University, who provided a sounding-board for many of the ideas that were incorporated into these chapters. Finally, she would like to acknowledge Mike Zigmond, who read chapters, made suggestions, and participated in many one-sided conversations about nineteenth- and twentieth-century Britain, with great patience and humor; and Evan Zigmond, for being an unending source of comic relief.

Empire, State, and Society: Britain Since 1830, First Edition. Jamie L. Bronstein and Andrew T. Harris.
© 2012 Jamie L. Bronstein and Andrew T. Harris. Published 2012 by John Wiley & Sons, Ltd.

Introduction

Why write a history of modern Britain? In the nineteenth century, Great Britain was the world's recognized superpower, with a daunting formal empire, networks of trade and investment outside its empire, and a formidable military. The geographical extent of British power was rivaled only by the opinion that the British had of themselves: as first in industry, first in culture, first in democratic institutions. By the twentieth century many of these points of pride had proven transitory. The story of British expansion and contraction is a rich and complex tale for the Western industrialized world. Whether it is also a cautionary tale will depend on one's politics as much as the historical record.

For American students of history in particular, British history continues to hold great interest. Britain is, after all, one of North America's distinguished ancestors, the source of many of its juridical and political institutions, its historically dominant language, and much of its literature and culture. In the twenty-first century, Britain remains one of America's staunchest allies, the fruits of the "special relationship" which developed during the Second World War. American students remain fascinated by modern British culture: the Beatles and the Rolling Stones, the royals and Monty Python, England's green and pleasant land, literary period dramas via BBC America, and the general "historicity" of an older society.

Modern British history reveals as much by its departures as its similarities. How was an abolitionist movement different in a country that contemplated no domestic institution of slavery? How did oversight of a vast and diverse empire interact with the formation of racial identities at home? How did demographic patterns and the environmental impact differ when industrialization took place on a small island rather than a large continent? The United States is often considered a country in which considerations of "class" have been irrelevant and white men were enfranchised from the 1820s onward. How then did workers' experience

Empire, State, and Society: Britain Since 1830, First Edition. Jamie L. Bronstein and Andrew T. Harris.
© 2012 Jamie L. Bronstein and Andrew T. Harris. Published 2012 by John Wiley & Sons, Ltd.

differ in a more hierarchical society in which they were specifically deprived of, and struggled for, the vote? Britain two centuries ago continues to fascinate because it was a country grappling with modernity in a language that we share, but with beguiling and dissimilar problems. The people who populated that world are enough like us to be accessible and yet different enough to raise fascinating historical questions.

The field of modern British history has undergone a transformation in the past generation. There is more material available than ever from which to draw – thick description about political culture, about the multifaceted experiences of people within Britain and within its empire, about the nature of national and regional identity. Long cognizant of class, historians have come to appreciate that a modern story of British culture cannot be told without weaving gender and race throughout the narrative rather than relegating them to boutique chapters. The story of empire took place not only in the seat of government at Whitehall and in the colonies themselves, but also impacted the lived experiences of ordinary Britons and influenced how they interacted with their state. Recent historical writing has broadened what we know about religion, gender, science and technology, transatlantic movements of ideas and people, and the interaction between people and their environment. We have tried to integrate these into a meaningful narrative from which students and faculty can derive both a coherent story and useful points of further exploration.

Empire, State, and Society proceeds chronologically and thematically. Within each broad time period we have divided material into separate chapters on politics, on society and economics, and on intellectual beliefs and cultural forms, varying between two and three chapters in each period according to the historical coherence of the resulting narrative. In the twentieth century the two world wars so demarcate their age that each receives a comprehensive chapter.

In contrast with the United States, where a weak federal system diffused power, Britain had a strong locus of power in Parliament – but it was far from being the only important site of power. Thus, our political narrative includes not only ministerial changes and Acts of Parliament, but also foreign affairs, political culture, the changing nature and institutions of local government, the relationship between Britain and various colonies, and notable shifts of emphasis within Britain's own regions. Looking broadly at political culture enables us to address larger interpretive questions: Was Britain relatively calm in the mid-nineteenth century because struggles to define nationhood or to retrench economically could be absorbed by the Empire? To what extent was Britain in the late twentieth century torn between its roles as special friend of the United States and as leader of a new European coalition? Our treatment of each period's social and economic history also engages the changing nature of class, families, work and leisure, of leisure culture and people's interaction with their changing environment and with the law, and of the different experiences of women and children and immigrants, providing readers with a rich appreciation of what it felt like to live through the period in question.

We also explore the intellectual and cultural reactions to and sensibilities within each period. How did the British think about and understand the paths they took through Utilitarianism, Evangelicalism, science, religion, and socialism? How did they construct or respond to modern art, Fabianism, decolonization, or economics? How did they generate ideas, how did they create cultural norms, and how did they criticize the assumptions of their own times?

This work begins in 1830, which does not align precisely with the commencement or conclusion of any major historical epoch. The Napoleonic Wars ended in 1815; the industrial revolution started much earlier and continued into the nineteenth century; Victoria's reign began in 1837; the first great Reform Act was not passed until 1832. This frees the book from having to begin with the beginning of an actual event, which is just as conceptually challenging as beginning in the middle. Chapter 1 lays the groundwork for both the structures of British society and politics in 1830, and provides a brief overview of the history leading up to our beginning. Readers interested in further exploration of the period before may wish to consult the excellent volume preceding ours in this informal series, *Imperial Island*, by Paul Kleber Monod.

1

Britain to 1830

In 1830, King George IV died and was succeeded by his brother the Duke of Clarence, who became William IV. William's rule was short – only seven years, and was flanked by powerful royal personalities both before and after. George IV (r. 1820–1830) had been a wonderfully disliked philanderer and decadent dandy. Queen Victoria's rule (1837–1903) spanned over six decades and represented the highest point of British industrial and imperial strength. Yet in his apparently timeless ceremonial coronation as king of Great Britain, William reminds us just how paradoxically new the kingdom of Great Britain really was. In 1830, it had existed only 30 years.

Great Britain signified an area of land encompassing one large island off the northwest coast of Europe, a smaller island further west (Ireland), and a host of still smaller islands scattered nearby (the Orkneys and Shetlands to the north, the Hebrides to the northwest, the Isle of Man to the west, and the Isle of Wight due south, among others). The total land mass was just over 120,000 square miles: slightly larger than the combined New England states, less than half the size of Texas, smaller even than France or modern Germany. Great Britain was neither geographically coherent nor, as a nation, very old, having been created by unifying Ireland with England, Wales and Scotland by legislative act in 1800. Scotland itself had been similarly united with England and Wales in 1707, and Wales in 1536. The United Kingdom in 1830 was thus already a state that had been absorbing its neighbors for three centuries.

Even in 1830, Great Britain was more than the sum of these small islands in the North Atlantic. In terms of population, the British Empire theoretically encompassed over one-fifth of all the world's inhabitants in 1815 – and this was even *after* the loss of 13 of the American colonies. What then did it mean to be "British" in 1830? Who governed Britain? Who worked, who spent, and how

Empire, State, and Society: Britain Since 1830, First Edition. Jamie L. Bronstein and Andrew T. Harris.
© 2012 Jamie L. Bronstein and Andrew T. Harris. Published 2012 by John Wiley & Sons, Ltd.

did people live? This chapter attempts both a static picture of the governance, landscapes, and societies of Britain in 1830, as well as an exploration of the many changes in politics, economic production, and ideas in the decades leading up to William's coronation.

Geography

The defining feature of British geography as a set of islands navigable by internal rivers and canals is its proximity to and reliance upon water. Water protected Britain from European conquest in this period: the most recent successful invasion from Europe had occurred in the Middle Ages.[1] Separation by 30 miles of water from continental Europe encouraged the British, perhaps more than most people, to explain their temperament with reference to accidents of geography. They saw themselves as different from Europeans in spirit, in culture, and in politics. One cannot read too much into this assertion of difference, since Britons also traveled abroad, had extensive commercial relations with European states, sometimes sent their children to be educated abroad, and had numerous cultural connections and exchanges across the English Channel, and across many other bodies of water besides. That they *saw* themselves as different is more telling than the possibility of difference itself.

The British Isles possessed a long coastline and many port cities. With extensive internal waterways, enhanced by eighteenth-century canal building, this meant ease of access to water transport – and transport by water was, in the age before railways, always less expensive and faster than transit over land. No point in Britain is more than 70 miles from the ocean, and most are far less distant from major rivers and canals.

Britain has extensive variations in its landscape. The North of England, north of a rough and imaginary line from Durham to Exeter, is relatively mountainous, rainy (over 40 inches a year), and less agriculturally productive than the South, due to the rockier soil. It is also where much of the mineral wealth resides: the iron, coal, tin, clay, lead, and copper that have been crucial to modern industrial development.

South of this imaginary line, the land is more gently rolling, with less but still considerable rainfall, enough to make portions of it still essentially swampland in the eighteenth century. Better drainage techniques had by then already begun converting these boggy areas into cultivable farmland. Wales and Scotland are more mountainous, and Scotland consists of both rocky highlands and hilly, agriculturally fertile lowlands. In both Wales and Scotland by the early nineteenth century, geography had influenced settlement patterns: population concentrated in coastal areas, in valleys, or on plateaus. Separated from Britain by water in some areas wider than the English Channel, Ireland has fewer large mountain ranges and

Key

The following counties are abbreviated:
Bucks = Buckinghamshire
Beds = Bedfordshire
Herts = Hertfordshire
Hunts = Huntingdonshire
Notts = Nottinghamshire

Map 1.1 Counties of Great Britain and Ireland in 1830.
Source: Paul Kléber Monod, *Imperial Island: A History of Britain and Its Empire, 1660–1837* (Oxford: Wiley-Blackwell, 2009).

more rain than most of Britain. Its temperature range is even milder than that of southern England, with warmer winters and cooler summers.

Britain's climate is unusually moderate given how far north most of Britain actually lies – Britain's latitude is about the same as Calgary in western Canada. In fact, warm air from ocean currents coming out of the Caribbean generally gives Britain a milder climate than many northerly continental European countries. This could lead to metaphorical overexertion, as an enthusiastic poet of the 1780s endowed Britain's climate with powerful attributes:

> Thy Seasons moderate as thy Laws appear,
> Thy Constitution wholesome as the year:
> Well pois'd, and pregnant in thy annual Round
> With Wisdom, where no fierce Extreme is found.[2]

Whether Britain owed moderate, wholesome, well-poised, or wise government to its weather is a fine point on which scholars may disagree, but the moderate climate certainly meant long growing seasons, mild winters and relatively cool summers.

Governance and Political Culture

Although in theory Great Britain was ruled by a monarch who headed the executive branch of national government, the governing structures had several layers with power diffused among them. To contemporaries British government presented several paradoxes: a strong state with a weak and limited monarchy; a ruling oligarchy that nevertheless paid lip service to public opinion; a nation that prided itself on a wide range of political and civil freedoms, yet was still in 1830 anything but democratic. Historians have called Britain since 1689 a "constitutional monarchy," yet there is no written constitution to be found, rather a set of political practices with legislative and customary boundaries of action.

Great Britain's national government consisted of the monarch and two legislative bodies making up Parliament: the House of Lords and House of Commons. The monarchy's powers had been dramatically reduced in the seventeenth century, and its range of operations came to rely on consensus. In 1830 the monarch needed parliamentary approval for all expenditure, which placed significant limitations on the ability to conduct foreign and military affairs freely. Only Parliament had the power to tax. The monarch appointed the Prime Minister, whose mission was to manage the crown's affairs in Parliament; but in practice, a Prime Minister could only govern if he could attract a majority of votes for key government legislation. And less formally, Parliament had made clear in the previous century that in times of extraordinary political instability, it could even presume to decide who would be the next king or queen.

Other areas of authority were implied: no monarch had vetoed legislation since Queen Anne in the early eighteenth century, though it was still theoretically possible to do so. The crown appointed new peers, which gave it influence over the House of Lords. The crown also controlled and appointed offices throughout the executive branch, including the civil service and armed forces, and granted all royal pardons (the only kind there were). Finally, the crown could dismiss a Prime Minister fallen out of favor, but still had to work through Parliament for fiscal resources. King and Parliament worked together, and though there were fears of *growing* executive power as late as the 1770s, the crown was by then quite circumscribed in what it could accomplish on its own.

The House of Lords comprised a varying number of hereditary peers, 26 bishops, and two archbishops. Peers inherited their titles of (in order of descending rank) Duke, Marquis, Earl, Viscount, and Baron.[3] To be a peer allowed but did not require one's attendance to government business in the House of Lords, so there was no absolute number of seats in that body; it depended on how many chose to participate at a given time. Some 360 peers voted on one of the most significant pieces of legislation in the 1830s, but most of the time far fewer sat in deliberation. The Lords often represented politically and socially conservative positions throughout the nineteenth and twentieth centuries, which meant that at many key points they could delay or obstruct legislation proposed by more liberal governments.

The House of Commons served as the more representative body, though it was representative only in an abstract and tenuous sense. Its 658 members represented the people of Great Britain "virtually." This meant in its eighteenth-century context that members of the Commons (or MPs, for Members of Parliament, a misnomer as nobody called a peer by that abbreviation) embodied all the different perspectives of the British people without actually being accountable to or elected by most of them. Indeed, contemporary politicians often boasted of their independence of electoral influence. Lord North claimed in 1784 – in Parliament – that members did not represent constituencies at all:

> To surrender their judgments, to abandon their own opinions, and to act as their constituents thought proper to instruct them, right or wrong, is to act unconstitutionally . . . They were not sent there . . . to represent a particular province or district, and to take care of the particular interest of that province; they were sent there as trustees, to act for the benefit and advantage of the whole kingdom. (Quoted in Briggs 1965: 98)

This was one position among several, however, as members often brought forward locally relevant legislation and acted on behalf of regional, local, and even personal interests.

Of the 658 total members, 489 held English seats; Scotland elected 45, Wales elected 24, and Ireland elected 100. English members came from counties (each of 40 counties returning two members), boroughs (ranging in size and legitimacy from cities and towns to deserted marsh, as in the case of Old Sarum which had no inhabitants at all, its residents having left for Salisbury centuries before due to bad drainage), and the universities of Oxford and Cambridge, each of which returned two members.

Voting rights were a patchwork in Britain before 1832. Generally, county residents paying 40 shillings per year in rent were eligible to vote. In some boroughs, nearly all taxpayers could vote; some were called "pot-wallopers" because anyone owning a pot in which to boil water could vote; in others, adult men earned the "freedom" of the borough and the right to vote there whether resident or not. On the other end of the spectrum, some borough seats were owned outright by individuals of wealth who sold seats to those sharing their sympathies and willing to pay. Nor was this last practice particularly secret; until 1807 such seats were still publicly advertised in newspapers. Many urban areas that had seen considerable population growth in the previous century had no representation at all until 1832.

Who served in the Commons? While it was an elected body, great landholders still dominated politics in the early nineteenth century, controlling the House of Lords, exercising direct influence over some two-thirds of all seats in the House of Commons, and serving in Cabinet posts. In urban constituencies, though, with less local influence deriving from landownership, this may have been less the case. In constituencies in London or Yorkshire, the "middling sort" might make their voices heard.

Nonvoters were not completely excluded from political participation. Through municipal politics, petitioning movements, voluntary associations, or the ability to finance (or withhold from financing) government debt, the middling sort had growing informal political influence that reformers increasingly sought to transform into a formal political role from the 1770s forward. In 1832 they achieved some measure of success. Locally, in areas such as poor law policy, policing, and parish government, even those without property at all could participate. In contested Parliamentary elections, the people arrayed in their numbers were essential: to raise their hands to nominate candidates at the outdoor "hustings"; to light their windows with candles, to wear symbolic colors and participate in parades through town; and even to eat roast beef and drink toasts at election-related banquets. In such ways political symbolism mattered.

By the early nineteenth century Britain's political leaders had developed a loose party system of Whigs and Tories, though these affiliations were so unstructured as to be only fair guides to political ideology. The monarch was supposed to be above party politics, but this was rarely the case in fact. Both party affiliations grew out of the late seventeenth century, and referred originally to those politicians in the 1670s and 1680s who either opposed the succession of the Catholic James,

Duke of York (Whigs), or supported him (Tories). While both Whig and Tory politicians came primarily from the landowning gentry, over the eighteenth century these early party labels had come to accrue other generally applicable meanings. Tories favored a less aggressive foreign policy, lower taxes, a powerful monarchy based on divine right rather than constitutional legitimacy, and a more exclusive Anglican Church. Whigs favored a more aggressive foreign policy in the service of commercial and colonial power and the taxes to pay for it, a constitutional monarchy, were less attached to the Anglican Church and more willing to tolerate Protestant religious dissent.

The wars with both the American colonies and revolutionary France altered these loose party alliances, so that by the early nineteenth century, Whigs had taken on the mantle of political reform, civil liberties, and increasingly, free trade. Tories, who had been in power during most of the wars with France, had cast themselves as protectors against revolutionary radicalism abroad and at home, and had become the party of order and repression in the course of their long period in office. A quarter-century of war against revolutionary France had both catalyzed British radicalism and its response: a series of laws both during the wars and in the years immediately following that curtailed civil liberties and stifled any possibility of Parliamentary reform. Tories also stood against free trade and for a system of protective agricultural tariffs. Even so, neither Whigs nor Tories had a developed party structure in 1830 that could ensure consistent votes on legislation or highly concerted political action, and it was not uncommon for individuals to start their career in one party and end it in another. A number of Parliamentary gadflies considered themselves "independent Radicals" and belonged to neither party, and party membership was not yet essential to a political career.

What did government mean in the early nineteenth century? How did most people feel themselves governed? The British state had for the previous century concerned itself primarily with war, foreign policy, and the means to pay for it: tax collection, trade policy and maintaining vast and intricate systems of credit and debt maintenance. In times of war in the eighteenth century (effectively over 45 years between 1700 and 1815), military and naval expenditure, combined with service on the national debt, averaged 85 percent of total expenses. More telling is how little by modern standards the state spent on civil government even in peacetime: approximately 18 percent in the early eighteenth century. Even that had fallen to 11 percent by the 1820s. Overall spending on civil government rose, but military spending and debt service rose even faster as wars became longer or more costly to prosecute.

As this budgetary breakdown suggests, domestic social legislation aimed at national issues remained a low priority, though this had begun to change, slowly, by the 1830s. "There was little expectation even as late as the 1840s that the central government should use a very significant proportion of national resources to attempt to ameliorate social injustice or even to promote economic growth; an expensive state was still usually equated with 'extravagance' and the perpetuation of unfair privileges" (Harling and Mandler 1993: 69). Relative to other European states at the same time, Britain's national government played only a modest role in the daily lives of its people. And yet relative to other European states, Britain managed to extract a considerable amount of tax revenue year after year: 20 percent of national output went into the state's coffers in various forms of taxation, twice the percentage squeezed out of its subjects by the French state.

The increasing cost of government, primarily through the high cost of waging war throughout the eighteenth century, brought changes in how the political orders saw the state once the long wars against France ended in 1815. Both Whigs and Tories now argued with varying enthusiasm that the structures of state government needed to become more efficient, more centralized, and less expensive. Historians once thought that this drive to modernize government in the early nineteenth century was driven by the new social pressures of industrialization and the new and more vital energies of middle-class men from industry. Recent work suggests that the movement to modernize government came instead from a very old-fashioned source: a desire to reduce the cost of government to taxpayers, especially to the wealthiest landowners who paid the largest share of taxes.

Similar movements to make local government more efficient, centralized and professional (against the decentralized, corrupt and amateur governance of the eighteenth century) took place, and often for similar reasons: the cost of social policy drove demands for efficiency and centralization, since those were the only conceptual ways to claim better services without raising taxes. In the early nineteenth century, and crucial to our story, this subtle shift, and the prioritizing of efficiency and frugality in expenditure, meant that the state remained poorly equipped, and not really inclined, to respond to the social, economic and demographic challenges of industrialization.

Despite the prominence of national events like wars in shaping our understanding of early nineteenth-century British history, most Britons came into contact primarily with local government rather than with the British state. Each county had a lord-lieutenant, appointed by the crown, and usually one of the most prominent landowners in the county. He led the militia in times of civil unrest, dispensed patronage in the form of minor offices, and served as a conduit for information between the county and the central government. The Justices of the Peace (JPs), also crown appointees and often local landowners as well, licensed ale-houses, decided bastardy cases, oversaw the capture of runaway apprentices or servants, fixed prices and wages in a number of trades and agricultural products, decided the interpretation and implementation of poor law policy, oversaw markets, appointed constables, assessed tax rates, and negotiated riots large and small until troops could be summoned. And those responsibilities were in addition to their more recognizably judicial roles as judges of the criminal law: hearing cases, deciding punishments in cases where they acted as judge and jury, and convening juries for serious crimes. Both lords-lieutenant and JPs came from wealthy families, and to serve in such positions was a recognition of one's local authority as well as a tacit claim that those with the greatest property had the greatest interest in preserving social stability.

Britain's Empire

Britain was more than just a disorganized collection of ancient nationalities and local governing bodies held together by a few strands of central government. It was also the center of an empire, and this had profound implications for its trade, its politics, its identity, and its culture. Even after the loss of the American colonies, Britain remained at war's end in 1815 the greatest imperial power in the world. Imperial concerns had played an increasing role in drawing Britain into military and naval conflicts throughout the eighteenth century, as imperial commercial connections came to be seen as more and more important and worth fighting for. Throughout the eighteenth century, Parliament, newspapers, magazines and public commentary focused on imperial topics: trade, war, governance, imperial architecture and foodways, and the racial, cultural and ethnic difference of "natives" everywhere.

But the term "empire" meant not a single kind of colony, a uniform system of governance, or even similar motives for acquiring and developing different plots of land. It did not mean in this period that all imperial subjects spoke the same language or received the same attention from London. The defining feature of the empire was its variability. There were the colonies of primarily white settlement: British North America, and later Canada; Cape Colony; and the colonies that would later combine to form Australia. There was the collection of states, governed partly by the British government and partly by the privately owned East India Company, that would become India. And there were acquisitions through previous centuries' war and piracy in the West Indies, the Caribbean islands dedicated to agricultural production through slave labor: Jamaica, Barbados, Trinidad and Tobago, and numerous smaller islands.

Colonies provided significant amounts of some goods, usually raw materials; but they also provided Britain with the financial and shipping resources to do business in other parts of the world. Of the ten largest British imports in the late eighteenth century, half were from Europe and only three were colonial in origin: sugar (primarily from the West Indies), raw cotton (also primarily from the West Indies in this period), and manufactured cotton and silks (from India – though this was changing rapidly). Fifty years later, Britain still imported most of its second largest import, sugar, from the West Indies, but its largest import, cotton, now came from the United States. Another significant import was timber, one-third of which came from British North America, primarily Canada. Some 30 percent of British exports went to colonial possessions in the first half of the nineteenth century, primarily to the West Indies but also significantly to Canada and India. Britain also did a large export business with the former American colonies, and with Latin America, which had never been part of the British colonial sphere.

A network of legislative acts – the Navigation Acts of the 1650s – defined that sphere economically as much as politically, binding Britain and its colonies with protective tariffs to ensure that colonial goods flowed more cheaply to Britain than elsewhere, and that British goods flowed more cheaply to the colonies than goods from other nations. The tariff system broke down in the early nineteenth century under the twin challenges of both ineffectiveness and the new political economy of free trade. In any case, by then British manufactures had become relatively less expensive globally, and so could flourish without tariff protection.

Along with iron and finished textiles, a different kind of export made its way from the British Isles to the British colonies: people. In the quarter century before 1815, about 180,000 people left England, Wales and Scotland; between 1815 and 1850, this number soared to 600,000 (with many emigrating from Ireland as well, particularly in the famine years of the 1840s). One-fifth of these emigrants traveled to imperial lands, the other four-fifths making their way to the United States.

The most controversial migrants were not voluntary, however, but forced. British imperial energies in the eighteenth century lay in the Atlantic: particularly in the vast network of shipping, finance, agricultural production, import and export underwritten by African slave labor. An average of 60,000 slaves crossed the Atlantic each year, bound primarily for the Caribbean in the early part of the century and, by its close, shifting focus to North America. They grew sugar, rice, indigo, cotton and tobacco, and served as domestic servants and even in some skilled trades. The British did not invent slavery, and indeed were part of a succession of European nations dominating the slave trade following the Portuguese, Dutch and Spanish. Still it was under the expanding Atlantic colonial economy, increasingly controlled by Britain, that slavery and the slave trade expanded most dramatically, up to its eventual abandonment under the pressure of the British anti–slave-trade movement in the early nineteenth century.

Colonies had been settled, acquired or won in such various ways and under such different kinds of British government that colonial rule remained haphazard in the early nineteenth century. Many of the Caribbean islands had self-governing assemblies, as had the American colonies before the revolution. Canada had institutions of representative government after 1791, as did Australia, which had been settled as a penal colony in 1788. Colonial governments always had a governor appointed in London, however, and local assemblies' legislation could always be overturned by the British Parliament. In 1815 this arrangement was formalized with the creation of the "crown colony," an entity ruled directly by the British state without need of local validation. This distinguished settler colonies from others, such as India, in which local rulers still ruled, and in which there was no need to introduce British styles of representative government as there were few British settlers to represent.

The Indian states had begun as purely commercial ventures with no thought of settlement in the seventeenth century. The East India Company, a joint-stock company chartered with monopoly trading privileges, owned its own ships, paid its own employees, and financed its own military protection, and in this peculiar manner carved out significant portions of India as British colonies by the late eighteenth century. The Company engaged in both peaceful and hostile trading actions that looked little different from local wars. Its employees made trading agreements with Indian princes that looked little different from treaties signed between sovereign states.

The Company collected taxes on Indian property for local rulers as part of these agreements, and so grew from a commercial operation into a vast administrative structure involved also in tax collection. It imported textiles from India, pepper from Sumatra and china, silk and tea from China. From the 1760s the Company began expanding its territory in India considerably, and its leaders expanded their responsibilities to include courts of law, armed forces, and many of the trappings of a state itself. In Britain, the Company and its leaders, with the great wealth they accrued, were often viewed as corrupt and beyond British control, and in 1773 Britain began to install government oversight on Company activities. Over the following decades, chartered company rule gradually gave way to direct government control, a process not completed until the state took over Company operations in their entirety in 1858.

Social Orders

In 1814, the Scottish author, magistrate and criminologist Patrick Colquhoun attempted a snapshot of British society in his *Treatise on the Wealth, Power, and Resources of the British Empire*. His statistical methods and accuracy leave much to be desired, but his numbers will do for a rough sense of who earned what and how in the early nineteenth century. Below the royal family and aristocracy (the "Highest Orders" comprising nearly 600 families) were the "Second Class," composed of non-titled gentlemen of considerable wealth (47,000 families), the "Third Class" of affluent clergy, lawyers, doctors, merchants, large manufacturers, and bankers (12,200 families), the "Fourth Class" of minor clergy, less notable lawyers and doctors, more modest manufacturers and merchants, prosperous shopkeepers and artists, and modest but independent farmers (233,650 families), the "Fifth Class" of small farmers, middling shopkeepers, and inn-keepers (564,800 families), the "Sixth Class" of artisans, agricultural laborers, and "others who subsist by labour in various employments" (2,126,095 families), the "Seventh, or Lowest Class" of paupers, vagrants, and criminals without any fixed labor (387,100 families), and a category of menial servants, separated out because the nature of their occupation precluded having families (1,279,923 individuals).

Colquhoun's remarkable precision should not be taken as accurate, but it provides us with a general analysis based on some of the widely shared assumptions of his era. He assumed that society was a hierarchy – an assumption few then would have questioned – and that the top of this pyramid belonged to people who had inherited titles and the land to go with them, implying also the income that derived from land. But this was not a society in which wealth or status was determined entirely by land or title, as the other "classes" make clear. The second class consisted of "gentlemen," a broad category in which income could come from several sources; the third and fourth classes were based partially on land but also on commerce or profession. British society then was a society in which few clear lines separated people and families in terms of status, but one in which status was if anything more important because of this very lack of clarity. It was not a polarized society of rich and poor, nor were wealth and status static; but it was a society of many layers shading into one another. Individuals possessed some social mobility, in that merchants could acquire titles, land and landed status, and their offspring could marry into nobility; yeoman (small farmers) could become tradesmen; tradesmen could become merchants. There existed large numbers of people between the mighty and the poor, and these, called the "middling sort" by contemporaries, themselves recognized many gradations of wealth, status, profession, and influence. Colquhoun also points out that many people were quite poor. The very poor worked as laborers or servants, in agriculture and manufacturing, or in whatever low-skilled or unskilled labor was locally available.

Given a society of many permeable layers, there was still the general belief that wealth carried with it obligations: to one's family first, of course, but also to one's civic environment (you were expected to pay taxes and serve in local offices), and to the less affluent around you. The other side of this was the deference and respect accorded to and expected by the wealthy. It is important not to overstate the degree or impact of this paternalism, or the exclusive monopoly of the affluent over civic or philanthropic activities. There were aristocrats who shunned responsibility, and conversely, there were many poor Britons who saw no need for deference – or who simply did not come into contact with the great families of the county. But the concept of a paternalistic ruling class retained force into the nineteenth century, well after actual paternalism had in fact greatly diminished.

Industrial and Other Revolutions

The starting point of this volume – 1830 – used to be regarded by historians as the endpoint of the industrial revolution. The first "industrial revolution" was seen as a collection of transformations in productivity, working conditions and power sources with dramatic results for urban change, population growth, wealth distribution, the landscape of political power and the physical landscape of industrialized Britain. At the end of the revolution, many people worked in factories rather than at home or in the fields, they lived in cities rather than the country, they derived power from steam rather than their own or their animals' labor, and vast wealth and poverty was created that shaped the contours of countless individual lives and also the very power of the British state. Without industrial change, Britain would not have become the great global military, imperial and economic power of the nineteenth century.

Contemporaries saw these changes as revolutionary as well. One author heralded in 1827 the massive consequences of the recent spread of steam power:

> To enumerate the effects of this invention would be to count every comfort and luxury of life. It has increased the sum of human happiness, not only by calling new pleasures into existence, but by so cheapening former enjoyments as to render them attainable by those who before never would have hoped to share them. Nor are its effects confined to England alone; they extend over the whole civilized world; and the savage tribes of America, Asia and Africa, must ere long feel the benefits, remote or intermediate, of this all-powerful agent.[4]

Alexis de Tocqueville, visiting the rapidly growing northern manufacturing city of Manchester in the 1830s, wrote in more mixed tones that "from this foul drain, the greatest stream of human industry flows out to fertilize the whole world." Karl Marx and Friedrich Engels based much of their early model of class conflict on what they observed in Manchester as well.

These observations capture the themes well and also several partially submerged truths: that contemporaries did not agree about the ultimate meaning of industrial change, though many thought it momentous enough; that it altered the patterns of human consumption by changing systems of production; that it had effects not confined to Britain but acting on a global scale; and that it would have long-term impact on the world's "savages" – as many Britons thought of peoples outside Europe – as well. Within these major themes and questions, what we know about and how we discuss industrial change have themselves been under constant revision since historian Arnold Toynbee coined the term and concept of an "industrial revolution" in 1884 (Toynbee 1961). In order to make sense of the concept, it is important to separate out several different transformations and take each in turn. For what at first glance looks like one process is really at least four: increased agricultural yield, changing patterns of population growth, expanding domestic and international consumption, and increased productivity in manufacturing. These four have led historians to argue that what we once saw as unified process taking seven decades now looks like a series of interconnected changes starting early in the eighteenth century and, in many ways, still only in its early stages by 1830.

Agriculture

A necessary precondition for increased manufacturing productivity was, in the eighteenth century, increased agricultural productivity – to feed more people at a lower cost, with fewer hands working the land. Yield on land rose dramatically, and for several reasons. Farmers traditionally left some land fallow each year to replenish soil nutrients, and began introducing clover and root crops such as turnips to those fields that both returned nutrients to the soil quickly and provided feed for livestock. As the agricultural yield per acre fell in some parts of continental Europe in the early eighteenth century, production actually rose in Britain.

Tight profit margins in grain led to economizing wherever possible, and while this meant lower food prices for consumers overall, many of the means of such economizing also had negative effects on less affluent farmers. Landholders wealthy enough to hire farm laborers had for centuries employed them by the year; now they employed by the week or even the day, allowing them to lay off when business was slow. Most dramatically, between 1760 and 1815, Parliament enacted over 3,400 Enclosure Acts, as landowners purchased common lands throughout the country, and purchased parcels of land from their neighbors as well to create larger holdings. Smaller plots meant less room to experiment with new crops or production methods. As a tangible sign of this, in the century after 1750, 200,000 miles of hedges were planted in England, as much as in the previous 500 years. With larger properties, farmers could experiment and increase productivity. Farmers also applied new fertilizers like seaweed, lime and guano, and drained marshlands to bring new fields under cultivation. Fields produced more for man and beast, and both increased their numbers as a result.

Population

In 1798 Thomas Malthus, a clergyman, published *An Essay on the Principle of Population*, arguing that population growth inevitably happened more rapidly than growth in the means to sustain a given population. This, he proposed, led to misery, hunger and early death for most people – and suggested certain limits to population growth as well. What Malthus did not know at the time of writing was that the population of Britain had been expanding at a fast rate for much of the previous century. About 13 million people lived in the British Isles in 1780, rising to 15.7 million in 1801 and 24 million in 1831 – close to doubling in a half-century. The population had begun to rise in the 1730s, and spurred on by low food prices and early marriages, increased more rapidly throughout the century. As the food supply supported greater numbers of people, the economy supported their employment as well. Had it not done so, cheap food would have been meaningless.

There were social consequences to this population increase. As coal and iron deposits were found in the North, and industries developed to extract and process them, the growing population found employment in new industries by shifting through migration from south to north. With shorter agricultural labor contracts, poor and landless farm laborers were less tied geographically to one place, and moved about the country more than in the past, placing strains on the system of poor relief that relied on a more stationary workforce. The nation was also becoming increasingly urban. In 1650, only one in ten English people lived in towns larger than 10,000; in 1800, nearly one in four did so. The growth of towns resulted not from improved medical care (they continued to be seen as places of ill health, deaths exceeding births until the 1770s), but from in-migration as the rural population grew faster than rural employment. By 1700 London eclipsed Paris as the largest city in Europe, and continued to grow rapidly. In the eighteenth century one-sixth of all English men and women lived in London at some point in their lives – a far higher incidence of metropolitan living than elsewhere in Europe.

Consumption and markets

More food supported more people, and people required more than food alone to live – much more to live well. Domestic demand for manufactured goods of all kinds thus rose throughout the century, and internal trade flourished with road improvements and construction of numerous canals that sped goods around the country faster than before. For example, the Leeds and Liverpool canal began construction in 1770 and finally opened in 1816. At 127 miles, it served as the primary mode of coal transport from east to west, cutting transport costs by 80 percent between Yorkshire and Lancashire. Around mid-century more durable and smoother roads were laid down, speeding up land transport for people, produce and manufactures alike. The trip from London to Manchester by coach took 80 hours in 1750 and only 30 hours in 1821 – and this was before railways. The quantity of traffic also increased: in 1756 one coach ran daily from London to Brighton, and by 1811 there were 28 coaches every day on the same route. All this pointed to greater domestic consumption. The average family purchased £10 of British-made goods a year in 1688, £25 in 1750, and £40 in 1811. Affluent families purchased far more. Foreign trade also increased, as British North American colonies became more populous and Britain gained access to vast new colonial markets in India, particularly after mid-century. British exports to the Americas grew 687 percent, for example, from 1700 to 1770.

Contemporaries remarked often on how this massive increase in consumption and prosperity was unique to Britain, and on the social implications it brought in its wake. Fortunately there was little agreement about these. Henry Fielding, writing at mid-century, blamed crime on increasing consumption of the wealthy, which inspired the poor to ape their betters and steal to do it right. Foreign visitors remarked more positively on the relative luxury of all the classes and the dispersal of wealth throughout the nation. And Samuel Johnson claimed that easy consumption put the British in thrall to fashion and novelty, so much so that they even wanted to be "hanged in a new way."[5]

Naturally the wealthy spent the most, but such was the nature of English society that every layer might aspire to the layer above, and conspicuous consumption was one way to appear to have gotten there. The closeness of different economic strata and lack often of clear demarcation meant that many people could emulate their social betters. Manufacturers responded to the ever-changing demand for newness, creating fashions that varied more and more rapidly as the century wore on – indeed, creating the concept of fashion as something highly impermanent. By the 1770s, this novelty manifested in ways both mundane, as new toys and pottery, and absurd, as outlandish wigs requiring special openings cut into carriage roofs.

This consumption of luxury goods by any but the rich was something new in itself. Economic theorists had earlier held that total consumer demand in a country was inelastic – the rich would purchase and the poor would barely get by with little surplus, making attempts to change or even consider domestic consumption irrelevant. The very word "market" had meant in the seventeenth century a fixed place where something was sold; in the eighteenth century it began to mean a potentially limitless demand for one's goods, if one knew how to manipulate people into wanting them. Luxury had previously been seen as something sinful; now it was an engine for economic growth. One observer noted at mid-century that envy itself "was a goad to industry and ingenuity even among the meaner sort who are spurred up to imitate this industry by the example of the rich." The man who bankrupted himself trying to spend like his social betters was nonetheless performing some good for the nation because he worked so hard to produce in order to support his material wants.

Productivity and industrial change

Throughout the eighteenth century, then, more food sustained more people, and more people purchased more things – but when we speak of the industrial revolution, we are also trying to explain the extraordinary rise in productivity that made possible the production of the things themselves. Higher productivity manifested itself in several ways. Real national output (the cost of goods produced nationally) grew slowly until about 1780, at about 1 percent annually; this then rose to 1.8 percent annually until 1800, and then more than 2 percent per year until around 1830. This type of continued growth, year after year, is unusual and has been pointed to as a "turning point" in British economic history. National exports rose from £9 million in 1780 to £22 million 20 years later – an impressive figure when one considers that Britain was at war against France at the later date. An international comparison gives a sense of the immensity of this change in productivity, at least in the most impacted field. In the mid-eighteenth century, the British domestically produced textile of choice was wool and had been so for a long time; silk was a luxury item. Cotton goods were typically made in such small quantities in Britain, and at such uncompetitive prices, that when the British bought cotton goods such as linens or calicoes, they imported them from India. In 1780 it took an Indian handspinner 50,000 hours to process 100 pounds of raw cotton into cloth. By 1795 in Britain, an automatic spinning machine, or "mule," did the same work in just 300 hours. It is no surprise, then, that by the middle of the nineteenth century, the direction of goods had reversed. As dramatic as the rise in cotton production had been, however, and as great an impact as cotton had had on exports and internal consumption, its effects can be placed in perspective when we remember that as late as 1830, only one person in 80 worked in a cotton factory.

While we associate "industrial" production with factory production, in fact productivity began to rise well before the adoption of large-scale centralized man-ufacturing. By the early eighteenth century, textiles, and particularly elements of the cotton industry, saw several significant transformations. Raw cotton went through several stages of production on its way to becoming cloth. The cotton was picked; carded to remove seeds, hulls and other debris; spun into thread; woven into cloth; and then dyed, cut and sewn into its final form. Already in the eighteenth century, then, there existed that "division of labor" that the Scottish economist Adam Smith credited with rising productivity (though he did not yet see it happening so dramatically in cotton in the 1770s). Through the "putting out" system, individuals contracted to spin and weave wool or cotton in their own homes, delivering the thread or cloth to merchants who supplied them with the raw wool or cotton and paid them on receipt of the finished cloth. A substantial amount of cotton production happened this way by the mid-eighteenth century and imports of raw cotton rose accordingly from £2.8 million in 1750 to nearly £60 million in 1800.

At first, these transformations were clearly beneficial to working people. Cot-ton cloth produced through the putting-out system allowed cottagers to take on some cotton spinning and weaving in their homes with minimal investment in machinery, and it allowed them to manage the time spent on cotton production within the context of their primary responsibilities of farming. It provided income that supplemented their agricultural pursuits and could be done at any time of the year, unlike many farming activities. Because parts of the productive process could be accomplished by different members of the family, it was a way for families to maximize the cash-producing output of women and children. During the course of the eighteenth century, however, increased productivity at various stages of the production process spelled a gradual erosion of the home spinner-and-weaver's contribution. Carding machines, flying shuttles to weave faster, and the spinning jenny (starting with 16 spindles in 1767 and expanding to 100 by 1800) all rapidly sped up the process of making cotton cloth and reduced its price. Steam power was first applied to spinning in 1785, and a year later, a power loom driven by horse, water or steam transformed weaving. Spinning and weaving had become so much more productive that until the early nineteenth-century invention of the cotton gin, the demand for raw cotton exceeded the supply.

The application of technology and steam power to cotton changed the relation-ships within the productive process. While cottagers could generally afford to own or rent spinning wheels and weaving looms, such applications as steam-driven power looms and large spinning jennies were beyond the reach of almost all la-borers (and too large for many households in sheer size as well). These massive machines were expensive and, once purchased, could be made quite profitable if they ran most of the time. This logic made factory production economically desirable, as employers laid out substantial funds to purchase equipment and then needed to bring workers to the equipment rather than the other way around. Once in the factory, owners advanced their production by integrating the timing of each stage of the process, which meant in effect that owners began to see their workers as part of the productive process itself. Factory workers thus traded inconsistent earning power and control over their own time (when working out of the home) for presumably consistent wages but far less control over their time, working conditions, and place of employment.

Why, then, would workers take on factory jobs? Factory wages often outstripped agricultural wages, and often outpaced wages for similar work done outside the factory as well. Inflation tended to increase faster even than factory wages in the late eighteenth century, so gains in real buying power (or the "standard of living") did not materialize until the 1840s for most workers. Adaptation to factory work, with its set and strictly enforced hours, holidays, meal times, break times, dress and mandatory sobriety, took place unevenly, and there was considerable tension throughout the late eighteenth and early nineteenth centuries between workers and employers over the new authority that employers attempted to exert at work. The stakes were large, since by the early nineteenth century employers asserted the right to influence or dictate the terms of workers' leisure as well.

Application of steam power to textile production had another powerful effect: it changed the relationship of people to their environment and determined the future of population growth, movement and density. Before steam, most large-scale manufacturing had to take place near running water, for Britain's streams and rivers ran many of the first-generation spinning jennies and looms. Thus, early factories were as likely to be outside of cities as in them. The modern image of industrialization and urban change derives from the later age of steam, which only gradually emerged in the late eighteenth century and became dominant by the 1830s. By then manufacturing could take place anywhere, and factories began appearing in cities and large towns to take advantage of proximity to a labor force. While industrialization and urbanization took place separately in the eighteenth century, and cities began growing independently and prior to major industrial change, by the end of the century the two movements had knit together as factories were increasingly located near people, and people migrated in search of jobs to where factories existed to hire them. The decision to locate factories near large population centers and sources of coal enhanced the northward-moving trend of the population, as cotton production grew most in the North. Population density nearly doubled, and in some cases more than doubled, in industrializing Lancashire, parts of Yorkshire, and Warwickshire. Birmingham, Bradford and Manchester all started the century as towns and ended as major urban centers.

Cotton was just one important force for economic change in Britain. By 1790 Britain had 150 cotton mills in operation; 20 years earlier there had been only 20 such mills. Soon some 7–8 percent of the entire national income came from cotton production. But other interlocking sectors also transformed as well, some of them spectacularly so. Coal, used in the early eighteenth century primarily to heat homes (much of the wood of Britain's great forest land having been built with or burnt in previous centuries), found a new use in powering blast furnaces engaged in smelting iron ore. Coal extraction rose from 3 million tons in 1700 to 10 million tons a century later. In 1728, 25,000 tons of pig iron was made; in 1788 this had more than doubled to 60,000 tons; and between 1788 and 1796, in a period of only *eight years*, this figure doubled again to 125,000 tons. Iron replaced wood in any number of uses: in architecture as rivets, screws and girders; in ships and bridges; in weapons, as well as household items.

Geography played a role in the pattern of industrialization, not only in the presence of water power at first and also of water transport, but also in the location of materials necessary to production. Tin, copper and lead made Cornwall a mining center; coal and iron together meant South Wales became a site of tremendous mining and smelting; the same was true of Birmingham. Most coal and iron deposits were found in the North, with very little found in the South near the urban centers of London, Oxford or Canterbury. The South had traditionally been a more prosperous agricultural region, the more mountainous North possessing poorer soil only capable of lower agricultural yields. Textile production originally thrived in areas that could not get by with farming alone, and so when cotton production took off it did so in places not known for their wealth, and drew population to those areas as well.

Social Stability and Instability

The powerful and potentially destabilizing forces of commercial growth, industry, rapid urban change, and the transformation of rural land ownership throughout the eighteenth century together pose important questions about social stability. The British state weathered these profound social and economic challenges without major convulsions, while undertaking numerous military conflicts. Other European states under similar pressures experienced revolution and social conflict on a vast scale. Why not Britain? Was British society in 1830 held together by bonds of loyalty, manufactured or real? Or was it a society on the brink of revolution under the stresses of industrial change and political challenge? It is too easy to say that, because no revolution occurred, British subjects harbored only loyalty, just as it is also too simple to say that every social or political tension was a nascent rebellion for the state to nip in the bud. In the years immediately following the Napoleonic Wars, popular radicalism and political unrest rattled the British political establishment, particularly in the context of massive and sudden troop demobilization, high food prices and domestic unemployment. Though revolution did not occur, it was certainly imaginable by a broad spectrum of British society.

We must content ourselves with speculations riddled with exceptions. We have already noted that British society, particularly rural society, was imbued with elements of paternalism and deference, which could have acted as means of stabilization. Two other kinds of cohesion merit consideration: law and customary practice, and religion and national identity.

Law and custom

Part of the ideological and economic inheritance of the early nineteenth century was a recasting of the meaning of customary practice. In the eighteenth century, custom and statute had provided support for a deferential social model that at the same time protected such rights of the common people as common land usage, food prices, wages, and working conditions. As this social model eroded, the state became less interventionist and more laissez-faire. At the same time, new technologies had transformed production in certain industries, population expansion created a vast pool of cheap labor, and new ways emerged to organize production that shifted control over working conditions from workers to employers. The state had been more proactive in the past out of a sense of preserving social order, and with the decline in such traditional concepts of order, new ways would have to be found to knit together the British people into a stable society in the face of tremendous social change. Two recent historians have written:

> Two nations faced one another in the post-war years and the divide between them was immense. What the post-war crisis revealed most clearly was that the ruling class was losing the capacity to govern . . . By 1820 . . . social reciprocities had greatly weakened. In a new social order in which custom and paternalism were marginal, in which new working-class identities were emerging alongside the growing economic power of the industrialist and the rule of the market, laws denouncing workers' associations and the haunting shadow of the military featured more conspicuously in the theatre of rule. (Hay and Rogers 1997: 208)

This transformation in the state's role did not happen immediately, but state protective regulations were dismantled over several generations. The government stopped encouraging prosecution for food profiteering in the 1760s, and by 1802 food markets were wholly unregulated. Wage-fixing by magistrates, sanctioned by the 1602 Statute of Artificers to prevent impoverishment, fell out of use in the mid-eighteenth century and was repealed in 1815. Apprenticeship requirements, which limited access to certain trades and thus protected wages in those fields, were repealed in 1814, having come under criticism by political economists and employers for decades. And as we have seen, the half-century after 1760 saw a tremendous number of Enclosure Acts, making common field usage rarer. Nor were these changes reciprocal, since many categories of workers were still criminally punishable for leaving work under the Master and Servant Act.

The result was an imbalance between the demands that the law exacted and the protections the law offered. Enclosure allowed higher yields and greater economic efficiency, but also less of a safety net for the poor. Loosened restrictions on trade meant access for poor into trades, but also dilution of wages and standards. The repeal of statutes that protected labor allowed employers to introduce newer and more productive machinery, which many workers saw as threats to their jobs.

The criminal law also helped to reinforce authority, drawing many layers of society into that authority so that it rarely appeared to be an exclusive tool of the elite. Eighteenth-century criminal justice relied on the gallows, and on the terror it inspired among the poor. The state had few of the resources to deter crime that would be available to later governments: it had limited policing and limited secondary punishments. Prosecution depended on the victims of crime themselves. In this context, the criminal law could only deter through fear of punishment. Over the course of the eighteenth century, the number of crimes for which one could be hanged quadrupled, nearly all of them crimes against property. The criminal law, then, served as part of the means by which the wealthy commanded the respect and deference of the poor. But the law was not only a tool of the rich, and indeed, most of the victims of crime, then as now, were the poor themselves. Nor was the criminal law "controlled" in any absolute sense by the rich; people of varying means played a role in determining what it meant. Men of property in Parliament made the law itself and served as judges, but people of quite modest means served as jurors, watchmen, constables, and other local officers who set the reality of enforcement. And the ultimate decision in whether or not to prosecute a crime lay with the victim, who could be of any level of wealth. The law served thus as a means of social cohesion both for the terror of the gallows as a deterrent and for the widespread participation that allowed a broad spectrum of British society to play a role in interpreting its meaning.

Identities and Beliefs

In the midst of dramatic economic change, after a quarter-century of bloody and costly war, was there a common experience of what it meant to be "British"? We have no surveys of British identity to guide us, nor mass media on which to base generalizations. The very borders of what constituted "Britain" in 1830 had only recently incorporated Ireland and, not that much earlier, Scotland. Nor did a common language provide a universal foundation. At the end of the eighteenth century, one in five Scots spoke only Gaelic, half of Ireland spoke only Irish Gaelic, and while the Welsh gentry were bilingual, a staggering 90 percent of the Welsh people spoke primarily Welsh. In the absence of ancient borders or common linguistic practice, historians have turned to common historical experience, ideology and religion to understand the nature of British identity.

The British saw themselves, their government, their social structures, their religion and even their climate as blessed, and in this rather blinkered self-satisfaction they may have been little different from residents of any other early nineteenth-century state. War can be a powerful catalyst for people to examine, reaffirm or critique their sense of national identity, and in the previous half-century they had experienced both demoralizing defeat in a colonial war and resounding victory in the longer conflict with revolutionary France. These wars should be placed in the larger context of both a century of commercial rivalry and outright war with different continental alliances that almost always included Catholic France. While religious belief played little direct role in the meaning of these conflicts, particularly as the century progressed, continuous warfare with the most powerful Catholic state solidified British identity as both Protestant and anti-Catholic, and referred Britons back to previous centuries' more overt religious conflict, beginning with the Reformation.

The term "Protestant" does not fully explain the theology of most Britons. Britain had, and still has, a close bond between church and state. The Anglican Church, also called the Church of England, was a blend of Protestant theology, with its emphasis on faith rather than works and a personal relationship to the divine rather than one mediated by priests, and a hierarchical structure similar to that of Catholicism, with authority over church policy and theology descending through two archbishops, 26 bishops, and numerous parish priests. The key structural difference was that the monarch served as the legal head of the Anglican Church, rather than the Pope.

Many early nineteenth-century Britons fitted uneasily if at all into this church structure. Aside from the rituals of birth, marriage and death, few would have attended church with any regularity were it not for the social expectation of doing so – and many did not attend an Anglican church at all. The religious upheavals of the sixteenth and seventeenth centuries had left British Protestantism with several variants outside the Church of England. There were Dissenters, also called Nonconformists, meaning any Protestant not taking Anglican communion: Presbyterians, Baptists, Congregationalists, Methodists, and Quakers. Some Catholics remained, though those numbers dwindled every decade: the 115,000 Catholics in 1720 had become only 69,000 by 1780. There were Jews, though not in significant numbers: probably fewer than 10,000 at any point in the eighteenth century. The Act of Toleration (1690) had guaranteed a generalized religious freedom, with certain political rights preserved for Anglicans. But proving oneself Anglican was a low bar for an easy conscience, and though legally excluded from office, several non-Anglican Dissenters and Jews became MPs, mayors and city leaders during the eighteenth century by practicing "occasional conformity": which meant they went through the ritual of paying Anglican tithes and taking Anglican communion once a year to pass legally as Anglicans.

The Anglican Church had been losing participants throughout the eighteenth century, though Methodism (which began within the Church but ultimately left it) inspired many adherents among the working poor, and Evangelicalism (which sought to transform the Church from within) tried to put the fire back into a faith that looked, by the 1780s, a little too tainted by Enlightenment rationalism and moderation. Evangelical leaders William Wilberforce and Hannah More wanted to revive spirituality among the rich to save souls, and also to reaffirm their moral credibility among the poor. In this way God's work could coincide nicely with the paternalism so necessary to social cohesion. Evangelicals represented a new kind of Puritanism, one aimed at the comfortable and complacent, and one that promised to make people of character, moral fiber, and religious conviction who could take that conviction actively into the world. At the center of movements to abolish the slave trade, educate the poor, and pursue a more righteous foreign policy, Evangelicals led the way. The virtuous fervor of the turn of the nineteenth century fed prominently into the Victorian mood.

While British Protestantism was fragmented, anti-Catholicism was more cohesive. Anti-Catholic sentiment in Britain was based in the common belief that Britain had to defend itself against invasion or subversion by Catholic states, which might encourage British Catholics to turn against their neighbors and help engineer revolt from within. Such a revolt, if successful, would make Britain into a dependency of another state and spell the end of British liberties, British government, a successful foreign trade policy, and British practice of Protestantism at home. Such fears of foreign intervention had a legitimate enough basis in the sixteenth and seventeenth centuries, when France and Spain had both attempted to foment rebellion, and in the eighteenth century when France had ties to the Scottish Jacobite rebellions in 1715 and 1745. English and later British Parliaments had passed a series of acts limiting Catholic practice in Britain: the Corporation and Test Acts (1663, 1673, and 1678) required Anglican observance to hold public office at any level. Catholics could not hold seats in Parliament, could not vote, and could not succeed to the throne, a limitation on very few individuals to be sure, but a symbolically powerful one nonetheless. Laws restricting property ownership, trade and civic rights for Catholics in Ireland were even more stringent – and it is worth pointing out that "British" identity contained an inherent core uncertainty once Ireland became part of the British state in 1800. To be fully British and Catholic was a contradiction in terms, resolved partially by the removal of restrictions on Catholics in 1829. Popular anti-Catholicism continued through the early nineteenth century, but popular religious toleration had also been growing for some time (and indeed, made possible Catholic Emancipation). Increasing numbers of Catholics fought in the British armed forces in the many wars of the eighteenth century, as well as the many colonial conflicts around the globe.

Britons saw themselves then as a Protestant people with unique liberties and particular claims to be civilized. They did not suffer under an autocratic monarch but had, in the context of early nineteenth-century Europe, a relatively limited royal authority. They possessed freedom from arbitrary arrest, a toleration of public demonstration, some participation in local government for the nonelite, jury trials and due legal process. Theirs was not a society of castes, and social mobility was at least plausible, albeit more possible for some than others. Famine, still present on the continent, no longer plagued the British Isles. They were not a militarized state, but a commercial state whose trade was protected by naval power, seen as the natural military force of a free people. And, lest we forget, Britons were a *free* people; the song 'Rule, Britannia' may not have said what Britons *were*, but the lyrics to the song made clear that they were not nor ever would be slaves.

All of this was partly true and partly wishful thinking. Britishness so defined underwent significant stresses from its military endeavors in the 70 years before 1830. Expansion of the empire throughout the late eighteenth century, particularly at the conclusion of the Seven Years' War (1763) brought in Catholics from Quebec, Hindus and Muslims from India, and indigenous peoples who were clearly not Christian, white or civilized in British terms. Empire meant ambiguity and paradox, and early nineteenth-century Britons were "an insular people, accepting concepts of authority, exclusiveness, and inequality so essential to Empire [who] had also espoused a political and economic liberalism which simultaneously undermined those foundations" (Porter 1999: 27). War against revolutionary France had led to limitations on civil liberties across the board, and postwar unrest led to further suspension of rights to assemble, to print, and to form associations. Jury trial had been in decline since the mid-eighteenth century as more minor crimes became subject to summary justice – judgment by one or two JPs without need of a jury of one's peers. And while Britons might not be slaves, and were squeamish about Britons owning too many slaves in Britain itself, they certainly bought, sold, insured, shipped, financed, and bought the produce of slaves largely without thought or regret. Eighteenth-century commerce and finance was predicated at many levels on colonial slave labor. But this too was complicated, as Britain was also the source of much anti-slavery campaigning; Parliament abolished the slave trade itself in 1807 and emancipated slaves in British colonies in 1833 (though the process of emancipation took several years).

Clearly, Britain in 1830 was a society in economic transition: a society whose legal and legislative structures lagged behind economic change. At the same time, strong institutional forces held the society together: the political primacy of the landed aristocracy, a widespread belief in the superiority of British liberties and institutions; opposition to Catholicism; the galvanizing nature of the empire and the wars against France. Over the next several decades, some of these hardy ideas were themselves challenged, as attempts were made to identify and resolve social issues, grant civil liberties to Protestant Dissenters and Catholics, and expand the franchise. The question of the meaning of British identity would undergo continual redefinition throughout the entire modern period.

Notes

1   William of Orange, who could be said to have invaded England in 1688, was actually invited by leading nobles and faced no resistance, so this seems not to count.
2   "The Isle of Wight" (1782), anonymous poem quoted in Briggs 1965: 8.
3   These titles can be confusing for several reasons. First, individuals can gain titles over their lifetime, so the title by which they are called can vary according to when they play a particular role. Second, individuals can hold multiple titles, in which case they are referred to by their highest title. Third, younger sons who do not inherit their father's title may be referred to as "Lord such and such," even though they are not peers and do not sit in the House of Lords. As with sports statistics, keeping track of such rules and their specific applications can occupy considerable energy.
4   D. Lardner, *The Steam Engine Familiarly Explained and Illustrated with an Historical Sketch of its Invention and progressive Improvement* (1827), quoted in Briggs 1965: 24.
5   He referred to the spread of the gallows drop, supposedly more humane than a slow asphyxiation caused by simply removing the support underneath the hanged individual.

References

Briggs, Asa (1965) *The Making of Modern England, 1784–1867*. New York: Harper & Row.
Harling, Philip, and Mandler, Peter (1993) From "Fiscal-Military" State to Laissez-Faire State, 1760–1850. *Journal of British Studies*, 32 (Jan.): 44–70.
Hay, Douglas, and Rogers, Nicholas (1997) *Eighteenth-Century English Society*. Oxford: Oxford University Press.
Porter, Andrew (ed.) (1999) *The Oxford History of the British Empire, vol. 3: The Nineteenth Century*. Oxford: Oxford University Press.
Toynbee, Arnold (1961) *The Industrial Revolution*. Boston: Beacon Press. First published as *Lectures on the Industrial Revolution in England*, 1884.

Further Reading

Colley, Linda (1992) *Britons: Forging the Nation 1707–1837*. New Haven: Yale University Press.
Eastwood, David (1994) *Governing Rural England: Tradition and Transformation in Local Government, 1780–1840*. Oxford: Oxford University Press.
Levine, Philippa (2007) *The British Empire: Sunrise to Sunset*. Harlow: Pearson Longman.
Porter, Roy (1990) *English Society in the Eighteenth Century*. London: Penguin.
Price, Richard (1999) *British Society, 1680–1880: Dynamism, Containment and Change*. Cambridge: Cambridge University Press.

Thompson, Edward (1963) *The Making of the English Working Class*. New York: Vintage.

Thompson, F.M.L. (ed.) (1990) *The Cambridge Social History of Britain*. Cambridge: Cambridge University Press.

Wahrman, Dror (1995) *Imagining the Middle Class: The Political Representation of Class in Britain, c.1780–1840*. Cambridge: Cambridge University Press.

Williams, Glynn, and Ramsden, John (1990) *Ruling Britannia: A Political History of Britain, 1688–1988*. New York: Longman.

2

Universal Suffrage and No Surrender
Politics at Home and Abroad, 1830–1867

It was a December evening in 1842, in Leeds. At 5:30 p.m. the doors were opened, to reveal that the music hall had been decked out in fine style for a party. Evergreens and artificial flowers hung from the rafters and entwined around handsome portraits of the gentlemen who were advocating the right of the working classes to vote: Feargus O'Connor and Thomas Slingsby Duncombe. Flags and banners festooned the walls, including one that read: "T.S. Duncombe, the unflinching advocate of the People's Rights." Over the next hour, men filed in, filling the tables in the music hall, and then took tea. Toasts were given to a document called the People's Charter, that among its Six Points called for the expansion of the right to vote to include all men over the age of 21. And then – to immense cheering – Thomas Slingsby Duncombe got up to speak.

The man who ascended the podium was tall, and straight, with a pleasant, symmetrical face, a tanned complexion, and curling dark hair.[1] In the broad tones of his Yorkshire upbringing, Duncombe announced that he was completely committed to their cause of expanding the suffrage (the right to vote). He assured his audience that being a Chartist and campaigning for the rights of working people was not a crime, and urged them not to relax their call for the right to meet in public and discuss their grievances. Invoking the rights of freeborn Englishmen, he told them that he believed that he was representing the traditional politics of his country by upholding Chartist ideals. Far from the inner London constituency that had elected him to Parliament, in front of a group largely composed of nonvoters, Thomas Slingsby Duncombe was giving a stump speech. Duncombe and his followers believed that if the working people gained the right to vote, they would be able to directly represent their interests for the first time: to protect the rights of labor, regulate the hours of factory work, and prevent the poor from being inhumanely warehoused.

Empire, State, and Society: Britain Since 1830, First Edition. Jamie L. Bronstein and Andrew T. Harris.
© 2012 Jamie L. Bronstein and Andrew T. Harris. Published 2012 by John Wiley & Sons, Ltd.

The English political system was in flux between 1830 and 1867 – and the nature of the organization of Parliament, and who should qualify for the vote, were at the center of the change. A combination of popular pressure and shifting political alignments facilitated the passage of the 1832 Reform Bill, which expanded the electorate and enfranchised many members of Britain's growing middle classes. But over the next 30 years, growing prosperity and trade and a series of challenges from the unrepresented forced the reconsideration of the issue. In turn, these pressures helped to shape the British political landscape from fuzzy and overlapping groups into political parties with clear and predictable positions on issues. While the parties were divided at home, consistent leadership in foreign affairs produced a popular, unifying realist policy that helped to force other countries to participate in British trade and acknowledge British governance.

Gaining the Reform Act

By 1830, critics of Britain's baroque and bizarre system of representation had been calling for change in the nature of Parliamentary elections for over 50 years. They had used every method at their disposal – including letter-writing "corresponding societies," newspapers dedicated to reform, political theater, and even the occasional riot. Combinations of artisans and members of the middle classes – no longer just a political phrase but identifiable leaders and groups – formed "Political Unions" dedicated to Parliamentary reform. They also sought to reform local government.

The Prime Minister in 1830 was Arthur Wellesley, the Duke of Wellington, and he had impeccable Tory credentials. Having brilliantly led England's army against Napoleon, he embodied English rationalism arrayed against ever-revolutionary France. Paradoxically, however, his ministry had seen political rights extended to non-Anglican Protestants in 1828, and to Catholics in 1829. In November of 1830, Wellington publicly declared himself against any further Parliamentary reform, at a time when the most vocal public opinion and the press favored it. He was forced to resign.

Wellington's resignation occurred against the backdrop of continuing popular unrest. After the long wars against Napoleon, bad harvests coincided with the demobilization of large numbers of troops, leading to unemployment and famine in the countryside. When landowners introduced threshing machines that decreased the need for workers to thresh crops by hand, the workers responded by burning hayricks, breaking machines, and writing anonymous threatening letters. The problem was widespread: historians recorded over 3,300 incidents between 1830 and 1832, concentrated in the south and east of England (Holland 2004).

Wellington's replacement as Prime Minister, Earl Charles Grey, saw that some kind of limited Parliamentary reform might satisfy the middle classes while at the same time holding off the threat of revolution (a threat that had arisen in the streets of France as recently as 1830, and so was very real and present). In 1831, he introduced a reform bill that proposed to redistribute a large number of seats from small boroughs to the large new urban areas and some counties. The old patchwork of qualifications for the borough vote would be replaced with a standardized franchise: anyone holding land, buildings, or a combination of both worth £10 had the right to vote.

The tortuous path that Grey's bill traveled on its way to becoming law illustrated the entrenched interests involved. After a 302 to 301 vote, the bill passed the House of Commons. Since the bill faced an uncertain future in the House of Lords, Grey convinced King William IV to dissolve Parliament and hold a general election, so that more reform-friendly MPs would be selected. Next, the bill stalled in the House of Lords, where a Tory majority defeated it soundly by 41 votes, fearing the first of many shocks to the Constitution.

Lord Grey asked the king to create new and more Whiggish peers, committed to passing the bill, and which would in effect erase the Tory majority in the House of Lords. When the king refused, the Whig ministers resigned, and were briefly replaced by Wellington. In the provinces and in the streets of London, reformers in their political unions demonstrated and even rioted, threatening to withhold taxes or even to inaugurate a potentially calamitous run on the Bank of England (a popular saying held that "To Stop the Duke, Go for Gold"). Under immense pressure, the king finally relented, agreeing to create up to 50 new peers. Faced with the threat of diluted power in both houses, the largely Tory peers passed the measure, which became law on June 7, 1832.

Parliamentary reform represented no triumph of the middle classes. The aristocracy continued to govern much as before, both representing themselves in the House of Lords, and being disproportionately represented in the House of Commons as well. The percentage of MPs of noble birth in the House of Commons had increased from 28 percent in 1801 to over 42 percent in 1830, and aristocrats occupied ministry posts and controlled patronage. The Reform Act of 1832 made some inroads into this power, decreasing the proportion of noble MPs to 27 percent in the 1840s and 1850s, but not until the 1890s was there a precipitous drop. Aristocrats could still shepherd bills through Parliament that promoted self-serving and locally beneficial infrastructure: turnpikes, railroad extensions, and the construction of docks.

The Reform Act did expand the electorate from about 400,000 to about 900,000 voters, out of a population of 24 million people. Although the electorate more than doubled, there was no permanent shift in power either from one political party to another or even from one economic interest to another. The degree of change varied by region: in England, one male adult in five now had the vote; in Scotland, it was more like one man in eight. New industrial cities were directly represented for the first time. Counterbalancing this, the interest of landowners was strengthened by the expansion of county seats and the Chandos clause, which enfranchised farm

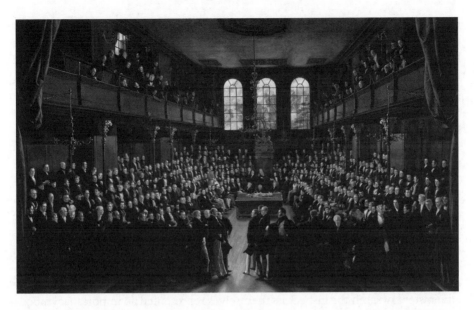

Figure 2.1 The first Reformed Parliament, elected in 1833, crowds into the House of Commons chamber in this painting by Sir George Hayter. (*The House of Commons, 1833* © National Portrait Gallery, London).

tenants paying £50 in rent per year (who, it was feared, would be forced to vote the way their landlords directed on pain of eviction). Some artisans were enfranchised by the new £10 householder franchise, but others, who had been able to vote by having become master artisans within their boroughs, or by virtue of paying taxes to support the poor (poor rates), were disenfranchised. The titled nobility and their children continued to predominate in Parliament – making up between 70 and 80 percent of MPs – and as cabinet ministers.

Government Energized

Although Parliamentary reform didn't usher the middle class into power, it did initiate a decade of relatively more activist government. Motivations for this new energy varied. Some Whig politicians felt that their high status conferred on them some social responsibility for the poor, but this was hardly new. Evangelicalism – the increased commitment to vigorous moralism within many Christian sects – created a sense of purpose among many in power and even more people outside of Parliament. Others – including the energetic civil servant Edwin Chadwick, who called for public health reform – were motivated by the idea that well-planned, efficient government policies could maximize human happiness. No matter what motivated any particular individual, the result was the discovery that social problems required political solutions. Those who would use the government at any level to address these problems were aided by technology: more daily newspapers, and greater public literacy, meant more public attention to the plight of overworked factory children, or West Indian plantation slaves, or contaminated public drinking water – increasing the pressure to act. The philosophy of Utilitarianism, and religious Evangelicalism, would also motivate legislators (these concepts are explored in more detail in Chapter 4).

The machinery of government was also refined. The 1830s and 1840s saw production of numerous Parliamentary "bluebooks," as Parliamentary Select Committees and Royal Commissions gathered evidence about social problems – interviewing witnesses ranging from factory children to doctors to mine owners – and recommended possible solutions. In some areas, as in factory reform and the reform of mine safety, inspectors were appointed for the first time to monitor implementation of new social policy. There were never enough inspectors to actually administer laws, but the inspectors themselves represented an important symbolic

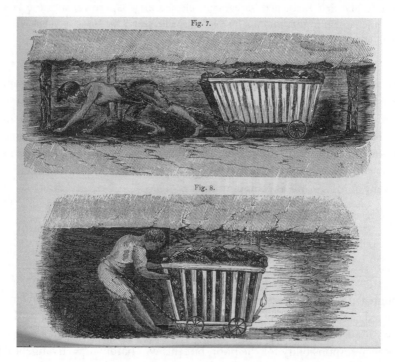

Figure 2.2 Illustrations like these, from an 1842 Parliamentary Report on Children's Employment in Mines, produced moral outrage and led to the banning from underground mine work of all women and of boys under the age of ten. (© The British Library Board B.S.Ref. 18 volume 17, 65).

shift from local initiative toward centralized expertise. When it came time to refine legislation, these inspectors could provide crucial, expert testimony based on their own first-hand knowledge.

The achievements of the Parliaments of the 1830s were impressive, if sometimes driven by seemingly contradictory principles. Thomas Clarkson, William Wilberforce and others had inaugurated Britain's first major social reform movement in the 1780s, to end Britain's participation in the trade in African slaves. While the first abolitionist movement succeeded in outlawing Britain's role in the shipment of slaves, slavery itself continued in Britain's colonies. The British economy was still firmly integrated with the products of West Indian slavery – particularly sugar. In 1833, after abolitionists had engaged in decades of agitation, petitioning, the publication of emotional tracts, and the minting of medals depicting shackled slaves, Parliament finally emancipated the slaves in its West Indian colonies, with a transitional period of involuntary "apprenticeship" that ended in 1838. Although changing economic realities may have played a role, the success of abolition gave the British moral credit that could be deployed elsewhere in the empire and in foreign affairs for the rest of the century.

Humanitarianism was acceptable only up to the point at which it appeared to conflict with the realities of the market. In 1834, after the issue of poverty was studied by a Royal Commission whose membership included several economists and the ever present Edwin Chadwick, Parliament passed a new Poor Law. It modified the older system of poor relief, by which poor rates were raised locally and subsidies paid to the unemployed, who could still live at home. The New Poor Law specified that subsidies to the poor should only be given inside a workhouse, where conditions were to be made "less eligible" – more unpleasant – than a struggle for survival on the streets. "Less eligibility" was envisioned in order to encourage the poor to use every resource to avoid destitution. In some counties, workhouse inmates were separated from family members, had their hair shorn, were assigned uniforms, and made to unravel rope from old ships to earn a scanty keep – but Poor Law Guardians in other counties resisted building such workhouses. As with many initiatives undertaken in this period, Parliament had the power to legislate, but local authorities retained the power of implementation, even though a larger government machinery was deployed.

The new Parliament also took up the issue of Britain's factory workplaces, especially those that operated 12 to 14 hours daily, spinning thread and weaving cloth. Like the movement to end the slave trade, the factory movement was a grassroots effort, although this one brought together well-meaning paternalists with the factory workers themselves. "Short-time committees," seeking a ten-hour workday for children, combined pamphleteering, public demonstrations, petitioning, and even the use of personal narratives and fiction. Earnest propagandists like Yorkshire's Richard Oastler, and MPs like Preston's Michael Sadler, conjured mental pictures of deformed factory children never seeing the light of day, losing their fingers to machinery and fearing being beaten by overseers, as the factory foremen were then called. Of course, drawing attention to the harsh conditions in factory workplaces helped to burnish the image of supporters of agriculture. In 1833, the movement earned a victory through legislation. In most factories, child workers now had to be at least nine years old, could only work an eight-hour shift and were promised a few hours of school per week. But Parliament resisted further reform, constrained by the perceived need to ensure British competitiveness in worldwide markets, by the belief that work was morally beneficial to children, and by the material truth that poor parents depended on their children's earnings to augment the family's income.

While the reformed Parliament's commitment to humanitarianism was ambiguous, its commitment to efficiency was clear. One of the most momentous pieces of legislation of the 1830s, the Municipal Corporations Act (1835) targeted the administration of towns and cities. It eliminated the old system of self-selecting "corporations" at the local level, and replaced them with city councils elected by ratepayers under the assumption that more responsive government would be more responsible and less corrupt as well. Even as Parliamentary politics continued to be dominated by the aristocracy, the middle classes and prosperous artisans now had an outlet for their public improvement energies. Boroughs that had never been formally incorporated could petition for incorporation, and large cities like Birmingham and Manchester did so. The mid-Victorian era became the moment of great pride in the possibilities of local government: massive town halls, libraries, and public bathhouses were built as monuments of this spirit. Town halls and libraries, in turn, cultivated the development of a greater public sphere – the politician Joseph Chamberlain later spoke to crowds of thousands about the expansion of the suffrage at Birmingham's town hall; libraries provided autodidact workingmen not only with "useful knowledge," but also with the knowledge they needed to contest their place in society.

Public health was another great concern ushered in by the reformed Parliaments. In 1842, utilitarian bureaucrat Edwin Chadwick produced a massive report, *The Sanitary Conditions of the Labouring Population of Great Britain*. It detailed the many unintended side effects of industrialization and urbanization, such as dank basement apartments lacking ventilation and lack of ready access to running water (water companies were still privately owned, and public pumps were often befouled with the microorganism that causes cholera). People who were crowded into slums without ventilation coughed on each other and gave each other tuberculosis; people without access to water to wash clothes suffered from lice-born typhus. All of this led, most dishearteningly, to a noticeable differential in expected lifespan between workers and members of the leisured classes. In Derby, for example, life expectancy for a member of the gentry was 49; for a laborer or artisan, it was 21.

The government had begun, in 1837, to register birth and death records. The computation of life-chance statistics for the first time, and the empowerment of local Boards of Health, allowed cities and towns to begin to combat the problems of public health. Beginning in the late 1840s, cities throughout Great Britain erected municipal bathhouses, water supplies, and massive sewer systems (like that designed by engineer Joseph Bazalgette for metropolitan London). Uncertainty about the way in which diseases were transmitted also led both to a distrust of churchyard burials and legislation forcing the construction of new cemeteries far from centers of population.

Not all of these measures were perceived positively by their intended beneficiaries; workers opposed state-imposed vaccination programs and formed "pig protection societies" to shield their pigs from attacks by local authorities, who it was feared would remove the animals for reasons of public health. Workers who could not afford running water, soap, or decent food saw the real public health question as one of decent wages rather than government programs. The public health missionaries often complicated their aims with a perception of working-class homes and neighborhoods as foreign, savage, and dirty. Ironically, they held this position even as they hired working-class women to come clean their own homes or do their own laundry.

Victoria and Her Ministers

While British political parties had yet to coalesce in the way that they would later in the century, in the 1830s there were two rough groupings that served as seats of power. The Tory or Conservative Party, stronghold of farmers and great landowners, had long been associated with maintenance of Britain's ancient institutions, particularly the monarchy and the Church of England. Any legislative change should be slow and incremental and as little as necessary to preserve the status quo. Sir Robert Peel restated these principles in a new form in the Tamworth Manifesto (1834). The Whigs were not revolutionaries either, but they were slightly better disposed toward political reform, cities, and manufacturing. Each nascent political party had its own clubs and stately houses for dining and socializing and scheming, although party organization did not penetrate down to the grassroots level.

After the short political debut as Prime Minister of the Tory Sir Robert Peel (1834–1835), this decade of accelerated government really belonged to William Lamb, Viscount Melbourne, a traditional Whig, who presided between 1835 and 1841. Well respected despite two brushes with accusations of sexual scandal, Lord Melbourne formed a close relationship with Queen Victoria, who acceded to the throne at the age of 18 in 1837 upon the death of her uncle, William IV. A 58-year-old widower, Melbourne quickly adopted Queen Victoria as his protégée, not only discussing matters of policy with her but also dining with her, riding horses with her, and spending up to six hours daily in her company. Victoria would in fact come to be known as the "Queen of the Whigs," so closely was she identified with Melbourne and his policies.

Although the powers of the British monarch were waning, certain facets of the king's or queen's responsibilities were still important. The existence of the empire made the monarch an important figure, binding together disparate peoples, rulers, and political systems. The monarch would also have a cultural impact at home – his or her preferences and fashions were likely to have an impact on popular practice, whether through widespread mimicry or popular revulsion. And although the responsibility of forming a cabinet almost always went to the political party with the most seats in the House of Commons, a monarch's preferences could still have an impact.

This last fact came to light in the Bedchamber Crisis, in which constitutional procedures were bent to cater to the Queen's personal scruples. After serving two years as Prime Minister, Melbourne resigned on May 7, 1839, in the wake of a lost vote in Parliament. As was customary when one party faced a no-confidence vote and resigned, the party in opposition – here the Tories under Sir Robert Peel – was asked to form a government. Peel accepted the invitation. He also asked the queen to show favor to the new government by replacing some of her Whig ladies of the bedchamber with Tories. Royal patronage in the form of such positions was still an important element of a monarch's relationship with the party in power. When she refused, not wanting to lose the company of her closest friends, Peel resigned, and Melbourne resumed power for another two years. The incident harmed the monarchy, by calling into question Queen Victoria's aptness for power and her willingness to abide by longstanding traditions.

Stability finally came to the monarchy after 1840, when Victoria calmed the fears of those worried about female monarchs by trading one male influence for another. Under intense pressure to agree to some suitor, she married her first cousin, 20-year-old Albert of Saxe-Coburg and Gotha. After a whirlwind courtship, Albert was duly naturalized, granted a public salary, and given the title of Prince Consort (setting a precedent about the titles given to the spouses of British queens). Queen Victoria was completely smitten, and the young couple gave birth to their first daughter nine months after the wedding. The second child – a son and heir – followed a year later, as did another seven children, at fairly regular intervals, over the course of the marriage.

Victoria's near constant state of pregnancy from 1840 to 1857, her intermittent postpartum depression, and her personal belief that women lacked leadership skills circumscribed her political role, giving Albert the opportunity to enlarge his as Prince Consort. When Melbourne's government finally, decisively fell in 1841, and the Tories were swept in, Albert provided a necessary transition by befriending Sir Robert Peel, who became the Tory Prime Minister. Albert also entertained visiting heads of state, wrote extensive policy recommendations directed to government ministers, and even participated actively on the committee that chose the public art and decoration for the new Houses of Parliament constructed in the 1840s. His crowning achievement was planning the 1851 Great Exhibition at the Crystal Palace in London, which showcased Britain's global commercial and manufacturing dominance. Although the satirical magazine *Punch* poked fun at Albert's German background, his assiduousness and seriousness helped to neutralize some of the sentiment that had grown up against the monarchy during the days of Victoria's raucous Hanoverian uncles.

The Chartist Movement

The fact that Victoria and Albert made a young and attractive couple helped to insulate the monarchy at a time of ferment in popular politics. The reformed Parliament, although it had governed boldly, did not yet include direct representation of the working classes, who had been left out of the 1832 Reform Act. Beginning in 1836 and 1837 in Manchester and Huddersfield and Bradford, the mass movement against the new Poor Law and its workhouses, which workers saw as dehumanizing, and the unfulfilled desire for factory reform coalesced into a palpable desire for change. Leaders like Methodist "political preacher" Joseph Rayner Stephens ascended the "platform" (often an upturned wagon in the middle of a field) amid large crowds, and encouraged workmen to demand bread or blood. Meanwhile, in London, a group of artisans and radicals styling themselves the London Working Men's Association formed a group for political gain and mutual assistance. They generated a list of six points that came to be called the "People's Charter," calling for annual parliamentary elections; equal electoral districts; vote by secret ballot rather than oral declaration; payment of Members of Parliament (which would enable working people to serve); no property qualifications for Members of Parliament (at that point the lowest amount of property that an MP could possess was £300); and, most importantly, a vote for every man over 21 years of age.

Some of these points harked back to the eighteenth-century Parliamentary reform movement; others reacted to legislation passed since 1832. The Chartists, as adherents of the People's Charter came to be called, explained their own movement as a reaction to perceived betrayal by the middle classes, who, in the Chartists' interpretation, had been given the vote in 1832 only with the help of working people's implied threat of national revolution. The middle classes' failure to repeal heavy taxation, combined with the insults of limited factory reform and the New Poor Law, were tarred as "class legislation" that a working people's Parliament (or a Parliament accountable to working people) would surely repeal. Although a few working-class women demanded the right to vote on the basis of natural rights, the Chartist movement presented its constituency as male, and women and children as subsidiary subjects whose interests would be protected by enfranchising their artisan and laborer fathers.

The Chartist movement burgeoned over the next two years, with help from gentleman leaders like Feargus O'Connor, a charismatic former Irish MP, and thousands of local working men (and a few women) who assumed leadership throughout England, Wales and Scotland. The movement puzzled Melbourne's government, since it combined traditional and constitutional protests such as petitions with more menacing varieties, like the threat of military or industrial action. A "national petition" calling for the adoption of the People's Charter garnered over a million signatures, and the Chartist National Convention, akin to a working-class shadow Parliament, met in London in early 1839. But the Chartists also armed and drilled in military formation, obtaining pikes and melting down pots and pans to make bullets. The government perceived an abortive rising at Newport in Wales in November of 1839 as part of a nearly successful national revolutionary strike. Trials followed, and many Chartists – including O'Connor – were jailed.

The Chartist agitation would continue as a disruptive backdrop throughout the 1840s. In total, the Chartists would present three national petitions, in 1839, 1842, and 1848, the last with over 3 million signatures. But the movement also spawned an entire institutional culture: a national political organization (the National Charter Association), Chartist churches and schools, Chartist newspapers and magazines, Chartist poetry and song, and even a land company designed to locate shareholders on their own tiny cottage properties through a lottery system. The constituency of the movement fell away after the presentation of the last petition on April 10, 1848. As nationalist leaders in Ireland agitated for repeal of the Union with Great Britain, and democratic nationalist movements surged on the Continent, special constables – men recruited from the ranks of London's civilians – blocked a bridge to prevent the Chartists from escorting their petition from the south bank of the Thames to the House of Commons.

After 1848, some Chartist leaders continued to support democratic causes abroad, and some moved into the Liberal Party, but the main mass of followers drifted away. Whether this was due to exhaustion of resources and tactics or to general satisfaction with the government and the economy is still a matter of historical debate. The Chartist movement had seemed to be the main threat to domestic political stability during the "hungry forties," a time of mass unemployment, wage stagnation, and high food prices fueled by the Corn Laws; Chartism's end ushered in a more conciliatory period of relations with working people.

Pressure from Without: the Church and the Corn Laws

The Chartists were not the only group that sought to pressure governments of the late 1830s and early 1840s. Protestant dissenters, having defeated the Test and Corporation Acts, now set their sights on removing other political and civil disabilities. They lobbied for a recognition of civil marriages undertaken outside of the Church of England; opportunities for higher education, since they were excluded from the ancient universities of Oxford and Cambridge; and an end to the onerous practice of having to pay church rates – essentially a tithe to support an Established Church to which they did not belong.

Also fighting against the Church of England were thousands of Irish Catholics, who campaigned to abolish the tithe as well (particularly since some parishes in Ireland had very few Anglican communicants). But these were not the only complaints of the Irish populace. The dumping of British textile goods in Ireland below cost had held back the development of native Irish industry. Peasant farmers were forced by absentee landlords to pay inflated rents, reaped no benefit of any improvements made to their farms, and could be evicted easily. Catholic civil emancipation in 1829 brought a cadre of 32 Irish Catholic MPs, led by Daniel O'Connell, into the House of Commons and thereby brought these issues into mainstream British politics. The nature of coalition government in the House of Commons made their support necessary and at times crucial.

In 1835, O'Connell and the Repealers (those against Union with Britain) con-cluded the Lichfield House Compact, an agreement with the Whigs to table the idea of Repeal for the time being as long as Ireland was fairly governed. When Sir Robert Peel was elected to head a Tory ministry in 1841, however, O'Connell shifted his tactics, forming the Loyal National Repeal Association and agitating again for repeal of the Union. While the Repeal agitation was at first met with state trials of key leaders, eventually Peel's government turned to trying to use Parlia-ment to remove some of the grievances of the Catholics. His decision, in 1845, to triple the grant made to the Maynooth seminary, one of the most important Catholic educational institutions in Ireland, garnered little thanks from O'Connell's Parliamentary wing, but elicited great outcries from hard-line Protestants. A wit from the British magazine *Punch* declared:

> How wonderful is Peel
> He changeth with the Time
>
> Turning and Twisting like an Eel
> Ascending through the Slime.[2]

Sir Robert Peel's most momentous change of policy involved the Corn Laws, on which he made a decision that split his own party in two and forced a dramatic political realignment. The Corn Laws prescribed a sliding scale to prohibit the importation of wheat until it reached a relatively high price. By artificially inflating the price of grain, the Corn Laws protected the agricultural interest by allowing landlords to charge higher rents to tenant farmers, while producing high food prices and major fluctuations in the price of bread for everyone else. Anti–Corn Law organizations formed in both Manchester and London in the 1830s, composed of members of the industrial middle class and artisans. Some were involved in the organization because they thought that it would increase their standard of living; others, because they felt that the high price of bread artificially forced industrial wages higher. The groups petitioned, held public meetings, struggled against the

Chartists for the adherence of working people, and published tracts. Two MPs, Richard Cobden and John Bright, whose names became synonymous with free trade, espoused the cause. By the mid-1840s – even before the Irish famine made the wheat question a critical one – Sir Robert Peel, the Conservative Prime Minister, felt compelled to act.

Peel's own Tory Party had been tremendously polarized over the question of Corn Law repeal. One faction, the protectionists, led by the backbencher Lord George Bentinck and the flamboyant young MP Benjamin Disraeli, argued strenuously against their repeal on the grounds that the agricultural interest was crucial for national prosperity and security. According to the protectionists, repeal of the Corn Laws would be the Tory Party's death blow. In the end, the party split over the issue. Some followers of Peel – led by their belief in free trade and economic retrenchment – gravitated by the 1850s to the newly coherent Liberal Party. In turn, Disraeli – whose Jewish ancestry might otherwise have made it difficult for him to get a foothold – gained great political capital and eventually led the Conservative Party.

Famine in Ireland and the Limits of Free Trade

The repeal of the Corn Laws came too late to avert the most serious demographic disaster Great Britain would face in the nineteenth century – the Irish potato famine. Preconditions for the famine had included absentee ownership of the land by Protestant landlords, combined with the renting of ever smaller portions of land – at high rents, and always under threat of eviction – to members of large, Catholic families. The ownership of such small plots of land had led to the development of a potato monoculture, and potatoes had become the central dietary staple for many Irish peasants. The fungal blight killed the potatoes in the ground, entirely wiping out the 1845 and 1846 crops.

Although one contemporary wag had compared Sir Robert Peel's smile to the handles on a coffin, he was not without empathy. His government established a Scientific Commission to study the extent of the blight, and a Relief Commission to distribute corn on the cob as a form of relief, and to provide unemployed workers with employment on public works as a means of survival. But when Peel's government fell in 1846, and Peel was replaced by the Whigs under Prime Minister Lord John Russell, relief was scaled back; and the government, far from the scene of death and destitution, did not feel the same urgency as the local relief committees on the scene. The principles of political economy which reigned at the time discouraged charity on the grounds that it sapped the ambition of the poor. Suffering had to be the will of Divine providence. Russell was also committed to the principles of free trade, and believed that the market would correct itself. All of this occurred against a backdrop of prejudice against the perceived racial and religious differences of the Irish peasantry.

The result was widespread hunger, death, and emigration. Historians approximate that, of a pre-famine population of 8 million, 1 million Irish people died during the famine from starvation as well as diseases, like cholera, that find better purchase in weakened bodies. Another million Irish people migrated, largely to North America, where many of them continued to nurture resentment against the British government. Emigrants cleared the way for the continuing chain migration of younger members of Irish families to America – a process that accelerated throughout the nineteenth century and ensured that the population in Ireland never returned to pre-famine levels.

Palmerston and Foreign Policy

The Chartist movement, the repeal of the Corn Laws, and the Irish famine all complicated domestic politics for British governments in the 1840s. At the same time, foreign policy allowed Britain to present a united front under a single leader. Lord Palmerston dominated the foreign office, serving for all but five years between 1830 and 1851, in a way that enabled his policies to continue during his periods out of office. The ultimate realist, Palmerston resolved that Britain would have no eternal friends, and no eternal enemies – the right policy was that which guaranteed Britain's interests. He had broad cross-class appeal; even many Chartists seemed to approve of Palmerston's bluster and patriotism and his active and forceful attempts to open other parts of the world to British business.

The need to maintain British prestige and commercial links abroad at all costs led to the decision in 1839 to send gunboats and marines to China in order to maintain an open market for opium. As one of the only British-traded commodities able to match the British thirst for Chinese exports, imports of opium into China facilitated British purchase of Chinese goods and preserved a balance of trade. Palmerston also waged war in Afghanistan (1838–1842) to protect British interests in India (a misadventure that ended with the wholesale slaughter of British troops). In the Don Pacifico affair (1850), he established the policy for the Royal Navy to intervene against foreign nations to protect the rights and business interests of British citizens – even those with a tenuous claim on citizenship – anywhere in the world. The combination of Palmerston's aggressive stance, the unmatched Royal Navy, and a system of alliances and regular meetings among the major European powers produced peace and stability for Britons at home.

Palmerston was no longer in the Foreign Office during the one major disturbance to the mid-Victorian Pax Britannica – the Crimean War. In 1854, France's Napoleon III and the Russian Tsar clashed over influence in southeastern Europe, and specifically over which country had the right to protect Christian interests in the Holy Land, then within the Ottoman Empire. In an attempt to prevent

Russia from expanding into Turkey, disturbing the European balance of power, and perhaps even menacing India, Britain and France declared war on Russia. Britain's naval focus resulted in the decision to invade the Crimea, where two cities were besieged (Kars and Sebastopol) and a series of naval skirmishes initiated, but the actions failed to rout Russian forces. As new telegraph lines relayed word of logistical problems to the public at home, and Britons learned that more British soldiers were dying of disease than in battle, public discontentment with the war grew apace. The territorial integrity of the Ottoman Empire was guaranteed by treaty at the war's end, but the indecisive and costly nature of the war itself caused many in Britain to wonder whether they had been deceived about their own military superiority. Ironically Palmerston, who had done the most to promote the idea of British military superiority, became Prime Minister during the war, and was widely supported for his role.

The 1850s have been referred to as an "age of equipoise," or counterbalancing forces. This was possible in part because the empire became a repository for British troops, imperial officials and civil servants, and surplus population in general, providing opportunities for employment and settlement on a global scale. Almost 200,000 white settlers migrated to the various Australian colonies in this period, outnumbering the indigenous Aboriginal population for the first time. Visions of a green and pleasant land down under conflicted with widespread hopes of easy riches, which seemed plausible enough after the discovery of Australian gold deposits. While the Australian continent would be settled by the British first through penal transportation and then the Gold Rush, New Zealand was colonized beginning in 1837 by the New Zealand Land Company, which hoped to create a utopian intentional community. Although the native Maori people were at first protected in their landownership by treaty, by the 1850s the British desire to respect indigenous property ownership had evaporated.

The year 1857 was momentous for the future of the empire, and for British public and official beliefs about its governance, as a major mutiny challenged the fundamentals of British rule in India. Throughout the previous decades, the East India Company had steadily consolidated its landholdings, all of which depended on the use of native Indian soldiers, or sepoys, who greatly outnumbered British troops in India. Grievances had been building against British rule among traditional rulers dispossessed by the growing British presence. Unwanted Westernization measures taken by the East India Company smacked of cultural imperialism: welcoming converts from Hinduism, encouraging Hindu widows to remarry against the tenets of their faith, and threatening traditional structures of authority by reorganizing land tenures. While dissatisfaction had long been simmering, the catalyst for revolt was the decision by the British army to equip troops with new Enfield rifle cartridges greased with fat from cows and pigs – cartridges that had to be torn open with one's teeth. A step less sensitive to both Hindu and Muslim sensibilities can hardly be imagined – and even though the Company quickly removed the cartridges from circulation, the symbolic damage had been done.

On May 9, 1857, the garrison of Indian soldiers at the city of Meerut witnessed 85 Indian cavalrymen paraded in chains for refusing to handle the Enfield rifle cartridges. The following day, three regiments present at the public humiliation revolted, releasing the captives and marching on Delhi in an attempt to restore the Mughal emperor, who had presided over large tracts of the subcontinent before the arrival of the British. The local British commander waited too long to react, and the result was a series of bloody battles between native Indians and the British colonial community. The episode was devastating to British confidence and shattering to those who lived through it. Twenty-eight-year-old Harriet Tytler, the wife of a British army officer in India, later recalled living under intermittent gunfire inside an ammunition storage hut for a month with her two toddlers and her unclad newborn. Most galling for her was not the experience itself – surely part of the construction of the mythical British "stiff upper lip" – but rather the feeling of betrayal by her family's longtime Indian servants. In the wake of the uprising, British soldiers carried out violent revenge against the rebels; then the government disbanded the East India Company and governed India through a crown-appointed Viceroy.

Despite having Palmerston at its head, the Liberal government of the 1860s seemed less firmly directed on foreign policy questions. The upwelling of nationalism in continental Europe had been difficult for the government to contend with, since it seemed in line with key principles of liberty and justice resonant with British liberalism, yet at the same time could be highly destabilizing to reigning continental aristocracies, with which British noble families had temperamental affinities. The government, led by Lord John Russell, came down on the side of Garibaldi and favored a united Italy in 1860, and allowed Bismarck to annex the duchies of Schleswig and Holstein in 1864, in the service of creating a united Germany.

Similarly, when 11 states broke from the United States of America to form the Confederate States of America, the question of the British government's posture became pressing, though not so much as to provide clarity in foreign affairs. The American South was a vital supplier of cotton to the mills of Lancashire, and many Southern plantation owners claimed kinship with the British aristocracy on grounds of a shared commitment to political leadership and a leisured lifestyle. But many transatlantic links had also been forged between American and British churches; between American and British abolitionists; and even between American and British working people – all of which militated against any reflexive decision to support the Confederacy.

The Union government and the British government sparred throughout the war – first, in November 1861, over the "Trent Affair," in which the Union navy removed from the *Trent*, a ship headed to London, two men who hoped to be the Confederate ambassadors to the Court of St James's. Another major issue, as Britain's former colony grappled with its future, was the secret decision by some British shipyards to build warships for the Confederacy. The *Alabama*, *Florida*, *Georgia*, *Rappahannock*, and *Shenandoah*, built in Liverpool, sank more than 150

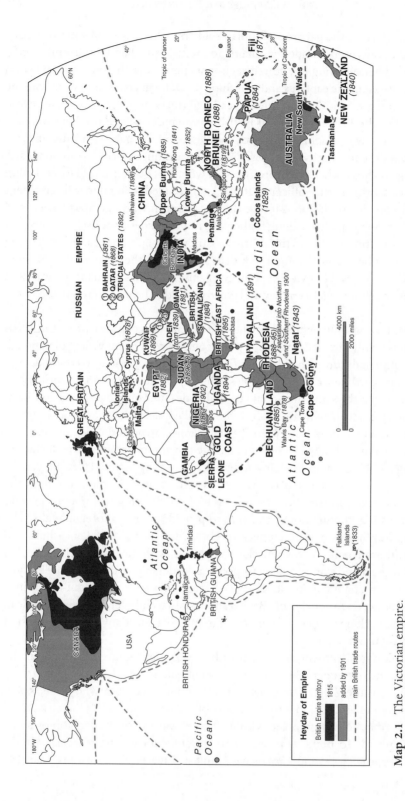

Map 2.1 The Victorian empire.

Source: Based on Nigel Dalziel, *The Penguin Historical Atlas of the British Empire* (London: Penguin, 2006), pp. 64–65.

Northern ships, and, the United States would argue, cost it hundreds of millions of dollars and significantly prolonged the war. The biggest threat to a Union victory, British government recognition of the Confederacy, never came, although Chancellor of the Exchequer Gladstone struck fear into the hearts of Northerners when he expressed his feeling that Jefferson Davis and the Confederacy had "made a nation." The feeling of crisis was averted with President Abraham Lincoln's Emancipation Proclamation of 1863, which transformed the Civil War from another apparently nationalist rebellion into a war about slavery, making British support for the Confederacy much more unlikely. If many antebellum Americans had been Anglophobic, the British government's inconsistent behavior during the war showed they had good reason for their ambivalence.

Realignment and the Second Reform Act

Within the British Isles in the 1850s and 1860s, as the economic dislocations of the 1840s receded, conflict was increasingly contained by constitutional methods, as the two parties defined themselves more clearly. The Corn Law had split the Tory Party, allowing the Peelites to find their free trade economic allies within the Liberal Party. William Gladstone, originally a Peelite Tory, served as Chancellor of the Exchequer under Lord John Russell and Palmerston, and set the stage for Liberal concerns by concentrating on rational government budgets, efficiency and retrenchment. Free trade began as a plank in the Liberal platform, and over the course of the century became dominant as the seemingly natural course of capitalism. The protectionist remnant of the Tory Party left behind by the decamping of Peel's followers was now led by Lord Derby, with Disraeli serving as Chancellor of the Exchequer. Derby headed two short "minority" governments, not having enough votes in the House of Commons to hold onto power.

"Whiggish" historians, looking at the nineteenth century for some greater progressive meaning, fastened on the expansion of the electorate, claiming that as some social groups became more prosperous, they were rewarded by being brought within what Gladstone called the "pale of the Constitution." A closer look reveals that the process of being brought within that pale was a contested one, and that it revolved around the question of British identity. The case of the Jews provides one example. There were approximately 20,000 Jews living in Great Britain in 1850, the majority of whom had been born in Britain; the great migration from Eastern Europe to London came 30 years later. The Jewish community, which dated from 1656, was prosperous, and attempted as much as possible to assimilate. Lionel Nathan de Rothschild, a member of the banking family, had first been elected to the House of Commons in 1847, but was barred from taking his seat by an oath that required people to swear "on the true faith of a Christian." Multiple "Jewish Disabilities" bills had been introduced to remove civil restrictions, but not until 1858 were voters in the City of London entitled to the service of the elected representative of their choice if that choice happened to be Jewish.

The electorate also continued to be metropolitan. Although the colonies surfaced periodically in debates over foreign policy – when the advisability of freeing the slaves in the British West Indies was debated, for example – colonial concerns were relatively invisible. The fact that residents of India or Canada or Australia had no direct representation at Westminster probably played a role. Whether the colonies benefited or drained the nation's resources helped differentiate Liberals from Conservatives. Colonial uprisings like the traumatic Indian rebellion of 1857 elicited Parliamentary discussion, but the militarism of the empire did not disrupt the otherwise liberal and progressive flavor of domestic politics. If anything, the empire became a place where military intervention was sometimes needed, which created an argument against using military force to quell domestic disruption. Britons, after all, were not the same as colonial natives.

The mid-century electorate also continued to be male. Not only did women lack the vote, but married women continued to labor under the political disability of coverture (which prevented them from owning property, including their own wages, suing, and being sued). The laws of the time made married women's earnings the property of even estranged husbands, and automatically granted custody of minor children to the father. Caroline Norton, a well-born friend of Lord Melbourne's who suffered brutality at the hands of her abusive husband and lost custody of her young children, not only became a cause célèbre from the 1830s on but also campaigned tirelessly for reform of the laws relating to women, divorce, and property ownership.

In 1857, the Divorce and Matrimonial Causes Act removed divorce matters from the control of Parliament and the ecclesiastical courts, making divorce possible through the law courts for the first time. Reflecting a social double standard, however, a husband needed only to prove that his wife had committed adultery, while a woman had to prove not only adultery, but also either incest, bigamy, cruelty, or desertion. The Act granted to wives who were separated from their husbands any money that the wives subsequently earned, and even made it possible for some wives to claim a maintenance payment from their husbands. It did not, however, affect the property rights of women living with their husbands.

To acknowledge the limitations of reform and the exclusive nature of British citizenship is not to deny all change, and in many ways, Parliamentary reform was the central political question throughout the 1860s. Despite the fact that many MPs felt ambivalent about reform, they had been under intermittent pressure to consider additional electoral changes since 1832. Reform Unions and other groups had pressed the issue through out-of-doors lobbying, and some Radical MPs, like Joseph Hume and Peter Locke King, argued for manhood suffrage.

Palmerston opposed reform, but upon his death in office in 1865, he was replaced with the more sympathetic Liberal Lord John Russell. Russell had once declared the 1832 Reform Act "final," and had been nicknamed "Finality Jack" as a result, but had come to see the cause of further reform as a positive good. Gladstone, Russell's Chancellor of the Exchequer, had been steadily gaining in popularity while circulating on speaking tours throughout the countryside, advocating a major expansion of the suffrage on moral grounds. The Reform League and various "Manhood Suffrage Associations" raised awareness of the reasons that workers deserved the right to vote. Workmen had become thriftier; they had become more educated; the confrontational, occasionally violent tone that had characterized the Chartist movement was largely absent.

Empire also played a role in the debate around the Second Reform Act. Radicals argued that although English men shared a common racial and ethnic heritage with British-born migrants who had left for Canada, or Australia, or the United States, it was only on British soil that they lacked the right to vote. British MP Robert Lowe, who had spent time in the colonies, argued that the colonial experience proved that democracy produced anarchy, the rule of mere numbers rather than the dominance of those with property and intelligence. Finally, the resurgence of reform as an issue coincided with the Morant Bay rebellion in Jamaica. Black Jamaicans, economically suffering under the incompetent Governor Eyre, and almost completely deprived of the vote, violently rebelled and British troops on the island responded by indiscriminately killing Jamaicans regardless of race, suffrage, or economic status. The result was Jamaica's conversion into a state whose administration and legislation came directly from the British crown, affirming the popular contemporary concept that only white men were fit for political inclusion.

In 1865, Lord Russell put forward a government reform bill, only to see opposition arise from within his own Liberal Party. Opponents, led by Lowe, favored a representation by "interest," arguing that since enough members of the working classes could already vote to represent that interest, watering down the electorate with more workers would only undermine the representation of other groups. Russell's government fell, as these Liberal opponents joined with Disraeli's Conservatives to defeat the reform bill. Conservatives formed a minority government against a backdrop of popular riots in favor of Parliamentary reform.

Hoping to move his party out of its minority status, Disraeli engineered his own reform bill in 1867. He showed great political flexibility, characterized by some as "opportunism," by working with any in the Liberal fold who would work with him, and accepting any amendments to his bill in those cases where he was clearly about to be outvoted. When it came time to vote on the Reform Act, Disraeli had put the Liberals into an untenable position: they could oppose the Act on partisan grounds, while undermining their history of public commitment to the issue, or they could vote for it, and at least cultivate the appearance of integrity on the issue.

The 1867 Reform Act extended the vote to all male household heads who had lived in a place for at least a year, paid at least £10 a year in rent, and were personally responsible for paying their own taxes. In the counties, the suffrage extended to those who owned property worth £5, or who paid £12 to rent property. Some smaller towns lost one or both seats, and their MPs were reallocated to larger cities. In all, about 1,120,000 voters were added to the 1,400,000 previously eligible, meaning that somewhere between two-fifths and three-fifths of working men now had the right to vote.

The 1867 Reform Act was a far cry from any endorsement of egalitarian democracy, and Disraeli himself had supported what John Bright called the "fancy franchises": granting extra votes to graduates of England's ancient universities, members of the learned professions, or men with large savings accounts. Nonetheless, there was great qualitative difference between the first and second Reform Acts in terms of both intent and consequences. The first Reform Act had addressed ancient constitutional grievances, including corrupt boroughs, but had, through enfranchising a limited portion of the middle class, solidified the continuation of aristocratic rule for the next 35 years. The first reformed Parliament dedicated itself to some social questions, such as public health, factory reform, and reform of local government, but in a paternalistic way, directed at subjects rather than citizens. This exclusionary focus in turn fueled the Chartist movement.

In contrast, the Second Reform Act answered most of the urgent questions raised by Parliamentary reform, and thereby ushered in a new age of constituency politics. Both Conservatives and Liberals found they had to be more organized, both at the national level, as "whips" enforced voting discipline, and at the local level, to register and canvass voters and circulate within their constituencies gaining popular support. A new electorate required that its needs be met in different ways: through the provision of housing, public education, regulation of the food supply, and the provision of public utilities. And just as the presence of the empire had helped to give rise to stability at home and to the creation, for the first time, of working-class male citizens, so this new political nation had to deal with larger questions of empire – of the fate of Ireland, of whether Britain ought to be expansionist or inward-looking, of the dying Ottoman Empire and an expanding Russian one.

Notes

1   "Thomas Slingsby Duncombe, Esq., MP for Finsbury," from *Supplement to the Illustrated News of the World*, 1859, L302 Duncombe, Islington Local History Center.
2   Quoted in Briggs 1965: 342.

References

Briggs, Asa (1965) *The Making of Modern England, 1784–1867: The Age of Improvement.* New York: Harper & Row.
Holland, Michael (2004) Swing Revisited: The Swing Project. *Family and Community History,* 7 (1): 87–100.

Further Reading

Briggs, Asa (1959) *Chartist Studies*. London: Macmillan.

Chase, Malcolm (2007) *Chartism: A New History*. Manchester: Manchester University Press.

Evans, Eric J. (1983) *The Forging of the Modern State: Early Industrial Britain, 1783–1870*. London: Longman.

Gash, Norman (1971) *Politics in the Age of Peel*. New York: Norton.

Hall, Catherine (1992) *White, Male and Middle Class: Explorations in Feminism and History*. Cambridge: Polity.

Levine, Philippa (2007) *The British Empire: Sunrise to Sunset*. London: Pearson Longman.

Mandler, Peter (1990) *Aristocratic Government in an Age of Reform: Whigs and Liberals, 1930–1852*. Oxford: Oxford University Press.

Stedman Jones, Gareth (1983) *Languages of Class: Studies in English Working-Class History, 1832–1982*. New York: Cambridge University Press.

Thompson, Dorothy (1984) *The Chartists: Popular Politics in the Industrial Revolution*. New York: Pantheon.

3

Dark Satanic Mills?
Economic and Social Change, 1830–1867

The 16-year-old boy, with heavy-lidded eyes and a vacant stare of a face, described his early life to the journalist. His father had died when he was an infant; his mother supported him and his brothers, taking any kind of work available and leaving them at home with only the house key and some bread and butter for lunch. There were times when she had pawned everything in the house and there was no food at all, and the boy and his brothers were so hungry that they cried. "She used to be at work from six in the morning until ten o'clock at night, which was a long time for a child's belly to hold out again, and when it was dark we would go and lie down on the bed and try to go to sleep until she came home with the food" (Mayhew 2009: 39). At age 8, the boy went to work to support his family, peddling green vegetables in the morning and nuts in the evening. By 14, he was spending part of his wages to take his girlfriend out drinking at the public house, and by the following year, had moved into his own lodgings. He had evolved a cynical philosophy of life: "In course God Almighty made the world, and the poor bricklayers labourers' built the houses arterwards – that's my opinion; but I can't say, as I've never been in no schools, only always hard at work, and knows nothing about it."

The young peddler, or "costermonger," had his reminiscences duly recorded by the author and social reformer Henry Mayhew, who printed them first in a series of articles and then as a book: *London Labour and the London Poor* (1861). Mayhew documented for his largely middle-class audience a culture completely foreign to their experience, despite its existence in and throughout the capital and many booming provincial cities. As an amateur ethnographer, Mayhew's work expanded on what the novelist and future Prime Minister Benjamin Disraeli had called in 1842 the "two nations" of England: the rich and the poor.

By 1830, iron furnaces, railroad tracks, and beam engines already dotted the English countryside, and the enclosure of fields and the improvement of agricultural

Empire, State, and Society: Britain Since 1830, First Edition. Jamie L. Bronstein and Andrew T. Harris.
© 2012 Jamie L. Bronstein and Andrew T. Harris. Published 2012 by John Wiley & Sons, Ltd.

techniques had already enabled or forced the transfer of workers from farm fields to factories. Quantitatively, the British economy was booming, with a steady growth rate of over 3 percent per year. Other important economic changes resulted from ideological and financial shifts – Britain's adoption of the banner of "free trade," even as it cemented the bonds of empire; its position as the creditor of the world and the willingness of the growing middle class to invest its savings in the growth of industry, both in Britain and abroad.

The economic growth that had characterized Britain since the mid-1750s continued into the mid-1850s, with cotton textiles, coal, and iron as the leading sectors. A growing population, combined with the need to import food, meant that Britain had to step up exports in order to compensate for that demand. Cotton and iron goods were both desirable abroad – exports were up to almost £50 million in the late 1830s – and had greatly increased production through inventions (iron-forging technologies, power spinning frames and looms) and new ways to organize production. At first, the relatively low wages paid to industrial workers meant little internal demand for products beyond the merest necessities; but by mid-century, falling prices increased workers' purchasing power and contributed to the growth of the domestic market. The nation's infrastructure also matured, as space and time were conquered as never before. The 1830s and 1840s saw the profuse growth of railway lines, from 600 miles of track at the time that Victoria came to the throne, to 6–7 thousand miles of track by the 1850s. The construction of the railways featured massive feats of civil engineering, including the two-mile "box tunnel" on Isambard Kingdom Brunel's Great Western Railway, constructed by 1,200 laborers over two and a half years. Telegraph communication (1837), penny post (1840), and the elimination of "local time" (1845) in favor of a national standard helped to unite Great Britain. Iron steamships like the *Great Britain* (1843), 1600 horsepower, propeller-driven and over 300 feet long, made transatlantic journeys safer and more commonplace.

After a brief but very painful dip from the late 1830s to the mid-1840s, the British economy underwent a boom period that lasted from 1847 to 1866. Exports to France doubled; investors became more willing to sink their capital into ventures in India and South America; and even the "cotton famine," the cutoff of raw materials from the American South at the beginning of the Civil War, proved an opportunity to find new sources of cotton and invest in updating cotton mills rather than a permanent setback.

The astounding population growth that had begun in the mid-1700s continued in the early Victorian period, but it was unevenly distributed; England and Wales, home to 13.8 million inhabitants in 1831, grew to 18 million in 1851 and over 22 million by 1870, through a combination of slightly lower death rates, immigration, and earlier ages of first marriage. In contrast, the population of Scotland remained just under 3 million people for the entire period, and Ireland, which began the period under study with 7.8 million people, had experienced a net decrease of about 2 million people by 1861, primarily due to the potato famine and out-migration. The relative urbanization of the population of the United Kingdom is striking; at mid-century, more than half of Britain's population lived in towns of 20,000 or more. In contrast, more than half of the people in the United States still lived on farms as late as 1900.

This demographic growth and internal migration put stress on both central and local governments, at a time when the acknowledged role of government was really very limited – and it also put stress on the environment. Because deliberate urban planning did not yet exist, noisome activities increasingly occurred close to dense concentrations of people. Cattle were slaughtered at markets in the middle of cities, and bits of their carcasses left to rot. Rivers ran through urban areas contaminated with sewage from industries like tanning and brewing. A sick child's soiled undergarments, washed near a public pump in London, provoked an outbreak of cholera that killed 616 people in 1854 (Summers 1989). Coal smoke, the by-product of both machinery and home heating, caused chronic respiratory problems and blocked out the sun for days at a time. Souvenirs from horse-drawn vehicles converted public streets into obstacle courses that women wearing dresses navigated at their own risk. By the summer of 1855, the Thames was so stagnant with sewage that it had begun to fester, as Professor Michael Faraday explained (in a letter that illustrates Victorian ingenuity as much as anything else):

> The whole of the river was an opaque pale brown fluid. In order to test the degree of opacity, I tore up some white cards into pieces, moistened them so as to make them sink easily below the surface, and then dropped some of these pieces into the water at every pier the boat came to; before they had sunk an inch below the surface they were indistinguishable, though the sun shone brightly at the time; and when the pieces fell edgeways the lower part was hidden from sight before the upper part was under water ... surely the river which flows for so many miles through London ought not to be allowed to become a fermenting sewer. (*Mechanics' Magazine* 1855: 29)

Contemporaries tried to make sense of industrial change and determine whether they saw an increase or decrease in wages, living conditions, and other indicators of people's well-being. Some observers characterized the changes as largely positive. Andrew Ure, a Scottish doctor who wrote extensively on industrialization, argued that the benefits of change – particularly increased industrial wages and lower prices for basic commodities – outweighed any negative consequences. Others felt that social costs outweighed any benefits. For example, opportunities for higher wages in urban areas led to a flight to overcrowded cities with poor amenities. The young Friedrich Engels brought his readers with him as he traveled through Manchester's working-class districts in 1844:

> Everywhere half or wholly ruined buildings, some of them actually uninhabited, which means a great deal here; rarely a wooden or stone floor to be seen in the houses, almost uniformly broken, ill-fitting windows and doors, and a state of filth!

THE POOR MAN'S FRIEND.

Figure 3.1 *Punch* cartoonist John Leech engaged in social criticism in his 1845 cartoon "The Poor Man's Friend," which shows a man living in destitute urban conditions, for whom death comes as a merciful relief. (Photo: IAM / akg-images).

> Everywhere heaps of *débris*, refuse, and offal; standing pools for gutters, and a stench which alone would make it impossible for a human being in any degree civilised to live in such a district. (Engels 1969: ch. 4)

In a thinly disguised gloss on Manchester, the novelist Elizabeth Gaskell had written in 1848 of the unpaved streets, heaps of ashes, pools of sewage, the poor living in cellars with their windows stuffed with rags (Gaskell 1998: 66). Critics of industrialization argued for social policies that improved living and working conditions, such as restrictions on child labor, and greater availability of poor relief.

The debate about the impact of the industrial revolution continues today. Conditions like poverty and child labor existed before industrialization, so that increased wages led to higher standards of living that outweighed drawbacks like crowding and pollution. People moved to towns and cities from rural areas largely because they expected their wage rates to increase, and this kind of movement helped some workers to break away from the comforting but socially static tradition that a man would follow in his father's trade or station in life.

Changes in wages do not tell the whole story, however, and contemporary reporting reveals anxiety and fear about the declining nature of urban life (Williamson 1981). The environmental lens of a "biological standard of living," that takes into account not only a person's rising or falling wages, but the whole interaction of the human organism with its environment, includes factors like disease, over-crowding, the efficiency of food markets, and environmental pollution. Between 1820 and 1840, the mean height of working-class men and women actually fell, compared to those who came before and after – suggesting that children, and/or pregnant women, were not receiving all the nutrition that they needed (Johnson and Nicholas 1992). As contemporaries observed, even though rural workers and urban workers were similarly poorly paid, rural workers survived better than their urban counterparts, with better access to healthier food supplies and fresh air. At mid-century, the life expectancy for infants born in Manchester and Liverpool was only 30 years, well below the national average of 41 years; but Glasgow had the most dismal statistic, with a life expectancy of only 27 years (Sretzer and Mooney 1998).

Social Structure: The Aristocracy

Part of why contemporaries wondered about whether economic change benefited the country was the highly disproportionate division of wealth and income. As noted in Chapter 1, Britain had been a stratified society for centuries. Legal institu-tions preserved the aristocracy's hold on political power through strict settlement and entail, which prevented imprudent estate-owners from selling off their lands by legally preserving them intact for the next generation; and through primogeniture, under which the oldest son in a family inherited all of the family's lands unless a will specifically made other arrangements. Some aristocratic families found themselves stretched thin by home renovations, lavish parties, and the support of large num-bers of family members and retainers. They were able to replenish their fortunes by intermarrying with daughters from wealthy families among the gentry, and through greater mechanization of agriculture, the improvement of farmland land, and royalties paid to them by mining and railroad companies.

Because few commoners were rewarded for their service to the crown with peerages – and then only if they had no children – aristocrats saw themselves as a group with racial, familial, educational, and economic advantages that made them uniquely suited to govern. Like the sons of plantation owners in the antebellum American South, the sons of aristocrats were freed by economic comfort to pursue the higher education (still in Greek and Latin and mathematics) thought vital for political leadership. It was expected in the early Victorian period that members of the aristocracy would have both a "country house" and a place in London, enabling them to link their rural constituencies with the seat of power, political news, and intrigue. Queen Victoria symbolically embraced about a couple of thousand of those at the top level of society each year, through levees and drawing room engagements, to which one could only gain entry through an aristocratic patron.

Increasingly, sons and daughters of the landed gentry, business magnates, and professionals also found their place at court as wealth trumped birth as the only path to a royal event. The London "season," as the annual social season/marriage market was termed, became longer and more hectic and crowded over the course of the nineteenth century, as the daughters and sons of the newly wealthy gained entry.

As noted in the preceding chapter, the aristocracy continued to govern after 1832 very much as before, and members of the aristocracy and gentry were still educated for political leadership. Children were raised among and by servants, largely separately from their parents. They received their earliest educations in nurseries, taught by governesses, and rarely saw their parents. Later, boys were sent to the great public schools like Winchester, Eton, and Harrow ("public" here meaning the opposite of its American meaning: private and dependent on endowments or on fees from students' families), which taught boys Latin and Greek, introduced them to other members of the ruling class, inculcated a belief in the superiority of the Anglo-Saxon race, and, by the 1860s, elevated the idea of an athletic body as well as a sound mind. Finally, it was on to the universities of Oxford or Cambridge for greater social exposure to others of the same class. As a result of the long-standing assumption that exposure to classical texts made men fit to govern and make moral decisions, the curriculum still focused on Greek, Latin, natural philosophy and mathematics. Newer emphases on subjects like modern languages and history were introduced at universities in Scotland and in London, but not at Oxford or Cambridge for some time.

Aristocratic women of the eighteenth century had participated indirectly in politics, choosing candidates to serve as MPs for proprietary boroughs, making speeches or dispensing cakes and ale at parties to support their chosen candidates, and even presiding over "salons," where intellectual and artistic greats met for discussion. By the 1830s and 1840s, however, under the influence of an evangelical ideal that separated "moral" women from the public eye, and a new politics that had begun to exclude nonvoters from political participation, these activities had come to seem much less typical or forgivable even for aristocratic matrons. Although they enjoyed participation in lavish social events, the London season, and the cultural life of towns like Bath, aristocratic women had little control over their own destinies, marriages, or even the number of children they bore. Aristocratic wives and daughters were expected to visit the sick, distribute customary food and drink at the holiday season, create model cottages for tenants, or support "coat clubs" and "boot clubs" to encourage rural laborers' thrift. Charity helped maintain the bonds of deference between rural workers and aristocrats and reaffirmed the latter's cultural dominance.

While the aristocracy and landed gentry held onto their political and economic dominance with little change before 1870, they did have to adapt to a more pervasive middle-class culture. Aristocratic concepts of manliness from the regency period – high living, womanizing, and dueling – became less pervasive than were thrift and moral sobriety. The meanings of economic "independence" were in conflict: aristocrats could earn income from rents rather than production, were expected to entertain lavishly, and spent much of their time in leisure activities like hunting and fishing, while for other social groups "independence" meant the ability to win bread to support a family. Religious evangelicalism operated on both the aristocracy and the wider culture. Just as Parliament in the mid-1840s moved decisively away from older mores by shutting down famous London gambling clubs like Crockford's, so Anthony Ashley Cooper, the 7th Earl of Shaftesbury, was moved by his own evangelical tendencies to dedicate his life to reforming child labor and providing schools for poor children.

The Middle Classes

In the late eighteenth century, "the middle classes" was a political term invented to express a political middle ground at a time of divisiveness. France may have been captured by radicals, but England was the land of the moderate middle. Those who discussed the middling ranks of society – no matter what term they used – tended to link them with all of the "positive" attributes of a stable society: masculinity, trade and commerce, moral seriousness and evangelical self-control, urban life, and a habit of socializing and acting to reform society through the formation of voluntary associations. Members of the middle classes saw themselves as exemplars of creditworthiness and belief in transparent and honest government. They defined themselves in opposition to both working-class wealth, amassed through bodily toil, and aristocratic wealth, earned through rents.

By the early Victorian period, an increasing number of people identified themselves in this way. Families with incomes between £50 and £400 a year increased from 15 to 25 percent of the population of Great Britain between the 1820s and the 1850s. In 1851, 28 percent of middle-class families earned their livings as owners of shops. Twenty-one percent were in such professions as law, medicine, the church, teaching, and engineering; although fields like medicine and the law were themselves minutely subdivided on the basis of education and clientele. Another 21 percent of middle-class families were supported by clerks, government agents, or bankers. Ten percent were farmers, 12 percent owned factories, 4 percent were in the hospitality industry as innkeepers, hoteliers, or tavern-keepers, and 11 percent were retired.

Those on the lower end of middle income who lived in cities were likely to own single-person enterprises and use mostly family labor, including that of their wives – but even an income of £300 a year was enough to hire a resident maid. Those members of the more modest middle classes who farmed generally leased or owned between 50 and 300 acres. They invested their money in houses and buildings, left real property to their heirs at death, and had limited access to credit from banks that might allow them to expand their enterprises. Many members of the modest middle classes belonged to "dissenting" congregations and had only local contacts. Residentially, these were the men most likely to live in economically mixed neighborhoods – perhaps running pubs or retail stores that catered to a working-class clientele.

In contrast, those in the upper ranks of the middle classes were more likely to be members of a partnership or trust and to employ a significant workforce, whether in industry or by running larger farms. They had access to credit from outside the family circle, and generated a surplus that could be invested in government securities, foreign infrastructure, or land. Members of the more prosperous middle classes had the educational advantage of private academies or the less prestigious fee-charging grammar schools, and their social circles tended to extend outside their provincial towns, to those in the same industry in other cities, or in London. Like more modest middle-class men, these wealthier men participated in voluntary societies, but tended to be leaders rather than members of the rank and file. They were more likely to be Quakers, Unitarians, Congregationalists or Anglicans than Methodists or Baptists, sects which had greater working-class appeal. The more prosperous sectors of the middle classes often lived in segregated neighborhoods in the city center, or, increasingly, in enclave-like suburbs.

Although many members of the middle classes had been enfranchised by the Reform Act of 1832, they did not vote as an economic bloc. Rather, their party affiliations often divided along religious lines, Tory Anglicans on one side, Liberal Nonconformists on the other. Party feelings could also be subsumed for the greater good of the towns, in whose politics men of the middle classes played a role at all levels. Manufacturers and large retailers served as town councilors and Poor Law Guardians and chaired voluntary societies. Men with less economic and political capital belonged to book clubs and societies that distributed religious tracts and visited the poor. Initiatives such as the perceived need to reach out to encourage thrift among members of the working classes, or the prospect of bringing docks and railroads to urban areas united middle-class men across the lines of economic and religious division. One example of the Victorian culture of voluntary association, the National Association for the Promotion of Social Science, founded in 1857, brought experts in many areas together to craft policy and advise Parliament on legislation. Eventually, this task would devolve to government experts, but in the mid-Victorian period, there was no social issue that could not be tackled by the right committee of volunteers.

The middle classes had varying experiences based on differences in income, political affiliation, and religious affiliation, but the most salient division for de-termining life experiences was gender. Although little boys and girls dressed alike until about age five – in long, curly hair and dresses with leading-strings – any similarity between the two ended soon after. Parents encouraged boys to pursue physical and outdoor play, sent them to receive formal education, and arranged for them to serve an apprenticeship or work in the family business. Girls were taught useful skills at a younger age, but only those that would fit them for marriage and parenthood: needlework and cooking, the skill of caring for younger siblings. Although the occasional liberal father saw value in educating girls for the sake of education, most received training in those attainments – the ability to play musical instruments, draw, or speak a little French – designed to make them ornaments for a future husband.

These early differences developed into completely different expectations for adult men and women. Middle-class men defined their masculinity largely through identification with the workplace, itself increasingly a space outside the home. Doctors, engineers, and others defined their professional identities for the first time through a process of exclusion on the basis of education and gender. Family ties were crucial to the success of many businesses, as Leonore Davidoff and Catherine Hall (1987) have documented; but this support existed alongside a potent "myth" that the best men pulled themselves up by their bootstraps. The popularity of this idea explains the success of Leeds newspaperman Samuel Smiles's best-seller *Self-Help* (1859), a book aimed at the upwardly mobile working classes. The book argued – through notable examples of self-made men – that individuals were responsible for their own future, and that if they persevered – even in the face of incredibly steep odds and against logic – they would win the appreciation of their families and the adulation of society.

While masculinity was largely defined by men's connection with the world of work, and commerce and political life, men's lives were not lived only in the "public sphere." To a much greater extent than aristocratic men, middle-class men played with their young children, made the major decisions regarding their children's formal education, gave them paternal advice, and participated in hands-on child care when their wives were ill. They took older children on walks, read aloud to them, held family prayers, saw to their sons' educations and apprenticeships and were encouraged to dote on and shelter their daughters. They were also largely in charge of family discipline – aiding the stereotype of the stern Victorian father.

In contrast, middle-class women were informed, through a vigorous cultural discourse, that their major role was within the home: marriage and companionship with their husbands, engaged but not suffocating mothering of their children, and thrift and orderliness as housewives, including the assiduous and time-consuming supervision of the servants, whose presence in the house was a crucial marker of entry to the middle classes. Much of the literature outlining a "domestic sphere" for women encouraged women to develop the personalities of husbands and children, without consideration of the idea that women might have personalities or interests of their own.

The Victorian middle-class home – more often rented than owned – was increasingly a center of habits of consumption that had trickled down from the aristocracy and gentry: full of bric-a-brac, heavy curtains and rugs, musical instruments, and ornate furniture. Often situated away from urban centers in new suburbs, such homes afforded much more privacy to their dwellers – sitting rooms for women, separate bedrooms for children, parlors for company, separate staircases and kitchens for the use of servants. Middle-class women aspiring to follow their social betters turned to Mrs Beeton's *Household Management* (1859–1861) to understand the separate tasks undertaken in larger country homes by scullery maids, nursery maids, footmen and butlers, even if they only had a couple of maids-of-all-work to manage.

In fact, Victorian middle-class women faced considerable structural barriers to a life outside the home. While women could bring property into a marriage, it became the property of their husbands, who could take for their own use even wages earned by wives during the marriage. Large families continued to be the norm. The average middle-class woman gave birth to seven children, at intervals of about 18–24 months, from the time that she married until about age 40. The large amount of time that many women spent pregnant and breastfeeding – and moral concerns about being visibly pregnant in public – encouraged many women to cultivate a small social circle of home and family. The middle-class home of the period had its own attractions, now that each family member increasingly had his or her own space, in the drawing room, nursery, or den. And because they were responsible for rearing their young children until it was time to enroll in school, and because they aimed to be educated conversationalists for their husbands, middle-class women were also encouraged to receive a basic education, and to read improving literature.

Middle-class women also contributed to the family economy and larger community. Women performed unwaged work alongside household servants, shopped and planned meals, and created and maintained the family wardrobe. All of these were so important to a middle-class family's survival that marriage was recognized as an economic partnership, and widowed men – especially those with small children – tended to remarry quickly. Conversely, a wife without the ability to manage these responsibilities could be as detrimental as no partner at all, as in George Eliot's novel *Middlemarch*, in which a promising young doctor is ruined by his wife's spendthrift ways.

Particularly among the lower middle classes, women had no choice but to work for money. They fed and housed pupils, coworkers, apprentices, and other lodgers, and ran small businesses in their homes. When husbands took teaching assignments, wives taught female students without any additional payment. Widows might completely take over their husbands' former responsibilities upon his death. Women also sometimes earned money for personal or family use by undertaking small-scale activities that could be done at home. There were a few women in science, but their role was envisioned as subsidiary to that of men, and limited to certain fields considered to be more passive than others (botanical collecting and drawing or astronomical observation, for example). For women who did write or draw, it was more acceptable for them to translate or illustrate the work of others rather than invent their own. There were important writers, like Elizabeth Gaskell, George Eliot (the penname of Mary Anne Evans), and Harriet Martineau, but they were rare. Some women who dared to participate in the public sphere chose pseudonyms to write about politics, or encouraged women to channel their political feelings through traditionally "female" activities like consumer boycotts (Gleadle 2005).

Both men and women of the middle classes increasingly made a mark for themselves as leaders through religious stewardship. The British government's 1851 census of religious observance revealed that middle-class people – and particularly the women among them – were more avid religious practitioners than members of any other class. Religion was a bridge to areas of public life that were described as private – churches as well as the homes they visited as part of missionary efforts.

Tight bonds between religion and the family structure in the nineteenth century helped to facilitate the cultural emergence of the middle classes. Middle-class families were supposed to be close: fathers provided for single daughters from beyond the grave with iron-clad annuities that supported them and kept them safe from predators, and poetry and song romanticized the love siblings were supposed to have for each other. But church membership helped to extend this feeling of brotherhood and commitment beyond the confines of the middle-class family; surely a comforting aspect at a time of great economic change. Young women volunteered as teachers in Sunday School; single men who moved to a new town could find other religious single men to socialize with through the Young Men's Christian Association (YMCA). Middle-class mothers founded missionary societies to find fellowship with each other and reach out to working-class women, whether such outreach was acceptable or not.

The Working Classes

The rich associational culture of the British middle classes meant that Britain's economic middle defined themselves, not only as those who were neither the wealthy nor the poor, but also those who most energetically acted in and upon society. In contrast, the working classes were defined by others: seen as the objects of reform, the nature of their lives is largely refracted through the agendas of the reformers. In the early Victorian period in particular, Select Committees and Royal Commissions began to focus on the physical details of workers' surroundings and their bodies, arguing that these were related (whether as cause or as effect) to lack of spiritual development, lack of morality, or lack of shame. People were more likely to believe that poverty was the result of a worker's moral failings than that it was a structural feature of capitalism.

Urban and rural working people experienced significantly different lives. Even as urbanization proceeded, small farms persisted because they grew more diverse crops than larger farms, which had narrowed production to wheat and cattle. Throughout the country in 1851, about half of all farms were still family farms of

50 acres or fewer. They relied largely on family labor, with all family members participating at harvest time; teenage children were still distributed to neighboring farms as servants, as they had been for centuries. Small farmers supplemented their income with work as carters, tavern-keepers, providers of raw materials like lime or gravel; women and children working at home made butter, collected eggs, and even wove hand-loomed cloth up until the 1860s, despite the fact that cheaper machine-made cloth was available. In some areas of the country, as in Lancashire, this tradition of family farming benefited from nearby industrialization, as demand grew among urban workers for perishable goods like milk, butter, fresh vegetables and berries.

Less self-sufficient were farm laborers, who could be hired either by the day, or on an annual contract. Rural workers continued to raise large families, planted and harvested, repaired fences, cared for farm animals, made butter and cheese, and served as domestic servants in others' homes. Although farmworkers' wages varied regionally, being higher in the North, most wages were meager, and workers depended on supplementing them either illegally (by trapping game) or legally (through cultivation of allotment gardens, pieces of land of less than an acre which were often rented to workers as, it was hoped, cures to rural poverty and idleness). Although some philanthropists took a greater interest in rural workers' housing, most laborers' cottages were run-down even compared with city slums. Many rural families lacked access to the kinds of cultural amenities available in cities and towns, although children were widely sent to Anglican Sunday Schools to learn basic literacy.

Crowded together, given access to newspapers and political meetings, and more alienated from their "social superiors," urban workers had a richer associational culture than did those living in the country. The "togetherness" of urban workers was reflected in the environment; the standard urban housing in the early Victorian period was the brick row house, many examples of which still survive in England's urban North. Workers lucky enough to live in these attached "two-up, two-down" houses enjoyed two rooms on the lower floor (generally kitchen and public areas) and two on the upper floor (generally sleeping areas). Because the rows of houses were built back to back, with only a small alleyway separating the "front" row of houses from the "back" row, there was no way to achieve ventilation through the houses, so workers shared each others' diseases and sewage and cooking smells as part of this togetherness. To add insult to injury, as many as a hundred people or more shared a single, too rarely emptied, earth toilet, or "privy," located at the end of the block or in the back alley; and they shared the need to bring in water from sometimes contaminated public pumps.

Less fortunate workers made do with cellar dwellings, in which a large family might be crowded into a single room in the base of a building. Public health reformers who visited these lodgings often noted damp, cracking walls, bugs, and vermin; but the lack of privacy inherent in Victorian working-class dwellings, with parents and children sleeping in the same room, appeared to bother such reformers as much as did the lack of access to ventilation and water. Morality could trump mortality as a cause for concern.

Particularly during the "hungry forties" (the 1840s), the lives of urban working people in the early Victorian period revolved around finances. Although some urban working people contributed on a regular basis to "friendly societies" organized through their workplaces or neighborhoods, providing some shelter for a rainy day, most working people had few assets and little savings. As a result, while the man of the house might skim off some amount from each week's pay for recreation and drink, other family members were expected to contribute their wages to a common fund, from which the wife planned meals and other expenses. Working people often could not afford to purchase food and other goods in any quantity – meaning that they paid more, for lower-quality food, than did other groups. This was especially true in those areas where workers were paid in "truck" – company scrip used in lieu of cash in some mining villages and redeemable only at a company store. So pervasive was this practice that even an 1831 Act outlawing truck was unable to eliminate its use. Yet even as they made do with poor bread and adulterated butter, they spent money that they did not have on funerals, wanting to avoid at all costs the stigma that came with a pauper's funeral. Poor women often depended on the ability to pawn family clothing and other items at the beginning of the week, and to redeem their pawned items at the end of the week. The British working classes exasperated social reformers when their priorities for consumption were so clearly inefficient in reformers' eyes.

While they could afford little, most urban workers were fully integrated into an imperial economy. A traditional diet of whole grains, root vegetables, and occasional fish, eggs and meat products had given way to a preference for white bread with a scraping of jam or butter, tea (from the East Indies) and sugar (from the West Indies), all of which contributed to workers' short stature and vitamin deficiency. Even when the family wage increased, nutritional benefits were not evenly distributed; within families, food tended to be rationed, with the largest and best portions of any protein source available (usually meat or eggs) going to fathers. Over time, malnutrition, pregnancy and breastfeeding wore down working-class women, although given the presence of workplace accidents and endemic diseases like tuberculosis, life expectancies for men and women remained similar.

As did some middle-class women, most working-class women supplemented the family economy through a number of measures that, while not given the same social recognition as breadwinning, were crucial to survival. They scavenged food or coal, repaired clothing, learned ways to stretch a small amount of food, took in lodgers, or performed outwork tasks, like sewing, within the home. Some women – especially female heads of household – also worked outside the home, but were largely confined to unskilled jobs. Gender itself played a major role in the definition of "skill" within a workplace: men who operated spinning mules were considered skilled because they did a job limited to male workers, whereas women who operated four weaving looms alongside them in the factory were considered

Figure 3.2 In this 1835 print, workers operate a pair of spinning mules. Each of the hundreds of spindles on each mule performs the work previously done by a single spinner. At right, below the machine, a piecer performs the dangerous task of cleaning the floor and piecing together broken threads. (© The British Library Board 1044.g.23, opposite 211).

semiskilled or unskilled. Considerations of "skill" also revolved around workers' ability to control the entry of other workers into a field, through mandatory apprenticeships or traditional practices of subcontracting.

Working-class children's experiences were the most different from those of their middle-class and aristocratic peers. Few very young children worked outside the home, but by the age of 10 or 11, about half of boys, and a significant number of girls, already earned wages. Child workers were particularly concentrated in textile industries producing cotton, silk, linen, and wool articles; their small bodies and small fingers were thought to be well suited for activities like getting under spinning frames to piece together broken threads. Children also worked underground in coal mines. Before legislation limited work underground to those over age ten in 1842, children as young as five or six sat in dark spaces, without candles, opening and shutting ventilation doors on which the health of all workers underground depended. Deprivation of sunlight caused short stature and rickets in these mining children, who spent much of their early lives in the dark with little human company. Preindustrial cottage industries like weaving or nail-making also called on the participation of all family members; but the environment in which work took place was very different by the 1830s and 1840s. Now, young workers worked steadily for up to 12 hours, at a pace determined by machinery.

Experiences of the workplace in the early Victorian period depended on a number of different variables. The location of the workplace was important. Coal miners shared similar experiences: long days underground, work alongside family members and children who tended mule carts or opened ventilation doors, the threat of constant danger from falling roofs and exploding gases, and pay by the volume of coal brought up. But coal miners in Northumberland and Durham were better organized, and more likely to be able to wrest concessions from their employers, than, for example, the miners of southern Wales. The age and skill level of a worker helped to structure his or her experience. An adult artisan working in a cutlery factory in Sheffield was more likely to be able to exert some control over the hours of his employment, and the steps he took to turn out a product, than was a child working to piece together threads or replace full spindles with empty ones in a textile factory in Lancashire. For many workers, the workplace was still a construction site, a small shoe shop, or a family-owned nail-making business, with the major change being increased demand for products rather than any introduction of machinery or division of labor.

Workers' experiences also depended on whether they were unionized. Beginning in the 1830s, workers attempted to build broad-based national unions. Formed in the 1830s under the stewardship of the philanthropist Robert Owen, the Grand National Consolidated Trades Union attempted cooperative production and sales. The National Association of United Trades came together briefly in the late 1840s as a merger of existing trade unions, and as a means of creating cooperative work for the unemployed. Successful unions created a sense of solidarity among workers, provided "journeymen" with work as they traveled from one town to another gaining job experience, and maintained their own mutual aid societies. But although unions were legal, employers opposed their existence, claiming they restricted the freedom of trade. Few workers were unionized by 1870 – about 500,000 out of a total workforce of 20 million – and those who were tended to have socially acknowledged work "skills" and some ability to control entry into the workforce.

Within the working classes, there was a hierarchy of status and opportunity. At the opposite end of the spectrum from the skilled tradesmen were the paupers, who made up 8 percent of the British population in 1841. Some were members of the pool of casual labor – unskilled construction helpers, many of them Irish immigrants – hard-pressed to cobble together steady enough employment to keep their families fed. Some of these men and women participated in the avid recycling industry: collecting old clothes to be made into paper, old bones to be made into china, or even night-soil (human waste) for use on market garden crops. Some purchased small amounts of produce or flowers and worked the pavement for long hours to resell them at a tiny profit. Others participated in theft or burglary, fencing their wares through the pawn shops (although the prospect of long jail sentences or even penal transportation to Australia made this a risky option). Voluntary charities for the urban poor were insufficient, and might require that recipients go through a complicated and judgmental interview process to ascertain eligibility. In order to qualify for government poor relief, men and women had to move back to the places where they had been born – because it was only there that they had a "settlement," or official entitlement to relief. These factors, in combination with the Poor Law's mandate that the poor be served in workhouses, meant that most people preferred to eke out an incredibly marginal living than to seek charity from the state.

Workers' leisure opportunities were structured by age, gender, and the rural-urban divide as well. Urban workers were segregated from members of the middle and upper classes in their leisure activities. For working men, public houses were important gathering places, providing not only much-appreciated alcoholic beverages, but also the opportunity to socialize, escape the demands of wives and children, hear newspapers read, and wager on bare-knuckle boxing matches and impromptu running races. Larger establishments were just beginning to experiment in this period with singers and circus acts, appealing to a younger crowd of women and men; these would become the kernel of the late nineteenth-century music hall. Working-class women and children had little opportunity for formal leisure activities: women relied on informal socializing as they hung washing on the lines; children invented games played in the streets.

Just as evangelical reformers had noticed the poor living conditions of many workers, so their leisure activities came under scrutiny. The fact that so much of male working-class leisure revolved around drink made many uncomfortable (and not just middle- or upper-class reformers – the "teetotal" movement for abstinence from alcohol had its roots among Northern workers in the early 1830s). Patrons attempted to provide "rational recreation" for working people. Mechanics' institutes, purpose-built buildings with middle-class or aristocratic patrons who provided libraries and practical classes for working men, proliferated in provincial towns in this period, as did Sunday Schools, but few of these were popular unless they could be taken over by working-class leaders. Many workers had a strong desire for respectability defined on their own terms, which revealed itself in wide reading at public libraries, or attendance at lectures on science, or participation in the cooperative movement, in which families clubbed together their funds to supply the basic necessities of life to themselves collectively at a wholesale price.

Reformers found workers' absence from church especially dismaying, although the religious census of 1851 did show church adherence was still strong among workers in rural areas and smaller towns. In Wales, the nonconformist chapel became a site of community strength; Methodism in particular attracted many working people before its peak in 1850; and Catholic church adherence was strong among the Irish immigrants of the industrial Northwest. But even the choice not to participate in organized religion was not the same as secularism; for all but a few committed secularists, nominal Protestantism was a key facet of British working-class identity, which differentiated them not only from Catholic immigrants but also the Hindu and Muslim residents of the growing British Empire.

The economic growth, rural-to-urban migration, and changing fortunes of social and economic groups in England, Wales, Scotland and Ireland between 1832 and 1867 were just one part of a drama taking place on a much larger stage, as Britain now had substantial footholds in North America, the Caribbean, India, Australia and New Zealand. Whether or not middle-class housewives, schoolboys at Eton, or hard-rock miners in Cornwall participated directly in the process of imperial expansion, the British government conducted that expansion largely on their behalf, and it affected all Britons economically, politically, and socially.

Before 1870, both the empire and other areas of the globe offered a sphere for investment and export, for those firms willing to take risks and wait a long time for returns. The availability of markets for British goods – not only in places like Australia and Canada, but also in the United States, Argentina, and Uruguay – meant that British firms could continue to pay workers relatively low wages, while at the same time expanding their output by calling out for other countries to practice "free trade." Britain's imperial experience also allowed it to provide the world with shipping and insurance services.

Like so many other experiences in the early Victorian period, the experience of empire was refracted through social class. The aristocracy and gentry found in the empire the opportunity for power and leadership; members of the middle classes read newspapers that covered imperial concerns, and traveled to imperial outposts as journalists, doctors, military officers, and members of the civil service. But even the working people who may not have known where their tea or sugar or hot cocoa were imported from were aware that the government regarded the empire as a place to be filled with Britain's "surplus population." Between 1788 and 1868, British courts deported 162,000 felons to the provinces that eventually became Australia. The six high-profile trade unionists deported to Australia in 1834, and the Chartist leaders later sent there in 1839, created a mindset that the colonies were to be feared – transportation to the other side of the world as a form of living death. Beginning in the 1830s, this vision began to change to one of the colonies as lands of opportunity. First Canada, and then Australia, became new lands that workers could reach through government or private assistance schemes. The "colonies of settlement," as these outposts of empire were called, promised the prospects of political participation, high wages, landownership, and social mobility – and even riches, after gold was discovered in Victoria in 1851.

By the 1860s, Britain had achieved a measure of peace and prosperity through industrial growth, imperial expansion, and increasing deployment of the ideology of free trade. This had come during extraordinary demographic growth, particularly in urban areas, leaving a legacy of tremendous wealth creation as well as poverty on a previously unrecognized scale. The economic and social forces unleashed by rapid industrial change fueled domestic and foreign politics for decades to come, and provided the context for equally destabilizing and creative intellectual developments through the mid and late Victorian period.

References

Davidoff, Leonore, and Hall, Catherine (1987) *Family Fortunes: Men and Women of the English Middle Class, 1780–1850*. Chicago: University of Chicago Press.

Engels, Friedrich (1969) *The Condition of the Working Class in England in 1844*. London: Panther Books. Originally published 1845. At http://www.marxists.org/archive/marx/works/1845/condition-working-class/ch04.htm (accessed Dec. 18, 2007).

Gaskell, Elizabeth (1998) *Mary Barton*. Oxford: Oxford University Press.

Gleadle, Kathryn (2005) Charlotte Elizabeth Tonna and the Mobilization of Tory Women in Early Victorian England. *Historical Journal*, 50 (1): 97–117.

Johnson, Paul, and Nicholas, Stephen (1992) Male and Female Living Standards in England and Wales, 1812–1857: Evidence from Criminal Height Records, *Economic History Review*, 48 (3): 470–481.

Mayhew, Henry (2009) *London Labour and the London Poor*, vol. 1. London: Cosimo Press. First published 1861.

Mechanics' Magazine (1855) Polluted State of the Thames. Vol. 63 (July 7).

Sretzer, Simon, and Mooney, Graham (1998) Urbanization, Mortality and the Standard-of-Living Debate: New Estimates of the Expectation of Life at Birth in Nineteenth-Century British Cities. *Economic History Review*, 51: 84–112.

Summers, Judith (1989) *Soho: A History of London's Most Colourful Neighborhood*. London: Bloomsbury. Extract at http://www.ph.ucla.edu/epi/snow/broadstreetpump.html (accessed June 29, 2011).

Williamson, Jeffrey G. (1981) Urban Disamenities, Dark Satanic Mills, and the British Standard of Living Debate. *Journal of Economic History*, 41 (1): 75–83.

Further Reading

August, Andrew (2007) *The British Working Class, 1832–1940*. Harlow: Pearson Longman.

Black, Jeremy, and McRaild, Donald (2002) *Nineteenth-Century Britain*. London: Palgrave Macmillan.

Flanders, Judith (2004) *Inside the Victorian Home*. New York: Norton.

Hobsbawm, Eric (1968) *Industry and Empire: The Birth of the Industrial Revolution*. New York: New Press.

Joyce, Patrick (1993) *Visions of the People: Industrial England and the Question of Class, c.1848–1914*. Cambridge: Cambridge University Press.

Morris, R.J. (2005) *Men, Women, and Property in England, 1780–1870*. Cambridge: Cambridge University Press.

Rose, Sonya (1992) *Limited Livelihoods: Gender and Class in Nineteenth-Century England*. Berkeley: University of California Press.

Thompson, Andrew (2005) *The Empire Strikes Back? The Impact of Imperialism on Britain from the Mid-Nineteenth Century*. New York: Longman.

4

Utilitarians, Evangelicals, and Empire
Intellectual and Cultural Developments, 1830–1867

The question of questions for mankind – the problem which underlies all others, and is more deeply interesting than any other – is the ascertainment of the place which man occupies in nature and of his relation to the universe of things. Whence our race has come; what are the limits of our power over nature, and of nature's power over us; to what goal are we tending; are the problems which present themselves anew . . .

Thomas H. Huxley, *On the Relations of Man to the Lower Animals*, 1863

In the midst of dramatic and often wrenching social change, few common traits link the many tendencies, impulses and developments we group together as "Victorian culture." Victorian cultural and intellectual life contained its own opposites: faith and doubt, anxiety and confidence, earnestness and hypocrisy. The industrial age saw both unparalleled wealth and growing awareness of poverty, and Victorians encouraged both cultural conformity and produced extraordinarily trenchant social criticism that retains its energy to this day.

Huxley's quote reminds us that the early Victorians self-consciously understood themselves as living through tremendous historical transformation, a sea-change in ideas, beliefs, politics, and social order. Behind them lay the static hierarchies of social order and clerical knowledge; before them lay a future of progress, reason, and a dynamic social structure. This future evoked optimism in those who believed it good and pessimism in those who saw only decline, but all understood that the world of their parents would be radically different than the world of their children, and in this respect the age really was new. It would be as bracing and destabilizing as if today, accustomed as we are to the constancy of change, we suddenly grasped that society and knowledge had *ceased* to change and would remain more or less the same for the next hundred years.

Empire, State, and Society: Britain Since 1830, First Edition. Jamie L. Bronstein and Andrew T. Harris.

What produced this new sense of continuous change? Undoubtedly the economic, demographic and environmental impact of industrialization profoundly challenged people's concept of a static social order. Wealth creation, widespread poverty, population growth, urbanization, new and much faster forms of transportation all contributed to the belief that the very foundations of their world were shifting under their feet. The growth of middle-class households that had begun in the previous century represented an implicit challenge to the idea that birth ought to determine wealth and political influence. More than that, the growth of an urban "working class," or even the growth of an articulate urban laboring population, posed a direct and threatening democratic question to political stability. If people could alter their social status, then what became of the assumption that fixed social status was a quality inherent in the very nature of society? With that question hanging, and with old elites losing their hold on the levers of social order, what force – moral, political or economic – would or could provide social stability? Who had the right to rule, and why?

Economic restraints on prices, wages and entry into certain trades through apprenticeships had all been loosened if not eliminated by the early years of the century, and so markets for labor and goods became more uncertain and more unstable. Population growth and increasing migration during the eighteenth century, accelerated by new labor demands in the early industrial era, meant more people living in new and often urban environments, freed from the ties of family, of community, and of the rural social hierarchy so much less prevalent in growing towns and cities. Nor was anxiety confined to the working poor; for all the prosperity of the mid-nineteenth century, middle-class Britons lived through dramatic economic cycles of boom and bust in credit, industry, and finance. Few were so affluent as to be free of the negative effects of economic fluctuation.

The social changes accompanying industrialization created fluctuating labor markets, but the fear of revolution – popular, dramatic, and violently bloody – hung over the decades of the first half of the century. The memory of the French Revolution of 1789, refreshed by European revolutions in 1830 and 1848, made all popular gatherings seem potentially more threatening – to the middle-class champions of public order, but also to poorer Britons, some of whom gloried in this threat and some of whom were just as leery of violent change as their more affluent neighbors. Benjamin Disraeli, novelist, Tory politician and ultimately Prime Minister, wrote that those with property saw "the masses" as enemies, and felt that "they might have to fight, any year, or any day, for the safety of their property and the honour of their sisters."

Victorian culture was not all fear, anxiety and social disintegration, of course. Industry and science suggested new sources of work, new discoveries about the natural world and new ways of improving individuals and even society in general. The same person who might look with horror on the social climbing and political ambitions of his servant or hatmaker could have come from similar roots just one or two generations earlier. One could value the fruits of social mobility and economic change so long as they accrued primarily to oneself. We seek here to outline the contours of both optimism and pessimism, and we begin with the foundations of belief in Victorian religion.

Religious Belief and Religious Practice

Britain – or rather England – had an "established" church, which meant that membership and attendance in the Church of England determined one's legal ability to vote and hold local or national office. Many non-Anglicans, including Presbyterians, Congregationalists and Jews, practiced "occasional conformity" as noted in Chapter 1, but even this skirting of the law rankled in the minds of many. The 1820s saw the repeal of the Test and Corporation Acts (which placed civil restrictions on non-Anglican Protestants) and passage of the Roman Catholic Relief Act (which removed restrictions on Catholics). For a brief period it looked as if England might continue down this road and disestablish its church entirely, removing that church's close connection with and influence over political life, but this did not come to pass. Instead of losing power through disestablishment, the Church of England became broader and its tenets less clearly defined throughout the century. In this it followed the place of religious belief throughout British society as a whole: society was becoming gradually secularized, acknowledging different sources of morality and knowledge itself in secular education and scientific discovery.

Concern about formal disestablishment caused tremors, but the really frightening prospect was more grassroots in nature. In 1851, the British government undertook the first Census of Religious Worship, in which the state sought to determine how many people attended religious services in church on a given Sunday, what church they attended, and what conclusions could be drawn about the shape of British religious life. The results were bleak, revealing, and misunderstood all at once. Only 7,261,032 people had attended services, and when one factored out those too young, old or sick to attend, that left over 5 million who could have gone to church and chose not to. This led to considerable hand-wringing about the irreligion of the working classes, whose lack of religious grounding fed into broader concerns about their immorality and hence the likelihood of social breakdown. Without the salutary fear of damnation provided by organized religion of any stripe, the argument on behalf of morality became murky, at least in the minds of the socially respectable churchgoing Briton. Even so, little evidence suggests that irreligion actually led to bad behavior among the working poor. As historian Asa Briggs pointed out, church attendance and religious homilies might encourage industry and thrift, but fear of unemployment and starvation were even more persuasive.

For all that it appeared to reveal at the time, the 1851 religious census needs to be seen in the context of both a more general and dramatic long-term population increase, and a rise throughout the century in the number of churches built, the number of active churchgoers, the number of children attending Sunday School, and the vitality, passion and variety of Victorian belief. While the census focused attention on the irreligion of many, we should not conclude that this snapshot of religious attendance equals either religious belief or a long-term trajectory of belief in itself. What, then, did Victorians think about faith and how did they practice it?

The established Church of England still had the most adherents at mid-century, followed by different nonconformist sects (Methodists, Congregationalists and Baptists, to name the largest). Anglicans and the nonconformist sects taken together had roughly equal Sunday attendance. Catholics made up a small minority (perhaps 750,000 in 1850), and Jews a far smaller one (35,000). There were significant regional differences: nonconformity dominated towns designated "chief manufacturing districts," and cities on the western coast saw higher numbers of Catholics, driven by Irish in-migration particularly after the 1830s. Scotland had its own established national church separate from the Church of England, the Church of Scotland (known as the "Kirk"), that differed in both theology and church structure from the Anglican Church. Its Calvinist theology emphasized salvation through faith alone, rather than behavior, to a greater degree, and its hierarchy consisted of different layers of assemblies rather than the more authoritative Anglican episcopal structure. Like the Anglican Church, the Kirk embarked on attempts to reach the growing populations of urban poor through early aggressive church-building campaigns. The state had limited capacity to support this, however, leaving the Scottish religious field fragmented among the established church and two offshoots: the United Presbyterian Church and the Free Church. By 1845, earlier than in England, the Scottish national church got out of the business of poor relief and had pulled back from education as well by 1872.

Although very much a minority religion in England, Wales and Scotland in the nineteenth century, Catholicism thrived, growing from under 100,000 adherents in 1800 to 750,000 in 1850. This tremendous increase came from the great numbers of Irish immigrants seeking work throughout the period, and in particular from heightened immigration during the famine in the 1840s. That most Catholics in England were poor immigrants did nothing to improve strains of anti-Catholic feeling going back centuries. As adherents to a religion whose members (in theory) and whose church leaders (in practice) owed allegiance to an external ecclesiastical structure, Catholics had since the Reformation been seen as always a potential source of disloyalty, and even treason, within the realm. Britain had often gone to war with Catholic France and Spain over faith, colonial possessions and commerce, and had absorbed Catholic Ireland by conquest, occupation and settlement, so the fear that some British Catholics might very well desire disruption of government was all too real. Protestant Britons also retained a residual belief that the papacy sought to bring Britain back under Roman Catholic control, though this was by the nineteenth century pure fantasy. Taken together, however, these factors help explain the tremendous outcry in 1850–1851 over a papal decision to expand the size and complexity of the English Catholic Church hierarchy. Violent editorials were published in newspapers, eminent English Catholics were burnt in effigy, and mobs harassed Catholic priests in public. It seemed that British fears of papal domination were coming true – but this proved ephemeral. The long-term trend throughout the century was not prejudice but gradual if uneven acceptance in British life.

Britain's Jewish population was quite small. The state had legally "admitted" Jews into the country in the 1650s under Oliver Cromwell, and numbers remained low into the nineteenth century, climbing from 25,000 in 1800 to perhaps 60,000 by 1880. Much of this increase was, as with Catholics, driven by immigration, albeit from Central and Eastern Europe rather than Ireland. Except for formally excluding them from Parliament until 1858, British laws did not discriminate against Jews any more than other non-Anglicans; unlike in most European countries, they were not required to live in particular areas, wear certain clothes or refrain from practicing specific occupations. Jewish men could vote and run for office in local elections. They had not yet separated into industrial working-class and affluent professional middle-class Jewish communities (as they were to do later in the century), and most were craftsmen and small shopkeepers. British anti-Semitism existed as an undercurrent but not a torrent of abuse – Benjamin Disraeli, who converted to Anglicanism at the age of 12, may have been whispered about because of his Jewish parents, for example, but this did not prevent him from becoming Prime Minister.

Socioeconomic factors often influenced (but did not determine) formal church membership: Anglican Evangelicals tended toward greater affluence, while middle-class Britons gravitated to nonconformist sects and Methodism in particular appealed to the working poor. These differences had something to do with the culture of a faith and a sense of group belonging, but also derived from the degree to which different beliefs and social outlooks could be more or less congenial to people of different means. A faith that emphasized the importance, immutability and even necessity of earthly suffering (such as Anglicanism) could be a harder sell to a working-class family interested in either explanation or amelioration of their own hardships. In contrast, the Methodist Church self-consciously ministered to the poor, and emphasized the brotherhood of congregants through intensely emotional "love-feasts" and small "classes" of worshippers.

All churches sought to respond to population growth, migration and urbanization by increasing campaigns of church-building and community outreach throughout this period and particularly before 1880, when the state began taking on a greater role in providing the social welfare services traditionally done by religious organizations. The Church of England built 5,500 new churches and added 11,000 parish clergy between 1830 and 1901; the major Scottish churches built some 1,800 churches and added 1,700 ministers in a comparable period. Formal church attendance does not encompass the whole of religious practice, however, and Sunday School attendance also rose throughout the first three-quarters of the century, though not sufficiently to keep up with population growth. Various societies

promoted belief and religious practice beyond any formal church structure: societies promoting temperance, religious literature, and dissenters' rights, and
missions to bring godliness and moral improvement to "heathens" abroad and
the unchurched at home. One such movement, the Christian Socialists active in
the decade after 1848, sought to fuse religious belief with working-class political
awareness and activism, and encourage cooperative associations that deliberately
emphasized the Christian elements of working-class political and social improvement. Although Christian religious organizations at mid-century remained socially
conservative in a general sense, espousing good works and salvation rather than
any significant changes in social structure, individuals motivated by personal evangelical beliefs played central roles in movements to address questions like public
health reform, child labor, and anti-slavery.

   The fate of Britain's religious denominations had been intertwined with its global
presence for centuries, and in the mid-nineteenth century imperial religious expansion and missionary work created both complex opportunities and challenges. In
theory, religious and political leaders saw the spread of British Christianity, British
commerce and British imperial authority as commingled and mutually supportive.
In practice these relationships proved more complicated. Religious establishments
in colonial contexts could be seen as part of a larger imperative to order, but
churches and missionaries sometimes had divergent goals from those of the state.
British denominations, Anglicans in particular, wanted to replicate in white colonies
their power structures at home, but it was increasingly difficult to impose any kind
of ecclesiastical uniformity on settlements consisting of immigrants from many
different churches. The state had no interest in expending political and real capital
in enforcing such authority overseas at the cost of colonial harmony. Furthermore,
as the Anglican Church increasingly lost the ability to define exclusive civic participation at home (with the repeal of the Test and Corporation Acts, and with
Catholic emancipation), it became impossible to do so in the newly settled white
colonies with their patchwork of different religious faiths.

   Missionaries occupied a different place in colonial settlements, and they concentrated their efforts not in white colonies but in the areas of exploration, commerce
and political control in India, Africa and other non-Christian regions. The London
Missionary Society developed thriving networks of schools and other services in
South Africa, and the Anglican Church Missionary Society had a significant presence in India. Local rulers sometimes requested the formation of missions in their
countries, as in Nigeria and other parts of West Africa. While the Anglican Church
had shunned missionary work in the eighteenth century, by 1843 an Anglican
could write that "it is no longer a question whether the heathen shall be left to
themselves . . . the Church [must] extend herself with the extension of our Empire,
even to prevent our country from becoming a curse to the pagan world" (quoted in
Porter 1999: 233). Missionary work abroad bent domestic gender norms, as women
signed on to teach women and girls in societies in which a male presence would
have been unwelcome. Missionaries played a powerful informal role in extending

British language, culture and religious beliefs abroad, and brought back stores of ethnographic, botanical and geographic knowledge on their return. British parishioners supported them financially, listened to their lectures when they came home, and followed their adventures through tracts and magazines aimed at every member of the family. Missionaries presented imperial peoples not as racially inferior, but rather as religiously ignorant, socially backward, and open to the uplift that Christianity offered.

Domestically, while each sect and faith in Britain faced considerable demographic challenges, many also experienced internal revival movements that sought to move religious belief away from the easygoing religious practice of the previous century and toward a more intense and personal religious experience. The most famous, the Oxford Movement, sent tremors through the Church of England in the 1830s. Since its inception during the Reformation, the church had included members (known as "High Church") who placed greater value on the authority of the church hierarchy and on the ceremonial aspects of music, liturgy, and external symbolism that supported inner devotion than, for example, on the text of the Bible itself. High Church Anglicans did not consider themselves Catholic, but their comprehension of the church's role in explaining the mystery of the divine had long been at odds with the more individually driven faith of the majority of Anglicans.

In the early 1830s, a group of Oxford scholars and theologians, concerned about the state's apparent secularism and its implications for English Protestantism, began publishing a set of 90 *Tracts for the Times*, a series of writings designed to revive the spirit of the church to its earlier presumed glories. Men like John Keble, Edward Pusey, and John Henry Newman all sought to bring English Christianity back to a pre-Reformation unity of worship, and in this had mixed results. In 1841 Newman published an article implying that Anglican and Roman Catholic theology were not so far apart after all, which took High Church Anglicanism considerably further than most people were prepared to go. He touched a nerve of anti-Catholicism and concerns about Ireland, and the offending article raised such opposition throughout the country that he was forced from his position at Oxford. Four years later, in 1845, he completed his own religious journey and, as if proving the worst fears about the Oxford Movement, converted to the Roman Catholic Church.

Doubt, skepticism, and atheism

Several forces undermined nineteenth-century religious belief. German literary scholarship from the 1820s onward cast increasing doubt on the literal and historical accuracy of both old and new testaments. Charles Lyell's geological work in the 1830s reinforced this doubt with evidence from the natural sciences that suggested that, contrary to Genesis, patterns of rock formation told a much longer story of the earth's development. And Charles Darwin's evolutionary theories (discussed further below) placed humans – surely the center of God's creation – and animals firmly within a changing natural world at odds with a fixed point of divine attention.

Not all who questioned religious orthodoxy traveled to atheism, though. Most probably stopped at indifference and some went as far as outright hostility, while some developed secular forms of religion to provide structure to morality, social welfare and worldview. Some atheists, freethinkers and other forms of organized irreligion (there was such a thing) even developed their own missionary societies, secular Sunday Schools and hymnals to do battle against the forces of organized religion among the working class, where unbelief had often been linked with radicalism and democratic political ideals. Many in the working class saw in the varieties of free thought a belief system that valued progress, improvement and curing social ills in this world rather than the next, and validated social mobility rather than the social stasis of most Christianity.

Most working people did not embrace any kind of atheism, though. Many remained Nonconformists (Methodists or Congregationalists, for example) and these non-Anglican forms of Protestantism continued to offer a powerful faith as well as the organizational grounding for social action. In theory Nonconformity focused the attention of the working poor on otherworldly salvation; in practice many took the lesson of equality before God, combined it with leadership opportunities within working-class communities, and emerged as fierce and effective labor leaders later in the century. Whether or not they became labor leaders or activists, for many working people, the education provided by both Anglican and nonconformist Sunday Schools was the only opportunity they had for acquiring basic literacy.

Science and the Experimental Worldview

As religious Britons (not just atheists) came to question the source and validity of biblical revelation, this temperament of doubt and skepticism spread throughout many layers of British culture and thought. We like to imagine the Victorians as unshakably certain in their rectitude and confidence, but in truth many Victorians regularly grappled with uncertainty about the scope, nature and accuracy of what humans could know about the world. John Stuart Mill wrote in a diary entry in 1854:

> Scarcely any one, in the more educated classes, seems to have any opinions, or to place any real faith in those which he professes to have . . . Those who should be the guides of the rest, see too many sides to every question. They hear so much said, or find that so much can be said, about everything, that they feel no assurance of the truth of anything. (Houghton 1957)

Coexisting with this absence of grounded truth was nonetheless a widely held belief in the power of human reason to explore the outer world as well as the innermost springs of human action and behavior. Reason carefully applied would lead to human progress, and science would feed that progress by eliminating natural and man-made miseries that eternally dogged the human condition. Of course, this belief in reason served as a solvent as well, for if theological explanations of people and the universe were undermined, scientific explanations had not yet been fully constructed.

The foundation for widespread optimism as well as anxiety about scientific pursuits lay in the popularity of science itself in every sphere. The Victorian era saw a proliferation of scientific societies, journals, exhibitions and controversies. Scientific questions made their way into cultural realms far from the laboratory or any other mode of deliberate experimentation, and imbued politics, literature, gender and theology with their flavor throughout the century. New plants and animals and technologies flowed in from around the world, filling Kew Gardens, the British Museum and countless lecture halls with their novelty – and with a broad cross-section of the public eager to take part. In the 1830s, the practice of science itself had not yet solidified into a profession, with subspecialties requiring specific education and courses of training. Many Victorians, men and women, were amateur collectors, classifiers, and experimenters – in short, scientists. By the 1860s this had begun to change, and the professional and the amateur were developing different and competing claims to veracity.

The outpouring of major works early in the period reveals the expansion and prevalence of this mindset. Thomas Carlyle's *Sartor Resartus* (1833–1834) both mocked and confirmed the omnipresence of scientific thought: "to many a Royal Society, the Creation of a World is little more mysterious than the cooking of a dumpling . . . Man's whole life and environment have been laid open and elucidated; scarcely a fragment or fibre of his Soul, Body, and Possessions, but has been probed, dissected, distilled, desiccated, and scientifically decomposed." Carlyle was right to notice. The 1830s and 1840s saw a range of seminal works published that spurred people's thinking in a range of scientific realms: John Herschel's *Preliminary Discourse on the Study of Natural Philosophy* (1830), William Whewell's *History of the Inductive Sciences* (1837) and *Philosophy of the Inductive Sciences* (1840), J.S. Mill's *System of Logic* (1843), and Charles Lyell's *Principles of Geology* (1830–1833). Carlyle may have rejected the claims of science's proper scope of authority, but he did so in the context of an extraordinarily prolific period for publishing scientists.

"Science" itself was not homogeneous, and contained within itself numerous disagreements about its own authority, the line between amateur and professional, and the audience and influence it might have. As an amateur whose work exercised perhaps greater influence than that of any other scientist of the period, Darwin himself represents the lack of professional training so common to the early Victorian period. Scientists were themselves as yet unclear about "what one could safely claim about natural law, nor was it obvious when, where, and to whom such claims could be made" (Winter 1997). Nor were the boundaries between disciplines yet clear – or rather, Victorians did not yet see the value in the disciplinary specializations now taken for granted. To sort those out with some success would take several generations and the establishment of numerous specialized journals, societies and educational programs. It was not, for instance, obvious to the mid-Victorians that experiments in phrenology (which proposed that character traits could be discerned from the shape of bumps on the head) or mesmerism (early hypnotism and communing with spirits) were fundamentally different than experiments with electricity or botanical fieldwork.

Charles Darwin's work in botany and biology provides a sense of how powerful an influence science had both within the scientific community and throughout society as a whole as fodder for metaphor, political argument and social critique. Darwin originally planned to pursue theology in college, but found his interest more suited to that of amateur botanical collector. A fortunate connection during his college years arranged for his invitation to serve as the ship's naturalist on the *Beagle*, which explored the coasts of South America and its Atlantic and Pacific islands in the 1830s as part of the British navy's grand design of mapping the world for trade. He gathered observations and drawings of animals and plants throughout these islands, and puzzled over the similarities and differences between different species. How did these differences come to be?

Darwin entered his scientific career having read Lyell's work on geology, which had suggested that, contrary to biblical accounts, the earth was much older and more changeable than once thought. Soon after his return to England, Darwin also read Thomas Malthus's 1798 work on population, which proposed that the number of humans would always increase faster than people's ability to feed themselves. The drive to reproduce always being checked by scarce resources, Malthus concluded from this unhappy scenario that the lot of humanity was starvation, misery and death through malnutrition and disease. Darwin took from Malthus a central insight: nature operated within the same constraints as people, and so the context of nature was one of an unending struggle for resources in which inevitably many organisms must perish. In other words, the natural world was unfixed and very likely undergoing constant change under the pressures of overpopulation and insufficient food.

Darwin's solution was the novel theory of natural selection, in which all plant and animal life constantly struggles for survival, and only those species best able to thrive and reproduce in their particular environments will last. Random variations in each species produce qualities that support or hinder its ability to survive – for instance, a bird with a longer beak will be better able to extract seeds from some kinds of pods, and so such a bird will stand a better chance than one without this random variation. Given limited food supply, nature then "selects" for the likelihood of survival in every generation of every organism, and thus species change and differentiate over countless generations of mutation. He elaborated on this theory first in *The Origin of Species* (1859), applied to plant and animal life, and then brought humans into natural selection in *The Descent of Man* (1871).

Figure 4.1 Charles Darwin's 1859 *Origin of Species* sparked skepticism among some who could not credit the idea that humans had evolved from apes. A *Punch* cartoonist here lampoons both Darwinism and an older, abolitionist image. (© The British Library Board P.P.5270.ah.206).

Natural selection proved troubling to contemporaries on several levels, and Darwin knew his work would generate controversy. He had held off publishing for many years in the certain knowledge that he would be branded an atheist. By the late 1830s he was beginning to doubt the authenticity of biblical miracles, and when he married in 1838, his father urged him to conceal his growing theological doubts from his wife. His intentions, however, were not to discredit religion or God but rather to advance understanding of the natural world. By the time he published in 1859, though, his work could only lead people to articulate the crisis of faith and doubt that had been germinating in British and European culture for several decades. In 1860, the British Association for the Advancement of Science staged a public debate on natural selection between Bishop Samuel Wilberforce and Darwinian advocate Thomas Huxley, during which Wilberforce famously asked Huxley whether he was descended from an ape on his father's or his mother's side. Huxley's response was less memorable, but Wilberforce's question captures the sense of what critics thought at stake.

Natural selection made the process of natural change look free of intent and God, and left Victorians wondering where God's design could be found if not in nature. If species had changed over time, then God could not also have created the world without flaw (let alone in six days, as told by Genesis), which in turn raised serious and disturbing questions about whether God had created people at all. Whatever their degree of religious observance, it was a commonplace that God created people in his image. Darwin's evolutionary theory suggested instead that people, and all species, emerged from a world of struggle rather than goodness, and chance rather than divine cause. A precocious young man of 16 read the *Origin of Species* and cursed "the rigorous logic that wrecked the universe for me and for millions of others" (Bannister 1979: 243). Furthermore, the natural world depicted within was a brutal one in which all species engaged in constant struggle and most would ultimately become extinct. If this was God's world, it was a world of malice, contention and destruction. Some attempted to see evolution as further proof of God's omnipotence as the designer of a self-regulating and self-improving system, but this was a slender kind of optimism.

Darwin's work not only shook the worlds of biology and theology, but by extension also influenced social and political thought as well, and in ways Darwin clearly never intended. Thomas Huxley, one of Darwin's earliest and most vociferous supporters, was one of several who believed in a foundation for morality based on the new science of evolution. What was ethically right was behavior that was rewarded by natural selection. This made people uneasy, for it implied that morality derived from impersonal (and not divine) forces, and that brutal nature provided the best object lessons for good human behavior. Late nineteenth-century imperial boosters thought natural selection justified colonial expansion and subjugation, for the economic and military superiority of Western powers could be seen as proof of its own naturally sanctioned success. Laissez-faire economics, needless to say, was eminently supported by natural selection applied to human behavior: governments should not attempt to meddle in what natural law decreed. Herbert Spencer, an engineer, editor at the recently formed *Economist,* and independent scholar whose work spanned several disciplines, sought to bring evolutionary theory into philosophy, ethics, and what would in future years be called sociology. His *Social Statics* (1851) and other works saw evolution explaining not only biological change but the essence of social progress as well, and Spencer saw society itself as an evolutionary organism.

Scientific research took place in venues influenced by social class, and science in turn became metaphorically applied to understand contemporary class and social order. A number of politically radical or democratic Britons, including many Chartists, embraced the less hierarchical and welcoming realms of herbalism, phrenology and spiritualism because those were less elitist in access. Geologists, by contrast, formed the Geological Society, which operated like a gentlemen's club and helped determine the course of research in that field. Not all scientists were born gentlemen: Michael Faraday, who worked on electromagnetic induction and electricity, had been born into poverty.

One paradox of Victorian science derives from its role as both powerful critic of inherited understandings of the natural world and, at the same time, upholder of many of the same social and cultural principles, replacing theologically based postulates about gender, race and social order with theories derived from experimentation and reason. Darwin's evolutionary theories, for instance, certainly upended any number of Victorian religious assumptions, but reaffirmed the belief in man's natural intellectual superiority to women. The solvent of reason might prove complete in the very long run, but Victorian scientists lived within their own culture and as such did not set out to remake it utterly.

The attitudes of scientists toward race were similarly ambivalent. Some tried to correlate presumed known character traits or mental abilities of different racial groups with anatomical characteristics. Used in this way, science could validate existing racial assumptions rather than challenging them. The birth of anthropology supported the search for ethnic groups untouched by Western culture and hence living in a "natural" state. This could easily become a way to confirm one's assumptions about primitivism and civilization as much as a means of critiquing those assumptions, since designating any group as "natural" could also underscore Western superiority and, ultimately, colonial rule as well. Victorian science, and the Victorian reading public, were not incorrigibly racist: the author of the derogatory *Negro's Place in Nature* was publicly hissed, and his work sold only 250 copies.

Victorian science thus operated within an imperial context in several ways. The Royal Geographic Society, founded in London in 1830, drew together robust audiences of cartographers, military and naval officers, colonial administrators, scientists, engineers, and politicians to share information, host lectures, and promote further exploration by securing funding from various public and private sources. The 1830s saw increased attention to exploration and the geographical imagination, as Britons sent mapping expeditions to destinations as diverse as British Guiana, Kurdistan, and the Arctic. They explored up the Niger and Zambezi rivers in Africa, and for several decades at mid-century, the travels of John Hanning Speke, Richard Burton and David Livingstone sparked considerable public interest in discovering the source of the River Nile.

Exploration undertaken to map land and sea for commercial ends brought Britons into contact with new plants, animals and insects to study and new cultures against which to measure themselves. Other less obvious connections were also made: British companies dominated the global telegraphy market, which expanded dramatically and globally after the first successful undersea cable was laid across the English Channel in 1851. Parts of Michael Faraday's subsequent work on electrical conduction and insulation – crucial steps in understanding electricity – were moved forward by specific problems noticed in Britain's cable telegraphy lines.

As science professionalized, some scientific societies and clubs became more exclusive as disciplines became more clearly defined. The Ethnological Society attempted to mitigate this by creating new public meetings open to women while maintaining its status as a gentlemen's club. Natural history proved particularly open and inclusive, and the mid-Victorian era saw an explosion of garden clubs, provincial societies, mechanics' institutes and public lectures that brought science into middle- and working-class lives. Novelists like George Eliot and Charles Dickens wove scientific issues into their fiction, and cartoonists, satirists and poets both upheld and poked fun at the pretensions of scientists to explain the natural world. It was not uncommon for Britons to experience the latest discovery or hypothesis firsthand at public lectures, demonstrations and experiments.

People in general read more about science throughout the nineteenth century (part of a growing trend in popular literacy, as discussed below). In 1815 there were five commercial science journals, and by 1895 there were over 80 in circulation. Nor was this interest only for scientists or devoted amateurs, but it made its way into children's literature as well. Nearly all middle-class children read Margaret Gatty's *Parables from Nature* (1855–1864) in school and experienced its short stories about nature and observation. Reverend John George Wood proved that science and theology could coexist with his *Common Objects of the Microscope* (1861), *The Boy's Own Book of Natural History* (1860), and many other books, in which he used the microscope as a way to tell a divine story through scientific observation. Some works were written explicitly for female audiences, such as *The Young Lady's Book: A Manual of Elegant Recreations, Arts, Sciences, and Accomplishments* (1859) which included chapters on botany, ornithology and geology and aimed at encouraging women's scientific knowledge. This was done in the context of traditional gendered femininity, but it also laid the foundation for young women as scientific observers in their own right.

The mid-Victorian years also saw the expansion and growing influence of social science – that is, scientific principles of investigation applied directly (and not only metaphorically) to social questions. If one could discover the laws of nature, could such laws also exist about human behavior, market conditions, and the broad dynamics of social change? This was not wholly new terrain. Adam Smith's *Wealth of Nations* (1776) had postulated "laws" of supply and demand, David Ricardo's *Principles of Political Economy and Taxation* (1817) put forward "laws" of wages and rents, and classical economics had developed out of these influences. Political economists treated economic questions as the aggregate of individual human choices, which could be understood, predicted, and even altered. What began in the realm of political economy spread to other disciplines, and the era also saw the creation of the National Association for the Promotion of Social Science (1857), the British Archaeological Association (1843), and the Anthropological Institute (1871), itself a product of the merger of two anthropology societies formed in previous decades.

Social Thought and Criticism

Victorian social and political thought – that is, how Victorians grappled with the big questions of social organization and values, the role of individuals and the state, and the nature of work – was profoundly and inevitably influenced by several transformations taking place in society and political life themselves. The industrial revolution generated tremendous extremes of wealth and poverty, and technological progress in mass communications allowed the effects of poverty to be widely appreciated for the first time. The French Revolution of 1789, and the more widespread European revolutions of 1830 and 1848, kept social unrest tied throughout this period to political upheaval. Those families that had become moderately affluent were not immune from this kind of anxiety, as these decades also saw boom and bust cycles in international trade, finance and credit markets. Few were so rich or so insulated as to be secure from one form or another of radical uncertainty, and attitudes toward social instability ranged from advocacy for state intervention to belief in the complete efficiency of unrestrained markets.

The two dominant cultural movements of the early nineteenth century, Utilitarianism and Evangelicalism, were no longer radically innovative by the 1830s and had become so influential as to be absorbed into the conceptual frameworks of many Britons. By 1834, both the philosopher Jeremy Bentham and Evangelical antislavery advocate William Wilberforce were dead, and they left behind acolytes who diffused the impact of their respective work throughout social and political thought and policy.

Bentham had held that the goals of government – indeed, the goals of all human behavior – should be to maximize pleasure and minimize pain. People and nations should judge the goodness or badness of a policy by how much pleasure (or how little pain) that policy added to the world. Utilitarianism was then an inherently democratic belief system, in that each individual's pleasure or pain should be taken into account – not some more so than others. It was also an optimistic belief system, in that it assumed we could both know the outcomes of our actions as a science, and that we could apply that knowledge toward social improvement.

Once it left Bentham's pen, the principle of utility became a powerful force for much that was good and some that was pernicious in Victorian Britain. A government assessed on its usefulness for the greatest number of its people would seek to improve their well-being, their health, their living conditions, and their laws, and indeed, Victorian social policy from the 1830s forward exhibited a powerful interest in social reform in all of these areas. The spirit of Bentham lived on in numerous Victorian Royal Commissions investigating prison reform, sanitary conditions, public health, criminal justice, education, and many other social problems, each one gathering voluminous evidence, producing legislative recommendations, and setting up oversight to make government an effective agent of social betterment. Utility was a solvent for inherited power or customary practice, since neither derived from a rational calculation of human benefit. The "greatest good for the greatest number" could also imply a more profound political shift toward representative government, but since autocratic government could in theory produce the same results, this should not be overemphasized. One of Bentham's best known and prolific followers, John Stuart Mill, doubted that democratic societies were necessarily the most utilitarian, because in practice most people lacked the education to make wise political decisions.

Intellectually, utilitarian thinkers valued things that could be measured, or whose effects could be measured, and this mindset produced mixed results. They tended to devalue abstract thought and reading for their own sake. It was better to do than to think; Victorian culture was a culture of results. Samuel Smiles, writing *Self-Help* in 1859 for working-class self-improvement, advised readers that "the experience gathered from books, though often valuable, is but of the nature of *learning*; whereas the experience gained from actual life is of the nature of *wisdom*; and a small store of the latter is worth vastly more than any stock of the former."

Utility also made its way into education far enough to be thought worth mocking by Charles Dickens, who famously parodied the stiltedness and soul-crushing narrowness of utilitarian thought when applied to young (and working-class) schoolchildren in *Hard Times* (1854). The aptly named teacher Thomas Gradgrind describes his teaching philosophy with an exhortation: "Now, what I want is, Facts. Teach these boys and girls nothing but Facts. Facts alone are wanted in life. Plant nothing else, and root out everything else." In a chapter entitled "Murdering the Innocents" Gradgrind attempts just that, denying the use of nicknames, discussion of circuses, and contemplation of appealing pictures under the common prohibition of anything or any topic not conducive to factual advance. Whimsy and wonder are forbidden. Of course, Dickens overstated his case to make a novelist's point: that utility and reason did not effectively encapsulate all there was to being human. The presence of novelists like Dickens and bombastic critics of rationality like Thomas Carlyle illustrates that although certain strains may have been dominant in Victorian thought, it was a great and noisy discussion rather than a monologue.

Utility did not always equal materialism, but an appreciation only for what was obviously useful could lead that way, especially when coupled with the unprecedented social mobility of the industrial age. Victorian critics lambasted their society for its ignorance of and indifference to aesthetics, its focus on work and riches, and the shallowness of its cultural tastes. John Sterling, in his *State of Society in England* (1828), lamented: "*Wealth! wealth! wealth! Praise be to the god of the nineteenth century! The golden idol! the mighty Mammon!* Such are the accents of the time, such the cry of the nation." Social critics from Carlyle to John Ruskin to William Thackeray called their countrymen to task for their limited horizons, and the poet Arthur Hugh Clough parodied the distorted values produced by exclusively material concerns:

> Thou shalt not steal; an empty feat
> When it's so lucrative to cheat . . .
> Thou shalt not covet, but tradition
> Approves all forms of competition.

Samuel Taylor Coleridge noted as early as 1817 that his countrymen "look at all things through the medium of the market, and . . . estimate the worth of all pursuits and attainments by their marketable value."

Victorians also imbued work itself with near mystical and highly moral values, not too surprising given the social and economic upheavals through which they lived. Work conferred character, or was at least an outward sign of moral virtue. The converse was also believed true: that lack of work signaled a moral failing. "There is always hope in a man that actually and earnestly works; in Idleness alone is their perpetual despair," wrote Carlyle in *Past and Present*, and Samuel Smiles preached a similar message to working-class Britons in *Self-Help*, basing national progress on the propensity of individuals to work hard. No matter people's affluence, though, the "culture" of hard work supported but did not create the conditions in which work mattered. The material rewards and ever present possibility of financial ruin combined to make work relevant in and of itself. Victorians may have celebrated this in order to validate the conditions in which people lived and the social order supported by people spending their time working rather than less productive pursuits.

Victorians generated the most profound criticisms of these materialistic tendencies. Essayist Matthew Arnold lamented the shallowness of material goods as goals in themselves, and the artist and art critic John Ruskin was not alone in arguing that that the same division of labor underpinning increased productivity had quite negative consequences for those doing that labor. Like Marx, Ruskin pointed out that modern factory production made manufactured goods cheaper but also deprived workers of any sense of dignity in their work, since they produced ever smaller pieces of the final product and were thus disconnected from their labor.

Raised in the spirit of Bentham's Utilitarianism, John Stuart Mill ultimately transformed its values and conclusions over a career of extraordinary and wide-ranging brilliance. The son of James Mill, a historian and friend of Bentham's, John Stuart Mill was a child prodigy taught to read Greek at three years of age, a radical journalist in the 1830s, and a prolific and influential author through the 1860s, while his intellectual influence continues to the present. In addition to the *System of Logic* mentioned earlier, he produced a body of work including the *Principles of Political Economy* (1848), *Considerations on Representative Government* (1861), *On Liberty* (1859), and, published posthumously, his *Autobiography* (1873). Mill gave intellectual weight to mid-Victorian liberalism and articulated some of its most pressing tensions; in this he both exemplified the movement and often went beyond it to positions seen by contemporaries as radical and by future readers as prescient. While he took from utilitarian thought its faith in the power of reason and its belief that the state should serve the greatest good, he also became critical of the democratic implications suggested by those beliefs. All people were *capable* of exercising political judgment, but most people were insufficiently educated to do so wisely. The greatest good for the greatest number would not, therefore, be best served by a democratic system of government. This suggested the need, furthermore, to move beyond laissez-faire social policies; the removal of civil barriers to success was not nearly enough to ensure equality of opportunity, and in this he opened the door for a split in the intellectual foundations of late nineteenth-century liberalism. In *On Liberty* he argued for the need to preserve individual freedom *in spite of* the power of the state and of public opinion, again showing remarkable farsightedness and laying the groundwork for subsequent critiques of mass politics.

The other great influence on Victorian thought and culture, the Evangelical movement, had like Utilitarianism diffused into a softer and broader component of the Victorian temperament. The late eighteenth century's religious enthusiasm had become a set of cultural imperatives toward individual and social improvement, and this meant tremendous emphasis on earnestness, sobriety, honesty, propriety, and virtue for its own sake. It also meant respectability in action and, importantly, in the judgment of others. These are all positive character traits; carried to extremes they looked like priggishness, social conformity, and hypocrisy. Walter Houghton argued in the mid-twentieth century that the Victorians "sacrificed sincerity to propriety . . . pretended to be better than they were . . . [and] refused to look at life candidly" (Houghton 1957). They held themselves and others to impossible standards of moral rectitude which few could actually attain. They valued conformity over individual expression as a bulwark against social change, political instability, and religious fragmentation.

Were the Victorians then more morally upright than previous or later generations? Did they value virtue to a greater degree because they said they did? Certainly the age was filled with exhortation, Temperance societies, and novels praising virtue and decrying vice, but it is unclear whether behavior itself had changed. Higher standards of conduct reflect both the prevalence of more stringent behavioral codes and also the constant and ongoing need to uphold those codes. If people really were more virtuous, they would not have had to write about virtue so aggressively.

If behavior remains a question mark, literacy and reading habits provide surer grounding. Victorians of all social classes read more than ever before. Parliament lifted the duties (state taxes) on paper, advertising and periodicals in the 1850s and 1860s, making print technology affordable for more people than before. Weekly and monthly periodicals boomed in number and readership, and the number of provincial papers rose from 200 in 1846 to 750 in 1865. The boom came not only from cheaper production costs but from a dramatic increase in the number of people able to read. According to government statistics, in 1845, 33 percent of men and 49 percent of women were illiterate. By 1871, these figures had fallen to 19 percent for men and 26 percent for women. Working-class Britons read broadsheets, popular ballads, sensational cheap weeklies, serialized novels, and Sunday papers. Some aspired to digest more than this, and David Newsome notes that "One self-educated Mancunian [a resident of Manchester] read the five volumes of Macaulay's history aloud to his neighbours, and sent the author a vote of thanks 'for having written a history which working men can understand'" (Newsome 1997). Perhaps the most telling point to be made about Victorian written culture is that in news, in literature, in social criticism and political awareness, Victorians were far better read than their predecessors.

They also viewed art in a greater number of venues. The early Victorian era saw the opening of several major new museums in London and major provincial cities: the Victoria and Albert Museum, the National Portrait Gallery, the Birmingham Museum and Art Gallery and the Walker Art Gallery in Liverpool (one can include the National Gallery itself, founded in 1824, if it is dated from its present site, to which it moved in 1838). The expansion of museum-going capacity reflected both civic and state interest in supporting the arts and a growing public aesthetic interest.

One of the most influential and diffuse artistic movements of the period, the Pre-Raphaelites, reacted against the formal and idealized painting styles in fashion since the eighteenth century. Dante Gabriel Rossetti and William Holman Hunt, with four other painters and a sculptor, met monthly from 1848 through the early 1850s. Calling themselves the Pre-Raphaelite Brotherhood, they sought to "go to Nature in all cases, and employ, as exactly as possible, her literal forms." As an 1852 reviewer wrote in the *British Quarterly Review*,

> If they were to paint a tree as part of a picture, then, instead of attempting to put down, according to Sir Joshua Reynolds's prescription, something that might stand as an ideal tree, the central form of a tree, the general conception of a beautiful tree derived from a previous collation of individual trees, their notion was they should go to Nature for an actual tree, and paint *that*.

So too with people, animals and all else: their goal was art as literal realism. They broke with painting from classical statues or other painters and desired to go to the source itself. Although their styles looked forward to near photographic depiction (photography had itself only emerged in rudimentary form in 1839), the subject matter looked backward to ancient, medieval and Renaissance content. Initially this meant critical opposition, as some saw the choice of content as expressing an overtly Catholic religious preference in the midst of the Oxford Movement. Over time, this faded with the fading of the particular religious controversy itself. More influential was the exact rendering of natural beauty, which looked very different from the idealized beauty depicted by artists for centuries.

In architecture, Gothic competed with classical styles, and the age tolerated and encouraged both of these and many others. In the midst of industrial expansion and the application of glass, iron and engineering on a greater scale than ever before (as in the structure of Crystal Palace, designed to display modern British economic prowess), Victorians sought to recover the Gothic look of archways, stone

Figure 4.2 An interior view of the British Nave of the 1851 Great Exhibition (© The British Library Board Cup.652.c.33).

construction, and internal and external ornamentation. No doubt the stately, time-less and reverent Gothic style served as a counter to the spread of smoke-belching factories, urban tenements, and the dynamism of industrial change itself. Both critic John Ruskin and architect Augustus W.N. Pugin saw in Gothic architecture styles that were both functional and expressed the medieval values of spiritual and social unity (in aspiration if not in fact). After Parliament burned to the ground in 1834 (an accidental fire having broken out during the deliberate incineration of ancient wooden accounting tools in the basement), Pugin and Sir Charles Barry designed the new Parliament buildings. Over the next quarter-century, their or-nately grand construction rose from the ground with Britain's growing economic and global power. Their designs reflected the belief that the Gothic style captured what was most organic about Britain's constitutional blend of royal, aristocratic, and common governance. Nor was this confined to the high culture of the elite or the intellectually sophisticated, for the Gothic style permeated many expres-sions of civic pride as well. The middle-class appreciation for Gothic architecture, coinciding with the economic forces driving the financial success of the middle class itself, suggests an ongoing ambivalence about industrial change at the root of British culture. As Britain industrialized and social change begot social conflict, Gothic styles provided a reassuring anchor to an idealized past and validated the economic might of the present.

References

Bannister, Robert (1979) *Social Darwinism: Science and Myth in Anglo-American Social Thought*. Philadelphia: Temple University Press.

Houghton, Walter (1957) *The Victorian Frame of Mind*. New Haven: Yale University Press.

Newsome, David (1997) *The Victorian World Picture: Perceptions and Introspections in an Age of Change*. New Brunswick: Rutgers University Press.

Porter, Andrew (1999) Religion, Missionary Enthusiasm and Empire. In Andrew Porter (ed.), *The Oxford History of the British Empire*, vol. 3: *The Nineteenth Century*. Oxford: Oxford University Press.

Winter, Alison (1997) The Construction of Orthodoxies and Heterodoxies in the Early Victorian Life Sciences. In Bernard Lightman (ed.), *Victorian Science in Context*. Chicago: University of Chicago Press.

Further Reading

Jay, Elisabeth (1986) *Faith and Doubt in Victorian Britain*. Atlantic Highlands: Macmillan.

Lightman, Bernard V. (ed.) (1997) *Victorian Science in Context*. Chicago: University of Chicago Press.

Parsons, Gerald (ed.) (1988) *Religion in Victorian Britain*, vol. 1: *Traditions*. New York: St Martin's Press.

Royle, Edward (1974) *Victorian Infidels: The Origins of the British Secularist Movement, 1791–1866*. Manchester: University of Manchester Press.

Wiener, Martin (1981) *English Culture and the Decline of the Industrial Spirit 1850–1980*. Cambridge: Cambridge University Press.

Wiener, Martin J. (1990) *Reconstructing the Criminal: Culture, Law, and Policy in England, 1830–1914*. Cambridge: Cambridge University Press.

5

Democracy and Empire
Politics, 1867–1910

In 1882, a charismatic figure calling himself the Mahdi (Messiah in Arabic) raised an army in the Sudan, a vast territory on Egypt's southern border. The Mahdi led a millennial movement against Western influence in the region that threatened Britain's tenuous colonial hold over the area. When an army of 11,000 British and Egyptian soldiers could not conquer him, the British government sent war hero General George Gordon to evacuate the 15,000 Westerners in Sudan's capitol at Khartoum (Hake 1914: 240–249). Gordon, his public profile enhanced by interviews with journalist W.T. Stead, was an avowedly Christian soldier and an avid and aggressive imperialist. He had previously led an army against the Taiping Rebellion in China (1850–1864), built roads through the Sudan, and exerted himself in suppressing the slave trade. He was seen publicly as the best man for the job.

Violence and frustrated diplomacy accompanied the attempted evacuation, and the British government's failure to send reinforcements put Gordon into a particularly weak military position. While Gordon waited fruitlessly for more men, the Mahdi's troops besieged Khartoum for over 300 days, with Gordon and about a thousand Egyptian troops inside. Lytton Strachey, writing many years later, described the battle of wills between General Gordon, who courted martyrdom and refused to take any route available to save himself, and Prime Minister William Gladstone, who hesitated to send additional troops because he thought Gordon was exceeding his orders. Gordon wrote in his journal:

> I will not leave the Sudan until every one who wants to go down is given the chance to do so, unless a government is established, which relieves me of the charge; therefore if any emissary or letter comes up here ordering me to come down, I will not obey it, but will stay here, and fall with town, and run all risks. (*New York Times* 1885)

Empire, State, and Society: Britain Since 1830, First Edition. Jamie L. Bronstein and Andrew T. Harris.
© 2012 Jamie L. Bronstein and Andrew T. Harris. Published 2012 by John Wiley & Sons, Ltd.

The Mahdi's soldiers killed Gordon and his men, mounted Gordon's head on a pike carried around town, and dumped his body into the Nile. Two days later, British reinforcements reached Khartoum and lifted the siege.

News of Gordon's death brought a public outcry against what now looked like cowardly and ineffective government indecision; Queen Victoria wrote an emotional note to Gordon's surviving sister; funds were raised for the support of the family; and Gladstone was pilloried by people, press and the political establishment for the way in which his anti-imperialism had apparently killed a hero. The circumstances of Gordon's death helped set in motion the decision to send a second expedition into the Sudan 13 years later, securing the region for Britain at high cost and little geopolitical gain (Strachey 1918).

As the domestic political impact of Gordon's death showed, the 1867 Reform Act had ushered in a new political world. Politically, the era of the independent Member of Parliament was over, replaced by a two-party system dominated until 1880 by Liberal William Gladstone and Conservative Benjamin Disraeli, and later by Gladstone alternating with other Conservatives. These alternating ministries provided a platform for working out the meaning of this party system for imperialism, nationalism, political participation, and the proper role of government Was Britain to be an empire leading the world, and could Britain afford such a vision? Should working people be brought within the pale of the Constitution, and if so, in what way? Should the Irish govern themselves or remain part of the British state?

Ultimately, after this brief period of relative two-party stability, each party fragmented along different fault lines. The Liberal Party split first over the question of Home Rule for Ireland in 1886. Later, the Unionist Party, comprised of the Conservatives and the anti–Home Rule Liberal Unionists, divided over the question of free trade and "imperial preference" (protective tariffs for commodity shipping and exchange within the empire), ushering in the Liberal Party again after a period of Conservative dominance. Joseph Chamberlain, once a radical mayor of Birmingham, played a leading role in both of these divisions. Internal struggles impacted, and were in turn impacted by, expectations that the world held for Britain as the dominant global power.

Reform and Inclusion

The 1867 Reform Act enfranchised some working men, but did not conclude the struggle over the meaning of political citizenship. The period after 1867 saw increasing attention to the political and civil enfranchisement of women. The 1857 Divorce and Matrimonial Causes Act had begun to address the worst inequities – protecting women's wages from confiscation by abusive or absent husbands – but after Parliament rejected an attempt by MP John Stuart Mill to advance a women's suffrage amendment in 1867, those in favor of expanding women's rights attacked incrementally. The Social Science Association began by supporting changes in civil laws affecting women's legal rights, as did leading Liberals Mill, Robert Lowe, and Jacob Bright.

Supporters introduced into Parliament the Married Women's Property Bill, which aimed to grant women the right make contracts, sue, and own their own earnings and inheritances. The Married Women's Property Committee, an advocacy group outside Parliament, produced petitions and pamphlets and held parties designed to attract adherents and raise awareness of their cause. Proponents of the legislation pointed to the United States, where such Acts had already been adopted in New York, Vermont, and Massachusetts. Those who opposed putting men and women on a more equal legal footing argued that changing the balance of power within the home would ruin marriages and deprive men of the prerogative of their wives' property. The debate in the House of Lords centered almost completely on the perceived inability of working-class women to make good financial decisions, and resulted in 15 of 17 provisions being stricken from the bill. Ultimately, the Act passed in 1870 enabled working women only to keep their wages, a far cry from the bill's original scope but one that still allowed the beginnings of financial independence.

Nor were women the only group energized by the debate around the 1867 Reform Act. While the 1850s and 1860s had been relatively quiet times for labor activism compared to the tumultuous 1840s, unions had evolved in several ways. Unionized workers banded together in the National Reform League in 1865, and in the London Working Men's Association in 1866, and built up internal funds and created infrastructures for mutual support. In the absence of any kind of social safety net, union funds were crucial for members who became sick or were injured on the job.

Infighting among the most skilled members of the organized trades led to a proposal by the labor unions in the Manchester area for an annual meeting of labor organizations which they called the Trades Union Congress (TUC), first held in June 1868. Like the National Association of United Trades for the Protection of Labour, which had been formed in the late 1840s, the TUC was a pressure group that might, it was hoped, sway MPs to support pro-labor legislation. The TUC represented over a million trade unionists in 1874, half a million in 1881, and over 800,000 in 1889, as trades councils and individual unions appeared and disappeared with peaks and valleys in the economy.

Even before members of the working classes entered Parliament in their own right, both Liberals and Conservatives consulted the TUC and other labor organizations in the hopes of winning the labor constituency. In 1872, the TUC formed a Parliamentary Committee of trade unionists, headed by Henry Broadhurst, to focus more specifically on exerting political influence, either by electing MPs or influencing sitting members. The need to exert this influence was palpable, since even the Liberal Party did not always produce legislation in workers' interests. Gladstone's first Liberal ministry delivered the Trade Union Bill to organized labor, giving unions the right to strike; but it also produced the Criminal Law Amendment Act of 1872, which made even peaceful picketing illegal.

At the same time that the TUC lobbied MPs, it also pursued a strategy of trying to elect working men into office, and this kind of direct representation carried with it many difficulties. Some of these had been pointed out by the Chartists: Members of Parliament were still unpaid, making it difficult for a working man to represent a constituency and feed his family. Another more cultural issue was the widespread admiration that many working people felt for their social superiors as a "natural" governing class. In 1869, a year after the TUC's first failed attempt to secure entry of working men into Parliament, John Stuart Mill encouraged union leaders to form the Labour Representation League. The hope was not necessarily to form a third political party, but rather to pressure the Liberal Party to attend to workers' issues. Even so, as a result of this organization and with the help of the miners' unions, two union candidates were elected in 1874, nine in 1885, and six in 1886.

Gladstone and Disraeli

The presence of two strong party leaders – Benjamin Disraeli and William Gladstone – helped to focus the meaning of "Conservative" and "Liberal" in the third quarter of the nineteenth century. Gladstone, born in 1809, was the son of a sugar planter who hoped to secure his sons' entry into society by sending them to Eton and Oxford. Gladstone began his political career as a Conservative, and believed in social hierarchies and meaningful class differences. He was also a High Church Anglican who saw religion as central to the morality of the state. When the Conservative Party split in 1846 over the repeal of the Corn Laws, Gladstone's sympathies remained with Sir Robert Peel, the party's divisive leader.

As Lord Aberdeen's Chancellor of the Exchequer, Gladstone distinguished himself through his attention to free trade. He also had a progressive tax policy, lowering taxes on everyday items like tea and sugar, while maintaining the income tax on the middle and upper classes. In 1859, after a long progression in that direction, Gladstone, like other Peelites, officially crossed the aisle and joined the Liberal Party. He then continued while Chancellor to eliminate taxation on many consumer goods and to encourage the Cobden-Chevalier Treaty (1860), which drastically reduced French tariffs on British manufactures and British tariffs on French wines.

Like Peel, Gladstone was a morally serious man. He cut down trees as a form of recreation, and thought it fit to "rescue" prostitutes through a one-man street ministry. Nonetheless, his willingness to enfranchise progressively larger sectors of the working classes on the grounds of their increasing morality, thrift and education, and his willingness to meet with the public directly through political tours and speeches, to give stump speeches, made "The People's William" a beloved political figure. Only his relationship with Queen Victoria was less than warm; she commented that "He speaks to Me as if I were a public meeting."

Disraeli too had begun his political life as a Conservative, but beyond that he and Gladstone had little in common. Disraeli was the son of Isaac D'Israeli, a literary scholar who had opportunistically converted his family from Judaism to Anglicanism when Benjamin was 12. After an abortive attempt at a public-school education, Disraeli, who had never quite fit in, was educated at home. Like his father, Disraeli aimed at a literary career, writing his first novel, *Vivian Grey*, when he was in his early twenties.

Once Disraeli had set his sights on politics, it took him five attempts to enter Parliament – experimenting with different combinations of mentors and political parties – before he was finally elected the Conservative MP for Maidstone in 1837 at the age of 33. In a society of polite and not-so-polite anti-Semitism, he was considered by most to be Jewish and thus an outsider, a status compounded by his flashy and puzzling taste in clothing. Annoyed at having been excluded from Sir Robert Peel's inner circle, Disraeli found his moment when the Conservative Party split over the issue of the Corn Laws. The Peelites, who supported Corn Law repeal, went one way, and Disraeli, who supported the cause of the agricultural protectionists, led the rest of the Conservative Party in the other direction.

Between 1868 and 1880, Disraeli and Gladstone alternated as Prime Minister, and thereby helped to cement the notion of two-party stability. Their ministries bear looking at in detail because, as each leader attempted to reach out to a wider electorate, his government advanced or presided over legislation the impact of which was to reorganize government to shoulder much more social responsibility.

Gladstone's First Ministry (1867–1874)

Gladstone's priorities during his first ministry were shaped by his desire for a morality-based politics. He was eager to address some of the larger inequities in Ireland, but was also determined to maintain social peace. Irish tenant farmers were mostly Catholic, and held long, expensive leases from largely absentee Protestant landlords. Gladstone's Irish Land Act (1870) gave tenant farmers some security of land tenure and the opportunity to sell the rest of their leases to another farmer, and also allowed tenant farmers compensation for the improvements they had made to leased farmland. A very few farmers were even enabled to purchase their holdings, using long mortgages underwritten by the government. The Act didn't solve the problems of evictions or high rents, however, and the resulting disappointment led Irish lawyer Isaac Butt in 1870 to form the Home Government Association. This group, later called the Home Rule League, advocated a separate domestic legislature for Ireland. Fifty-nine candidates advocating Home Rule won seats in the 1874 Parliamentary election.

Gladstone's pursuit of reform was both comprehensive and remarkably coherent, as most of his legislation sought either to eliminate discriminatory barriers to talent or to make government less expensive and more efficient. W.E. Forster's Education Act (1870) took a step toward free public education. The Act allowed the creation of locally elected school boards in places inadequately provided with public education. The boards could levy taxes to pay for nondenominational Christian schools for children aged 5–12. The legislation reflected a compromise between the Liberal Party – which included many non-Anglican Protestants – and the Conservative Party. It left the Church of England as the leading provider of elementary education (a Tory priority), but also promoted the improvement of society through the cultivation of improved citizens (a Liberal priority).

A new civil service examination system (1871) opened almost all government departments to talent, making government more efficient and answering some of the clamor for such changes that had followed the Crimean War. Reforms in the army shortened enlistment periods, eliminated the punishment of flogging, and prohibited officer candidates from purchasing their commissions. The University Tests Act (1871) allowed non-Anglican professors to teach at Oxford and Cambridge, further limiting the Anglican monopoly on education. The Secret Ballot Act (1872) achieved one of the Chartists' demands by introducing written secret ballots, although some contemporaries felt that a truly manly voter should be proud to declare aloud his choice of candidate. Finally, the Judicature Act (1873) eliminated much waste and confusion that had erupted from England's dual system of courts of common law and courts of equity. Common-law courts ruled on the basis of previous case law; courts of equity, dealing largely with property matters, could make exceptions when statutes provided no legal remedy in inequitable situations. The Judicature Act created a single court system with one court of appeal and one supreme court, although this provision was never carried out, and the House of Lords retained its responsibility as the court of appeal.

While in opposition, and against the better judgment of some Conservative Party members, Benjamin Disraeli had become party leader. He proposed a new union of Conservatism with working-class interests, a long-running theme in Disraeli's political career. As the leader of the Young England political movement in the 1840s, he had famously written that Britain was composed of two nations: the rich and the poor. He also tied the Conservative party to an explicitly imperial mission. As he told a Crystal Palace audience in 1872, "If the first object of the Tory party is to maintain the institutions of the country, the second is, in my opinion, to maintain the Empire of England" (Crangle 1981: 7).

Disraeli's Second Ministry (1874–1880)

Disraeli's second ministry demonstrated his commitment to working people and to the empire. The Factory Act (1874) limited the workweek to 56.5 hours for women and children and raised the minimum working age; and the Sale of Food and Drugs Act (1875) outlawed some of the egregious adulteration plaguing the British food supply (recent scandals had revealed instances of milk infested with pus, and "pepper" partially composed of floor sweepings). The Artisans and Labourers' Dwellings Improvement Act (1875) enabled communities to knock down unsafe slums. The Conspiracy and Protection of Property Act (1875) legalized trade union picketing, and the Employers and Workmen Act (1876) – the name a substantial departure from the "Master and Servant Acts" of the past – equalized the criminal liability of employers and workmen. Finally, the 1880 Employers' Liability Act capped many years of lobbying by trade unions for some form of guaranteed payment for workers injured on the job. Although many of these Acts were permissive rather than mandatory, in the aggregate they seemed like a remarkable social program.

Abroad, Disraeli advanced a "forward policy" which involved expanding and consolidating Britain's positions in the world, particularly protecting India and shipping routes to India and the Far East. He arranged for the Rothschild banking house to purchase 44 percent of the shares in the Suez Canal, when Egypt's ruler, the Khedive Ismail Pasha, made them available. In so doing, he prevented the canal from falling into the hands of a competitor European nation that might purchase a significant part of its ownership. He also engineered the Royal Titles Bill (1876), which transformed Queen Victoria into "Empress of India," a symbolic move much to her delight. But a forward policy carried a great deal of risk. Wars against native Zulu warriors, in an attempt to protect British interests in the South African Transvaal (1879), and in Afghanistan, in an attempt to consolidate British power there (1878), were difficult to prosecute, undermined British claims to racial and social superiority, and provided the Liberal Party with ammunition to argue that the tremendous expense of empire weakened Britain in the long run.

The most serious challenge to Disraeli's foreign policy came in Turkey. As the Ottoman Empire crumbled, nationalist movements grew in the Balkans, and the Turks responded to them with violent repression. The Turks put down an 1876 uprising among Bulgarian Christians, leaving 15,000 dead; reports of horrible atrocities – piled skulls, burnt corpses – began to make their way into the British press. Disraeli dismissively referred to the reports as "coffee house babble," and this callous reaction to the suffering of fellow Christians filled Gladstone with righteous indignation. Gladstone in turn published a pamphlet that questioned Disraeli's commitment to a Christian foreign policy. Popular enthusiasm for this point of view brought Gladstone out of retirement, to face cheering crowds and rouse them with his always stirring, often hours-long oratory.

The Bulgarian atrocities motivated Christian Russia – an eagerly expansionist state – to declare war on Muslim Turkey, on the pretext of protecting Christians within the Ottoman Empire. The dangers posed by Russian expansionism propelled the British government to intervene. A popular music-hall song expressed English

Figure 5.1 In this *Punch* cartoon, Prime Minister Benjamin Disraeli presents Queen Victoria with the title "Empress of India," much to her delight. Due to his Jewish background, Disraeli was often depicted as "foreign" by cartoonists. (From *Punch*, April 15, 1876. Photo: IAM/akg-images).

feeling and also introduced the term "jingoism" – meaning a warlike nationalism – to the language (Jenkins 1996: 124):

> We don't want to fight but by Jingo if we do
> We've got the ships, we've got the men, and got the money too!
> We've fought the Bear before, and while we're Britons true
> The Russians shall not have Constantinople.

Ultimately, Russians did not try to take Constantinople, although they did attempt to impose unacceptable peace terms on the Turks. Disraeli intervened in the negotiating process and gained the admiration of diplomatic Europe. Germany's Chancellor Otto von Bismarck supposedly commented, "Der alte Jude, das ist der Mann!" (essentially, "The old Jew, that is the man!") (Packenham 1992: 57). Queen Victoria elevated Disraeli to a peerage as the Earl of Beaconsfield.

Seemingly, the only one unhappy with Disraeli's performance was Gladstone. Not only had Disraeli been cavalier during the Bulgarian atrocities, but he had also abandoned Liberal principles of thrift and retrenchment in pursuit of imperial baubles. "The central strength of England lies in England," Gladstone had noted. Gladstone's solution to the Disraeli problem was to tour Scotland giving stump speeches, on the expense of empire and the immorality of forcing other nations to bend to Britain's will. This "Midlothian Campaign" (1879–1880), named for the region in Scotland in which Gladstone spoke, marked a populist strategy that a few politicians had practiced before but which Gladstone perfected. Gladstone's speeches attracted women and children, and spurred the production of political souvenirs and banners emblazoned with Gladstone's picture and nickname. Disraeli was too ill – and in any case of the wrong temperament – to do his own political campaigning, and the Conservatives were defeated in the election of 1880 in a landslide.

Gladstone's Second Ministry (1880–1885)

Gladstone's second ministry, and the death of Disraeli (1881), ushered in a new era in which the Liberal Party had a freer hand. As always, one of Gladstone's primary interests was Ireland, which he now approached with both carrot and stick. The carrot was the Land Act (1881) that gave Irish land tenants the "three Fs." These were the right to transfer ownership to new tenants (free sale), the right to remain on the land without fear of eviction (fixity of tenure), and the right to pay a reasonable rent (fair rent) as determined by a "Special Land Court" set up by the Act. The Coercion Act (1881), on the other hand, imprisoned leaders of the rebellious Irish Land League and effectively calmed its tactics. Gladstone saw what he was doing in Ireland as bringing the benefits of liberalism and rational dialogue to a thorny political issue. Others in his party were appalled at what they perceived as sacrificing the principles of right governance in order to negotiate with uncontrollable nationalists. Underscoring the latter viewpoint, in May 1882, Gladstone's niece's husband, Lord Frederick Cavendish, the new Irish Secretary, was murdered in Dublin's Phoenix Park by members of a group calling themselves the Irish National Invincibles.

In addition to his work with Ireland, Gladstone's second ministry saw the passage of the Third Reform Act (1884) and the enfranchisement of 1.76 million male householders. It enfranchised most of the country's agricultural workers, who, although they lived in Conservative districts, were open to promises of "three acres and a cow." In 1885, in part as a result of the electoral expansion, the Conservatives failed to win a majority of rural county seats for the first time. After this, in order to improve success, the party attempted to exclude voters from the polls through questionable registration tactics, and tried to produce low-turnout elections at which working people would be the least likely to vote. It also mobilized party volunteers through the Primrose League, which held social functions and raised money to support Conservative candidates. Critically, and fatefully, the 1884

Reform Act also harnessed the Liberal Party to the issue of Home Rule, since it tripled the Irish electorate; by 1885, 85 out of 103 Parliamentary seats for Ireland were held by Home Rulers.

Gladstone's second ministry also saw a revived interest in amending the 1870 Married Women's Property Act. That legislation had been fatally flawed: it gave women the right to their wages but no way to sue husbands who had illegally taken those wages. It also freed a husband from a wife's debts brought into the marriage, but gave creditors no way to sue the wife to be repaid (a flaw that was corrected in 1874). After 12 years of lobbying to correct these deficiencies, and on the heels of a more liberal women's property Act passed for Scotland (1881), the Married Women's Property Act (1882) finally granted much of what women and their advocates had been seeking. Women gained the right to sue and be sued and the right and responsibility for each member of a couple to support the other spouse. A second Act in 1884 gave spouses the right to testify against each other. Since the initial legislation of 1870, though, a societal sea-change had occurred regarding women's separate legal personhood, and neither of the Acts of the 1880s elicited much public fear or debate. Finally, although Gladstone claimed to see no special imperial role for Great Britain, his second ministry involved Britain expensively in a war in South Africa (1881), an invasion of Egypt (1882), and the Gordon disaster in the Sudan.

Home Rule, Joseph Chamberlain, and the Liberal Unionists

The 1884 Reform Act was followed by a general election, and, as with that of 1867, the Liberals returned with a majority. Gladstone's third ministry (1885–1886) was his shortest, crushed by the issue of Home Rule for Ireland. Why did Gladstone become such an avowed advocate of Home Rule? Britain's white settler colonies, which had been awarded the right to rule themselves under the theory of "responsible government" (the idea that the executive in each nation should be responsible to its own Parliament), served as an example for Gladstone as he crafted his bill for Irish Home Rule (1886). But Gladstone also saw the abuses occurring in Ireland as evil. They roused him to ire in the same way as had the Bulgarian atrocities of the 1870s.

The Home Rule Bill proposed to move all legislative powers for Ireland to a bi-cameral legislature located in Dublin, with MPs in one house and peers and elected senators in the second house. The proposal split the Liberal Party in two. Almost 100 Liberal politicians gravitated to a new Liberal Unionist Party, combining belief in Ireland's continued integration with Great Britain and traditional Liberal support for small government and free trade. Since aristocracy and large landowners were slightly overrepresented among Liberal Unionists, this new group fell, socially and ideologically, between Liberalism and Conservatism (Lubenow 1986). With the defection of the Liberal Unionists, the vote against Home Rule ushered in six years of Conservative Party rule, as the Conservatives solidified themselves as the party committed to preserving the empire, and Liberal numbers fragmented.

The Liberal Unionists were led by Joseph Chamberlain, a new kind of politician for a new age. The son of a nonconformist screw manufacturer, Chamberlain began his political career as mayor of Birmingham from 1873 to 1896 and exemplified a kind of municipal social policy that came to be called "gas and water socialism." During his mayoralty, Birmingham was cleaned up through a Town Improvement Scheme, provided with gas and water distribution, and glorified with a new city center. By the time he stepped down, one American observer called Birmingham "the best governed city in the world" (Watts 1993). Even before being elected MP for the first time in 1876, Chamberlain espoused a number of progressive issues: manhood suffrage; free public elementary education; county governance reform; national councils for Scotland, Wales, and Ireland; disestablishment of the Church of England; and salaries for Members of Parliament. Eventually, these were enumerated together as Chamberlain's "Unauthorized Programme" (1885), seen by Gladstone as much too radical, but extremely popular with the newly enfranchised working classes.

With Disraeli deceased, leadership of the Conservative Party passed to Lord Salisbury (with ministries in 1885–1886 and 1886–1892), who, as a consummate aristocrat, had little interest in the working classes or domestic policy generally. He focused primarily on foreign affairs, and held the posts of Prime Minister and Foreign Minister in tandem. Salisbury's ministries coincided with the steady, warlike drumbeat of what came to be known as the "New Imperialism," as France, the United States, Germany, and Britain raced through Africa in the last quarter of the century, annexing any "unclaimed" portion, no matter how unprofitably in the short run, in the hope that these lands would act as a buffer state in case of imperially driven war, or could be cultivated or mined for oils or diamonds. By the 1880s the colonizing powers were willing to sit around the negotiating table and carve up the continent. This they did at a conference held in Berlin in 1884–1885, and at a second international conference in 1890.

Gladstone had a brief fourth ministry from 1892 to 1894, during which he again took up the question of Home Rule. The issue was now more complicated, because in 1890, the Irish Parliamentary Party – which had evolved out of the Home Rule League – had split over a scandal surrounding the divorce of leader Charles Parnell. In 1893, Gladstone introduced a second Home Rule Bill. The first Home Rule Bill would have excluded all Irish MPs from Westminster; the second allowed 80 Irish MPs to stay in Westminster, but only to vote on Irish issues. The House of Commons passed the bill over great objections, since Gladstone had uncharacteristically miscalculated by over £300,000 the cost to the British government. The House of Lords killed the bill, and Gladstone retired in 1894 having apparently broken his party over the Irish issue and with no resolution in sight.

The Boer War

During his third ministry, Liberal Unionist leader Lord Salisbury (1895–1902) encouraged a war in South Africa intended to annex the Boer republics of the Orange Free State and the Transvaal. (The term "Boer" derived from the Afrikaans word for "farmer.") British interest in South Africa dated from the 1870s, when gold and diamonds had been discovered in sufficient quantities to make it appear that the region had enormous mineral wealth. Two Boer republics, the Transvaal and the Orange Free State, determined to maintain their independence. Under Disraeli's government, Britain had annexed the Transvaal (1880) and fought an expensive conflict against the Zulus. In 1881, the Transvaal was lost again, as the Boers, white settlers of Dutch ancestry, proclaimed independence. The British worked around the Boers to secure other parts of South Africa, most notably Cape Colony to the south of the Transvaal, presided over by Cecil Rhodes, the head of the British South Africa Company. Rhodes's publicly expressed desire to bring the world – including the United States – into the British Empire was shorthand for some of the ambitions of the New Imperialists.

In 1886, discovery of gold in the Boer-governed Transvaal precipitated an onslaught of British immigrants intent on riches, often as laborers working in the mines. The Boers, a conservative, nationalistic, and pastoral people, viewed outsiders with deep suspicion, though they welcomed immigrant labor in the gold mines. Paul Kruger, President of the Transvaaal, tried to discourage foreigners from settling there; they were heavily taxed and deprived of civil rights in the government of the Transvaal or in the city of Johannesburg where many lived. Furthermore, unregulated growth led to crowded and unsanitary living conditions.

By 1895, the foreigners living in Johannesburg (almost exclusively Britons), who outnumbered the Boer population in the Transvaal two to one and who paid 90 percent of the taxes, seemed to be on the verge of rebellion. Cecil Rhodes conspired with his friend Leander Starr Jameson, a British doctor, to lead a force of private mounted police from the British province of Bechuanaland to Johannesburg in the hopes of instigating such an uprising and creating the conditions for British government intervention. Jameson's raid on December 29, 1895 failed to spark any insurrection, and Jameson's men were stopped near Johannesburg and surrendered to Transvaal soldiers. Although the British government disclaimed any responsibility for the Jameson raid, the Boers – and many members of the British public – felt that the British had indeed been responsible (although opinion divided on whether that was a good or a bad thing). The German Kaiser's public congratulation to Kruger on thwarting the rebellion compounded bad feelings between Boers and Britons, and this bit of clumsy diplomacy exacerbated the atmosphere of cold war and the naval arms race developing between Britain and Germany.

In 1898, Transvaal residents overwhelmingly reelected Paul Kruger to the presidency. Shortly afterward, a minor police incident sparked the war so long desired by Cecil Rhodes. During an arrest, a Boer policeman killed an English workman named Tom Edgar. While the Transvaal's foreign population thought the killing was murder, the policeman was not only acquitted but also commended for his actions by the judge. The foreign community in the Transvaal petitioned the British government for redress, and attempts at diplomacy between the British government and the Boers followed. The talks broke down repeatedly, and in October 1899 the two countries went to war.

When war began, the combined Boer forces from the Orange Free State and the Transvaal numbered about 50,000. While Britain had vastly greater military strength around the world, there were only 14,750 British troops in the area, who were therefore greatly outnumbered by mounted soldiers intimately familiar with the terrain and desperate to protect their farms, families, and country. Had the Boers been able to defeat the British quickly they would have been victorious, but British reinforcements arrived and the war settled into a prolonged state of siege of three towns: Ladysmith, Mafeking, and Kimberley.

Faced with guerrilla warfare and a seemingly fluid line between fighters and civilians, Lord Kitchener made the decision to pen the Boers into what were termed "concentration camps," to cut off informal supply lines to the Boer troops. Twenty thousand Boers died of disease and malnutrition in 14 months – a breakdown of morality in wartime that horrified the public. The war finally ended in 1902 with British annexation of the Orange Free State and the Transvaal, after the deaths of 22,000 British troops, the expenditure of about £222 million, and a dramatic reevaluation of British military and moral superiority both at home and abroad. It was sobering that a war between the world's greatest imperial power and a colony of farmers could go so poorly.

While the Boer War was the most important British military action in the last quarter of the century, the rest of the empire continued to bulk large in both symbolic and military importance. In 1885, the Indian National Congress was formed, seeking more representation of native Indians in British rule. Ironically, British direct rule in India after 1858 had made the Congress's existence possible, by bringing political unification and a common language and education to an increasing number of Indians. Inexpensive postal rates, the spread of printing presses, and expansion of British-funded railways also fostered Indian nationalism. Nationalist leaders included members of a small but growing class of lawyers, businessmen and teachers inspired by the writings of John Locke and Thomas Jefferson, and by the lives of European freedom fighters of the nineteenth century. The British government failed to take the Congress seriously, but the Congress had real complaints, including the disproportionate British profit gained from large Indian construction projects and the comparative inability of native Indians to advance within the Indian Civil Service. While the Congress would not take many concrete steps toward independence in the era before the First World War, it nurtured some of the leaders who became significant later.

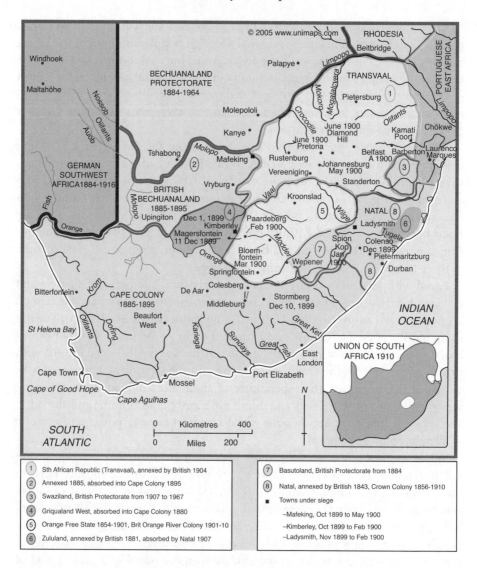

Map 5.1 The Boer War and the formation of South Africa.
Source: Based on "South Africa 1899–1910" © 2005, www.unimaps.com.

The "colonies of settlement," or predominantly white British emigrant colonies, also continued to absorb large numbers of British settlers. Between 1861 and 1900, 7.5 million people left the United Kingdom. Over a million went to Australia and New Zealand, 800,000 to Canada, and a few hundred thousand to South Africa. While some argued that maintenance of ties with these colonies was essential for the absorption of "surplus population," this argument was undermined by the fact that the largest majority of emigrants – about 5 million – migrated to the United

States. British settlers in the far corners of the late nineteenth-century empire tried hard to maintain contacts with their motherland. They sent their children home to British public schools and universities, and encouraged a "marriage market" in which British debutantes arrived in India every year to be married off to the local British elite. The Anglican churches in Australia and New Zealand imported their clergy from England throughout this period, which meant a continuous infusion of English culture. Although voting rights and the pattern of government varied from British norms, the settlement colonies continued to share British cultural preferences as well as political allegiance to the British monarch as head of state.

Beginning in 1903, Joseph Chamberlain attempted to capitalize on imperial organization by proposing a system of "imperial preference," which represented a retreat from the mid-century reliance on free trade. Chamberlain sought to unite Britain, Australia, Canada, New Zealand, and South Africa in a customs union, promoting his idea as one that would lift the wages of British working people. Chamberlain also proposed a more formal and binding union of these nations for imperial defense. Neither of these suggestions succeeded due to the strong opposition of the sitting Chancellor of the Exchequer, who, like most British economists of the period, was a staunch believer in Free Trade (Murphy 2001).

Disraeli's and Gladstone's policies in the 1870s and 1880s had also forced Britain's continuing involvement in the disintegrating Ottoman Empire. As a result, Britain found itself pulled in during 1895–1896, when Turks brutally put down Armenian demonstrations by killing approximately 30,000 Armenians. Disagreements within the Cabinet kept British intervention in the region to the maintenance of some naval vessels off the coast of Turkey, but for a while a revival of Crimean-style military intervention to block possible Russian invasion of Turkey seemed likely.

Although Britain supported an "open door" or equal access policy in China, Salisbury's Cabinet was beset by the problem of other countries carving out spheres of influence there, and Britain ended up leasing Wei-hai-wei as a naval station in 1898. Two years later, the British were stunned by the anti-Western Boxer rebellion in China, but again reacted indecisively due to Salisbury's drifting leadership. More successful for Salisbury were Britain's ventures in the Sudan, as the death of General Gordon was finally avenged at Omdurman (1898) – a military victory mythologized in the 1939 movie *The Four Feathers*.

In contrast to Gladstone's avowed policy of trying to push through Home Rule for Ireland, Salisbury's ministries combined coercing leaders of uprisings there with addressing Irish social problems. The first strategy was evident in the 1887 Irish Crimes Act, which could result in the imposition of martial law in turbulent areas; the second was the promulgation of Land Purchase Acts of 1885 and 1888 enabling Irish farmers to purchase their lands, backed by government Treasury money. The Congested Districts Act (1890) provided for publicly funded economic development, the construction of infrastructure, and the amalgamation of unprofitable farms into larger entities, and in 1898, the County Councils Act facilitated more local control over governance (Jenkins 2005).

Although aside from Chamberlain the leaders of Salisbury's government had little understanding of or sympathy for "the masses," some reformist domestic policies were implemented. Local government was finally extended from towns and boroughs to counties through the Local Government Act of 1888. County councils could now undertake such actions as providing for sanitation, inspecting and registering slaughterhouses, and sanctioning plans to build new workers' dwellings. Legislation approved under Conservative ministries also provided rural workers with allotments of land to cultivate for their own gardens, expanded building programs for urban workers' housing, and prohibited the employment in factories of children under 11 years old. And despite the fact that unions were receiving bad press in the 1890s, ministers increased their consultation with union leaders. The Workmen's Compensation Act of 1897, passed under a Conservative ministry, closed some loopholes in earlier legislation, making compensation for workplace accidents more certain.

The late nineteenth century also saw major changes in the governance of London, by far Britain's largest city. After 1855, London had been governed in a dispersed way, through parish vestries in the larger parishes, and district boards composed of parish vestrymen for the smaller parishes. In addition, the Metropolitan Board of Works was in charge of such major infrastructural improvements as drainage, lighting, and street paving. In 1889 the London County Council, led by a party of progressives, replaced the old Board of Works. The LCC's responsibilities expanded over time to include education and public transportation, along with the repair of infrastructure and the protection of property through fire departments.

In creating a more centralized umbrella for local government, the LCC conflicted with the older tradition of vestries providing for themselves. It soon came under fire by Salisbury's Conservative governments, which sought to shift some of its power and responsibilities to new metropolitan boroughs within London (achieved through the London Government Act of 1899). Joseph Chamberlain felt that returning some of the power to these municipalities would engender civic pride – and, in fact, buildings like the Finsbury Town Hall, opened in 1895, rivaled the large structures that had been built in at mid-century in thriving Manchester or Bolton. The impact, over time, had been to "reduc[e] the number, while retaining the multiplicity, of local authorities in the capital," from over 300 local authorities before 1855, to 38 in 1855, and 28 in 1899 (Harvey 1999). The LCC and the metropolitan boroughs counterbalanced each other.

As the century drew to a close, the Conservative Party remained in power, and the Liberal Party retained a tenuous vibrancy through collaboration with the Independent Labour Party (founded in 1893) and Irish Home Rulers. Liberal Party chief whip Herbert Gladstone and labor leader Ramsay MacDonald informally agreed that the Liberals would allow some seats to be contested by working-class representatives, in return for which MacDonald would rally trade unionists to support the Liberal Party. This informal agreement was adopted despite the fact that some workers were becoming more radical than Liberal: in 1894, the TUC adopted an amendment calling for nationalization of the means of production (a government takeover of key industries). In 1900, the Labour Representation Committee brought together unionists, the ILP, Fabians and Social Democrats, and put forward 15 Labour candidates at the general election.

In 1901, in the wake of an expensive strike on the Taff Vale railway in Wales, the British courts held that trade unions could be held financially responsible for the illegal actions of their members. This could be ruinous in practice; in the Taff Vale strike alone, the Amalgamated Society of Railway Servants ended up owing £42,000 in costs and damages. Although the Taff Vale decision is often – and rightfully – seen as a great setback for the union movement, it caused trade unions to flock to affiliate themselves with the Labour Representation Committee.

A New Century

Anxieties had raged about the cultural meaning of the looming new century since before 1890. They appeared to have even more significance when, just three weeks into January in 1901, Queen Victoria suffered a fatal stroke at the age of 81. Her death was immediately followed by mourning across the globe. Eighteen battleships and 12 cruisers escorted Victoria's coffin to Portsmouth; crowds thronged the streets of London as the coffin made its way to Windsor Castle; crowds even in New York had to be turned away from her memorial services. At the age of 59, Prince Albert Edward, an enthusiastic practitioner of hunting, golf and horseracing, who had been waiting his entire adult life for this moment, ascended to the throne as Edward VII (Clausen 2001).

The Liberals had lost power in the "khaki election" of 1900 – so-called because it was held during the repatriation of British soldiers from the Boer War. In 1905, they swept back into power, riding a new wave of concern with social reform. Over the next eight years, the Liberals enabled the provision of free school meals and school-based medical examinations; pensions for some of the elderly; and secondary-school scholarships for deserving students. Factory and mine safety regulations were overhauled, and, in 1911, workers and employers began to pay into a compulsory health-insurance scheme. David Lloyd George, a popular Welshman who moved from the position of President of the Board of Trade to Chancellor of the Exchequer, gave the Liberals a new fiscal policy. It walked a fine line between Labour's working-class constituency and the Liberals' traditional middle-class constituency. Lloyd George favored a social safety net financed by direct taxation (income taxes on the wealthy) rather than indirect taxation (taxes on vices like tobacco and alcohol widely viewed as working-class "necessities"). The "People's Budget" he presented in 1909–1910 therefore departed substantially from the ideal of retrenchment and government reform which the Liberal Party had pursued from the 1850s onward. The Budget provided for spending on eight new "Dreadnoughts," or large battleships, as well as old-age pensions, and unemployment insurance. The Budget was paid for by a combination of unprecedented taxes on the value of land, income taxes, higher licensing fees on the alcohol trade, and a "supertax" on the highest incomes.

The People's Budget was popular in the country for the way it made the wealthiest Britons pay their share. But since some of the wealthiest Britons had their own representation in the House of Lords, they used that body to vote down the Budget. Liberal Prime Minister Herbert Asquith called the vote against the People's Budget a rejection by the Lords of the time-honored values of the British Constitution, since the House of Commons had primary responsibility for money bills. Parliament was prorogued and a general election called. The Liberal Party lost seats in the election, but not enough to lose control of the government, since the Irish Nationalist Party remained in coalition with them. The Budget finally passed the House of Commons for a second time in April of 1910, and was passed by the House of Lords. The House of Lords had made a severe error, however; the original veto of the legislation had drawn attention to the way in which this ancient body stood as a stumbling-block to the requirements of a society seeking to build a social safety net. The logical consequence was to pare back the power of the House of Lords in the 1911 Parliament Act.

The Boer War aside, the late nineteenth century had been a period of political accommodation and change, illustrating the way in which the expanded electorate exerted pressure on political leaders to cater to constituencies. Although the Conservative and Liberal parties differed on their visions of the role and extent of the empire, the nation was held together by its commitment to imperial trade, and by the image of its reigning figurehead. But the year 1910 drew to a close with a new monarch, a new defense budget, and the beginnings of a new social safety net supported by taxation. In some ways this "Edwardian" period maintained many continuities with what had come before, with Britain imperially in the ascendant, two parties peacefully in and out of power, the monarchy and the aristocracy still exerting symbolic leadership, and the working classes steadily increasing in political representation. Over the next four years, however, Irish Nationalists and Unionists, advocates of votes for women, and trade unionists became more militant, and the House of Lords found its power radically curtailed. And while these sorts of challenges had been successfully contained in the nineteenth century, in 1914 Britain was dragged into the kind of global conflict that had not been seen since the Napoleonic Wars, forcing the government to accommodate radical rather than incremental change.

References

Clausen, Christopher (2001) The Great Queen Died. *American Scholar*, 70 (Winter): 41–49.
Crangle, John V. (1981) English Nationalism and British Imperialism in the Age of Gladstone and Disraeli, 1968–1880. *Quarterly Review of Historical Studies*, 21 (4): 4–12.

Hake, Alfred Egmont (1914) The Death of General Gordon at Khartoum, 1885. In Eva March Tappan (ed.), *The World's Story: A History of the World in Story, Song and Art*, vol. 3: *Egypt, Africa, and Arabia* (Boston: Houghton Mifflin, 1914). At http://www.fordham.edu/halsall/islam/1885khartoum1.html (accessed Dec. 15, 2008).

Harvey, A.D. (1999) London's Boroughs. *History Today*, 49 (7): 15–17.

Jenkins, T. (1996) *Disraeli and Victorian Conservatism*. New York: St Martin's Press.

Jenkins, T. (2005) Lord Salisbury and the Unionist Ascendancy, 1886–1902: Understudied and Undervalued, Does Lord Salisbury Not Deserve Better? *Modern History Review*, 16 (3): 13–18.

Lubenow, W.C. (1986) Irish Home Rule and the Social Basis of the Great Separation in the Liberal Party in 1886. *Historical Journal*, 28 (1): 125–141.

Murphy, Derrick (2001) Joseph Chamberlain: Radical and Imperialist. *Modern History Review*, 12 (3): 27–30.

New York Times (1885) Gordon's Diary. July 12.

Packenham, Thomas (1992) *The Scramble for Africa: White Man's Conquest of the Dark Continent from 1876 to 1912*. New York: Avon.

Strachey, Lytton (1918) *Eminent Victorians*. New York: Putnam's. At http://www.bartleby.com/br/189.html (accessed Dec. 15, 2008).

Watts, Duncan (1993) Juggler Joe: Radical and Unionist. *Modern History Review*, 5 (1): 20–23.

Further Reading

Bentley, Michael (2001) *Lord Salisbury's World: Conservative Environments in Late-Victorian Britain*. Cambridge: Cambridge University Press.

Biagini, Eugenio (2000) *Gladstone*. New York: St Martin's Press.

Martin, Ross (1980) *TUC: The Growth of a Pressure Group, 1868–1976*. Oxford: Clarendon Press.

Murray, Bruce K. (1980) *The People's Budget, 1909–1910: Lloyd George and Liberal Politics*. Oxford: Clarendon Press.

Parry, Jonathan (1993) *The Rise and Fall of Liberal Government in Victorian Britain*. New Haven: Yale University Press.

Porter, Bernard (2004) *The Lion's Share: A Short History of British Imperialism, 1850–2004*. Harlow: Pearson Longman.

6

The Decline of the Aristocracy
Economic and Social Change, 1867–1910

In the first week of July 1885, W.T. Stead, the editor of London's *Pall Mall Gazette*, published the first installment of "The Maiden Tribute of Modern Babylon," an exposé of child prostitution and white slavery practices in London. Audiences read of young girls being stolen from their family homes under the pretext of being hired as domestic servants, having their virginity checked by unscrupulous women doubling as abortionists and midwives, and then being secreted away to brothels where their virginity was sold for as much as £30. They read of young girls being tied down and deflowered in basement rooms especially constructed to muffle their screams.

The first installment culminated with the story of Lily, an adorable 13-year-old with dark hair and eyes, who was knowingly sold into prostitution by a dissipated mother who cared only for drink. The young innocent was inspected by a madam, found to be a virgin, confined in a room, and dosed with chloroform.

> A few minutes later, the door opened, and the purchaser entered the bedroom. He closed and locked the door. There was a brief silence. And then there rose a wild and piteous cry – not a loud shriek, but a helpless, startled scream like the bleat of a frightened lamb. And the child's voice was heard crying, in accents of terror, "There's a man in my room! Take me home; oh, take me home!" (Stead 1885)

Stead's article – distributed in part by the Salvation Army when W.H. Smith newsstands refused to sell what they considered smut – caused an instant outcry for passage of an Act to raise the age of consent. Stead's interest in the plight of young London girls revealed much that was typical of late Victorian England: a concern with urban vice and decay, and the desire for "social purity." But the picture

Empire, State, and Society: Britain Since 1830, First Edition. Jamie L. Bronstein and Andrew T. Harris.
© 2012 Jamie L. Bronstein and Andrew T. Harris. Published 2012 by John Wiley & Sons, Ltd.

of Stead's heroism became muddier when Stead's rival newspaper investigated further and found that "Lily" was actually Elizabeth Armstrong, whose father had not consented to her sale into prostitution, and that the man in the bedroom, the purchaser of a 13-year-old virgin, had been none other than Stead himself. Stead's concern with social reform was admirable, but he had much less concern for Elizabeth Armstrong as an individual than he had with the notion of proving the presence of child trafficking in London.

If continuing differences in power between men and women, the wealthy and the poor, the well-meaning and the depraved, were at the center of Stead's plan, these differences were also central to the way in which Stead and his accomplices were punished. Stead, without whom the plan would never have been conceived or executed, received a sentence of three months in jail, most of which was spent in a white-collar prison. Rebecca Jarrett, the woman who had found Armstrong for Stead, was sentenced to six months' imprisonment, on the grounds that she had misled Stead by claiming the parents' full knowledge and cooperation. Louise Mourez, who had examined Elizabeth Armstrong for evidence of virginity, was sentenced to six months at hard labor and a stern warning that were she really an abortionist as alleged, her penalty would have been much more severe. Stead's punishment reflects judicial protection for the welfare of a working-class girl, and the state's broader acceptance of responsibility for those of lesser legal or economic means (Plowden 1974).

The state that was coming to accept greater social responsibility was at the peak of its imperial influence in the late nineteenth century. Cities like Manchester, Liverpool, and Leeds, empowered by their status as the workshop of the world, were in full flower, with impressive architecture, large public works projects, theaters, libraries, and mechanics' institutes. London was the largest city in the world, with a population that would grow from 3 million in 1861 to over 7 million 50 years later, and whose technological wonders, including underground public transportation, were a model for others to follow. The empire and empire-building were still central to British prosperity and the British definition of self. That definition was becoming more cultural and racial than it had been earlier in the century, with imperialism increasingly pushed forward by international competition from other colonizing powers.

But below this outwardly projected confidence there crept more than a little doubt. British society continued to be extremely stratified, with large differences in the life expectancy, standard of living, and life experiences of rich and poor. As the first industrial nation, Britain experienced the downside of economic maturity earlier than other nations that had industrialized later. In some areas, like finance and shipping, the British were far out ahead of the pack – 80 percent of the world's new ships were built in Britain in the 1890s, most of them on Clydeside in Scotland. But in other areas new economic competitors like Germany and the United States menaced Britain's long-held manufacturing superiority. Faster transportation meant that British agriculture had to compete with farm products from all over the globe, putting the welfare of the British farmer – and the aristocratic landholder to whom he paid rent – in jeopardy. Traditionally less powerful groups asserted themselves more loudly, including married women without property rights and workers without the opportunity to combine into unions.

A Great Depression?

Traditionally, the period between 1873 and 1896 has been seen as a "great depression" in British economic history – but it was a depression of culture and confidence rather than statistics. Although annual economic growth slowed to just under 2 percent, there was no absolute decline, but rather a softening of the expectation that the British would dominate economically in the absence of real competitors. Having been constructed first, the machinery in British industrial plants was older and less efficient than that installed later in German and United States factories. Moreover, the United States, with its relative labor shortage that made machinery more necessary, was beginning to innovate in some areas – transportation and farm implements, for example – in ways that left the British behind. The British economy depended heavily on cotton textiles, iron, and shipbuilding. Britain had no advantage in newer industries like chemical manufacturing and was increasingly undersold by the United States and Germany in the steel industry.

Part of the difference stemmed from managerial culture. In the United States, for example, the late nineteenth century was the age of the limited liability corporation, with its army of middle managers and the possibility of horizontal integration (cornering the market on a single product) or vertical integration (controlling every aspect of production from raw materials to marketing). This organizational form enabled great economic powerhouses like Nabisco, American Can, and the meatpacking plants Swift and Armour. In contrast, as late as 1930, 70 percent of British firms were still personally managed by a single family. In the early Victorian period, this "family fortune" management style had helped to harness the energy and funds of family members, consolidating and promoting firms like Wedgwood and Bentley (the potters) and Cadbury (makers of chocolate). By the late nineteenth century, however, the personal management of British firms revealed certain pitfalls; the idea that the firm existed to advance the "family name" might make it less flexible, less likely to transition into inexpensive mass production, and less likely to innovate. If families newly rich felt tempted to invest their fortunes into landed estates and large country houses rather than back into the firm, a firm might not keep pace with the demands of the times. Finally, British technical education also lagged behind its German and American peers, which in turn meant fewer engineers and other skilled workers in British industry.

Part of the challenge British manufacturers faced came indirectly from state policies. Even though Britain's dominions – New Zealand, Canada, Australia, and

South Africa – did not have to purchase British goods if there were superior substitutes available, the British could fall back on their empire in a way most emerging industrial powers could not. Especially before 1900, this empire still came at great cost. If governments attempted to foster a cultural preference for British goods in the colonies, British firms would have little pressure to innovate. Furthermore, when it came to finding markets for investment, the presence of "safe" investment options meant that the thrifty British middle class was not forced to invest in British domestic firms. The continuing British commitment to the ideology of "free trade" made it harder for the British to compete in places outside of their empire, given that Germany and the United States were firmly committed to protectionist policies at this time, levying tariffs that made imported manufactured goods more expensive.

Operating under these restrictions, the British firms that did succeed made a name for themselves as custom producers of high-quality specialty items not available elsewhere. One Sheffield cutlery factory alone produced 10,000 different patterns of penknives. Such specialization required a well-trained workforce, which meant that British firms were less likely to benefit from increased productivity by standardizing the movements of their workpeople on assembly lines (known as "Taylorism" after its proponent Frederick Taylor), as was happening in the United States (Lloyd-Jones and Lewis 1994).

While British industrial growth slowed, the nation's financial sector grew. Service sector jobs represented half of new jobs created between 1841 and 1911. Some of these jobs came from the transformation of consumerism: chains like W.H. Smith (newsagents and bookstores) and Boots (pharmacies) could buy and sell in bulk, and a new advertising industry took advantage of color printing processes to pioneer long-running ad campaigns linking domestic products with enjoyment of imperial conquest. Retail stores benefited from new inventions, like the telephone and the typewriter, and, after 1896, from the additional mobility represented by the automobile.

The economic picture was also mixed by region. London in particular was able to survive the late nineteenth-century "Great Depression" nicely due to a combination of high demand for products, a large number of small and specialized workshops, and a labor force that was flexible about transferring from one career path to the next (Johnson 1996). Scotland, with its mineral deposits and navigable rivers, benefited from its dominance in shipbuilding, and South Wales dominated in coal exports. Ireland, predominantly agricultural, generally lagged in economic productivity. While Belfast was a modern industrial city with a thriving textile sector, most industries in Ireland were still low power and aimed at providing farmers with shoes and clothing, and processing their farm produce into food and beverages.

If the picture for British industry was mixed, the picture for agriculture was more uniformly bad. Between 1876 and 1900, Britain's farmers of wheat experienced a crisis, as prices dropped worldwide. Arable farmers in the South and East of England were the first to be hit, as strong cultural preferences for growing wheat caused

Figure 6.1 The invention of color printing processes sparked a flourishing advertising sector in Victorian Britain. Images of empire were among the most popular themes in advertisements. Here, tobacco is associated with patriotism and military service, but also with the luxurious East. (National Archives. Ref. COPY 1/185 folio 8).

them to resist changing to animal husbandry. At the time, farmers were receiving mixed price signals about what their next move should be – some argued that they should turn to dairying, citing a boundless demand for milk products in Britain's growing urban areas. Others promoted market gardening of vegetables and fruits, but these pursuits required a lot of hand labor at a time when farmers were trying to decrease the amount that they spent on wages. Other arenas that would have been fruitful were written off because they were not "real farming" – including raising pigs, which had long been done unsystematically as a hobby, and raising chickens, long thought of as women's work. Farmers dismissed as peasant solutions cooperative marketing schemes for dairy products that worked elsewhere in Europe. A government Board of Agriculture was set up in 1889 to disseminate research, and some universities began to offer courses in agriculture, including some directed at women. Some of the most creative landholders made other uses of their land – building housing developments, exploiting underground mineral deposits, or renting out some of their larger buildings to tenants or to schools; but many just saw their businesses fail (Hunt and Pam 2002). Agricultural failures were clustered most closely in the South and East of England in the 1870s and 1880s, but by the 1890s, bankruptcies had spread to Wales, Cornwall, and the area of present-day Cumbria (Perry 1972).

The transformation of English agriculture in the Great Depression had a serious effect on the power of the aristocracy. The fact that landlords were at the top of the social hierarchy, and that people looked to them for financial advice, made it even harder to change agricultural policy quickly. The price shocks occurred in a period in which many landowners were investing heavily in farm infrastructure, building new barns and cottages and mending fences. This resulted in debt burdens that could only be resolved by taking out mortgages or selling off land – a combination of events that led to a decline in the fortunes of some aristocratic families. The number of people directly under the influence of the rural gentry declined, as the number of male workers employed in agriculture decreased from a quarter of the workforce in 1851 to 12 percent in 1901.

A debate about the morality of land ownership patterns throughout Great Britain also undermined the economic foundations of the aristocracy. In Ireland, tenant farmers led by the Land League agitated for fair rents, fixity of tenure, and free sale. They met evictions with all kinds of extraparliamentary protest, including rick-burnings and boycotts. Members of the Irish land-reforming leadership in turn toured Scotland, agitating for wider land reform legislation. In the Scottish highlands in the 1880s, immiserated small farmers, who also lacked security of tenure and were required by law to subdivide their holdings, conducted a struggle for land law reform that coalesced into the Highland Land League – although it was unable to stem the great tide of Scottish highlanders who voted with their feet by emigrating.

In England, John Stuart Mill's Land Tenure Reform League sought free trade in land, and an end to primogeniture (the legal requirement that an oldest son inherit a family's land), entail, and strict settlement (both methods of tying up land for future generations of a family and making it impossible to subdivide and sell). Henry George, an American politician, was warmly received in Britain in the early 1880s; his *Progress and Poverty* (1879) proposed a "single tax" on land as the solution for disparities of wealth. A cheap sixpenny edition sold 100,000 copies in four years. For many, peasant proprietorship, or at least wider landholding, seemed to offer a firmer basis for social harmony than the concentration of land in the hands of a few families; Jesse Collings spearheaded a land reform campaign in 1885 calling for "Three Acres and a Cow," thought to be the minimum that peasant farmers needed to support themselves.

While aristocrats lost economic and social ground in the late nineteenth century, and the middle classes grew under the influence of jobs in the professions, education, retail and the clerical sector, British working people experienced mixed changes in their fortunes. Those in trades like glassmaking and shipbuilding, who had job skills that were consistently in demand, found that their "real wages" (the basket of goods and services that wages will buy) improved, due to decreasing prices for necessities. Year-to-year incomes were not predictable, since employment opportunities whipsawed from one year to the next with the health of individual companies. Still, with the exercise of a little thrift during the good times, skilled workers could more easily afford the working-class dietary staples of bread, flour, butter, lard, mutton, bacon, sugar and tea.

In contrast, unskilled workers suffered during periods of cyclical unemployment, which occurred in 1878–1879, 1885–1887, and 1893–1895 as part of the boom-and-bust cycle of global capitalism. The unemployed had historically been able to survive by pawning clothes and collecting outdoor relief, in those areas where relief outside the workhouses was still being offered. But a movement against outdoor relief starting in the early 1870s made it much harder to collect this support. Private organizations like the Charity Organization Society, founded in 1869, argued that flawed morals caused poverty, and refused relief to those who did not fit into the category of the "worthy poor" (mostly widows, children, and people with physical disabilities). The percentage of the population receiving some form of aid from the Poor Law Guardian declined from 10 percent in 1865 to 5.6 percent by 1900. Those who did have work were encouraged to save through the mechanism of trade union funds or friendly societies, but some workers and radical politicians also began to argue that the government should provide jobs for the unemployed on public works like roads and bridges. By 1905, the Royal Commission on the Poor Laws and Relief of Distress – which included the sociologist of poverty Charles Booth among its members – would evaluate some of these municipal programs and propose unemployment insurance as a more efficient method of helping the poor. Whether or not people in the United Kingdom experienced the late nineteenth century as a "Great Depression" depended on economic sector, inheritance, skill level, and individual factors of geography.

Population and Cities

Population growth caused some of the most trenchant problems in the late nine-teenth century. With the exception of Ireland, which had not yet recovered from the demographic calamity of the Famine, Great Britain experienced steady popula-tion growth in this period: from about 23 million in England, Wales, and Scotland in 1861, to about 37 million in 1901. This great population increase occurred de-spite the net outward migration to the empire and particularly to the United States. Scotland, where the service sector opportunities available in many English towns were lacking, was a particular source of outward migrants.

Demographic increase was accompanied by internal migration from rural areas and small market towns lacking in employment opportunities to nearby manufac-turing centers. During the decade from 1871 to 1881, the urban population of Great Britain increased by 19.63 percent, while the rural population rose only 4 percent; some of this rural-to-urban migration was "surplus" women moving from rural areas to take up situations as domestic servants, and it was offset by middle-class

Figure 6.2 Victorian poor relief was based on the idea that only certain classes of people – including these small children – constituted the "deserving poor," and that others should not be entitled to poor relief. Apparently the support provided by the Charles Thompson Poor Children's Mission in Birkenhead in 1905 did not include shoes. (National Archives. Ref. COPY 1/481).

suburban movement, but the rest was due to the relocation of industry from towns and villages to metropolitan areas.

Housing stock failed to keep pace. The worst overcrowding occurred in Scottish and Irish cities, but slum districts throughout the United Kingdom menaced human health through poor water supplies, filth, and the more abstract threats of crime and "degeneracy" from new migrants who neither spoke English well nor came from so-called Anglo-Saxon stock. Well-meant "slum clearance" programs knocked down some of the least sanitary, most overcrowded housing, but it was not thought to be the role of the state to provide good alternate housing, and displaced workers simply moved to, and overcrowded, neighboring slums. In London, moving slaughterhouses out of the city center and providing more street lighting was supposed to produce a more alert, neat, and tractable urban citizen.

Those who managed to avoid the most overcrowded slums benefited from improvements in the state of medicine in the last third of the nineteenth century. Some of the improvements were related to major discoveries, like Joseph Lister's use of antiseptic medical practice at the Glasgow Infirmary in 1865, and the increasing belief in the idea of contagion through some invisible agent as the cause of disease, rather than exposure to "miasmas" or bad air. The capstone of this progress came in 1875, when German physician Robert Koch successfully proved the germ theory of disease. Now, attention could be focused on insulating the well from the ill, and on finding medicines tailored to individual diseases. Public health improved due to better water supplies, the replacement of earth closets with indoor plumbing, the provision of public baths, less adulterated foods, and a better standard of nutrition that enabled bodies to combat disease. Deaths from infectious diseases, like cholera, dysentery, tuberculosis, typhoid, diphtheria, and scarlet fever, fell especially sharply. Life expectancy at birth for England and Wales increased from 41 years in 1851 to 43 in 1871 and 46 in1900, although even in 1900 there were significant differences between life expectancy in large cities (46) and rural areas (56.5) (Boyer 2004: 291).

Decreasing death rates combined with the increasing medicalization of death to change the cultural meaning of death and its attendant symbolism and cere-monies. At the beginning of the century, death had been a bedside family drama, a seminal religious moment that helped family members to determine whether or not the sufferer was going to heaven. By the end of the century, it had become a potentially painful biological process, only really understood by doctors, and from which patients should be protected. Dead bodies, once dressed for burial in kitchens by midwives or family members, were now handled by undertakers. The commodification of death increasingly removed people from direct contact with the corpse.

Municipal reformers and public health advocates thought they knew how to combat disease, but the moral and sexual dangers posed by the city were a trickier problem. The streets were places where prostitutes endangered the respectability of any woman who would go out in public. Men of ill repute, "cads," "mashers" and men-about-town, blended in with respectable gentlemen on the darkened streets. Gambling, drunkenness and assault posed moral, physical, and fiscal dangers. To penetrate the urban darkness might even bring death; during a brief scare in 1862–1863, a serial garroting murderer had people walking with their hands on their throats. And most notably, the eight murders and eviscerations of prostitutes perpetrated by "Jack the Ripper" in 1888 focused Londoners' attention on the little-known lives of poor East Enders, including new Jewish immigrants.

In fact, the environment of cities had an impact on private as well as public lives, although often not in the most feared ways. Unskilled urban workers faced economic uncertainty that led to older brides and grooms, as people who might have married in their early twenties postponed weddings until a time when they were more steadily employed. This in turn led to smaller but more prosperous families. The 1870 Education Act provided for school boards to oversee public primary education in places where the voluntary system proved inadequate. While fees were still charged, these were now subsidized so that the poorest parents might be responsible for a penny worth of tuition a week, or for no fee at all. Increasing regulation of the hours of labor provided opportunities not only for children to attend school but also for their parents to take advantage of new commercial leisure opportunities: music halls, pubs, professional sports teams, and museums allowed for a better mix of labor and leisure. The invention of the bicycle represented inexpensive mobility on demand. Still, particularly for children from dark and overcrowded homes, the streets remained the center of working-class public space, full of daily drama and the site of pickup games conducted with scavenged materials.

A Dynamic Working Class

Unionization was one of the most dynamic features of the last third of the nineteenth century. Those working people who lived in depressed agricultural areas found a moment of optimism in the campaign of Joseph Arch, who organized rural laborers in England's southern counties. Farm workers had traditionally been hired on yearly contracts that included both a weekly wage and a set of perquisites (inexpensive if shoddy cottages, flour, and perhaps a small garden allotment). Under Arch's leadership, they threatened to walk off the job if their pay was not increased. Arch's unions may have promoted a temporary increase in farm wages by as much as 3–4 shillings per week. His campaigns had a domino effect among nonunionized farms as well, as farmers offered laborers comparable wages in order to compete. Membership in the agricultural union movement peaked in 1874, with about 122,000 workers, representing 15 percent of the agricultural workforce (Boyer and Hatton 1994).

For urban workers, the last third of the century was a time of great ferment in the union movement, through a struggle between unions, employers, Parliament, and the courts to define the role trades unions could play. Unions had come under attack in 1866 over the "Sheffield outrages." Trade unionists then practiced "rattening," or hiding the tools of coworkers who refused to join unions, which escalated to injuring and even killing those who would not join. In 1867, the British courts in *Hornby v Close* held that trade unions were illegal associations that restrained trade. Feeling embattled, Northern union organizers called the first of their annual Trades Union Congresses in 1868 in Manchester; by 1872, the TUC represented 250,000 members. Political mobilization resulted in the election of the first two MPs from labor backgrounds (1874): Thomas Burt and Alexander MacDonald, both of them colliers by trade.

The 1880s and 1890s witnessed the expansion of a new age in unionism. By 1888, about 750,000 workers were unionized, representing about 10 percent of working men, and union activity was much more visible than it had ever been. Women workers at the Bryant and May match factory, who were exposed daily to phosphorous that broke down their jaws, forced to work 12-hour days, and fined for using the toilet, went on strike with the support of Fabian activist Annie Besant. Workers were portrayed sympathetically by the popular press, and Bryant and

May were forced to hire back the striking workers and correct working conditions. A highly public dock strike in London, lasting five weeks in late summer 1889, imparted great hope for union members of the newfound benefits of collective action. John Burns, the leader of the port workers, led daily parades of striking workers through the East End, suggesting the novel idea that even unskilled and semiskilled workers could be organized. Previously, the tradition that only skilled craft workers could be unionized had alienated the unskilled and divided the labor movement. The ideological impact of the "new unionism" was intense, sparking copycat strikes; throughout the country, even schoolchildren walked out of their schools, demanding shorter tasks, easier homework, and an end to lessons. By 1892, total union membership had doubled, reaching about 1.5 million workers.

Changing Roles for Women

The period saw opportunities for women change, even as their normative roles remained largely the same. Working-class women still found themselves in the most abject position. Whether they were married or living in common-law relationships, domestic violence and unwanted pregnancies were common, due to the cultural expectation that wives' bodies belonged to their husbands. Women were often deserted by their partners in hard times, and had to learn to cobble together survival strategies that might involve taking in boarders, taking in assembly work to be done in the home, scavenging useful items from the streets, and, most particularly, pawning items and redeeming them on a weekly basis. Women were challenged within the family economy by the tradition of husbands and sons of holding back the money they needed for leisure and beer, and paying wives a scanty sum with which the women were expected to keep up respectable appearances. The assumption that men required the best and largest portions of food in order to work meant that many working-class women were still regularly poorly nourished.

Women who did go out to work were still prohibited by custom and animosity from entering the skilled trades. They were marginalized by existing trade unions, and welcomed only into new women's trade unions supported by the National Federation of Women Workers and the Women's Trade Union League. They were also the subject of "protective" legislation, which regulated women's work in industries thought to be harmful to their future fertility (since waged work was still considered a temporary stopgap and motherhood the ultimate goal for women).

The challenges that had faced lower-income women throughout the century were compounded by a new concern with prostitution, immorality, and "white slavery." Prostitution had long been an expansive concept, encompassing habitual working girls, working-class women who might be susceptible to the offer of monetary or other treats for sexual favors in times of hardship, and "fallen women" of a higher social class who had been seduced or promised marriage and then deceived. These class distinctions were blurred by a series of "Contagious Diseases Acts" passed in 1864, 1866, and 1869, and designed to decrease prostitution by decreasing the numbers of working prostitutes. The CD Acts met the problem of prostitution from the supply side, by enabling policemen to preemptively arrest women suspected of being prostitutes, turn them over to doctors for forcible examination of their genitals, and detain those suspected of having syphilis or gonorrhea against their will in "lock hospitals" for up to three months. Women who refused to comply could be imprisoned. Similar Contagious Diseases legislation was passed in Britain's colonies, where prostitution was seen as doubly offensive, since it was an offense against racial purity as well as sexual self-control.

The first-wave feminism of the late nineteenth century considered protecting women from the sexual appetites of men to be part of its goal. Josephine Butler, daughter of a good Liberal family, headed the Ladies' National Association, a lobbying group formed to combat the CD Acts. In the first year of her campaign she traveled 3,700 miles and addressed 99 meetings, arguing that the CD Acts offensively singled out women as the sole cause of prostitution, and subjected all women who happened to be in the public sphere to preemptive arrest and suspicion. Butler continued her campaign into the 1880s, and expanded her activities as a social reformer into opposition to the "white slave" trade, or trafficking of young girls for the purposes of sex. She worked with W.T. Stead in his attempt to expose the white slave trade, but escaped the ensuing scandal.

Late Victorian middle-class and upper-class women could use the popular image of women as the more moral sex to overcome limitations on their participation in public life, but there were also attempts to grant women more formal civil and political rights. During the debate over the 1867 Reform Bill, John Stuart Mill (unsuccessfully) introduced an amendment to enfranchise women by changing the legislative language of citizenship from "man" to "person." The Third Reform Act (1884) provided another opportunity for discussion about whether or not women should have the right to vote; a surprisingly large minority of the House of Commons – 135 members – supported such a proposition. While women could not yet vote for MPs, they did in 1870 gain the right to vote for and serve as members of school boards, and, after 1894, the right to vote for members of local government as well. Property law changed too. The 1870 Married Women's Property Act allowed married women to keep their own wages, and a related 1882 Act expanded property rights and gave married women the right to buy, sell, and own property in their own right.

One major change in women's lives required no Act of Parliament. The 1870s saw the beginning of a great decline in fertility. English and Welsh couples who married in the 1880s produced, on average, between two and three children, in contrast with six or more children for those married in the 1870s or earlier. Irish rural couples who married in the 1880s still produced an average of five children, but this marked a great decrease from eight or more children earlier in the century.

After the 1880s 40 percent of couples had one or fewer children; very small families were more prevalent among professionals, the salaried, those with older wives, and men whose jobs kept them away from home for long periods of time. Charles Darwin and his wife embodied these changes. They had had a total of ten children; but the six children who lived to adulthood only gave birth to or sired nine grandchildren among them.

Why were families becoming smaller? After 1870, when primary school education became compulsory, and parents were deprived of their children's paychecks, the expense of having any children at all rose. Smaller families were also seen as beneficial. They could enable upwardly mobile working people to put their children through school, or allow middle-class women to spend more time working or in other pursuits outside the home. Due to the relative absence of reliable barrier methods of contraception, the fertility decline was managed through periods of marital abstinence, with larger spaces between the births of children, and the last child born when a mother was in her late thirties rather than after age 40.

While most women continued to be wives and mothers, and the Victorian home continued as the axis around which they turned, the needs of that home and the whole panoply of related goods and services could now be provided in ways that increasingly brought women into the public eye. Department stores like William Whiteley's, the "universal provider" – which provided food as well as clothing – opened in the second half of the nineteenth century. These stores could take up an entire city block, and dazzle the eye with multiple stories, mirrored interiors, red carpets, glinting chandeliers, and piles of products (the sheer opulence of the retail environment helped to disguise the fact that the goods for sale may have been produced under sweatshop conditions). As women made use of omnibuses and trams to leave their immediate neighborhoods and travel to London's West End, they faced both the delights of conspicuous consumption that supposedly threatened to deprive them of their rationality, and the chance to fall into all kinds of dangers (see Rappaport 2001: 32). Observers wondered whether respectable women would rub elbows with prostitutes, now that ready-made clothing gave women the opportunity to dress like their social betters. Would respectable women have secret assignations with men whom they met on the streets? Would they be tempted to shoplift? Would they – as the *Saturday Review* suggested – become like "oriental potentates", drifting away from thrifty behaviors in search of the newest trifles?

The shopping-crazed woman was not the only composite stereotype created by the press in the last third of the nineteenth century. Writers also summoned up the "new woman" – the embodiment of a set of practices supposedly embraced by young women of the time. New Womanhood had been made possible by an expansion of opportunities to women, including the opening of Girton College in 1869, where women could receive higher education, and the entry of a few women into the medical profession. In contrast with their forbears, who, it was claimed, depended on men and saw marriage and children as women's highest estate, the "new woman" was socially and economically independent. She might live alone, or with other employed women; she might work in a field formerly closed to women (including clerical and retail positions); she might take up the new fad of the bicycle or favor "rational dress," might smoke cigarettes, or even have romances without being married. Whether regarded with admiration or a sense of patronizing amusement, such single women were a constituency without precedent, and therefore potentially destabilizing.

Economically, the United Kingdom made the transformation into the twentieth century as a superpower, with great strengths in shipping, finance, and communication, good internal infrastructure, and improving cities. Industrially, Britain was achieving relatively slower growth, and agriculturally, it was having trouble competing in a world market, but the nation's imperial influence was still undisturbed in its own eyes, and in a world of competing empires, this was still extremely important. The hungry forties were now far in the past. The domestic market was beginning to expand and standards of living were improving, although unemployment remained a problem that was attacked in an uneven way. Socially, the nation was greatly transformed, particularly in urban areas, as women, trade unionists, and members of the United Kingdom's own internal periphery contended for greater civil and political rights, economic opportunities, and social recognition. The pace of change in the political and economic realms had accelerated, forcing a cultural reevaluation that will be discussed in the next chapter.

References

Boyer, George K. (2004) Living Standards, 1860–1939. In Roderick Floud and Paul Johnson (eds), *The Cambridge Economic History of Modern Britain*, vol. 2. Cambridge: Cambridge University Press.

Boyer, George, and Hatton, Timothy (1994) Did Joseph Arch Raise Agricultural Wages? Rural Trade Unions and the Labour Market in Late Nineteenth-Century England. *Economic History Review*, 47 (2): 310–334.

Hunt, E.H., and Pam, S.J. (2002) Responding to Agricultural Depression, 1873–1896: Managerial Success, Entrepreneurial Failure? *Agricultural History Review*, 50 (2): 225–252.

Johnson, Paul (1996) Economic Development and Industrial Dynamism in Victorian London. *London Journal*, 21 (1): 27–37.

Lloyd-Jones, Roger, and Lewis, Myrddin J. (1994) Personal Capitalism and British Industrial Decline: The Personally Managed Firm and Business Strategy in Sheffield, 1880–1920. *Business History Review*, 68 (3): 364–411.

Perry, P.J. (1972) Where Was the "Great Agricultural Depression"? A Geography of Agricultural Bankruptcy in Late Victorian England and Wales. *Agricultural History Review*, 20 (1): 30–45.

Plowden, Alison (1974) *The Case of Eliza Armstrong: A Child of 13 Bought for £5*. Extract at http://www.attackingthedevil.co.uk/pmg/tribute/armstrong/bailey/sentence.php (accessed Aug. 2011).

Rappaport, Erika (2001) *Shopping for Pleasure: Women in the Making of London's West End.* Princeton: Princeton University Press.

Stead, W.T. (1885) The Maiden Tribute of Modern Babylon. *Pall Mall Gazette*, July 6. At http://www.attackingthedevil.co.uk/pmg/tribute/mt1.php (accessed Aug. 2011).

Further Reading

August, Andrew (2007) *The British Working Class, 1832–1940.* New York: Longman.

Black, Jeremy, and Macraild, Donald M. (2003) *Nineteenth-Century Britain.* London: Palgrave Macmillan.

Cannadine, David (1999) *The Decline and Fall of the British Aristocracy.* New York: Vintage.

Floud, Roderick, and Johnson, Paul (eds) (2004) *The Cambridge Economic History of Modern Britain*, vol. 2. Cambridge: Cambridge University Press.

Koven, Seth (2004) *Slumming: Sexual and Social Politics in Victorian London.* Princeton: Princeton University Press.

Robbins, Keith (1983) *The Eclipse of a Great Power: Modern Britain, 1870–1975.* London: Longman.

Reay, Barry (1996) *Microhistories: Demography, Society and Culture in Rural England, 1800–1930.* Cambridge: Cambridge University Press.

Thirsk, Joan (ed.) (2000) *Cambridge Agricultural History of England*, vol. 7. Cambridge: Cambridge University Press.

Walkowitz, Judith (1992) *City of Dreadful Delight: Narratives of Sexual Danger in Late-Victorian London.* Chicago: University of Chicago Press.

Wiener, Martin J. (1982) *English Culture and the Decline of the Industrial Spirit, 1850–1980.* Cambridge: Cambridge University Press.

7

Faith and Doubt?
Cultural Change, 1867–1910

I have seen no such rapid or complete change as that which took place in the eighties and nineties . . . like one of those catastrophes which the geologist used to postulate in order to explain the alterations in the earth: sudden, immense, and, I think, irrevocable.

E.E. Kellett, As I Remember, 1936

[T]he most salient characteristic of life in the latter portion of the nineteenth century is its speed, and the question to be considered is – first, whether this rapid rate is a good one, and next, whether it is worth the price we pay for it? No doubt we "do" more, but is "doing" everything, and "being" nothing?

W.R. Greg, "On Life at High Pressure," 1875

Roger Charles Tichborne, an Englishman raised in France, heir to an aristocratic title and fortune, disappeared at sea on a trip to New York in 1855. He left behind a grieving mother who never accepted the fact of his death. In 1865, Lady Tichborne received word that a man claiming to be her long-lost son had turned up in Australia. Summoned to England, the "Tichborne claimant" was welcomed and acknowledged by Lady Tichborne and by many of Roger's former friends and acquaintances, despite the fact that the man claiming to be Roger could neither speak French nor knew many details relating to the person he claimed to be. In fact, the impostor was Arthur Orton, a rotund former butcher who was originally from Wapping, in East London. But while Lady Tichborne was alive, the family believed what she needed it to believe.

Upon her death, representatives of the legitimate heir to the Tichborne estate sued Orton, attempting to establish his identity as an impostor and a usurper of an

Empire, State, and Society: Britain Since 1830, First Edition. Jamie L. Bronstein and Andrew T. Harris.
© 2012 Jamie L. Bronstein and Andrew T. Harris. Published 2012 by John Wiley & Sons, Ltd.

aristocratic fortune. The case of the Tichborne claimant, which opened in 1871, became the kind of media sensation that was only possible because of cultural changes in the last third of the nineteenth century: increased working-class literacy and the emergence of a press that capitalized on titillating scandal. The Tichborne affair also emphasized certain continuities in late nineteenth-century British cultural life; many working people continued to support Orton's claim to the fortune even as the true heir won against Orton in court, and Orton was eventually convicted of perjury. The dream that a common man might be an aristocrat under the surface appealed, against evidence to the contrary, to the popular imagination, suggesting a blurring of boundaries in an increasingly fluid social order.

Mass Culture and Popular Literacy

With improvements in living conditions for the working poor after mid-century came rising literacy, new forms of entertainment and association, and new state structures to support elementary education. The population had risen significantly from 26 million in 1871 to 37 million by the end of the century. As manufacturing spread from textiles to a wide range of industries, these additional people found work, and with work and increasing real wages (wages remaining steady while prices of consumer goods fell) came a measure of expendable income previously unknown on such a scale. Illiteracy had been falling since before the 1870 Education Act, and in 1871, 19 percent of males and 26 percent of females could not read, down significantly from mid-century. The Education Act, and subsequent legislation expanding state support for public elementary education in 1886, were grounded on the assumption that if the working class was going to participate in political life, it would be irresponsible to allow them to vote without preparing them for informed citizenship. The new state-supported "board schools," so called after the local boards created to govern them, served far more students than the existing collection of denominational schools, upper-class public schools (really private), and a scattering of experimental schools for the poor. They promised national efficiency in providing elementary education, at the same time limiting the influence of religious instruction and local educational patronage.

Catering to this expansion of the working-class reading market was the widespread development of inexpensively produced newspapers. While middle-class readers viewed the cheap new press as sensationalist and xenophobic, by the end of the century hundreds of thousands of Britons received their news from such papers as the *Daily Mail, Daily Telegraph*, and the *Pall Mall Gazette*. The papers' expansion was partly a product of the end of the tax on printing newspapers which removed the last "stamp duties" in 1855. Telegraph cables completed over the next two decades made worldwide information transfer more rapid, and the cost of paper also declined as the technology of papermaking changed. The new press featured more accessible writing styles, as seen in William Stead's exposé on child prostitution in the *Pall Mall Gazette* during the 1880s. While the new papers attempted to move away from the highly formal style of Britain's more established press, some aimed at a more literate working-class readership as well. Robert Blatchford's *The Clarion* sought to bring socialism to the more educated masses after 1891 and helped solidify respectable working-class support for labor political activism. By the 1890s, the new press had expanded readership to include nearly a million readers for the largest papers. Cheaper technology and lower costs of production matched the interests of a rapidly expanding and more literate population. This allowed the mobilization of mass politics and the creation of mass culture as never before, evidenced also by the expansion of music hall attendance. A modest footnote to rising literacy was increased writing as well: Britons wrote and sent more letters through the postal service over the second half of the century, rising from 32 per capita annually in 1871 to 60 in 1900.

Figure 7.1 The circus, the music hall, and miscellaneous exhibitions like this display of an early robot were popular entertainments in late Victorian popular culture. (© The British Library Board EVAN. 1879).

Religion and Spiritualism

The relationship of the British state to formal religion changed in the late Victorian period. The Anglican Church underwent several disestablishment crises, in which it seemed for a time that it would no longer serve as the established church tied to the state's authority, and support that authority throughout the realm. With the reduction of civil disabilities imposed on Nonconformists, and their presence in the reformed Parliament after 1832, liberals and radicals often called on the state to sever or reduce its formal support for a state church as a relic of a more religious past. If Britain was an increasingly pluralist nation and empire, what logic could support government financial support and regulation of a church that explicitly served only some of its citizens? Nonconformists also resented the Anglican Church's control over elementary education – a control non-Anglicans subsidized with their own tithes until 1868. "Disestablishment" covered a range of such issues – access to political power for non-Anglicans, control of schools, direct state financial support, ownership of church property – and over the course of the nineteenth century several of these were addressed. When William Gladstone was Prime Minister, many hoped or feared that he would support disestablishment of the Anglican Church. While he did so in Ireland, where the church was disestablished in 1869, the liberal leader did not pursue this action in England and without Parliamentary support the matter died. The Church of Scotland survived similar disestablishment movements in the 1870s and 1880s, but also saw its influence over such areas as elementary education decline.

The attenuation of the Church of England's relationship with the state was mirrored by a decline in formal church attendance. By 1902, only one in five Londoners attended church on Sunday. Each of the major religious denominations sought to reach out to new migrant and working-class populations at home and imperial populations abroad. Each also became in the late nineteenth century less authoritarian in its hierarchy and less doctrinaire in its beliefs, and many religious institutions tolerated internal dissent among leaders that would have earned expulsion in an earlier time.

Diversity and theology

The hinge of increasing doctrinal toleration within denominations is illustrated by the treatment of John William Colenso, Bishop of Natal in Africa and hence a clergyman of the Anglican Church. Colenso, like many educated persons of the mid-nineteenth century across Europe, was influenced by the new scholarship coming primarily from German authors who applied linguistic and historical analysis to the Old and New Testaments. As bishop of the newly established see of Natal, his mission was in part to bring the Zulu to Christianity, a responsibility bolstered by a literal belief in the Bible's authenticity. But the new scholarship cast doubt on this literal truth. His own translation of the Old Testament into Zulu led increasingly to intellectual skepticism and a variety of theological differences with the Anglican hierarchy:

> I have arrived at the conviction – as painful to myself at first, as it may be to my reader – that the Pentateuch, as a whole, cannot possibly have been written by Moses, or by any one acquainted personally with the facts which it professes to describe, and further, that the (so-called) Mosaic narrative … though imparting to us, as I fully believe it does, revelations of the Divine Will and Character, cannot be regarded as historically true. (Ingram 1863)

While Colenso's faith was unshaken by this intellectual realization, some of his peers were not so willing to maintain the possibility of faith without a literally authentic word of God. Combined with Colenso's relative respect for Zulu culture, this also made him highly suspect as an agent of imperial progress. Amid calls for his resignation in South Africa and Britain, he was deposed and excommunicated for heresy by the Bishop of Cape Town in 1863. This ruling was overturned by the Privy Council itself, an advisory body to the monarch, which asserted that the Anglican Church did not have such authority over churchmen in the colonies. It also meant, critically, that so-called "broad" church perspectives on scripture, doctrine and faith could be tolerated within Anglicanism, even if, in this instance, the toleration was imposed by the state itself. This was no small thing, given that Anglicanism derived its authority in part from its establishment as the religion of the state.

Heterodox religious belief, and the occasionally resulting public outcry by traditionalists, was also seen among Scottish Presbyterianism in the 1870s, when William Robertson Smith, Professor of Hebrew and Old Testament at the Free Church College in Aberdeen, similarly applied current literary scholarship to the Bible and was expelled from the faculty. By the 1890s, both main branches of the Scottish church, the Church of Scotland and the Free Church, had relaxed the strict Calvinist idea of predestination (that salvation and damnation had been predetermined by God), allowing a deliberate lack of clarity around the role individual choice played in this process. The Nonconformists felt the same influence of biblical scholarship and science-induced doubt, as even did English Catholicism, committed as it was for much of the century to a staunch opposition to all things modern and secular. By the late 1880s, though, relatively little hubbub ensued when Oxford Anglicans (some of them inheritors of the Anglo-Catholic Tractarian movement earlier in the century) published a treatise entitled *Lux Mundi* that accepted the ideas of evolution and the now not so new biblical criticism. Charles Darwin, they wrote, was not the enemy of Christianity but its friend – for evolution reaffirmed the presence of God throughout the natural world rather than a divine absence. That *Lux Mundi* came from the theologically Catholic part of Anglicanism suggests the degree to which a faith might come to accept new and diverse influences under its respective umbrellas.

Finally, in the more open religious environment of the late nineteenth century, some Britons found a home in noninstitutional belief systems that lay in the gray area between science and religion, such as spiritualism, astrology, or the movement to commune with the dead through séances. Members of the Society of Psychical Research, founded in 1882, sought to explore the persistence after death of the soul, or some form of consciousness, and included spiritualists, skeptics, and early psychologists. Nor was this entirely a fringe element of British intellectual life. While the naturalist Alfred Russel Wallace's scientific career underwent considerable harm as a result of such interests, the SPR's membership included a range of highly respected establishment figures: a future Prime Minister (A.J. Balfour), a popular novelist (Arthur Conan Doyle), a Cambridge philosophy don (Henry Sidgwick), and the editor of the *Dictionary of National Biography* (Leslie Stephen). The SPR served as a working forum for nascent psychology as well, and published the first English account of Sigmund Freud's work in 1893. One of the SPR's notable successes, its investigations of the séances of the famous medium Madame Blavatsky, exposing them as deceptions, nonetheless did not lead to a decline in popular interest in communicating with the dead. The declining hold of formal religious belief combined with new scientific insights to create a broad area between science and faith within which such practices flourished in the late nineteenth century.

Religion and social services

While changing interpretations of theology in the age of Darwin and Liberalism occupied church leaders of all faiths, how did most people participate in and experience religious life? To what degree did the strict moral exhortations of the age define people's religious or moral behavior? The Victorian insistence on moral probity, often undergirded by participation in church-related activities and devotions, was itself complicated by middle-class Victorians' intent on using religious observance as a way to support social orderliness. In the late nineteenth-century world of rapid urbanization, dizzying scientific change, and the rise of mass working-class participation in politics, Victorian religion waged an ongoing battle against the forces of disorder and change. At the same time, formal and informal religious groups generated extraordinary voluntary social services in education, relief of poverty, and temperance.

In absolute terms, the number of new churches and additional clergy continued to increase mightily. For instance, the two main Scottish Presbyterian churches added 1,800 churches and 1,700 ministers between 1843 and 1901. Similar growth occurred to scale among Anglicans, Congregationalists and Methodists. It was, however, never enough, for the population growth of the period, combined with immigration, served to keep growth in church capacity perennially behind the overall growth of British society. Many working-class Britons, moreover, were not successfully brought into the religious fold, preferring to spend their Sundays in other more leisurely pursuits and often resenting the alliance between churchgoing and the temperance movement.

The late nineteenth century brought a flourishing of church-related, or at least religiously inspired voluntary societies that made up part of the vitality and breadth of religious participation if not belief itself. With the state's increasing involvement, regulation and support of elementary education after 1870, the influence of the Anglican Church over local schooling declined, and with rising educational standards, the church found it difficult to keep pace with schools underwritten by the public purse. The rise of voluntary societies aimed at improving the manners, morals and behavior of the working classes at home and converting non-Christian imperial subjects abroad more than made up for the church's diminishing role in domestic education. This rise grew out of several strands in different faiths. Evangelicals within the Anglican Church had been active in temperance and anti-slavery societies for decades; Protestant Nonconformists (primarily Congregationalists, Quakers, and Baptists) turned from their earlier emphasis on individualistic self-help to a broader sense of social responsibility; Catholics drew on their connections to the large influx of working-class Irish immigrants to emphasize their role in alleviating poverty and labor unrest.

The voluntary societies that grew out of these impulses were often organized and galvanized by middle-class women, who found in social reform many opportunities to make powerful contributions within acceptable cultural boundaries. While earlier generations of middle-class women would have worked, the fact that this was no longer expected did not remove the desire to put their abilities into service. One of the most famous of these groups, the Salvation Army, began when Evangelical minister William Booth sought to bring conversion to the urban masses and realized that salvation might succeed better if paired with social activism and the salvation of people's earthly bodies as well. Evangelicals, Catholics and Nonconformists all set up "missions" in poor urban areas, particularly in London's East End, to create recreational centers, schools, and homes in which ministers lived among the poor they served. The Band of Hope, begun in the 1840s in Leeds, flourished in the last decades of the century; members enrolled working-class children as young as six and both taught the menace of alcohol consumption and organized athletic and other recreational activities to create fulfilling lives free of drink. The Band of Hope appealed to a modest segment of the working class, many of whom would as parents have to strive for respectable middle-class stature in order to see this as a worthwhile activity for their children. The Young Men's Christian Association likewise targeted youth for early training in the habits of a moral life, a flavor of which can be found in Frederick Atkins's *Moral Muscle, and How to Use It: A Brotherly Chat with Young Men*: "Life is not a thing to be played with . . . It is a stern fight, in which the warrior must have ceaseless energy, keen foresight, and strong faith, if he is to win success and have an honorable record. The firing will not be done with toy pistols" (1890: 11). Manliness, Atkins argued, was godliness, and he used the language of conflict and battle to win over his presumably young male readers.

Unbelief

While many late Victorians reconciled science and faith without difficulty, some chose a variety of what was called at the time "freethought" and what we would now refer to as either atheism or agnosticism. It is easy to lay all this at Darwin's door, but the crisis of faith associated with natural selection had been percolating for decades – Lyell's geological assault on the Genesis creation story, linguistic unraveling of the Old Testament's historical authenticity, and even Adam Smith's invisible hand in economics all challenged the concept of an omnipotent God before Darwin published a word. While Darwin attempted to keep his private religious skepticism out of his public science writing, and more liberal theologians sought to see God in natural selection, a growing number of late Victorians concluded that religious belief was simply incompatible with modern life. Charles Bradlaugh, founder of the National Secular Society and a proponent of birth control, was elected Member of Parliament in 1880. He famously refused to swear his oath of allegiance on a Bible and was thereby prevented from taking his seat in the House of Commons until 1886. Notably, his constituents supported his cause, knowing his beliefs full well. Thomas Huxley coined the term "agnostic" to mean a scientific incapacity to know God's purpose, distinguished from atheist in that atheists were certain of God's nonexistence. A scientist, said Huxley, could not know such a thing, and sought to create in agnosticism a less confrontational approach to religious belief. Societies to promote atheism and agnosticism formed, such as the International Federation of Freethinkers, along with journals such as *The Freethinker*, whose founder, G.W. Foote, was convicted of blasphemy and sentenced to a year in jail. Leslie Stephen, the editor of the *Dictionary of National Biography*, was an agnostic, and made the case that despite common fears, agnosticism did not oppose ethical behavior: "I now believe in nothing, but I do not the less believe in morality. I mean to live and die like a gentleman if possible."

The Birth of "Society"

One of the most important trends in Britain in the last quarter of the nineteenth century was the tension between laissez-faire, or classical liberalism, which favored small government and an economy free from regulation, and what became known as "new liberalism," whose proponents held that human freedom could only be achieved if government played a role in the provision of public services, including utilities and education. The philosopher Herbert Spencer, influenced by the ideas of Charles Darwin, believed that mankind was constantly evolving in a better direction; but Spencer also believed that only in a state of the greatest liberty and freedom from government regulation could a person maximize his abilities. For Spencer, society existed to serve the individual.

Other liberal social thinkers, like the philosopher T.H. Green, agreed with Spencer that mankind was capable of moving in a positive direction, but they saw a role for the shaping of human capability by "society," an intermediate body between the individual and the potentially coercive government. For the benefit of society, government could provide access to education, water, reasonably decent housing, culture through libraries, and other amenities, without which movement forward was unlikely. Rather than a crutch that might limit individual expression or talent, this was seen as a reward for those ambitious enough to take advantage of new opportunities. In the words of future Prime Minister Herbert Asquith:

> Liberty ... is not only a negative but a positive conception ... To be really free, [people] must be able to make the best use of faculty, opportunity, energy and life ... It is in this fuller view of the true significance of Liberty that we find the governing impulse in the later developments of Liberalism in the direction of educa- tion, temperance, better dwellings, an improved social and industrial environment; everything, in short, that tends to national, communal, and personal efficiency. (Kazamias 1966: 83)

The late Victorian period was the zenith of "civil society" – a compromise between individual power and state power, in which enabling legislation often came from Parliament but localities had the opportunity to put into practice mandates to provide for the general welfare. At the same time, this period saw a transition from the bracing and individualistic "Victorian values" to a more complex social under- standing of problems like poverty, unemployment, delinquency, and prostitution. Some, like the Owenites, had claimed as early as the 1830s that personalities were formed by the environments that nurtured people, rather than being acts of sheer will – but now these views found endorsements from both academic sociologists and practical politicians. Sociologists Bernard and Helen Bosanquet, for example, advocated the idea of society itself as an organic whole, with individuals and so- ciety improving together in a mutually reinforcing way. As the Bosanquets saw it, providing the poorest families with good environments and training in thrift, nutrition and childcare would provide those who cared to take the opportunity with a way out of abject poverty. Those who did not cooperate were left to their own devices.

Conflicting views about the responsibilities of society and the nature of the individual found themselves expressed in many ways – including debates about the nature of crime and punishment. Advocates for the abolition of the death penalty argued that it was carried out so rarely that it could not possibly serve as a deterrent; that the state ought not to play the role of executioner; and that witnessing executions degraded the moral character of a people. Proponents of the death penalty – including, rather surprisingly, John Stuart Mill – argued just as trenchantly that for the criminal underclass, nothing short of the fear of death would effectively deter criminal behavior. After a Royal Commission studied the matter between 1864 and 1866, the state ended public executions, addressing fears about the degrading impact of witnessing executions but reserving their punitive purpose. The death penalty itself remained for crimes like treason and murder for another century.

A similar struggle characterized thought about the nature of juvenile offenders. Laws passed in 1854 and 1857 had for the first time provided reformatories and industrial schools, into which children between the ages of seven and fifteen were housed separately from the adult criminal population. Judicial reformers argued that exposure to adult criminals resulted in depraved, habitual young offenders, and that even those children who had not committed crimes, but who lived on the streets without visible means of support, could benefit from this state wardship. On the other hand, local jurists had so much discretion in sentencing that, into the 1890s, young teenagers still received prison sentences for minor "crimes" like vagrancy on the grounds that they should have known better and deserved punishment rather than gentle guidance.

Increasingly, the discovery of social problems was based on empirical research and attempts at statistical analysis. As Henry Mayhew had in the 1850s, Charles Booth set out to observe poverty in London in the 1880s – but while Mayhew had been fixated on the exoticism of London street-sellers and their lack of religious beliefs, Booth concerned himself more with the economic well-being of workers who earned below a "line of poverty," the wages necessary to subsist at all. To determine the nature of various neighborhoods and understand working-class survival strategies, Booth interviewed clergymen of every denomination, teachers, and policemen, and himself traveled through London's neighborhoods. He also had a staff of paid and unpaid workers – including women – who collected data on his behalf. Beatrice Potter, who eventually married the Fabian socialist Sidney Webb, spent days among London's poor East End Jews, getting a sense of their culture and even going "underground" as a sweatshop worker. The first volumes of Booth's social survey, *Life and Labour of the People in London*, began to appear in 1889, running to 17 volumes by 1903.

Booth set an example followed by other reformers, including the more organized Seebohm Rowntree, who interviewed York housewives and asked them to record all of their income and weekly expenditures in notebooks in order to calculate the poverty line. While Rowntree felt that most social ills – drinking, child neglect, and gambling – were caused by poverty rather than the other way around, he also lamented the growing unfitness of the "British race" itself. This idea that the British belonged to a superior "white race" threatened by the physical degradation of its own workers was common in the late nineteenth-century imperial context.

To the left of New Liberal thinkers, socialists argued that some basic level of amenities ought to be a birthright. Beginning in the 1850s, "Christian Socialists," led by F.D. Maurice, had turned away from the severity and individualism that had been advocated by Evangelicals in the 1830s and 1840s. Sharing the belief that all were part of the Incarnation, the Kingdom of Christ on earth, the Christian Socialists believed that suffering should be alleviated rather than endured as a worthy spiritual trial. Religious concern with social welfare continued throughout the century: in London's Bethnal Green neighborhood, for example, Stewart Headlam founded the Guild of St Matthew, a body intended to promote working-class religious observance as a tool of cultural uplift, but also to lobby the Church of England to support social change. Headlam had a significant following, and held positions on the London County Council.

Like their counterparts in Italy, Germany, France, and Belgium, secular socialists were eager to work together with the new labor movement and enfranchised working class. They used new county councils to provide urban areas with sanitation, transportation, education, and water supplies, moving the responsibility for these from private, for-profit companies to the state, supported by taxes. In London, the Fabians, who exercised influence on the London County Council, practiced what came to be called "gas and water socialism," favoring a slow evolution toward more municipal responsibility for the general welfare. Their society's name echoed that of a Roman emperor who had overcome his enemies through attrition and wearing down rather than through direct attacks, and came to stand for an incremental progressive social policy.

The socialist urge for "what ought to be" also found expression in widely read novels and pamphlets. Print designer William Morris wrote *News from Nowhere*, a novel about a traveler from the present who awakes in a deindustrialized, postrevolutionary version of Britain's future. Money and greed have been eliminated in Morris's utopia; sturdy, rosy-cheeked Pre-Raphaelite beauties of both sexes now labor in fields and workshops for the sheer joy of their craft. Notably, even the land is healthier in Morris's vision: choking fogs have been eliminated and the Thames is clean. Manchester Fabian Robert Blatchford, editor of the *Clarion* newspaper, penned *Merrie England,* a series of socialist tracts inspired by Morris's vision. Two million copies were sold at football grounds and other workers' gathering places by the *Clarion's* "red van," and their ideas became part of a culture of politically infused choirs, cycling clubs, and "Cinderella Clubs" for children.

Like Progressivism in the United States, the late nineteenth-century impulse toward social engineering in Britain encompassed voluntarism (belief in individual volunteerism rather than government-sponsored reform) and individualistic reforms as well as socialism in both its radical (controlling the means of production) and Fabian varieties. Toynbee Hall, a settlement house in East London where members of the middle class were intended to live side-by-side with humble workers,

Figure 7.2 This 1901 cartoon from the socialist newspaper *Justice* urged British working people to focus their energies on domestic improvement rather than getting involved in foreign wars and imperial adventures. (© The British Library Board Colindale).

provided services like nutrition classes and daycare as well as a model for genteel manners and culture. The American reformer Jane Addams made several visits to Toynbee Hall, and eventually emulated it by founding her own settlement community, Hull House, in Chicago.

William Booth, founder of the Salvation Army, was also a voluntarist who sought to help the poor. His 1890 book, *In Darkest England and the Way Out,* set forth the testimony of those living on the streets in their own words, and argued that even the most downtrodden should receive the necessities of life. People snapped up 115,000 copies in four months. Between 1886 and 1906, the Salvation Army served about 4 million people, founding shelters and rescue homes, providing nursing and childcare, and providing striking dock workers with food. It even built model match factories intended to avoid the jaw disintegration caused by yellow phosphorous matches. In his play *Major Barbara,* the Irish-born satirical playwright George Bernard Shaw poked fun at Salvationists for being middle-class martinets, but in reality, the organization's leaders included many who had come from the ranks of common workers, and who saw in the organization a chance for social uplift. Clashes with labor unions over temperance and the payment of union wages prevented the Salvation Army from combining with the labor movement in any long-term way.

The unemployed had historically been able to survive by pawning clothes and collecting outdoor relief, in those areas where relief outside the workhouses was still being offered. But a movement against outdoor relief starting in the early 1870s made it much harder to collect this support. Private organizations like the Charity Organization Society, founded in 1869, argued that flawed morals caused poverty, and refused relief to those who did not fit into the category of the "worthy poor" (mostly widows, children, and people with physical disabilities). The percentage of the population receiving some form of aid from the Poor Law Guardian declined from 10 percent in 1865 to 5.6 percent by 1900. Those who did have work were encouraged to save through the mechanism of trade union funds or friendly societies, but also began to argue that the government should create jobs for the unemployed on public works like roads and bridges. By 1905, the Royal Commission on the Poor Laws and Relief of Distress – which included Charles Booth among its members – would evaluate some of these municipal programs and propose unemployment insurance as a more efficient method of helping the poor.

Science and Social Darwinism

Darwin's work continued to reverberate with his application of natural selection to humans in *The Descent of Man* (1871). Humans, he argued, evolved from primates, and as *The Origin of Species* made the animal kingdom the subject of random mutation subject to no divine order, so he now asserted that people themselves arose not from God's image or intent, but through the same countless species variations driven by chance. Darwin's natural selection was not the only evolutionary theory to account for how species changed over time. The French botanist Jean-Baptiste Lamarck had posited earlier in the century that species could intentionally adapt to their environment and then pass on these adaptive traits, a level of willful change wholly at odds with Darwin's more random and mindless alterations. Throughout the late nineteenth century, many often conflated the two very different theories of evolution, particularly in the realm of applying the concept of evolution to a broad range of social issues well beyond botany.

A range of authors asserted a connection, or at least a metaphorical similarity, between explanations of biology and explanations of industrialization, imperialism, or class conflict. Darwin himself resisted such implications, insisting that his work had scientific value alone; Huxley also thought scientists would gain professional and public credibility precisely if they refused to lend their expertise to nonscientific phenomena. In the 1850s Herbert Spencer had used a Lamarckian adaptive framework to argue for social change from individualism to altruism – hence science supported a more collectivist state or more generous social services for the disadvantaged. Francis Galton's *Hereditary Genius* (1869) drew a different conclusion. Since the 1860s, "anthropometrists," who specialized in taking human physical measurements, had been measuring the facial angles and skull capacities of people of all races and both genders, to substantiate their claims that black and Asian people were less intelligent than white people, and that women were less like white men than like children or the "subject races" (Fee 1979). In Galton's assessment, some races inherently produced more talent than others, and those would be more globally successful in competition or conflict with races of lesser natural ability. His solution did not end there; it would in itself have lent scientific credibility to imperial aggression, but he went further, to propose artificially sup-pressing negative traits and promoting positive abilities – what he called Eugenics. Anglo-Saxon conquest through imperialism was therefore a foregone conclusion, and other groups – the Aborigines of Australia, the First Nations of Canada – were "dying races" destined to perish in the name of progress.

Natural selection, then, was deployed to support a wide range of political and social positions, no matter what Darwin and Huxley might think of their scientific validity. Even Huxley was not immune to the lure of applying science to social explanation. In later years he turned away from his support for laissez-faire eco-nomics and came to conclude that human behavior was fundamentally different from the behavior of the natural world rather than, as many contemporaries would have it, fundamentally analogous. In 1893 he famously stated that "social progress means a checking of the cosmic process at every step and the substitution for it of another, which may be called the ethical process; the end of which is not the survival of those who may happen to be the fittest . . . but of those who are ethically the best" (Davis 1907: 234).

Science and technology led some to explicitly pessimistic views about the progress of modern culture. W.R. Greg continued his paper on modern life (quoted in the epigraph above) as follows: "The rapidity of railway travelling produces a chronic disturbance in the nervous system, and the anxiety to be in time, the hur-rying pace, cause a wear and tear as well as accelerated action of the heart, which kills or injures thousands" (Greg 1875). What if people adapted to precisely those deleterious conditions that marked modernity? Could humans adapt *effectively* to dirtier, noisier and more crowded cities in a way that nonetheless marked an overall decline in species health?

Alfred Russel Wallace also came to startling conclusions about the lessons people might draw from biology. He rejected the stance of the professional scientist as removed from social concerns, and moved late in his career towards more radical social criticism deriving from evolutionary concepts. By 1890 he argued in *Human Selection* that

> when we have cleansed the Augean stable of our existing social organization, and have made such arrangements that *all* shall contribute their share of either physical or mental labour, and that all workers shall reap the *full* reward of their work, the future of the race will be ensured by those laws of human development that have led to the slow but continuous advance in the higher qualities of human nature. (Wallace 1890: 331)

Only in a socialist society, when females were freed from financial necessity to choose the most desirable husbands, could social progress really occur. A quarter-century later, in *The Revolt of Democracy* (1913), he went further still, arguing that capitalism had worked not for but against progress, leaving much of society in poverty: "the principle of competition – a life and death struggle for bare existence – has had more than a century's unbroken trial under conditions created by its upholders, *and it has absolutely failed.*"

The late Victorians also explored the underpinnings of gender and sexuality, in the process both affirming and challenging traditional beliefs about the roles and capacities of women. Popular cultural anxieties about women working outside the home, and in an ever more stimulating public sphere, led to physician William Gull's identification of anorexia nervosa in the 1870s. This medical condition, which included weight loss, listlessness, and nervousness, was seen as the result of an underdeveloped neurological system exposed to the rush of modern life. In 1889, Patrick Geddes and J. Arthur Thompson published *The Evolution of Sex*, in which women's weakness was recast as strength, since their greater "altruism, intuition and common sense" made them complementary to men. These attempts to apply scientific inquiry to understand gender and sexuality came against a backdrop of increasing educational opportunities for women, declining legal and public acceptance of domestic violence toward women, and the early promotion of contraception, all of which expanded the sphere of female agency in the family and in the workplace.

The specter of New Womanhood elicited a backlash from the Eugenics movement, aiming at promoting "good breeding" and perpetuation of the Anglo-Saxon race. "Craniometrists," a branch of the anthropometrists, called into question the idea that women, with their tiny brains, could determine their own social role. Any version of women's lives that prioritized careers and citizenship over marriage and mothering would decrease the number of English children born to "good families" (while working people continued to reproduce) and result in a general degradation of the supposed Anglo-Saxon race. This was especially dangerous in a late nineteenth-century imperial context. Women had been welcomed into the empire – particularly into its white colonies – as reproducers, intended to counterbalance wildly skewed sex ratios. With British world possessions at their largest extent, who would shoulder what Kipling called the "white man's burden," if English women stopped reproducing?

Late Victorian masculinity was also shaped by its imperial context. Physical contests such as those provided by public school sports were thought to provide young men with a clean healthiness to help them ward off the sensuous temptations of India and other colonial climates. Boys could read about the exploits of big-game hunters and conquerors of the African continent in the *Boy's Own Paper*, a newspaper for children, and even if they were destined to be retail clerks and never leave England's shores, could themselves still fantasize about violent foreign conquest. On the other hand, the late nineteenth century also saw the

cultural assertion of alternative sexualities. A group of bohemians calling themselves the Aesthetic Movement wore their hair long and favored art for art's
sake, and there were all kinds of cultural codes for homosexuality, such as the
wearing of a green carnation. Publicly, though, there was no tolerance for it, as
the trial of Oscar Wilde in 1895 demonstrated. The pugnacious father of Wilde's
much younger lover Lord Alfred Douglas had publicly accused Wilde of sodomy,
a crime under English law. Wilde had responded by suing the father for libel,
but the evidence unearthed during the case resulted in Wilde's own arrest for
"gross indecency." Wilde's celebrity as a playwright and poet could not save him
from scandal and imprisonment. He was sentenced to two years at hard labor in
prison.

Late Victorian natural and social sciences, then, contained no single message
about the lessons nature might provide for race, gender, class, or social policy.
Rather the lessons of science were diverse and offered metaphorical support for
a wide range of answers to questions of how states, economies, or people ought
to act.

Arts and Artists

Late Victorian and Edwardian high culture was increasingly dominated by a sense of
national decline, a reaction against the pieties and conventions that had permeated
British middle-class sensibilities for much of the century, and an artistic shift toward
seeing the process of creativity itself as a form of social criticism. Authors had
used literature as social commentary of their own times throughout the century,
but the gentle pricking of social convention of Dickens or even George Eliot
sharpened into the more biting commentary offered up by George Bernard Shaw,
Samuel Butler, and E.M. Forster. Samuel Butler's novel *The Way of All Flesh*,
published posthumously in 1903 but written 30 years earlier, skewered Victorian
propriety and hypocrisy, and set the stage for the early twentieth-century British
intellectual's revulsion for the previous generation's materialism, complacency and
self-righteousness. In a passage that might stand in for a generation's rejection of
its collective parents, he advised:

> To parents who wish to lead a quiet life I would say: Tell your children that they are
> very naughty – much naughtier than most children. Point to the young people of
> some acquaintances as models of perfection and impress your own children with a
> deep sense of their own inferiority. You carry so many more guns than they do that
> they cannot fight you. This is called moral influence ... They think you know and
> they will not have yet caught you lying often enough to suspect that you are not the
> unworldly and scrupulously truthful person which you represent yourself to be, nor
> yet will they know how great a coward you are. (Butler 1917: 30)

George Bernard Shaw moved to London as a young man and wrote plays that illuminated a range of social problems from poverty to women's suffrage to sexual anarchy. E.M. Forster published *Where Angels Fear to Tread* (1905) and *Howards End* (1910), the latter of which used a domestic drama to poke at the shallowness of material wealth and the indecent contempt of the rich for Britain's working poor. William Morris, socialist, designer, scion of the arts and crafts movement and novelist, looked backward for answers rather than to the future. In *News from Nowhere* (1890) he saw moral regeneration in the connected social order of England's medieval past.

Several of the more prolific social critics before the war, including Forster, Leonard and Virginia Woolf, Lytton Strachey, economist John Maynard Keynes, and the art critic Roger Fry, associated in varying relationships of friendship, marriage, affairs and intellectual kinship that collectively came to be known as the Bloomsbury Group, after a neighborhood in London of that name. Primarily from affluent families (most had met as college students at Cambridge), they comprised an informal group of extraordinarily talented artists, novelists and intellectuals. They challenged convention in the candor of their speech and their relationships, in .their commitment to the ideal of the aesthetic, and by the fact that they all read and critiqued each others' work and valued this mutual criticism more than any criticism from outside their group.

Aesthetics and sensibilities

Something changed as well in the larger aesthetic sensibility and cultural purpose of the artist. At the end of the century artists began turning away from an interest in art as illuminator of the world and instead strove to illuminate the artist's own experience. This movement reflected the belief that the purpose of art, and by implication the purpose of the artist, was to express the brilliance of creativity itself. Some artists, calling themselves "decadents," thus removed themselves from fitting into society in order to explain it and consciously sought to live free of social conventions. Art had a life outside of public approval or even public relevance. Walter Pater, writing in *The Renaissance* (1873), articulated the artist's ideals: "getting as many pulsations as possible into the given time. Great passions give us this quickened sense of life." In the years just prior to the First World War, art critics Roger Fry and Clive Bell used exhibitions of new, Post-Impressionist painting to suggest that rather than necessarily showing reality or telling a story, art should serve to elicit emotions from the viewer. Thus modern art was supposed to represent a stripped-down aesthetic of forms and rhythms, and an embrace of French values rather than utilitarian English values (Saler 1998).

To the extent that artistic production has social origins, this shift was in part a reaction against the rise of popular culture, a popular press, and increased mass participation in public life. The "public" with its middlebrow artistic appreciation for landscapes and portraiture would never approve of the more experimental work at the core of the true artist's creativity. Pater's quote above about stimulation also echoes W.R. Greg's 1875 comment on the speed of modern life. Urbanization changed human perception: the presence of crowds, tall buildings, artificial illumination and night life had the potential to transform the city-dweller. Governments reacted to the bustle of urban life by cleansing and clarifying: trying to banish offensive sights and smells, crime and slaughterhouses. Train travel had already sped up the pace of life; telegraphy, and then wireless, sped up the pace of communication. Artists were, like everyone else, living in a society of increased pace, noise and activity, and if some feared mental deterioration, artists at the turn of the century sought to capture this more destabilized sensibility through painting, writing, and sculpture.

The rapidity of technological change and accompanying fin-de-siècle nervousness forced Britons – and writers in other countries–to confront their future and wonder whether utopia or dystopia lay in store. H.G. Wells sketched out elaborate tales of the future meeting the present: a traveler voyages from the 1890s to centuries in the future in *The Time Machine*. Wells's protagonist discovers that humankind has bifurcated into the Eloi, a race of beautiful people living above ground, and the dark and twisted Morlocks who lived within the earth's crust and support and serve the Eloi, and eventually eat them. Without social reform, technology would not erase the gulf between the the upper and the lower classes. Wells's dystopic tale reveals the possibility that technological progress could just as easily lead humanity into an unpleasant future as into a positive one.

The cultural anxiety *about racial decline*, fed by a mix of increased economic and imperial competition, increased working-class political power, the New Woman, and Social Darwinism, was catalyzed further by Britain's protracted and bitter war with the Boers. That the world's greatest military power could be ground to a standstill by apparently ill-armed and barely civilized farmers cast grave doubt on Britain's ability to maintain its status should it ever be challenged by a more advanced competitor, of which there were several waiting in the wings. An army report of 1902 found that 60 percent of British males were physically unfit for service, and a subsequent government Committee on Physical Deterioration emphasized that the problem overwhelmingly existed among the rapidly increasing urban poor. The combination of imperial greatness and pageantry with these troubling indicators of national decline pointed many politicians and authors toward the example of ancient Rome, in whose greatness could also be found the origins of future decay. Urban dwellers focused on entertainment rather than vigorous exercise or wholesome agricultural labor, a popular desire for luxury rather than moral improvement, a failure of strong character and strong leadership, scandal in the highest levels of society: all these characterized both the Roman and British empires at their zenith. A 1905 pamphlet, *The Decline and Fall of the British Empire*, made this alarming point to great popular acclaim. One reader, Robert Baden-Powell, editorialized on its behalf and shortly thereafter founded the Boy Scouts to arrest this decline by raising boys to become tomorrow's fitter, stronger and better prepared soldiers.

National and Imperial Cultures

Provincial cultures and national integration

Under the pressures of increasing news circulation, faster travel, and nationally sponsored education, "Britain" came into more integrated being than ever before. Despite the earnest advocacy of linguistic and artistic "native traditions" as the underpinning of Scottish, Irish, and Welsh nationalism, Gaelic language and dialect were in decline as local languages retreated to rural areas. In Wales, the percentage of the population who could actually speak Welsh declined from 54 percent to 44 percent in the two decades after 1891, and in Cardiff, the largest city in Wales, only 6 percent did so in 1911. In Scotland a 1908 newspaper comment remarked that fewer Scots spoke in local dialect, since ability to speak widely understood English meant broader employment opportunities throughout Britain. It is not surprising that as internal migration increased the number of English and Scottish mine workers in South Wales, and with English as the language of commerce, government and the professions, that this period also saw a resurgence in Welsh cultural nationalism. Challenged by an increasingly integrated British state, Welsh scholars like John Morris-Jones sought to revive and popularize Welsh language and literature through translation of poetry into Welsh, guides to Welsh grammar, and Welsh literary competitions.

Time itself also came under state standardization. An 1880 Act (the so-called Definition of Time Act) referred to the doubts about whether official time referred "in England and Scotland to Greenwich time, and in Ireland to Dublin time, or to the mean astronomical time in each locality," suggesting considerable variation in time measurement between different places within what is, after all, not a very large country, and legislating only two fixed time zones. The ongoing extension of railways throughout Britain further brought more Britons into contact with each other and eroded local and previously more insulated cultures.

Empire and national integration

The late Victorian empire permeated many aspects of British culture and offered both a context within which to understand cultural life and many of the particular themes, stories and developments that fed into it. Imperial wars and expeditions furnished ongoing examples of British valor, heightening a patriotic sense of Britain ruling the world through both enlightened values and military might. This was not always factually true, for Britain suffered a number of more problematic episodes that threatened to cast doubt on this belief in the rightness of British imperial superiority – the Indian Mutiny of 1857 had foreshadowed this insecurity and the protracted war with the Boers made it more pungent. Nevertheless, the last decades of the nineteenth century saw empire displayed widely at home, and often to working-class audiences, through music hall productions, popular songs, and popular literature. Civic organizations and clubs displayed panoramas – three-dimensional and highly elaborate displays of battles or notable explorations. Exhibitions of global manufacturing, technology and culture assumed increasingly imperial tones as more raw materials came from colonies, and as more British goods were sold in colonial markets. Music, art, cultural artifacts – even native village displays with real natives – were all presented to the British public, and made their way into the British awareness of their imperial domain. Imperial themes worked their way into the British elementary school curricula, especially as the state played an increasing role in mass education after 1870. Youth literature captured the popular imagination through the *Boy's Own Paper*, which started circulation in 1879 with 200,000 copies and rose from there, and which often featured imperial contexts for adventure and instruction.

Imperial culture allowed Britons, particularly elite Britons, to imagine empire as just as hierarchical as their own society. For while much of popular and high culture celebrated British racial superiority and used Social Darwinist frameworks to justify white Britons' rule over the less enlightened, and often nonwhite, peoples of the world, imperial culture also rested on a traditional social vision of social orders organized according to status rather than race. When the British ruled, they looked for native status-holders with whom to partner, seeing in these representatives of their respective peoples a similar attention to the importance of social hierarchy as the proper ordering of a stable society. Aristocrats yearned for a social hierarchy where they could rule unimpeded, and this nostalgia found a home in the British Empire, where there were still many opportunities for the nobility and gentry in the civil service (particularly in India). While never forgetting the nature of "whiteness," upper-class Britons formed alliances with chiefs and native leaders, bestowing upon them the Order of the British Empire and other trappings of British service. In the non-white stretches of empire, large estates and retinues of servants – each with his or her own niche in the running of the household – could be maintained in ways no longer possible in Britain itself.

Britons saw their empire as both a collection of diverse ethnic groups, religions, cultures and races, often less enlightened than Britain itself, and as a collection of cultures whose social organization looked similar to the vanishing British social order of birth and inherited status. So while Social Darwinism justified British rule throughout British culture based on presumed racial superiority, Britain's much more ancient attachment to deference, symbolic prestige and a landed social order also underlay the mechanics of imperial rule.

These themes of imperial grandeur found full expression in Queen Victoria's Diamond Jubilee in 1897, a massive orchestrated pageantry celebrating the monarch's 50 years of rule and, at the same time, celebrating the reach and splendor of the empire over which she ruled. The Queen, accompanied by 50,000 soldiers from across the empire, all in local uniform, paraded through London to attend a Thanksgiving service at St Paul's Cathedral. Before the procession, Victoria sent a telegram of gratitude to all the outposts of empire around the world: "From my heart I thank my beloved people." In a curious mix of the very old and the very new, the Jubilee was also captured on an even newer technology than the telegraph, for it was filmed as well.

While imperial themes permeated British culture, avant-garde art from closer to home made a later entry into the British imagination. Virginia Woolf famously said after the Great War that human character had changed "on or about December 1910." She referred to the London exhibition, Manet and the Post-Impressionists, which brought the work of Manet, Picasso, Van Gogh, Seurat and other contemporary European painters to a British viewing public. While outside of Britain these artists had made their way into high culture already, Britain had remained relatively insulated from modern European trends in art throughout the late nineteenth century. The new painting, with its departure from any attempt to convey images realistically, shocked and horrified most British viewers – so that it may be too much to say that human character actually changed as a result of exposure, for British character at least initially rebuffed Post-Impressionist art. A prominent poet wrote that the exhibition was "either an extremely bad joke or a swindle." One of the few sympathetic critics claimed that while French artists were pushing the boundaries of painting and representation, British painters instead sold their talent for commercial advertising – an echo of the many literary critiques of Victorian materialism. The exhibition revealed the chasm between British and European high culture in the minds of most Britons, a cultural sense of profound national difference that was severely tested in the war to come. In culture, in social relations, and in the pace of technological change, Britain in the years before 1914 comprised a volatile mix of creativity and tension that underlay and accelerated the fragmenting international order.

References

Atkins, Frederick (1890) *Moral Muscle and How to Use It*. Chicago: Fleming Revell.

Butler, Samuel (1917) *The Way of All Flesh*. New York: E.P. Dutton.

Davis, James Richard Ainsworth (1907) *Thomas H. Huxley*. London: E.P. Dutton.

Fee, Elizabeth (1979) Nineteenth-Century Craniometry: The Study of the Female Skull. *Bulletin of the History of Medicine*, 53 (3): 415–433.

Greg, W.R. (1875) On Life at High Pressure. In *Proceedings of the Royal Institution*, vol. 7. London: William Clowes.

Ingram, Rev. George S. (1863) *Bishop Colenso Answered by His Own Concessions and Omissions.* London: William Freeman.

Kazamias, Andreas M. (1966) Spencer and the Welfare State. *History of Education Quarterly*, 6 (2): 73–95.

Saler, Michael (1998) Making It New: Visual Modernism and the "Myth of the North" in Interwar England. *Journal of British Studies*, 37 (8): 419–440.

Wallace, Alfred Russel (1890) Human Selection. *Fortnightly Review*, n.s., 48 (Sept.): 325–336. At http://digitalcommons.wku.edu/dlps_fac_arw/5/ (accessed Mar. 14, 2011).

Further Reading

Cannadine, David (2001) *Ornamentalism: How the British Saw Their Empire.* Oxford: Oxford University Press.

Hynes, Samuel (1968) *The Edwardian Turn of Mind.* Princeton: Princeton University Press.

Kern, Stephen (2003) *The Culture of Time and Space.* Cambridge: Harvard University Press.

Lightman, Bernard (ed.) (1997) *Victorian Science in* Context. Chicago: University of Chicago Press.

Newsome, David (1997) *The Victorian World Picture: Perceptions and Introspections in an Age of Change.* New Brunswick: Rutgers University Press.

Parsons, Gerald (ed.) (1988) *Religion in Victorian Britain*, vol. 1: *Traditions.* New York: St Martin's Press.

Stansky, Peter (1997) *On or About December 1910: Early Bloomsbury and its Intimate World.* Cambridge: Harvard University Press.

Thompson, F.M.L. (1988) *The Rise of Respectable Society: A Social History of Victorian Britain.* Cambridge: Harvard University Press.

8

In Flanders Fields
Britain and the Great War, 1910–1918

It was August 27, 1917, in the midst of the campaign that came to be called the Third Battle of Ypres. Edwin Campion Vaughan, a low-ranking British officer, herded his troops up the flooded and bombed-out roads near Langemarck in West Belgium under heavy mortar fire. He and his fellow soldiers escaped into a pillbox, a German concrete machine-gun emplacement, to find within two dead Germans and an unconscious German officer who was bleeding to death. Before the German officer came back to consciousness, Vaughan fixed his tourniquet; after the German awoke, Vaughan gave him water and offered him food. In return, the German offered him a lump of sugar from inside his tunic. "It was crumbling and saturated with blood so I slipped it into my pocket whilst pretending to eat it." After a few minutes the German officer began to feel better. As Vaughan wrote, "He told me how he had kept his garrison fighting on, and would never have allowed them to surrender. He had seen us advancing and was getting his guns on to us when a shell from the tank behind had come through the doorway, killed two men and blown his leg off." The Great War was not a war about ideology, as soldiers oscillated between attempting to kill each other and expressing their shared humanity (Carey 1987: 474–476).

The Great War represented a tragic failure of diplomacy. Rather than representing ancient warring dynasties, George V of England, Tsar Nicholas II of Russia, and Kaiser Wilhelm II of Germany were cousins. Although all of the powers involved in the conflict were interested in colonial expansion, the war was not initially about territorial conquest. Rather, it was precipitated by a naval arms race, by entangling alliances among major European powers, by war plans that provided no flexibility, and by the way in which nationalism in the former Ottoman Empire destabilized the balance of power. To enter a war, as the British would, in

Empire, State, and Society: Britain Since 1830, First Edition. Jamie L. Bronstein and Andrew T. Harris.
© 2012 Jamie L. Bronstein and Andrew T. Harris. Published 2012 by John Wiley & Sons, Ltd.

order to keep a promise about defending a neutral country, was an optimistic and perhaps even a naive decision; it's hard to say whether Palmerston would have approved.

Although the war was unnecessary, it was not, at first, unwelcome. Young men of the British upper classes, raised on the war stories of ancient Greece and Rome, believed that war was a glorious testing ground for masculinity, and rushed to volunteer before they could lose the opportunity to fight. The British could also muster up plenty of willing imperial troops, particularly those from Australia, New Zealand, India, and Canada, to fight in Turkey and Africa as well as in Europe.

But the same new technologies that had made possible the consolidation of a powerful empire could also take it apart, body by body. The war brought mechanisms of mass destruction: the machine gun, the hand grenade, the tank, the airplane, and poison gas. Troop movements were coordinated by radio, and reconnaissance carried out through aerial photography. The Great War was the first war to feature aerial bombardment of cities – by German zeppelin. It was the first war to see combat in the skies, as pilots (called "aces") in tiny biplanes attempted to shoot each other down. The Great War provided a rude awakening about the new nature of warfare and raised questions about whether war ever again ought to be thought of as an extension of diplomacy.

Rumbles of Thunder

In the four years leading up to the outbreak of war, Britain experienced domestic instability. Beginning in 1910, workers struck on the docks, in coal, in the cotton industry, and on the railroads. The local strikes had some able leaders; Tom Mann, who led the Liverpool transport strike, was a self-educated Communist machinist who advocated syndicalism (rule by trade unions). None of the strikes was particularly effective until, in 1912, leaders of the major trade unions decided to club their strength together into what they called the Triple Alliance, and to jointly negotiate with the government. By 1913, the number of workers in trade unions had grown to 4 million. The Triple Alliance of rail, transport, and mineworkers' unions had called a major strike for the summer of 1914, but because of the press of world events, it never took place.

Within Ireland, Nationalists and Unionists struggled over the disposition of Home Rule. At the time of the Act of Union between Great Britain and Ireland in 1801, the number of Members of Parliament allocated to Ireland at Westminster had been fixed. The Famine caused migration and starvation, so that there were fewer people living in Ireland at the end of the century. In addition, while Ireland's population had fallen, that of the rest of Britain had grown. The overrepresentation of the Irish population gave the Irish an electoral advantage in Parliament. Furthermore, the Irish MPs became a crucial swing bloc. The Catholic Nationalist

European Alliances and the Start of World War I

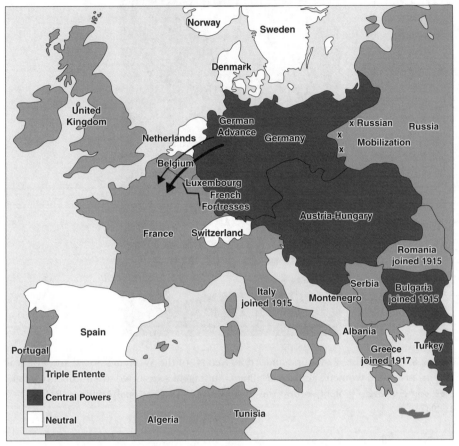

Map 8.1 European alliances and the start of the First World War.
Source: National Archives, at http://www.nationalarchives.gov.uk/pathways/
firstworldwar/maps/europe1914.htm.

Party allied strategically with the Liberals, while the Unionist Party in Ireland – mostly Protestants living in the six northern counties of Ulster – coalesced with fellow English Unionists to oppose Home Rule.

The passage of the 1911 Parliament Act, which significantly curtailed the power of the House of Lords, meant that the third Irish Home Rule bill, introduced in 1912, had a better chance of passage than previous Home Rule bills. But the Unionists in Parliament, having lost the ability to veto the legislation in the House of Lords, now turned to action outside Parliament. They encouraged the Ulster Unionists, and their fiery leader Sir Edward Carson, to threaten that if Home Rule passed, they would rebel and refuse to recognize the authority of an Irish parliament. The

Figure 8.1 Christabel Pankhurst and Annie Kenny, of the Women's Social and Political Union, advocated women's suffrage. Militant "suffragettes" resorted to a number of strategies, some of them violent, before the First World War. (National Archives. Ref. COPY 1/494).

Home Rule Bill passed, but a plan by the government to move troops into Ulster quickly fell apart, pushing Ireland to the brink of civil war. Fifty-seven British army officers stationed at Curragh offered to resign their commissions rather than fight against the Ulster Volunteers. The Great War broke out before an Irish civil war could, but none of the underlying issues surrounding the status of Ireland had been resolved.

Women also self-mobilized in the years leading up to the Great War, forming organizations that advocated for the right to vote. These organizations differed only slightly in the ends they sought, but differed dramatically in their tactics. The National Union of Women's Suffrage Societies favored such tactics as petitioning, publishing essays, giving speeches, and supporting parliamentary candidates who favored women's suffrage, but these moderate methods made little headway. The Women's Social and Political Union (WSPU), led by Emmeline Pankhurst and her daughters Christabel and Sylvia, advocated show-stopping acts that were impossible to ignore. They blew up mailboxes, vandalized paintings and golf courses, and broke windows of politicians' country houses. Most unforgettably, Emily Davison attempted to grab the king's horse at the 1913 Derby – possibly to hang a WSPU flag on the animal. But instead she was hit directly, and knocked unconscious, fracturing her skull: she died four days later. The government responded to these provocations by jailing female demonstrators and law-breakers. When women protested their confinement by going on hunger strikes, they were forcibly fed to keep them alive during their confinement. Forcible feeding produced nothing but negative publicity for the government, as propaganda from the time shows imprisoned British women with arms and legs pinned by matrons and doctors, fed with formula passed down a nasal feeding tube into the stomach. Thinking better of the idea, the government in 1913 passed a piece of legislation nicknamed the Cat and Mouse Act, which enabled the police to arrest women, free them once they were weakened by their hunger strikes, and rearrest them once they had gained their physical strength back. As with the trade union situation and the Irish situation, the "woman question" was a struggle that would only be defused by the onset of war in Europe.

The Outbreak of War

Turmoil on the domestic front had to some extent distracted the Liberal government from the buildup to war on the Continent. In the decades prior to war, considerations of realism in foreign policy had led to the formation of two competing forces in Europe. One was an actual military alliance: Germany was allied with the ethnically and linguistically diverse Austro-Hungarian Empire. France and Russia were also militarily allied. Britain was weakly allied with France, the two countries having signed an "entente cordiale" in 1904.

Britain's overriding policy toward Europe had been the same throughout the nineteenth century: to ensure a balance of power, so that no single country could threaten British interests by gaining dominance on the Continent. As Germany became economically more powerful, Germany and Britain both embarked on a naval arms race: Germany because naval power was perceived as central to its desire for imperial power, and Britain to offset the German threat to its own imperial trade routes. As First Lord of the Admiralty, Admiral Fisher had overseen a program to build Dreadnoughts; the 18,000 ton, turbine-engined ships were more massive than any other warships that existed. News that the Germans were building warships had sparked the cry for an additional eight Dreadnoughts to be built.

The initial catalyst for the war did not directly involve Britain. The heir to the Austro-Hungarian throne, Archduke Franz Ferdinand, paid a diplomatic visit to the capital of Serbia, a newly independent country that had once been part of the Austro-Hungarian Empire. Members of a radical resistance organization called the Black Hand assassinated Franz Ferdinand and his wife, Sophie. The

Austrians demanded that the Serbs discover the killers and bring them to justice, presenting the Serbs with an ultimatum for compliance. Although the Serbs
complied with the ultimatum in almost every respect, the Austrians declared
war, causing the Serbs to turn to their ally, Russia, for help. The Russians began to mass troops on Russia's western border, as Russian military planning
assumed that if they came to the Serbs' aid, it would bring them into conflict
with Austria-Hungary. As Austria-Hungary in turn had an active alliance with
Germany, Russian forces would inevitably be drawn into conflict with Germany
as well.

The massing of Russian troops triggered the German war plan, known as the
Schlieffen Plan, named after the man who had been the German war minister
in the early years of the 20th century. The Schlieffen Plan had been designed
to accommodate the fact that Germany was flanked by two powers, both allied
against it: Russia to Germany's east, and France to Germany's west. German
military officials determined that the best way to meet any threat by either France
or Russia was to go on the offensive with lightning speed. The Schlieffen Plan
called for German troops to race through neutral Belgium in a wheeling motion
that would enable them to overcome France's weak system of defensive forts,
surround Paris and crush France, and then return to the Russian front to defend or
attack against the Russians before the slower Russian forces advanced too far into
Germany.

It was the Belgian question, ultimately, that would bring the British into the war.
Britain had guaranteed the neutrality of Belgium through an 1839 treaty. When
war broke out and the Germans swarmed through Belgium, this forced the British
government's hand. Sir Edward Grey, the Foreign Minister, who had been non-
committal about British participation, appealed to the House of Commons, citing
the inhumanity of the Germans in invading a neutral country, and the importance
of British honor and completion of commitments. Parliament enthusiastically supported the notion of going to war; even the Liberal Cabinet was almost united
in support of British intervention. The years of Germany's economic, naval and
imperial advance had brought it into repeated potential conflict with Britain, and
so the invasion of Belgium proved a pretext rather than a decisive reason in itself.
The British declared war against Germany on August 4, 1914.

Raising an Army

Lord Kitchener, the leader of the British Expeditionary Forces (BEF), predicted
that this war would require not only British financial support for French troops,
but also major British army and naval involvement: a tall order for a country that
maintained only a small regular army, and relied on its naval forces. A Parliamentary
Recruiting Committee convened, and generated more than 13 million leaflets

with patriotic appeals, and a million posters, by January 1915. Despite the fact that recruitment was more rapid from the cities than from the countryside, the government's propaganda emphasized a narrower version of national identity: primarily rural, English, Conservative, and patriarchal: Men were to fight for the land of Shakespeare, for apple-cheeked English maidens and children, and green and pleasant farms (Coetzee 1992). Two thousand civilian volunteers circulated in the localities to sign young men up for service, and young women distributed white feathers – symbols of cowardice – to men who did not volunteer (Douglas 1970). This initial recruitment campaign was extremely successful, with more than 2.5 million British men signing on.

What motivated men initially to volunteer for war when there was no immediate threat to their own country? In the decades leading up to the Great War, public schools and boys' literature had both hammered insistently on the themes of the glory of war and patriotism, the honor of death in battle for one's country, and preparation for armed conflict. Within the public school tradition, nothing fit boys better to be good imperial Britons than games, since they promoted such virtues as muscular masculinity, dedication to the team, and good sportsmanship: not winning at any cost, but demonstrating a sense of self-mastery and fair play were uppermost. This martial spirit had helped recruiting during the Boer War, and it was exploited again at the outbreak of the First World War, with excellent results.

After the first year of the war, many veteran soldiers of the British army had been either killed in combat or allowed to leave military service. The number of men coming forward to volunteer for the war declined sharply. In response, the government conducted a census in July 1915 of all the men remaining in Britain who were of military age, excluding workers in critical industries and the medically unfit, and discovered that of 3 million theoretically fit men available for the army, the remaining single men were unlikely to come forward to volunteer without some compulsion. By 1916, the Military Service Act involuntarily recruited all bachelors and widowers who were without dependent children and between the ages of 18 and 41. Men were excused from duty if it was in the national interest for them to continue in their current jobs.

Tribunals set up throughout the provinces dealt with the new phenomenon of conscientious objectors. Men seeking exemption from service were asked about their religious and moral beliefs, and many were offered exemptions if they would consider alterative service that seemed sufficiently self-sacrificing: work with ambulance corps, in factories producing medical supplies, or as farm laborers. Men who had long affiliated themselves with pacifist churches like the Quakers often were exempted from service; those who objected to the war on political grounds (socialists, for example), were less likely to be taken seriously (McDermott 2010).

The results of conscription were impressive. In peacetime, the British army had comprised just 400,000 troops. At the height of the conflict, there were 4.5 million men in the armed forces, or one British man in three. In contrast with previous generations of British troops, these were not career soldiers, and in fact, the military leadership doubted whether urban men in particular had the stomach and the constitution for combat. Soldiers were trained in hand-to-hand combat in order to make them more aggressive. Men who were too young or too old for the military could gain experience in the Volunteer Brigade (jokingly nicknamed "Grandpa's Regiment"), which conducted weekly drills. As the age of military service was extended during the war, these men were incorporated into the army (Beckett 1985).

The First World War was the last war in which troops from all over the empire participated enthusiastically. Almost a million Indians fought in the war, most in the Middle East, and 150,000 on the Western Front. Australians and New Zealanders were sacrificed by the thousands in an abortive 1915 attempt to gain control of the Dardanelles Straits, a strategically crucial waterway in Turkey. Fifteen thousand men from the British West Indies fought against the Turks. Two hundred thousand Canadians fought in the First World War, of whom more than 60,000 were lost in battle. Over 200,000 Irish men fought on the side of Britain during the Great War – encouraged by the fact that the nationalist leader John Redmond had thrown his weight behind the conflict.

The Great War for the British Soldier

What experiences bound these men together? On the Western Front, where BEF troops participated alongside the French, military action quickly stalemated into trench combat, in earthworks miles long that accommodated men and supplies and even horses. Trench warriors experienced unremitting artillery barrages and strafing by machine guns mounted in the opposite trenches. At intervals, troops were encouraged to "go over the top": to climb wooden ladders from the trenches into the area separating the contending sides. This "No Man's Land," often a wasteland of barbed wire, burned trees, and scarred landscape, had to be crossed before troops could use their bayonets to take the trench opposite. The fact that troops crossing No Man's Land were running directly into machine-gun fire from the enemy's front trench meant that troops gained little terrain and suffered appalling casualties.

The combination of constant stress and exposure to the goriest sights of wartime psychologically overwhelmed some soldiers, a condition called "shell-shock" (Jones 2006). At intervals, troops rotated to the reserve trenches or even to areas behind the lines to rest and regroup. They were deloused (soldiers at the front were often infested with lice), had access to French food and wine, and received advanced training in special military skills. The on-again, off-again nature of combat in the First World War made many soldiers cycle between periods of high excitement and periods of boredom, between enthusiasm and disillusionment.

For some participants, including the writers Robert Graves, Wilfred Owen, and Siegfried Sassoon, the actual conditions of war were far removed from what they had been led to expect. Wilfred Owen took the title of his war poem "Dulce et Decorum Est" from the Latin "Dulce et decorum est pro patria mori": "How sweet and honorable it is to die for one's country." While this motto was taken seriously – it was carved in the chapel of the military academy Sandhurst in 1913 – in Owen's poem it is used ironically. The troops in his poem are not brave soldiers shooting at the enemy; they are bent double like old beggars, exhausted, dragging themselves through mud. The soldier who dies in the poem does not die on the parapet with a gun in his hand, but rather bumping along in a cart after having been subject to a gas attack; his face is twisted in agony, his lungs frothing with blood. Death came not with honor or ancient virtue, but with sickening and futile misery (Norgate 1989).

Although they are the most famous British poets who fought in the First World War, Sassoon and Graves and Owen were not the only soldier-poets of the war. Writers like Owen Seaman, who as the 53-year-old editor of *Punch* was not about to go to the front lines, attempted to stoke patriotism throughout the conflict, as in his "Pro Patria" (Seaman 1914: 26):

> Others may spurn the pledge of land to land,
> May with the brute sword stain a gallant past;
> But by the seal to which *you* set your hand,
> Thank God, you still stand fast!

It was possible for a soldier to see all of the blood and gore of shattered bodies and still see something redeeming about the conflict: the way in which combat might temporarily transcend class barriers, for example, or create intense male friendships in a way not possible in peacetime. And feelings about the war could be complicated or ambiguous: some soldiers were motivated by a vision of war as masculinity, or were thrilled to fight and even kill; but they also might resent the poor decisions made by those higher up in the chain of command (a resentment felt by soldiers throughout history). Understanding the feelings of soldiers is not a straightforward process, either, since both letters and diaries served as means for reinterpreting conflict both to the soldiers themselves and to family at home. No man wanted to picture himself as a coward or fearful at a time when manliness didn't readily accommodate those feelings.

Major Battles

BEF soldiers on the Western Front in 1914 and 1915 stopped the German forward advance in Belgium at the Battle of Ypres in October–November 1914. After that, the two contending sides settled down on either side of a trench stretching 400 miles from Switzerland to the Belgian coast (Marshall 1964: 140). In one way, the immobility of the troops was advantageous; the war became institutionalized, with trenches developing light-rail systems to serve them, intersecting communications and mess trenches, coal dumps, and ambulance runs. But the drawback, of course, was an immense number of casualties as the price for a few feet of terrain.

The scale of the butchery led the British government to think about opening another front in order to attempt military success somewhere more promising. The Ottoman Empire had joined the war on the side of Germany and the Austro-Hungarian Empire in August of 1914. This jeopardized British access to oil and to areas of the Middle East where the British already had control. Working with First Sea Lord (head of the naval service) Fisher, Winston Churchill, who was First Lord of the Admiralty, drew up plans for an invasion of the Dardanelles Straits, a crucial entry point to British possessions. In January of 1915 the British navy tried to assault the Dardanelles, only to be repulsed by Turkish artillery. Churchill then fell back on a contingency plan, a ground invasion of the Gallipoli peninsula by troops from the Australian and New Zealand Army Corps (Anzacs). The Anzacs were ordered to debark onto bare and scrubby beaches with nowhere to shelter from Turkish artillery emplacements. Then, failing to take advantage of their numerical advantage, the British military leaders on the ground ordered these troops to dig trenches. This gave the outnumbered Turks the time they needed to bring in reinforcements. Meanwhile, German U-boats destroyed three waiting British battleships. After months of waiting in terrible conditions, contracting typhus and cholera and sunstroke, the Anzac troops tried and failed to break through the Turkish lines at Suvla Bay in August 1915. In November, the imperial troops were finally evacuated. The death or injury of a combined total of 35,000 Anzac troops in the midst of a defeat helped to disillusion Australians and New Zealanders and to threaten their support for British policies well after the war ended.

In 1916 Lord Kitchener drowned when his ship sank; Lloyd George was appointed to replace him as War Minister. Unfortunately, Lloyd George gave a free hand to Sir Douglas Haig, now commander of the British Expeditionary Forces in France, who had risen in the ranks beyond the level of his abilities. Convinced by the French commander Joseph Joffre that it was the only good option, Haig agreed to mount a major offensive in the summer of 1916 at the River Somme in the north of France. The Somme was an area where the Germans had been left alone long enough to entrench extremely well, with fortified and electrified bunkers. After five days of bombardment, Haig expected his forces to be able to claim the German trenches, but English artillery that was supposed to destroy the barbed wire of No-Man's Land failed to do so. As a result, almost 60,000 British troops were killed while flailing along into open fire.

While the incessant battle was being fought (and not going well) on the Western Front, the Allies were picking off the former colonies of Germany, Austria-Hungary, and the Ottoman Empire. In Africa, Boer-led troops under generals

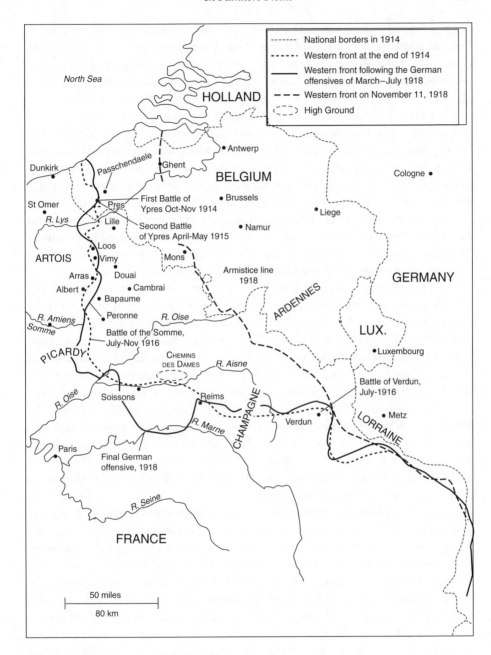

Map 8.2 Major battles of the Western Front.
Source: Based on Holger H. Herwig, "War in the West," in *A Companion to World War I*, ed.
John Horne (Oxford: Wiley-Blackwell, 2010), pp. 50–65.

Louis Botha and Jan Smuts attacked German troops protecting the colonies of German Southwest Africa and German East Africa. Small craft battled it out on Lake Tanganyika. British Nigerian soldiers and French Equatorial African forces fought against the Germans of Cameroon. This theater of war had been concluded by January 1916, ensuring the end of the age of German colonialism in Africa.

The prospect of oil had drawn British attention to the Ottoman colonies of the Middle East. An attempt against Turkish troops in what is today Iraq failed in 1916. In 1917, however, under the leadership of General Allenby, and helped by an Arab rebellion fomented by officer T.E. Lawrence (known after the war as Lawrence of Arabia), British imperial troops captured Jerusalem. The Middle Eastern campaign was expensive – almost ten times as many men died of diseases than died under fire – but it would also be fateful for the course of subsequent world events. Arthur Balfour's 1917 letter to the Jewish banker and peer Lord Rothschild promising Palestine to the Jews as a national homeland became one of the key documents supporting the founding of Israel after the Second World War.

The First World War was a world war not just because combatants engaged in both hemispheres, but also because neutrals were caught up in the conflict the world over. Britain and Germany had both laid undersea cables linking their countries with their own allies and with neutral nations. These cables were important not just for coordinating war plans, but also for disseminating information about the war to neutral countries in a way that presented one or another of the combatants in a flattering light. When war began, both countries tried to isolate the other by cutting cables and disabling radio transmitter stations in neutral countries. The British, whose undersea cable infrastructure was much more extensive, and who had more ships that could lay (and therefore cut and repair) cable, survived with more of their communications infrastructure intact (Winkler 2009). The solidity of the British telecommunications system enabled the British to court the United States from the beginning of the conflict.

When the war broke out, Britain blockaded the European coastline in an attempt to stifle German shipping. This worked well enough as long as the traditional rules of naval warfare were followed, although the German sinking of the passenger liner *Lusitania* in May 1915, killing 1,200 civilians, 10 percent of them American, sparked international outrage. The year 1916 also saw the war's one major naval battle, the Battle of Jutland, but it failed to dislodge the British blockade. In order to overcome the naval stalemate, the Germans declared unrestricted submarine warfare in 1917, meaning that German submarines would now target the ships even of noncombatant nations. Although Lloyd George was able to keep down the amount of shipped goods destroyed by using large and protected convoys, the declaration of unrestricted submarine warfare helped the US President, Woodrow Wilson, bring the United States into the conflict on the Allies' side. The final element that pushed the United States into the war was a bizarre misstep on the part of a German diplomat, who offered the Mexican government assistance to win back Texas, New Mexico, and Arizona, in return for a Mexican attack against the United States. The "Zimmerman note" had been boldly (or foolishly) sent to Mexico using the American undersea cables. On April 2, 1917, the United States declared war on Germany.

Although the Americans wished to deploy rapidly, mobilizing a large army proved difficult and they were slow to arrive. While the American troops were in transit, the British experimented with some novel military techniques. For example, General Herbert Plumer masterminded a massive tunneling campaign under the German lines at Messines. British troops placed mines – over a million pounds of explosives – underground at 22 different places and then detonated them simultaneously, blowing the top off the Messines ridge and killing 10,000 German troops instantly. Unfortunately, the Messines victory was followed up by a costly land campaign in thick mud, which undermined the victory's value.

By early 1918, the Allied armies on the Western Front were exhausted. On March 3, Russia, now under the control of the Bolsheviks after a year of domestic turmoil and revolution, signed a separate peace with Germany in the Treaty of Brest-Litovsk. This eliminated the Eastern Front and freed the Germans to pursue one last energetic push to the west. A million American troops landed just in time to meet the Germans as they were breaking through the British and French trenches. The Allied counteroffensive against the Germans came between April and October of 1918, and culminated with the Kaiser abdicating and Germany suing for peace.

The Great War on the Home Front

There was no unitary British civilian understanding of the Great War. Rather, both the experience of war on the home front and its memorialization in later decades varied with the class, gender, geographic region of origin, and chosen roles of the individuals who experienced those years. For those whose lives were interrupted by a unique moment of war service, the war might not have borne out the reasons for such sacrifice. Those whose war service continued the work they had done before, and would do after the war, might not have heroic expectations about war work at all.

Before the war, women's labor had been funneled into work which could be broken down into individual, low-paid tasks and classified as unskilled or semiskilled, and in which unions could not muster opposition to women workers. As a result, women had continued to be paid less than men. In contrast with male workers, who averaged around 28 shillings a week, about 80 percent of women workers made less than 17 shillings a week, with some making much less. Only 10 percent of working women were unionized in 1914. All of this changed with the war. Women replaced men in civilian jobs when possible, enabling an unprecedented proportion of male Britons to enter the conflict under arms. A million women worked in munitions factories, but women also worked as train and bus

Figure 8.2 The First World War afforded many women the opportunity for better-paid jobs in factories. These women worked in a Coventry munitions plant. (National Archives. Ref. MUN 5/164/1124/40).

conductors, retail and administrative clerks and typists, and trained nurses (who tended to be working-class women who had been doing this sort of work before the war). Women who had previously worked as ill-paid maids were able to get better waged work for the duration of the conflict, causing a momentary shortage of domestic help. Even middle-class women, who were not expected to engage in paid work, joined the Red Cross's Voluntary Aid Detachment units. VAD nurses, attracted to the prospect of making some of the same sacrifices made by their boyfriends or brothers, lived in substandard conditions and worked 12-hour shifts changing dressings and bedpans; they saw death on a regular basis and risked, or lost, their own lives.

For many women in war work, the change from routine was tantalizing and exciting, and afforded a higher wage, but the short duration of the war did not change the patterns of women's employment in any lasting way. Although women could be paid less than men, employers believed that more capital had to be invested in industrial processes where women were employed, since women could do repetitive tasks but could not perform the same skilled tasks as men. This analysis convinced employers to rehire male workers after the war. Nor did women's appreciation for home and family decline during the war; war work was thought to be fine for single women over 18, but women's central ambition was still expected to be marriage and a family. Most of the women who adopted "male" jobs for the duration of the war bowed out at the end of the conflict (McCalman 1971).

Civilians not only assumed some of the jobs of missing soldiers, they also remained tied to troops in the field through correspondence. This was a literate army at a moment that marked the high point of personal letter-writing; soldiers of the British Expeditionary Forces sent 8 million letters home every week. Most soldiers tried to spare their loved ones the worst details of combat, trying to lighten the burden of worry on those at home. Only the occasional candid letter summarized the horrors of war. One soldier wrote to his wife about the British wounded: "There are occasions when one must resist the entreaties of [wounded] men . . . and leave them to get in as best they can, or lie out in the cold and wet, without food, and under fire, as they often have to do for days and nights together" (Fletcher 2009).

The home front was also linked to the fighting front through shared sacrifice. While Britons were better fed than the civilian population on the Continent, food shortages persisted during the war, with women and children from working-class households having to spend hours standing in queues to buy basic necessities at inflated prices. In January 1917, a Food Production Department of the government replaced the system of self-directed private farming with government direction. Grasslands that dated from the nineteenth century were plowed up and farmed, with an eye toward producing more wheat and potatoes, and more sheep were pastured on common grazing land to make up for these converted grasslands. In the short run, high prices were extremely beneficial for farmers, and the few farm laborers who hadn't volunteered or been drafted were able to take advantage of higher wages (Crowe 2007). After some discontent (although no rioting), the government finally, in January of 1918, began a program of rationing. Within a few months the rationing program extended to all of the major staples of the British diet except bread (Hunt 2010).

Finally, civilians were also tied to the front through news about casualties and deaths. Telegrams carried information about the loss of loved ones; some time later, families might receive a package containing the personal effects of the deceased. Wartime VAD nurse Vera Brittain recalled her fiancé's effects arriving at his mother's house, completely mud-stained and covered in blood, with holes marking the entry and exit wounds of the fatal bullet (Brittain et al. 1998). These wartime deaths came at a time when attitudes toward death were in transition. Parents were no longer as used to losing children in infancy as they had once been, and there was neither time nor resources nor social sanction for the elaborate mourning displays that had been so characteristic of the nineteenth century. Families who had lost loved ones were therefore eager to make those deaths meaningful by making the conflict itself meaningful.

The First World War did not completely put a stop to cultural production. Both on the home front and on the battlefront, recorded music continued to play the increasingly important role that it had played before the war. Fewer gramophones were produced, but more records were consumed – from 3.3 million records in 1913 to 5 million in 1919. Popular music hall performers like Harry Lauder sold tens of thousands of records. On the front, common soldiers gravitated toward songs like "Keep the Home Fires Burning," "The Long, Long Trail," and "It's a Long Way to Tipperary" (along with soldier-generated parodies like "That's the Wrong Way to Tickle Marie"). In addition to music sung while marching, troops delighted in the gramophones that existed behind the lines, and a constant trade flourished in records from London and Paris (Hiley 1998).

The new technology of film continued to attract audiences. Picture palaces gave young people, especially those who were courting, a place to go to enjoy some private time, or to meet with friends. Theater owners tried to emphasize their social responsibility by holding benefits for refugees and soldiers, and educated the public through official war films and newsreels. Roll of Honour films, locally produced films of photographs and biographical information about local soldiers serving or killed in battle, were screened to patriotic piano music and elicited enthusiastic applause. Feature-length war films like *The Battle of the Somme* gave audiences a tiny window onto the horrors of battle, showing dead and wounded soldiers and the process of "going over the top." Audiences also delighted to see comics like Charlie Chaplin provide more escapist fare.

The War in Government

One of the major historical themes of the wartime period is the decline of the Liberal Party, and its replacement by the Labour Party as opposition to the Conservatives. Due to the enfranchisement of workers, in the last decades of the nineteenth century the Liberals had been forced to make alliances with the new Labour Party. "Lib-Lab" agreements specified that the Liberals would not put up candidates for certain Parliamentary seats that were able to field Labour candidates. The Liberals also began to shift leftward, pursuing policies like land reform and providing the rudiments of health care and social insurance in the 1909 "People's Budget."

At the beginning of the First World War, the eclipse of the Liberals as a major party was not a foregone conclusion. Herbert Asquith ably conducted the first two years of the war, engineering entry to the war with the Liberal Cabinet almost intact. Only over time did the government have to betray Liberal principles, expanding the state's authority and minimizing civil liberties during wartime. Noncitizens were confined in camps, and many Germans left Britain or were deported. The Defence of the Realm Act allowed the government to bypass Parliamentary approval in prosecuting the war. In 1915, the Ministry of Munitions was created. Not only did it supervise 2 million workers, it also had the power to control what was produced by whom in the private sector. A Treasury Agreement negotiated between the government and the major trade unions suspended the right to strike legally for the duration of the conflict. Work rules were relaxed, enabling workers with fewer skills to do jobs once reserved for more senior and more skilled workers. A Department of Information was established, later becoming a ministry, to screen all incoming information about the war and provide progovernment propaganda. This proved increasingly necessary as the war continued, since, for example, conscription in 1916 was controversial, and the failed Gallipoli campaign sharpened criticism of one-party government in wartime and led to a coalition of Liberals, Conservatives, and Labour.

The revival of the Irish question also had implications for the Liberal Party. In 1916, Irish nationalist and former diplomat Sir Roger Casement was arrested entering Ireland after having high-level contact with the Germans. He had agreed that, in return for German military support of an Irish rebellion, the Irish would hinder the British war against Germany. When the plot was discovered, Casement was tried and executed for treason. In the immediate aftermath of his arrival in Ireland and his arrest, a breakaway faction of Irish rebels led by Patrick Pearse and James Connolly carried out a rebellion to overthrow British power in Ireland by force. In the 1916 Easter Rising, 1,800 volunteers attacked key government buildings in Dublin, including the post office. The rebellion was soon quashed, and its leaders executed after courts martial. The British response to the rebellion, while hardly surprising, polarized Nationalist opinion in Ireland. The crackdown helped to advance the fortunes of the Sinn Fein party, which would engineer the formation of the Irish Free State after the war.

In 1916, the Liberal Party leadership split in a way that helped usher the party to its eventual demise. Prime Minister Herbert Asquith was replaced by David Lloyd George, who had replaced Kitchener as Secretary for War. Lloyd George attracted some censure from his fellow Liberals for presiding over a Cabinet that, while it had some Liberal and Labour support, was mostly Conservative. From then on, the Liberals themselves were divided into Lloyd George partisans and Asquith partisans.

Although the leadership split undermined the Liberal Party, Lloyd George was an effective Prime Minister. He rearranged the government to be more flexible in wartime, appointing five ministers to a special inner Cabinet, which coexisted alongside a more traditional Cabinet of 23 members. Ministers were appointed to be in charge of particular elements of their own expertise – labor, food rationing, shipping, munitions. The official agreement between workers and the government began to break down toward the end of the war, due to discontent over rising prices. To try to stem the discontent, the government instituted rationing, which covered cheese, bacon, butter, tea, and meat, and price controls were imposed on other staple food items.

As in all democratic countries in wartime, the British government faced the important task of keeping the population fixed on the importance of the war effort. Conscription and rationing were one part of that effort, but electoral reform was the other part. Women, soldiers, male domestic servants, and other men who were not household heads (adult sons, for example) still lacked the right to vote, and as the war dragged on, it seemed important to acknowledge the contributions they made by recognizing them with full citizenship. The 1918 Representation of the People Act added 8 million voters to the electorate, enfranchising all men over 21, all soldiers over 19, and women taxpayers/householders over 30 (about 80 percent of women of that age group), radically increasing the total percentage of adults enfranchised from 28 percent to 78 percent (Todd 2006). For the first time, soldiers and sailors would be able to vote by mail from the field. A separate 1918 Act allowed women to serve as Members of Parliament.

The Impact of the War

The failure of the German offensive of 1918, the crumbling of Germany's ally Austria-Hungary, and the entry of the United States into the war made armistice negotiations possible. Finally, on November 11, 1918, an armistice went into effect. In the near term, the Great War was demographically devastating for the British Isles and the colonies of settlement. A total of 720,000 British men had died – one in eight of the 6 million Britons who had fought in the war (DeGroot 1999). Put another way, Britain lost 1.6 percent of its population. Furthermore, Britain had lost a generation of leaders; one out of every four graduates of Oxford or Cambridge who were under 25 in 1914 died in the war, and these affluent and educated young men would have provided much of the next generation's pool of leadership talent. The demographic disaster of the war had implications for Britain's ties with its colonies of settlement as well; Australia lost 1.2 percent of its population, and New Zealand 1.5 percent, demographic calamities that helped tie the families of the dead soldiers to the empire with bonds of commemoration (Winter 2002).

The Great War also changed traditions for the memorializing of the war dead. In 1917, the Imperial War Graves Commission was formed, to mark the site of all of the war dead of the British, the Empire, and British allies. Soldiers who had died in combat were memorialized on the battlefields where they fell, which were turned into over a thousand cemeteries. The nations that participated in the conflict were also given the opportunity to erect national memorials on certain battle sites. For example, a Canadian war memorial was erected at Vimy Ridge, where, in 1917, the massed Canadian forces had fought together for the first time, losing over 3,600 in battle but gaining some territory that had been thought impossible to claim (Baldwin 2010). The names of over 11,000 Canadians who had died on the

Western Front and whose bodies had never been found were inscribed on the monument, surrounded by preserved battlefield and ringed by a new pine forest. The memorial meant not only to commemorate the heroism of the dead and remind visitors of their sacrifice, but also to present visitors with the opportunity for a spiritual experience (Hucker 2009).

Towns and villages across the British Isles and the colonies erected their cenotaphs to the war dead. Simple, stark, white columns, some inscribed with the names of those who had been lost, they were a far cry from the larger-than-life statues of generals on horseback who had glorified earlier conflicts. The day on which the war ended continues to be remembered as Armistice Day, and it is the custom to buy a paper poppy, and put it into the buttonhole of your jacket. The paper poppies commemorate the flowers that grew wild over the battlefields-cum-cemeteries of Belgium. In the words that John McCrae used to commemorate his friend's death in battle in 1915:

> In Flanders fields the poppies blow
> Between the crosses, row on row,
> That mark our place; and in the sky
> The larks, still bravely singing, fly
> Scarce heard amid the guns below.

The war wreaked financial as well as individual devastation, transforming Britain from the most financially solvent nation in the world into a debtor nation. Many factors had combined to cause this state of affairs. Some key industries like textiles were already in decline because they could be produced more cheaply elsewhere. It had been necessary to trade in dollars in order to secure the help of the United States in wartime, and the exports of Great Britain had generally suffered due to the redirection of labor into the war effort. Britain had also financed the military efforts of other countries without any hope of getting reimbursed. The national debt rose from £650 million in 1914 to almost £8 billion (in US billions, equal to £8,000 million as the British used to measure it) by 1920, which would have an impact on any government provision of social welfare during the Depression of the following decade (Rubinstein 2003).

The war helped accelerate a change in attitudes about the proper role of government in areas like education, housing, and social welfare. This was made possible in part by increased taxation during the war, which made continued taxation possible once the war ended. But the exigencies of total war also forced a reevaluation of what government owed to its citizens in return for profound individual and collective sacrifice. Before the Great War, only a limited number of soldiers had been rewarded with the ability to marry officially and to have their wives and families maintained by the army. The Great War could not have been carried out without the mustering of many who were already married. To their wives and children the government gave "separation allowances," separate government grants paid to the families while husbands were serving. The payment of such allowances as a matter of right foreshadowed the post–Second World War welfare state, and also enhanced the health of women and children by giving them their own, dedicated funds for the first time (Pedersen 1990).

The Great War stoked British nationalism, accelerated change in the status of women, and accelerated the centralization of the state, all characteristics associated with twentieth-century modernity. It also destabilized the worldwide financial system, disillusioned individuals and governments about the desirability and even the sanity of military intervention, and left hundreds of thousands dead. But the victors of the conflict, including US President Woodrow Wilson and Prime Minister David Lloyd George, could at least rest assured in the confidence that this would be the war to end war . . . at least until the next war.

References

Baldwin, Jerome (2010) Canadian Capture of Vimy Ridge. *Military Heritage*, 11 (4): 26–33.

Beckett, Ian (1985) Aspects of a Nation in Arms: Britain's Volunteer Training Corps in the Great War. *Review Internationale d'Histoire Militaire*, 63 (11): 27–39.

Brittain, Vera, et al. (1998) *Letters from a Lost Generation – First World War Letters of Vera Brittain and Four Friends: Roland Leighton, Edward Brittain, Victor Richardson, Geoffrey Thurlow*, ed. Alan Bishop and Mark Bostridge. London: Little, Brown. Extract at http://www.guardian.co.uk/world/2008/nov/14/first-world-war-vera-brittain (accessed Nov. 8, 2010).

Carey, John (ed.) (1987) *Eyewitness to History*. New York: Avon.

Coetzee, Franz (1992) English Nationalism and the First World War. *History of European Ideas*, 15 (1–3): 363–367.

Crowe, Hilary (2007) Profitable Ploughing of the Uplands? The Food Production Campaign in the First World War. *Agricultural History Review*, 55 (2): 205–228.

DeGroot, Gerard (1999) A Lost Generation? The Impact of the First World War. *Modern History Review*, 11 (1): 18–21.

Douglas, Roy (1970) Voluntary Enlistment in the First World War and the Work of the Parliamentary Recruiting Committee. *Journal of Modern History*, 42 (4): 564–585.

Fletcher, Anthony (2009) Between the Lines. *History Today*, 59 (11): 45–51.

Hiley, Nicholas (1998) Ploughboys and Soldiers: The Folk Song and the Gramophone in the British Expeditionary Force, 1914–1918. *Media History*, 4 (1): 61–76.

Hucker, Jacqueline (2009) Battle and Burial: Capturing the Cultural Meaning of Canada's National Memorial on Vimy Ridge. *Public Historian*, 31 (1): 89–100.

Hunt, Karen (2010) The Politics of Food and Women's Neighborhood Activism in First World War Britain. *International Labour and Working-Class History*, 77: 8–26.

Jones, Edgar (2006) The Psychology of Killing: The Combat Experience of British Soldiers during the First World War. *Journal of Contemporary History*, 41 (2): 229–246.

Marshall, S.L.A. (1964) *World War I*. Boston: Houghton Mifflin.

McCalman, Janet (1971) The Impact of the First World War on Female Employment in England. *Labour History*, 21: 36–47.

McDermott, James (2010) Conscience and the Military Service Tribunals during the First World War: Experiences in Northamptonshire. *War in History*, 17 (1): 60–85.

Norgate, Paul (1989) Wilfred Owen and the Soldier Poets. *Review of English Studies*, 40 (160): 516–530.

Pedersen, Susan (1990) Gender, Welfare, and Citizenship in Britain during the Great War. *American Historical Review*, 95 (4): 983–1006.

Rubinstein, Walter (2003) *Twentieth-Century Britain*. London: Palgrave Macmillan.

Seaman, Owen (1914) Pro Patria. In *Songs and Sonnets for England in Wartime*. London: John Lane.

Todd, Selina (2006) Flappers and Factory Lads: Youth and Youth Culture in Interwar Britain. *History Compass*, 46: 715–730.

Winkler, Jonathan (2009) Information Warfare in World War I. *Journal of Military History*, 73 (3): 845–867.

Winter, Jay (2002) Migration, War and Empire: The British Case. *Annales de Démographie Historique*, 1: 143–160.

Further Reading

Brittain, Vera (1978) *Testament of Youth*. New York: Penguin.

Carnevali, Francesca, and Strange, Julie-Marie (eds) (1994) *Twentieth-Century Britain: Economic, Cultural and Social Change*. Harlow: Pearson Education.

Dangerfield, George (2011) *The Strange Death of Liberal England: 1910–1914*. Piscataway: Transaction. First published 1935.

Fussell, Paul (2000) *The Great War and Modern Memory*. Oxford: Oxford University Press.

Hammond, Michael (2006) *The Big Show: British Cinema Culture in the Great War, 1914–1918*. Exeter: University of Exeter Press.

Joll, James, and Martel, Gordon (2006) *The Origins of the First World War*. London: Longman.

Kingsley Kent, Susan (1987) *Sex and Suffrage in Britain, 1860–1914*. Princeton: Princeton University Press.

Liddington, Jill, and Norris, Jill (1978) *"One Hand Tied Behind Us": The Rise of the Women's Suffrage Movement*. London: Virago.

Pennell, Catriona (2009) British Society and the First World War. *War in History*, 16 (4): 506–518.

Watson, Janet (2007) *Fighting Different Wars: Experience, Memory, and the First World War in Britain*. Cambridge: Cambridge University Press.

9

Nationalism and Depression
Politics, Economics, and Social Change, 1919–1939

It was 116 degrees Fahrenheit that May day in 1930. Reporter Webb Miller had walked six miles to the place where over 2,000 of Mohandas Gandhi's followers had congregated to protest the tax on salt that the British had levied in India. Miller watched as the men, dressed in homespun dhotis and caps like their imprisoned leader, approached the stockade, behind which native Indian policemen and their British commanders guarded the salt deposits. The police ordered the crowd to disperse, but they continued marching, until the police were ordered to attack. "Not one of the marchers even raised an arm to fend off the blows. They went down like ten-pins. From where I stood I heard the sickening whacks of the clubs on unprotected skulls," Miller wrote in the *New Freeman*. By the end of the day the police had injured 320 protesters; two had died. As the only foreign correspondent present, Miller produced testimony that was crucial to the strategy of satyagraha, or nonviolent resistance. The purpose of satyagraha was to call into question Britain's possession of the moral high ground in its colonies. If the colonizing power, rather than protecting the colonized, was using state-sanctioned violence to bash in their skulls, then surely it was time for the colonizing power to leave (Miller in Carey 1987: 502).

Although at first peace in Western Europe seemed to have been secured after the Great War, the 1920s were characterized by challenging conditions within Britain's empire, particularly in Ireland and India. The financial consequences of the war – Britain's debt and the decline of some of its leading industries – led to widespread unemployment and labor unrest; the demographic consequences led to a reevaluation of gender norms. Two strikes and widespread unemployment testified to the inability of either the Conservative Party or the newly empowered Labour Party to find a political answer to the problem.

By the end of the 1920s, economic instability had spread to the United States, deepening the worldwide crisis. As it had during the Great War, Britain turned to

Empire, State, and Society: Britain Since 1830, First Edition. Jamie L. Bronstein and Andrew T. Harris.
© 2012 Jamie L. Bronstein and Andrew T. Harris. Published 2012 by John Wiley & Sons, Ltd.

a national coalition government, and by the end of the 1930s the economic picture had begun to improve. On the other hand, the preoccupation with economic and imperial policies, and the reaction against the militarism that had led to the Great War, enabled Britain's governments to turn inward, away from the growing danger posed by Hitler and Mussolini. By the time it became evident that there was no line in the sand that Hitler would not cross, it was too late.

Negotiating Peace

When the Great War ended in November 1918, the sitting Parliament had been extended three years past its normal lifespan, and an election was called. Onlookers saw the 1918 election as a referendum on the leadership of wartime leader David Lloyd George. Many Liberals felt that by working with the Conservatives during the war he had betrayed the Liberal principles of peace and nonintervention; members of the Labour Party considered Lloyd George a Tory. To secure the election, he handed out "coupons" of approval to those parliamentary candidates whom he considered to be loyal, nationalistic and anti-Bolshevik. Nothing could match the popular appeal of his call to make Britain a country "fit for heroes." His Tory-Liberal coalition swept into power with 478 seats, and Lloyd George created a Cabinet drawn equally from both parties.

The first priority was to work with the other victors of the Great War to outline the postwar order. Thus, Lloyd George traveled to Versailles in 1919 as one of the "Big Four" leaders, to conduct negotiations for the peace, along with Vittorio Orlando of Italy, Woodrow Wilson of the United States, and Georges Clemenceau of France. Wilson's Fourteen Points, outlined in a January 1918 speech before the US Congress, structured the discussion. Wilson's points fell into three general categories. The first identified the specific problems that had led to the war: secret treaties, arms races, commercial protectionism, and interference with neutral shipping. All of these, Wilson hoped, would be eliminated in the new world system. The second category of points dealt with the emergence of nationalism. Wilson advocated the national self-determination of peoples as the principle that would help to both redraw the map of Europe and determine the fate of the Central Powers' former colonies. To the extent possible, each ethnic group should have its own physical borders: there should be no nation without a state. The final point was in a category all by itself: the formation of the League of Nations. The League was intended to be a supranational entity such as had never existed before, providing member nations with an opportunity to use rationality and diplomacy to address problems before they came to conflict.

The Treaty of Versailles failed to bear out Wilson's optimism. By the terms of the treaty, Germany was demilitarized, shorn of its coal-producing region, and made to pay reparations to Britain and France that it could ill afford. Czechoslovakia,

Yugoslavia and other new states created out of the former Austro-Hungarian and Ottoman empires retained ethnic minorities within their borders, and so retained the potential for internal warfare. The colonies of the losing powers were confiscated and parceled out to the winning powers to protect as Mandates under the League of Nations system. Most galling for the Germans was the clause that demanded that they accept the responsibility for the conflict. The Germans felt so dishonored by the document that at first nobody would agree to sign it; only after renewed war was threatened did representatives step forward. The Weimar Republic, Germany's first ever democracy, thus came into existence with many impossible burdens for a barely established state. John Maynard Keynes, a young British economist who attended the negotiations, warned in *The Economic Consequences of the Peace* (1920) that the treaty would result in instability for Germany's first democratic government, and create the potential for another war out of its overly punitive emphasis on war guilt and reparations.

At the time, however, Keynes was destined to be a Cassandra, and Western Europe seemed to be entering a period of peace and tranquility. The 1921 Washington Naval Conference embodied this new spirit of cooperation. Five powers – the United States, Britain, Japan, France, and Italy – agreed to a moratorium on naval shipbuilding, and set a ratio for the size of their navies at 5:5:3:1.75:1.75 respectively (meaning that for every 1.75 French or Italian ships, Japan could build 3 and Britain and the US could build 5). The "spirit of Locarno" – a term coined after a 1925 peace conference was held in Switzerland – prevailed, as France, Britain, and Germany's first democracy, the Weimar Republic, among others, agreed to guarantee the existing borders of Europe and to use diplomacy rather than force to achieve their goals. By 1928 over 120 countries had agreed, through the mechanism of the well-intentioned and toothless Kellogg-Briand pact, that they would no longer resort to war as an instrument of policy.

Even the challenge of the Russian Revolution appeared to be contained. The Bolshevik Revolution and ensuing civil war in Russia, which replaced the Tsarist government with Marxist-Leninist institutions, made Britain's postwar government uneasy. Would socialist utopianism have repercussions at home? Glasgow, with its shipyards on the River Clyde, had been an especially active site of labor radicalism during the war, and erupted into a mass strike in January 1919 that came to be referred to as "Red Clydeside." But this labor radicalism failed to shift the overall political current; the British Communist Party, established in 1920, would have only a few thousand members throughout the decade.

Empire in the 1920s

Some of the most daunting challenges faced by the Lloyd George coalition government concerned Britain's outlying areas and empire. Ireland had erupted into civil war in 1919, after the election of 73 MPs from Sinn Fein, the Irish Nationalist party. These members refused to meet in Westminster and called themselves the parliament, or Dail, of a new Republic of Ireland. War lasted until 1921, with Sinn Fein's military arm, the Irish Republican Army, squaring off against demobilized British troops who had fought in the First World War. Lacking discipline, these British "Black and Tans" were accused of torturing the civilian population. Lloyd George's government extended Home Rule to Ireland in 1920, but it was too little and too late; only the Protestants in Ulster recognized the Home Rule settlement. As the war continued, David Lloyd George negotiated with Eamon de Valera, the head of the Dail, to recognize Southern Ireland as the Irish Free State, while the six counties of Northern Ireland remained part of the United Kingdom. Power was transferred to the Irish Free State in January of 1922, temporarily removing the great question of Ireland from Britain's political agenda, although the exodus of the Irish MPs from Parliament shifted the balance of power in Westminster toward the Conservatives. Ireland itself erupted into civil war.

India also posed challenges for Britain's first postwar government. Edwin Montagu, Secretary of State for India, studied the question of the administration of India and produced a series of suggestions, the Montagu-Chelmsford Reforms, which became the Government of India Act (1919). The Act established "diarchy," a system of joint rule between the British government (embodied by the Viceroy), and legislative councils of native-born Indians. The portfolios of both of these were divided so that the Indians were in charge of domestic affairs, and the crown controlled security and foreign policy. This division of labor gave momentum to Indian nationalism by signaling the likelihood of eventual decolonization. The same year, British military commander R.E.H. Dyer ordered his troops to fire upon an unarmed crowd of demonstrators at Amritsar in the Punjab, killing 379 people and injuring 1,208 more (unofficial estimates say as many as 1,000 were killed). Many of those on the scene died when they jumped into a deep well to avoid being killed in the firefight. Eventually Dyer would be censured for his action, but not before the Amritsar Massacre had become a galvanizing event for Indian nationalism.

The Massacre coincided with Mohandas Gandhi's emergence as the recognizable leader of the nationalist movement. Gandhi, the son of the prime minister of a small princely state, was raised an observant Hindu, and married very early. After an expatriate education at Oxford, he moved to South Africa and took up a law practice. It was there that he first used the technique of nonviolent resistance, to try to force the government there to repeal some of its color-based "pass laws" that had been levied against the Indians living in South Africa.

Upon his return to India, Gandhi adopted the life of simplicity and poverty in which the majority of Indians lived. He advocated a movement in favor of Indian Home Rule by cooperating with Muslim leaders, encouraging the industry of homespun cloth, and promoting education, a national language, and the improvement of hygiene. The campaign included many kinds of civil disobedience against the British in India: blocking trains from running, withholding taxes, and encouraging Indians to avoid the British tariff on salt by making their own salt from salt water. The initial period of satyagraha concluded in 1922 when a mob set fire to a police station and 22 policemen burned to death, but it was just the beginning of a long struggle.

As Canada, New Zealand, South Africa, and Australia built their own export sectors, Britain no longer supplied as much to the empire. The government strove to retain imperial commercial ties by promoting Empire Shopping Weeks, creating the Empire Marketing Board, and, in 1924, an Empire Exhibition in London, but migration to the empire was slowing and cultural and economic ties were wearing thin. The 1929 Colonial Development Act provided funding for infrastructure in Britain's African colonies, but there was never a clear sense of whether Africa should be expected to provide mainly raw materials, or a labor force, or should begin to emerge as a source of military might, as India had long been.

The Great Depression and the Postwar Political Order

While these challenges to Empire were substantial, at the time they appeared to pose a smaller risk to Britain's power than the internal threat of economic instability. The economic threat was multifaceted. First, Britain emerged from the Great War a debtor nation – to the tune of $1.1 billion borrowed from the Americans, who insisted on having their debts repaid. Two debt agreements, the Dawes Plan (1924) and the Young Plan (1929) enabled the United States to loan money to Germany, which paid the reparations owed to Britain and France, which repaid the United States.

A second problem was more structural. Britain faced challenges from countries like Japan that not only paid lower wage rates but also had industrialized later and could outfit with much newer technologies. The shipbuilding industry found itself held back from selling ships in some parts of the world by other countries' protective tariffs, and the coal mining industry suffered from the absence of either advanced technology (much mining was still done with pick and shovel) or economies of scale (many coal concerns were very small and poorly capitalized). Alarmingly, these staple industries were also geographically concentrated in the North and West of England, in effect focusing the hardship in particular regions. A shift to new consumer industries like furniture production was possible, but given that this required new sets of skills not possessed by coal miners or shipbuilders, new factories tended not to locate in the North. As a result, the growth of jobs that did take place in the interwar period occurred almost entirely within the South.

Britain's economy faced barriers to modernization. Middle management, which had appeared in complex firms in the United States in the 1870s and 1880s, finally began to catch on in Britain in the 1920s and 1930s. Companies merged with other companies and evolved complicated organizational structures, financial branches, legal branches, and international subsidiaries – a big change from the "personally managed firms" of limited size of the past. Centralized decision-making at the top level required standardization in practices on the shop floor, removing some of the autonomy that workers had enjoyed. But while British firms adopted branches and middle management, "mass production" on the Ford model was a much harder sell to these companies. Some historians have theorized that the strength of trade unions in Britain made it hard for firms to introduce Taylorism, the assembly-line method of working whereby functional foremen instructed workers in the "one best way" of performing their repetitive factory tasks. Other historians have noted that, with no sign of the availability of a mass domestic market for certain goods (like cars) and with export markets shrinking, British firms did not see an advantage in retooling their plants for mass production. The smaller size of British firms, and the greater number in the market compared with American firms, also helped to promote and sustain less capital-intensive manufacturing.

Each government in the interwar period passed some legislation intended to ameliorate the Depression or to expand the economy by improving the workforce or the infrastructure. Lloyd George's concerns centered, as they had during the era of the People's Budget, on economic burden-sharing and providing the working classes with opportunities and a higher standard of living. Parliament passed the Fisher Act (1918), over the outcries of manufacturers. The Act mandated free public education for all children from age 5 to age 14 and the creation of "continuation schools" for part-time training of students up to age 18. The Housing and Town Planning Act (1919) obligated local authorities to meet the shortage of inexpensive housing by build new rental housing, promising them reimbursement from the Exchequer. The Unemployment Insurance Act (1920) provided unemployment insurance to low-waged workers (except farm workers and domestic servants). If workers had made more than 30 weekly contributions, were out of work and actively seeking work, were willing to take domestic servant positions if ordered to do so, and could pass a "means test" by having less than a certain income, they qualified for benefits. During the 1920s, household heads were entitled to unemployment payments of 17 shillings a week, with an extra 7 shillings for each dependent adult living in the home, and 2 shillings for each child (Eichengreen 1987). Those who did not qualify for unemployment insurance, or who needed their payments to be extended by an additional amount, might still qualify for some kind of social welfare under the Poor Law. Pregnant women, infants, and young children could also qualify for assistance provided by municipalities on medical grounds.

Although these reforms helped to maintain Lloyd George's personal popularity, he was still vulnerable. Falling coal prices, combined with a reprivatization of coal mines that had been government-run during the war, led to massive wage cuts for coal workers. The miners responded by going on a three-month strike. The other member unions of the "triple alliance," transport workers and railroad workers, threatened to take part (although they ultimately did not). The 1921 miners' strike ended when the coal mine owners agreed to locally negotiated guaranteed wage rates, although the miners would have preferred a national wage.

Lloyd George was also vulnerable without a party backing him. His vulnerability reflected a political shift during the interwar period, as the Liberals came to be replaced by Labour as the country's second major party. In 1922, Lloyd George's government fell over its flagrant propensity to sell aristocratic titles as a source of state revenue. The leader of the Conservative Party, Andrew Bonar Law, was asked to form a government. In the general election that followed, no party had a Parliamentary majority. The Conservative Party gained 38 percent of the vote, but the Labour Party and the two factions of the Liberal Party (split between followers of Herbert Asquith and Lloyd George) were nearly tied in their electoral accomplishments, each having earned 29 percent of the vote. It seemed probable that the next time the government changed, the Labour Party would have its turn to lead.

Stanley Baldwin replaced Andrew Bonar Law as the leader of the Conservative Party (1922–1923). As Joseph Chamberlain had done decades earlier, Baldwin favored tariffs, hoping that rejecting free trade and embracing protectionism might help with the nation's unemployment problem. But because this represented a significant change from British free trade policy and ideology since the 1850s, Baldwin felt that only another general election could provide the government with such a mandate. Here, he seems to have miscalculated badly. In the 1923 general election, Baldwin's Conservative Party lost 87 seats, which not only put an end to Baldwin's plan for tariff reform, but also ushered in the first Labour ministry under Ramsay MacDonald (1924).

Born to a Scottish servant girl and an unknown father, MacDonald had a background in Fabian politics and had worked as a white-collar clerk. But while his background was more humble than that of some other prime ministers, the Labour Party under his leadership was not particularly revolutionary. MacDonald filled his Cabinet with established politicians, and focused on social reform, rather than the more radical step of nationalizing industries. MacDonald also continued to emphasize homebuilding, presiding over the passage of a new Housing Act, which increased grants available to municipalities to build houses. The first Labour ministry was short; as Lloyd George had done, MacDonald fell into personal disrepute. It was alleged that he had granted aristocratic titles in exchange for a car and some stocks in the McVitie biscuit company. Conservatives and Liberals both opposed MacDonald's plan to sign treaties with the Soviet Union. Then, it was alleged that his Attorney-General had failed to prosecute the editor of the *Workers' Weekly* newspaper, who was accused of inciting British troops to mutiny. The discontent led to a general election and Labour's fall from power.

Stanley Baldwin's second ministry (1925–1929) was more successful than his first. Baldwin brought in Winston Churchill as Chancellor of the Exchequer, helping to rehabilitate Churchill's reputation after the Gallipoli campaign in the Great War. Another achievement was the clarification of Britain's relationship with its colonies of settlement. They had long demanded a clarification of their governing relationship to the mother country, and in 1926 Britain granted them the right to determine their own foreign policies. The autonomy of these states – guaranteed in 1931 through the Statute of Westminster – meant that although they shared a common head of state, the British monarch, they were no longer subject to direction from the government at Westminster.

As it has in many times and places, widespread unemployment resulted in a dialogue about employment and race. The 1905 Aliens Act had restricted immigration for the first time and allowed for the deportation of foreign paupers, and the 1919 Aliens Restriction Act barred foreign nationals from the civil service. In the interwar period, merchant shippers sought to compensate for lower profits by hiring sailors from the British Empire, who were paid less than white sailors, required to work longer hours, and due to their labor contracts, were not free to quit their employment. British unions responded by rhetorically attacking black workers for taking "white" jobs. Eventually the government responded with the Special Restriction (Coloured Alien Seaman) Order (1925) containing the first official legislative definition of race, and later created special second-class passports for nonwhite workers.

Between 1921 and the middle of 1926, 57,000 people were employed on government-funded public works projects. The Ministry of Transport also employed large numbers on the construction of new arterial roads. John Maynard Keynes's theory of economics proposed that direct government spending on jobs was likely to produce even more jobs in the private sector, as poorer people receiving wages immediately spent their earnings on necessities. But in contrast with the United States during the 1930s, "Keynesian economics" – which required purposely unbalancing budgets – was not a great motivator for successive British governments. Instead, the Treasury favored "sound money" policies, seeking to maintain the value of the British pound by pegging it to gold, on the grounds that this was essential to confidence and eventual investment (Garside 1985; 1987). When the pound was returned to the gold standard in 1925 – over Keynes's loud protests – the result was higher interest rates (holding back business investment) and lower wages. This situation lasted throughout the 1920s and into the 1930s. Unemployment rose to more than 17 percent of workers in 1921, declined to 12 percent the following year, and then remained at least 10 percent every year through 1939. In the worst year of the Depression, unemployment reached more than 20 percent (Rubinstein 2003: 110).

Although Keynesian economics was not on the agenda, Baldwin was determined to reach out to the working classes. The Widows, Orphans, and Old Age Contributory Pensions Act (1925) provided a guaranteed source of income to widows and their children and to those over 65. But these overtures were cut short by a second major strike. Miners, facing wage cuts and longer hours, threatened industrial action. Baldwin responded by appointing a committee to study the issue, and then, as per the committee's suggestion, paying government subsidies to the mines to maintain wages at current levels. Baldwin clashed with his own Cabinet, members of which saw such payments as blackmail. Lord Birkenhead summed up this frustration by noting that he would say that the miners' leaders were "the stupidest men in England, if we had not frequent occasion to meet the owners" (Mowat 1968: 300).

A Royal Commission was appointed, and in early 1926 it recommended reorganization of the mines and the removal of the government subsidy to miners' wages. Employers proposed extending miners' hours of work, and reducing the wages of all miners, and warned the miners that if they refused to agree with these new terms, they would be locked out of the mines beginning May 1, 1926. On May 3, 1926, the General Council of the Trades Union Congress supported the locked-out miners by calling a general strike. Over the next nine days, the strike marshaled almost 2 million workers in various industries. Skirmishes broke out in the North of England and in Glasgow; strikers broke windows, pitched coal, and stopped the trains from running. The violence was particularly intense in Scotland, where rail workers and coal workers lived in close proximity to each other and supported each other. The few trains that managed to make it into stations might have every window broken by thrown missiles, and threats to strikebreakers were common. On May 10, the Flying Scotsman, the train that plied the route between Edinburgh and London King's Cross, was derailed in Northumberland after colliers pulled up the tracks.

Ultimately, the General Strike failed, as hundreds of middle-class people seeking to perform manual labor volunteered for service, protecting Britain from grinding to a halt. In addition, truckers, representing an alternate modern method of

Figure 9.1 Workers at Crewe demonstrated during the 1926 general strike. (© Hulton-Deutsch Collection/Corbis).

shipping goods, were not unionized, and other trade unions lacked the personnel to effectively stop deliveries around the country. Having run out of money to pay strike benefits, the Trades Union Congress called off the strike without having achieved any concessions.

But the end of the strike was not the end of the tragedy. In Wales and in the North of England, the mine lockout continued, forcing miners' families onto the poor law rolls as local union strike funds were quickly depleted. Poor law unions, already in debt from 1921, and hamstrung in their attempts to borrow funds, were forced to be cheap in paying out benefits. Teachers described miners' children going without food or shoes, and carrying smaller children on their backs to receive donated breakfasts. Labour councils around the country, co-op stores, and well-meaning people who read about the plight of the miners donated food, and many strikers and their families took their meals at communal soup kitchens.

After the strike, miners lost their entitlement to a national minimum wage. The Trade Disputes Act (1927) made further general strikes illegal; disgruntled workers dismissed the law as "class legislation." The way that the government responded to the strike helped to shift public opinion back toward the Labour Party. In the 1929 general election, Labour once again pulled ahead, and Ramsay MacDonald gained a second term.

Changes for Women

The emergence of a new two-party system in the postwar period occurred against the backdrop of significant new debates about Britain's national identity. What was the proper social and economic role of women? Should Britain be primarily rural or urban? Should Britain embrace new technologies, or did they pose a danger to national cohesion?

Historians have argued that the loss of so many men in war, and the permanent disablement of so many others, led to a shift in gender roles during the interwar period. Some argue that the war transformed manliness itself from the crusading, adventurous colonial spirit of the nineteenth century into that of the insular village dweller: a "feminization" of British society. In turn, women's opportunities were changing. The dominant female image of the 1920s for contemporary writers may be the perpetually unmarried spinster – there were 1,096 women for every 1,000 men in Britain in 1921 – but many other young widows had only been married for days or weeks before they lost their husbands at the front, leaving them with nothing but a widow's pension of a pound a week. This demographic shock created a need for many single women to support themselves.

Working women had historically dominated three fields: textile production, clothing construction, and domestic service. In turn, men had dominated fields requiring hard physical labor, or those in which heavy capital investment required a large investment in long-term training of the workforce, and hence paid higher wages. Now, new fields like auto manufacture, electrical fabrication, and the chemical industry began to hire large numbers of semiskilled women workers to staff assembly lines.

Women's labor participation rates in the interwar period depended on several factors. For most working-class women, workforce participation was a stage of life, peaking when a woman was in her late teens. Labor force participation also varied geographically, depending on local traditions. Sixty-two percent of women in Blackburn in the West Midlands had paid employment at some time in their lives, but only 11 percent did in South Wales, where many women skipped this stage of life entirely and married at a younger age (Hatton and Bailey 1988). In areas where work was available, women tended to cease to participate in the labor force when they married, only resuming it again if by misfortune they became household heads. This cessation of work was due to two factors: working-class cultural traditions, which caused husbands to oppose married women's work in favor of the "family wage," and an informal "marriage bar" that persisted at many companies. Married women were also expected to dedicate their labor to the unpaid work of keeping up the home: work that was becoming more labor intensive as standards of cleanliness rose.

While child-bearing and child-rearing had been largely beyond the reach of the state before 1918, the Maternal and Child Welfare Act of that year helped to establish a total of 3,000 maternal and infant welfare clinics over the next 12 years. These clinics served as home bases for health visitors, who visited women in their homes after childbirth and monitored the welfare of infants. Many working-class men feared that these health visitors would meddle in their families' lives, or that the clinics would give their wives a place to go outside of the home. The state established Fathers' Councils to make this level of government intervention seem less strange, and to educate working men about "scientific" infant-care (in the 1920s, doctors thought children should be picked up as little as possible, and should be fed on a strict schedule). Nonetheless, particularly in working-class communities, gender roles remained rigid; women jealously guarded the tasks of hands-on parenting, and men were exempt from most parenting except when there was no female caregiver available. Only smaller families would reduce this child-care burden: the birth rate continued its nineteenth-century decline, reaching 2.2 births per woman in the late 1920s (Thane 1990).

Legislative changes in the interwar period helped to reshape and expand opportunities for women as well. The inclusion of women over 30 in the voting electorate in 1918 was significant, and the Sex Disqualification Removal Act of 1919 gave women the right to receive university degrees, and to participate in the professions and in civil service positions equally with men. The Act also made it unlawful for companies to institute an official "marriage bar" to prevent married women from working. In 1928, a debate over the reputedly negative moral effects of the "flapper vote" (the stereotypical young woman of the 1920s was a boyish-looking, footloose girl known as a "flapper") concluded with the lowering of the female voting age from 30 to 21. At last, women could now vote on the same terms as men. On the other hand, women's dominance in the electorate failed to translate into instant dominance or even numerical significance in the House of Commons, where the number of women representatives remained below 15.

The Matrimonial Causes Act (1923) gave women equal grounds for divorce with men, and in 1925, women gained equal rights of guardianship of minor children. New property laws passed in 1926 and 1935 gave women equal rights to own and dispose of property as well. On the other hand, protective legislation aimed at women in the workplace often focused on the negative impact of long hours on their ability to serve as wives, reproducers, and mothers: for example, the 1937 Factory Act prohibited women from working more than 48 hours per week. Once all women had the vote, the nature of the legislation changed; but the gender of the legislators would take much longer to change.

Tradition and Modernity

Was postwar Britain to be a technocratic, scientific, urban and electricity-powered nation? Or was the real and enduring Britain its traditional rural countryside? Stanley Baldwin, Conservative Prime Minister in the mid-twenties, celebrated rural England. As he noted to the Royal Society of St George in 1924:

> The sounds of England, the tinkle of hammer on anvil in the country smithy, the corncrake on a dewy morning, the sound of the scythe against the whetstone, and the sight of a plough team coming over the brow of a hill, the sight that has been in England since England was a land, and may be seen in England long after the Empire has perished and every works in England has ceased to function, for centuries the one eternal sight of England.

In 1926, Patrick Abercrombie, Professor of Civic Design, who had written *The Preservation of Rural England*, called for the formation of a task force on preservation, which was founded as the Council for the Preservation of Rural England. This lobbying group intended to protect the countryside from "ribbon development," development along roads between rural villages and cities, creating conurbations of continuous settlement. The mid-1920s also saw the Rural Lore movement in Welsh schools, in which children learned of the place names, the customs, and the historical figures of rural Wales in particular – simultaneously helping to build appreciation for the countryside and a sort of covert Welsh nationalism.

In 1898, in a reaction to poorly planned nineteenth-century cities, Ebenezer Howard had written *To-Morrow: A Peaceful Path to Real Reform*. His book suggested that England should strive for garden cities – urban areas surrounded by agricultural greenbelts that would supply them with food. The first garden city was built at

Letchworth in 1903, but the garden city movement really emerged as a cultural force after the First World War, with the building of Welwyn Garden City 25 miles north of London. Not only was Welwyn Garden City centrally planned, with low density development, broad, tree-lined avenues and an impressive but walkable city center, it also became the site of a successful "New Town" experiment in the 1920s, planned around community schools, libraries, swimming pools, cultural amenities, and playing fields, with a ring of communally owned agricultural land around the edge.

While many expressed nostalgia for a rural England that may never have really existed, others embraced the twentieth century, the age of electricity. The United Kingdom lagged behind other European countries and the United States in applying electrification in manufacturing. Electrification allowed those countries lacking large coal deposits to catch up to their economic competitors; never having been in this situation, Britain could only lose out relative to other nations, and hence moved slowly. As late as 1930, electricity drove only 38 percent of the British textile industry's machinery, compared with 83 percent in the United States. Nonetheless, there was incremental change: in 1913, electricity drove 23 percent of overall British industrial plant, rising to 49 percent in 1925 and 61 percent in 1929 (Beltran 2005).

Government publications promoted home electricity as a clean fuel, a "silent servant" that enabled women to escape the need for awkward relationships between employers and domestic servants by allowing women to use labor-saving house-cleaning devices instead. By 1939, two-thirds of British homes had been electrified. The silent servant did not liberate women from housework, however. Poorer families expended little of their income on "labor saving" devices for women, preferring to spend their money on luxuries that added enjoyment but did little to take away from housework, like radios and visits to the movies. And for the middle classes, as labor saving devices became more affordable, they were substituted for the work of servants, causing housework to expand to fill the time available.

The drive toward modernity was also represented in the interwar period by increased personal mobility. The late nineteenth century saw the bicycle revolutionize personal transportation; the early twentieth saw the bicycle eclipsed by the motorcycle. Britain dominated motorcycle production; during the interwar period British industry produced 300 different motorcycle brands (in contrast with just three makers in the United States by 1931) and in a single year, Britain built 147,000 motorcycles. In the early 1920s, 496,000 motorcycles traveled British roads compared with just 474,000 cars. The continuing expense of cars held back the development of the British auto industry. While in the United States Ford sold its Model T for $270, or about £60, in Britain the same car cost £169 due to the higher costs of labor and the failure to adopt continuous processes in factories. Even so, by 1939, automobile ownership had come within the reach of the middle classes, with one car for every five British families.

Britons saw that automobiles encouraged independence, personal flexibility, and discovery of previously remote areas of the country, helping to promote the tourist industry and enable a feeling of national cohesion. Cars also brought mobility to farm families for the first time. Automobiles caused traffic jams as well as motor vehicle accidents on insufficiently modernized roads (in the 1920s, the annual average fatality rate from motor vehicle accidents exceeded that of the early 2000s, despite the vast increase in the number of cars on the road). Some pessimists even blamed autos for a dip in morality, since the car gave rise to the lovers' lane.

Experiencing the Depression in the 1930s

By the end of the 1920s the Depression had increased disparities that already existed between wealthier and poorer parts of the nation. In some industrial cities, like Liverpool and Glasgow, the unemployment rate was 25 percent, as demand evaporated for coal, steel, ships, and textiles. Industrial Wales, the North of England, and parts of Scotland also suffered from poor public health facilities and high infant mortality rates. Governments practiced "industrial transference," assisting the migration of almost 340,000 people from 1928 to 1938. Workers were transported from depressed areas to new factory towns; parts of Durham and of South Wales, once thriving industrial areas, were classified as "derelict" and beyond hope. The government also offered financial incentives to companies willing to locate industrial plants in depressed areas.

Unemployment also operated differentially when it came to age and gender. Migrants, youth, and women workers were in demand because they could be paid less than their experienced adult male counterparts. A 1935 survey of wages across all industries indicated that men earned an average of 64.5 shillings a week, women over 18 earned an average of 31.3 shillings, boys under 21 earned 23 shillings, and girls earned an average of 16.3 shillings (Scott 2000: 451). The oldest workers, those in their fifties and older, were much less likely to get jobs again once they had lost them. As a result, the 1930s initiated the postwar trend among working people toward a period of "retirement" between the end of work and the beginning of ill health. Unemployment also differentiated on the basis of social class: while fewer than 2 percent of managers and employers found themselves unemployed at the height of the Depression, the rate of unemployment was more than 20 percent among unskilled workers – those who could afford it least.

Because it cost six times as much to employ a man on a public works project as to provide him with a direct unemployment payment, the government provided direct welfare payments, and promoted small vegetable gardens and occupational unemployment centers as a way for the unemployed to spend their time. George Orwell mercilessly skewered these centers – where, among other occupations, men learned how to weave grass baskets. In his 1937 book *The Road to Wigan Pier* he provided a vivid, visceral snapshot of life during Britain's Depression, gleaned through experiences living with miners and in cheap boardinghouses throughout

Britain's industrial North. He described the social impact of the family means test on welfare payments. Rather than just assessing the income of the unemployed family member, the new means test looked at total family income. This pushed the disabled elderly out of the houses of their relatives who were still employed, and into cheap boarding houses, where they didn't count as members of their families and could collect benefits in their own right.

Orwell also described the substandard housing in which many of the poor lived. He described families in Wigan still living in nineteenth-century back-to-back housing, with communal toilets in the alley behind, paying high rent for dwellings afflicted by insects, damp walls and poor upkeep. Even worse, due to the shortage of rental housing even at inflated rents, some families lived in caravans measuring only 450 cubic feet – a mixture of "gypsy caravans," broken-down buses, and wagons with tent-fabric stretched over the top, without electricity or running water.

Coalition Government and the Depression

Would the second Labour government find an innovative strategy for dealing with the economy? For his second term as Prime Minister (Labour, 1929–31; National Government, 1931–5), Labour's Ramsay MacDonald appointed many old political hands, and few people with any background in manual labor. Notably, the government incorporated the first woman Cabinet member to serve, Margaret Bondfield, who became Minister of Labour.[1] In a Parliament divided among Conservatives, Labour, and the Liberal Party, Labour lacked a Parliamentary majority, which made it difficult for the government to follow through on any initiative. Even worse, the government lacked a coherent economic stimulus plan. Two separate committees empowered to advise the government on financial steps suggested raising taxes and cutting back on government spending, including spending on unemployment payments. The prospect of a Labour government cutting back sharply on unemployment relief led half of MacDonald's Cabinet to oppose this idea. But rather than step down as Prime Minister, MacDonald became the head of a new national coalition government, in which the Liberal Party held most of the Cabinet positions.

The need for a change of financial strategy had become evident when the United States economy crashed in 1929, creating a domino effect in the rest of the world. When the United States could not afford to import goods, other countries could not sell their exports to the US market, and experienced their own crises in which they were importing more from abroad than they were selling. The United States levied a high protective tariff to combat the Depression. But the Smoot-Hawley tariff (1930) led to a wave of retaliatory tariffs from 23 trading partners, most notably Canada. The imposition of tariffs slowed foreign trade. The picture was especially bad for farmers: the entry of new food producers onto the world market had led to a sharp drop in the price of food.

The globalization of depression forced the British national government to act more decisively and to pull the pound off the gold standard and then suspend its debt repayments to the United States (1931). The value of the pound immediately dropped from $4.86 to $3.40, making British exports more affordable abroad. The government also finally broke with the free trade ideology pioneered in the Victorian era, erecting a 20 percent import duty on all but British Empire-made goods by 1932. Adopting these protectionist measures stopped other countries from selling their steel in Britain at prices that undercut the British steel industry. Britain's colonies and former colonies became part of the "sterling area," a free-trade bloc whose rules were determined in London.

Popular Politics

With the unemployment rate hovering around 22 percent, many people became more politically adventurous and experimental. As in the United States during the 1930s, a tiny Communist Party – which increased its membership from 2,756 to 7,478 in 1931 alone – argued for a Soviet-style solution to the economic crisis (the Soviet Union was the one developed country that seemed to onlookers to be enjoying relative prosperity; the degree of repression practiced by Stalin was not well known until later). In contrast with the United States, Britain's Communists were not able to join together with many other groups in a united effort that might have made them more effective. Nonetheless, they were significant because they helped to fuel the National Unemployed Workers' Movement, which promoted public demonstrations of thousands of workers against the "means test" in the early 1930s. In addition, just as idealistic young Americans joined the Lincoln Brigade to fight on the side of the Spanish socialists and communists in the Spanish Civil War (1936–1939), about 2,000 of Britain's left-wing youth also packed up their weapons and set off to Spain to oppose the fascist armies of Hitler's Spanish ally, Francisco Franco. About a quarter of those who went were killed before the war ended.

On the other end of the political spectrum, Oswald Mosley had begun his political career as a Conservative MP, parted with his party on the question of Ireland, and then joined the Independent Labour Party. He encountered little support within MacDonald's government for his plan of increased government spending, and so founded the British Union of Fascists (BUF), which emphasized youth, activity, and central planning, all dressed up in black shirts, fascist salutes, and a cult of personality around Mosley. By 1934, Mosley had become an open adherent of Adolf Hitler, a fact which helped to marginalize the BUF. In 1936, Hitler was one of only six guests who attended Mosley's wedding to Diana Mitford – a wedding held in the drawing room of Nazi Propaganda Minister Joseph Goebbels.

Figure 9.2 Hunger marchers paraded through London in 1932 to protest the government's handling of the economic depression. (© Hulton-Deutsch Collection/Corbis).

Consumption Patterns

The devaluation of the pound was crucial in promoting British recovery from the Depression. After 1931, interest rates on borrowing fell, which led, in turn, to more business investment. Over a million council houses (municipal low-income housing) were built during the interwar era. Workers were not the only ones leaving British cities for lower-density housing. Middle-class semidetached homes accounted for 2.5 million new homes built in this period. Houses could now be bought with as little as 5 percent for a down payment and on a mortgage over a term as long as 30 years. By 1938, 32 percent of homes were occupied by their owners – and over 60 percent of middle-class homes. Population pressures also eased; within a 20-year period, the amount of "urbanized" space in Britain increased by 50 percent, while the number of urban dwellers grew by only 10 percent (Whitehead and Carr 1999).

By the mid-1930s, the Depression had begun to abate as new industries producing consumer goods (cars, vacuum cleaners) and housing construction emerged as dominant economic sectors. With annual economic growth rates of more than 3 percent, the United Kingdom economy recovered much faster than other major industrial economies. Although the economy as a whole was improving, living standards were still held back by low wages. Whether they worked in agriculture, service or industry, families spent up to half of their total expenditure on food, and another one-quarter to one-third on housing. Consumer goods were more widely available, but still unaffordable, and whereas the widespread availability of consumer credit in the United States made it possible to buy almost anything from clothing to cars "on time" (that is, by paying the total cost over a period of time), hire purchase, as the same thing was called in Great Britain, was less available. To the extent that members of the working class increased their purchasing power, it was for things like radios, inexpensive ready-made clothing, commercialized leisure activities like admission to dance halls and cinemas, and a diet with more protein, fruit and vegetables, rather than for buying their own houses, furniture, cars, washing machines, or other large appliances.

Only for those in the middle classes was the interwar period a time of great consumer change. Modest earners in the middle classes expended only about 35 percent of their weekly budgets on food and rent, making the new array of consumer durables and semidurables more affordable. Thus, although the vast majority of homes had electric irons by 1939, and almost 39 percent of British homes had radios by 1938, only 27 percent had vacuum cleaners, and 3 percent had refrigerators and/or washing machines. For the most part, consumer goods were evaluated not only on their affordability, but on the basis of whether there were any other reasonably close substitutes able to get the job done (Scott 2007: 171).

Nationalism and Its Discontents

As the Depression eased, the question of the status of Britain's colonies reemerged. Britain's grant of autonomy to its colonies of white settlement through the Statute of Westminster (1931) helped to revive Indian nationalism, since India had been left out. A series of Round Table Conferences was held (1930, 1931, 1932) to negotiate the grounds on which India could be granted Dominion status. The Indian National Congress boycotted the first Round Table Conference, which coincided with the Salt Satyagraha described at the beginning of the chapter, but Gandhi attended later conferences. The Government of India Act (1935) granted native Indians provincial self-government and a majority of seats in India's Parliament, although it also forbade the legislature from discriminating against British commercial interests. Recognizing that the end of British rule in India was coming, the Indian civil service began withdrawing English civil servants and replacing them with native Indians.

While Gandhi represented India's Hindus, Muhammad Ali Jinnah's Muslim League demanded to be recognized as the representative agency of all Indian Muslims, and opposed the construction of any postcolonial state in which Hindus would have a permanent legislative majority. Given that two-thirds of those in India were Hindu, the Muslims feared that they would be disadvantaged. It was becoming clear that the withdrawal of the English from colonial rule would leave India in a divided state.

Palestine, a British League of Nations Mandate since the early 1920s, was also becoming more difficult to manage. The British had at first been supporters of the Zionist movement to unite European Jews in a homeland of their own; the 1917 Balfour Declaration had identified Palestine as a potential site, and a wave of Jewish migration to Palestine had followed. But by 1936, as a result of the Arab Revolt, which occurred in response to this migration, the British government began to back away from that commitment. The Revolt began in April of that year with the declaration of an Arab general strike by the Higher Arab Committee. By 1937 the strike had become an armed insurgency, to which the British responded with press censorship, collective punishment through fining and the destruction of houses and livestock, and even the use of Arab prisoners to clear land mines. Yielding to tactics that put pressure on the civilian population, along with mass arrests, and split by dissent from within, the Arab Revolt collapsed in 1939. But its end was accompanied by Britain's decision to prevent future violence by restricting the number of Jews allowed to migrate to Palestine (Norris 2008).

Both the political right and left had agreed that it was more crucial for the British to concentrate on their domestic problems and the struggles of empire than to attempt to police Europe. National opinion strongly opposed rearmament or forceful intervention abroad. The majority at a 1933 debate of the Oxford Union (the university's student debating society) famously voted that under no circumstances would they fight for king and country. In another episode, in a famous by-election in East Fulham, in London, in 1933, a candidate running on an explicitly antiwar platform trounced a local Tory who wanted to rearm. The by-election was taken as a plebiscite on war as an instrument of foreign policy.

The British determination to avoid war coincided with a burst of expansionism by other states. In their quest for a "Greater East Asian Co-Prosperity Sphere," the Japanese invaded neighboring Manchuria in 1931 and absorbed it into their empire as Manchukuo. When in 1933 the League of Nations censured Japan, that country responded by withdrawing from the League, and the following year repudiated its naval agreements from the previous decade and embarked on a massive naval building program. The Japanese then began to exert pressure against the Nationalist government in China, following up with a full-scale invasion in 1937. Japanese atrocities committed against Chinese civilians in Nanking in December of that year were a foreshadowing of things to come. The League of Nations issued protests, but these carried little meaning in the face of determined Japanese militarism.

The League of Nations proved to be equally impotent against Italy under the charismatic Fascist Benito Mussolini, who in 1934 oversaw an Italian invasion of Ethiopia, intended both to evoke the glories of ancient Rome and to serve as payback for the Ethiopian victory over the Italians at Adowa in 1896. Anthony Eden, the British Cabinet minister in charge of League of Nations affairs, tried to appease Mussolini with a grant of Britain's own land in the region, but this offer was rejected. The League of Nations attempted an embargo against Italy, but the Italians were quickly victorious and the Ethiopian emperor fled.

The most high-profile failure of the League of Nations was its inability to stem the expansion of the newly rearmed German state. Head of the National Socialist German Workers' Party (the Nazi Party), Adolf Hitler assumed power as Chancellor in 1933. Under his leadership, Germany withdrew from the League of Nations (1933), took over German coalfields that had been awarded to France by the Versailles treaty, and then began to rearm, against that treaty's clauses (1935). After Hitler and other German leaders blamed the Depression and German embarrassments of the interwar era on the Jews, the Nuremberg Laws disenfranchised German Jews as citizens, depriving them of professional employment and of education, barring them from public accommodations, and prohibiting intermarriage between Jews and Gentiles.

The British tabloids were distracted from the assault on human rights in Germany by a bit of old-fashioned scandal. George V had been a popular monarch, who had celebrated his twenty-fifth anniversary of rule in 1935. Upon his death, he was succeeded by his son Edward VIII. Suave and dashing and unmarried in his forties, Edward had a history of inappropriate love interests. His flames included an American who had been divorced once and separated once, and a married woman, before he finally took up with the American-born, previously divorced Wallis Simpson, who was still married for a second time. Simpson quickly procured a divorce, but by early December of 1936 her affair with the heir had become a public scandal. As titular head of the Church of England, Edward was barred from official marriage to a divorced commoner. But he had few other options if he chose to maintain his relationship: The Conservative coalition government ruled out the idea of a morganatic marriage (with a spouse of lesser rank, where any children could not succeed to the throne). Edward himself ruled out the idea of a royal mistress. Unable to deal with his double life, he signed a declaration of abdication on December 10, 1936, then married Ms. Simpson the following year in a ceremony boycotted by all the royals. His brother ascended the throne in his place.

Shortly after George VI's coronation in early 1937, Stanley Baldwin, who had headed the national coalition Cabinet for two years, was replaced as Prime Minister by another Conservative leader, Neville Chamberlain. Although Chamberlain's role in the appeasement of Hitler is well known, and came in the postwar period to stand as a symbol of an inappropriate policy when faced with an ambitious dictator, at the time only Winston Churchill appeared to think that appeasement was a serious mistake. Chamberlain reasonably feared that Britain, having failed to rearm sufficiently, could not follow through on any threat that it might make, and therefore should not threaten Hitler but placate him. In March of 1938, Hitler's troops occupied Austria, solidifying the amalgamation of the two countries with a trumped-up popular referendum.

When Hitler called for the annexation of that part of Czechoslovakia called the Sudetenland in 1938 – home to, among others, the "Sudeten Germans" –

Chamberlain personally flew to Munich to meet with Hitler to try to preserve the peace. Chamberlain's own writings betray a combination of regret and doubt about the course he was taking, but he returned from the Munich conference proclaiming "peace with honour." At the same time, fearing that Hitler was a madman, Chamberlain tried (unsuccessfully) to negotiate a series of interlocking defense pacts, and successfully bolstered both supply to the army and the size of the Territorial Army, Britain's volunteer reserve forces. As it happened, the peace with honor was very short; it was broken by the German invasion of Poland on September 1, 1939. Chamberlain issued an ultimatum to Hitler to remove his troops from Poland, and delayed as long as he could before declaring war, waiting for the French to join England; but finally he could wait no longer, and war was declared on September 3.

The 20 years between the end of the First World War and the beginning of the Second had begun to illustrate tradition's inability to contain new problems. When unemployment was structural, an outcome of Britain's aging industrial plant and declining trade with its empire, and hunger marchers wearing blankets were closing in on London from the industrial North, the gold standard and free trade were untenable. When Irish and Indian nationalists were willing to, respectively, take up arms against Britain and sacrifice themselves nonviolently, their determination called into question the notion that Empire was somehow good for the colonized. When the League of Nations demonstrated the limitations of internationalism, dictatorial expansionism eliminated isolationism as an option. Successive governments were reacting rather than acting. With the declaration of war, the crisis of confidence ended.

Note

1   Bondfield's appointment predated by several years Franklin Roosevelt's assignment of
    the post of Secretary of Labor to the first woman Cabinet secretary in the US, Frances
    Perkins.

References

Baldwin, Stanley (1924) What England Means to Me. At http://whatenglandmeanstome
    .co.uk/?page_id=121 (accessed Dec. 15, 2010).
Beltran, Concha (2005) Natural Resources, Electrification, and Economic Growth from the
    End of the Nineteenth Century until World War II. *Revista de Historia Economica*, 23
    (1): 46–79.
Carey, John (ed.) (1987) *Eyewitness to History.* New York: Avon.
Eichengreen, Barry (1987) Unemployment in Interwar Britain: Dole or Doldrums? *Oxford
    Economic Papers*, n.s., 39 (4): 597–623.

Garside, W.R. (1985) The Failure of the "Radical Alternative": Public Works, Deficit Finance and British Interwar Unemployment. *Journal of European Economic History*, 14 (3): 537–555.

Garside, W.R. (1987) Public Works and Mass Unemployment: Britain's Response in a European Perspective, 1919–1939. *Archiv für Sozialgeschichte*, 27.

Hatton, T.J., and Bailey, R.E. (1988) Female Labour Force Participation in Interwar Britain. *Oxford Economic Papers*, n.s., 40 (4): 695–715.

Mowat, Charles Loch (1968) *Britain between the Wars*. Cambridge: Cambridge: University Press.

Norris, Jacob (2008) Repression and Rebellion: Britain's Response to the Arab Revolt in Palestine of 1936–1939. *Journal of Imperial and Commonwealth History*, 36 (1): 25–45.

Rubinstein, William D. (2003) *Twentieth-Century Britain: A Political History*. London: Palgrave Macmillan.

Scott, Peter (2000) Women, Other "Fresh" Workers, and the New Manufacturing Workforce of Interwar Britain. *International Review of Social History*, 45: 449–474.

Scott, Peter (2007) Consumption, Consumer Credit and the Diffusion of Consumer Durables. In Francesca Carnevali and Julie-Marie Strange (eds), *Twentieth-Century Britain: Economic, Cultural and Social Change*. Harlow: Pearson Longman.

Thane, P.M. (1990) The "Menace" of an Aging Population. *Continuity and Change*, 5 (2): 283–305.

Whitehead, J.W.R., and Carr, Christine M.H. (1999) England's Interwar Suburban Landscapes: Myth and Reality. *Journal of Historical Geography*, 25 (4): 483–501.

Further Reading

Carnevali, Francesca, and Strange, Julie-Marie (eds) (2007) *Twentieth-Century Britain: Economic, Cultural and Social Change*. Harlow: Longman.

DeGroot, Gerard (1999) A Lost Generation? The Impact of the First World War. *Modern History Review*, 11 (1): 18–21.

Fisher, Tim (2005) Fatherhood and the British Fathercraft Movement, 1919–1939. *Gender and History*, 17 (2): 441–462.

Hardy, Dennis (1992) Utopian Communities in Britain in the Early Twentieth Century: The Example of New Town. *Communal Societies*, 12 (1): 90–112.

Jeremy, Paul (1977) Life on Circular 703: The Crisis of Destitution in the South Wales Coalfield during the Lockout of 1926. *Llafur: The Journal of the Society for the Study of Welsh Labour History*, 2 (2): 65–75.

Johnson, Paul (ed.) (1994) *Twentieth Century Britain: Economic, Social and Cultural Change*. Harlow: Longman.

Moss, Norman (2003) *19 Weeks*. New York: Houghton Mifflin.

Mullay, A.J. (2003) Off the Rails: The Scottish General Strike, 1926. *History Scotland* (Nov.–Dec.): 28–36.

Pugh, Martin (1999) *State and Society: A Social and Political History of Britain*. London: Oxford University Press.

Pugh, Martin (2006) The General Strike. *History Today*, 56 (5): 40–47.
SarDesai, S.R. (2008) *India: The Definitive History*. Boulder: Westview.
Sheridan, Dorothy (1984) Mass Observing the British. *History Today*, 34 (4): 42–46.
Tabili, Laura (1994) *We Ask for British Justice: Workers and Racial Difference in Late Imperial Britain*. New York: Cornell University Press.

10

Culture and Ideas between the Wars, 1919–1939

Vera Brittain defied her middle-class, provincial family's expectations. Although her parents' hopes firmly focused on her brother, and she was expected to be little more than an ornamental middle-class wife, she applied to and was accepted to an Oxford University women's college on a scholarship. She also fell in love with Roland Leighton, the son of a well-known London literary family, and they had a brief and romantic courtship. Leighton left England to fight in the First World War, and in 1915 he was killed just when he was supposed to be coming home on a Christmas leave. As a tribute to the sacrifice that Roland had made, Brittain spent the rest of the war as a Volunteer Aid Detachment (VAD) nurse in England, Malta, and France. She threw herself into her work, lived in spartan and uncomfortable conditions, and sought out the most grueling labor, changing bedpans and unpleasant dressings in the hope of feeling some kind of redemption. At the very least she hoped to cleanse herself of survivor's guilt.

Roland Leighton was not the last young man Vera Brittain lost in the war. By 1918, he had been joined in death by Brittain's beloved brother Edward, and by two of her best male friends, one of whom had been blinded and whom she had agreed to marry out of a sense of duty. War's end left her with nothing; she had been robbed not only of her loved ones, but also of her sense of direction. Ultimately, she became a writer and a crusader for internationalism, and although she felt as though most of the joy in her life had died along with the casualties of the First World War, she intended her future activities to stand as monument to those who were lost. Her memoir *Testament of Youth*, published in 1933, illustrates the way in which Britons grappled with the great losses of that war and tried to move on.

The First World War had been demographically devastating for Europe. Although Vera Brittain experienced exceptional personal losses, the cenotaphs that still dot many British villages and towns remind us that the experience of loss was

Empire, State, and Society: Britain Since 1830, First Edition. Jamie L. Bronstein and Andrew T. Harris.
© 2012 Jamie L. Bronstein and Andrew T. Harris. Published 2012 by John Wiley & Sons, Ltd.

felt everywhere. A full decade passed before the wounds of wartime healed enough to address these issues in full-length fiction and memoir. For many postwar writers, the war had forced a rethinking about the nature of patriotism and the advisability of war as a means of foreign policy. Many who had fought and survived were disillusioned about the Victorian generation that had sent its young men to die in heaps on the fields of Belgium and France. In contrast, those who had lost relatives in the war wanted to believe that their sacrifices had had a purpose and would not be forgotten, and so the themes of mourning and loyalty to the dead were common in short stories published in the popular press (Korte and Einhaus 2004).

Robert Graves, who was born in 1895 to a family of substantial pedigree, and educated in English public schools, volunteered to join the army in 1914, shortly after he was accepted to St John's College, Oxford. He was commissioned as a lieutenant, served on the Western Front, and was wounded twice. He also witnessed other men collapse mentally under the strains of constant shelling. Like the American Civil War memoirist Samuel Watkins, whose *Company Aytch* mixed autobiographical war memoir with fictional and humorous elements, Graves incorporated ironic or funny anecdotes into his writing. Also like Watkins, his purpose in melding fact and fiction was to achieve the distance necessary to critique those who sent the troops into war in the first place, sacrificing so much for what turned out to be so little. Graves's memoir and those of others of his generation helped to advance the idea of the war participants as a "lost generation," bound together by their experiences in ways that literally could not be comprehended by those who had not been in the trenches (Lunn 2005).

During the war, women had had many new opportunities to participate in war work and patriotic efforts that had previously only been open to men. Whereas many middle-class women had experienced isolating prewar lives, war work allowed them to bond together with other women. In wartime and the immediate postwar period, literature reflected that excitement, although not without controversy. Women authors like Virginia Woolf, Vita Sackville-West, and Radclyffe Hall included lesbian protagonists in their literary works or wrote openly about their lives and relationships. Hall's novel *The Well of Loneliness* (1928), which describes the life and relationships of a "sexual invert," was prosecuted for obscenity in both Britain and the United States. Woolf outlined a feminist writers' project in a series of lectures in 1929 at Cambridge University's two women's colleges. She sketched out a long history of women writing, and conveyed the need for every woman who aspired to write to have "a room of her own" and the time to study and concentrate (Gilbert 1983). Coming a decade after many women gained the right to vote, Woolf's emphasis on economic independence makes the point that political participation was only part of modern feminism.

In addition to leading to attempts to grapple with the legacy of the war and a reevaluation of gender roles, the Great War accelerated prewar artistic and literary rejections of tradition. The Bloomsbury Group of writers and artists noted earlier embodied this reaction from the turn of the century to the start of the Second

World War. Roger Fry and Clive Bell continued to bring awareness of modern art to Britain, including movements like Cubism, which portrayed various viewpoints on a single object simultaneously, Surrealism, which embraced images from dreams or from the subconscious, and Expressionism, which used exaggerations of color and shape in order to heighten the emotions of viewers. Sculptors like Henry Moore and Barbara Hepworth reduced the figures that they each sculpted into mere suggestions of the human form: for Hepworth, a "mother and child" might be a smooth alabaster pebble nestled in the curve of another piece of alabaster. Jacob Epstein sparked controversy with a sculpture that melded a stocky, pregnant female body with a head like a concave African mask; one of his sculptures, installed in a public park, was so controversial that it was repeatedly vandalized. All of these modern art movements demanded more of the viewer than did the more standard representational visual art of the nineteenth century, and some viewers were uncomfortable with these new expectations.

Literary modernism also courted controversy. It disrupted popular expectations: poets wrote verse that did not rhyme, and novels had broken, nonsequential narratives. Virginia Woolf's novel *Orlando* follows the adventures of the title character from the Elizabethan era to Woolf's present, with the protagonist not only living hundreds of years, but also experiencing a change of gender along the way. James Joyce's *Ulysses* mixes the events of a single day with the narrator's own interior monologue, creating an unusually challenging reading experience. Modernist writers made heavy use of symbolism and streams of consciousness, and allowed different narrators to retell the same story in their own voices within a single work. Nineteenth-century novels had been plot-driven; modernist novels sometimes required that the reader labor mightily to discover what the plot actually was.

These writers spanned the spectrum of political beliefs. T.S. Eliot, a major modernist poet and author of the most famous poem of the interwar period, *The Waste Land*, became extremely conservative after 1927 and gravitated toward both fascism and anti-Semitism. In contrast, many of the modernist authors remained politically progressive, including Julian Bell, John Cornford, W.H. Auden, and Stephen Spender. These four saw the Spanish Civil War (1936–1939) as an epic clash of civilizations played out on a diplomatic stage, and traveled to Spain to participate in the conflict, either to fight, or to observe and report. So many artists participated in the Spanish Civil War that Stephen Spender called it the "poets' war."

Although many literary modernists produced works that became part of the canon of great literature, their works had less appeal to the masses than did "middlebrow fiction" by writers such as J.B. Priestley, Winifred Holtby, and Hugh Walpole. Detective novels written by Agatha Christie and Dorothy Sayers gained widespread popularity as readers guessed the murderer from hints dropped in earlier chapters. Family magazines for the middle classes that dated back to the nineteenth century also remained popular. The interwar period saw an explosion of interest in amateur writing; middle-class aspiring writers formed "writers' circles" in many major cities, writing for commercial outlets or for privately circulated handmade magazines. Self-taught members of the working classes had their own intellectual culture, reading poetry and fiction that appeared in journals like *New Writing*, attending night classes, and writing their own works (Hilliard 2005).

If the average interwar Briton read anything on a daily basis, it was likely to be the newspaper. Each newspaper had its own presumed audience and political slant. *The Times* remained the newspaper of record. The *Morning Post* was conservative and government focused; the *Manchester Guardian* was liberal, and the *Daily Telegraph* focused on commerce. The *Daily Mail*, while not yet considered a working-class newspaper, appealed to women and children, and was the closest thing in Britain to the kind of "yellow journalism" that had become prevalent among the American newspapers owned by William Randolph Hearst. Committed left-wingers could choose between the *Daily Worker* and the *Daily Herald*.

While modernist art and literature achieved a foothold in Britain in the interwar period, modernist architecture found much less favor. Civic architecture under construction was still designed in the classical style; actual modernist architecture was incorporated into public buildings mainly by a few continental architects (like Walter Gropius) who migrated to England. Architects designing private houses gravitated toward Tudor and Arts and Crafts forms. Some cinemas and hotels incorporated elements of Art Deco during the 1930s, as did much interior decor and furniture, continuing that movement's influence from before the war.

Leisure and Sport

While "high culture" – dance, the opera, art museums, modernist literature – had its place, "mass culture" continued its ascendancy in the interwar period, aided by an increasing ethos of government responsibility for popular recreation and leisure. New geographic spaces opened for mass leisure. Parks, swimming baths, sports fields, and lawn-bowling greens were established by local government. Some leisure opportunities thus appealed to people of widely divergent class origins and skill levels. Voluntary organizations like trade unions had their own leisure-time activities and even ran their own vacation camps for working-class families. The first "theme parks" were established in the interwar period, as were commercial resorts like Butlin's, which provided all-inclusive vacations with schedules packed with activities.

But while the space for leisure was growing, time had still not caught up. Most manual workers needed to work constantly and earn wages in order to support themselves, making vacations an unaffordable luxury. Vacations with pay were only guaranteed with the 1938 Holiday with Pay Act, which even then only legislated that workers receive three consecutive days off.

The enjoyment of leisure also varied with a worker's age and gender. As long as they were employed, young men and women who were not yet married had the most disposable income to spend on enjoyments like dancing and the movies. They also spent money on "flash" clothing, and promenaded up and down to see and be seen. Married men, whether they turned over their pay packets to their wives or doled out money for "housekeeping," held back some amount that they used for such entertainments as smoking, gambling, and buying drinks at the pub. Working-class men also patronized activities like "all-in," or no-holds-barred wrestling, which had very few rules and were seen as disreputable by the more affluent. Working-class women had the fewest opportunities for leisure time. Their workday had no boundaries; their leisure activities were often limited to informal socialization with neighbors while performing outdoor chores. Even when working-class families saved up enough money to enjoy an annual holiday at the seaside, women continued to perform their regular cooking and cleaning roles.

The possession of a private space for recreation defined leisure for the middle classes. Middle-class women's leisure centered on novels, the home, and on informal entertaining featuring card games like whist and contract bridge. Middle-class men took to gardening and home repair; and for those who didn't have sufficient property to grow a garden, some towns and cities provided allotments that people could rent and cultivate. Bowls and lawn tennis became popular activities. The theater was also a social obligation for members of the urban middle and upper classes, and the playwrights who had been most popular before the First World War – particularly George Bernard Shaw – were still in vogue. The young comic actor Noel Coward began writing plays in the 1920s, and by 1925 had four plays running simultaneously in London's West End. Coward later became an extremely popular songwriter, and both wrote and appeared in films during the Second World War. Provincial theaters emerged, spreading the opportunity for both increased theatergoing and amateur theatricals.

Middle-class children who could afford them had new toys to play with, and yo-yos and roller-skating became popular. Teenagers tended to remain in school rather than work; they thus had little disposable income to participate in commercialized leisure activities, but the Boy Scouts and Girl Guides were still popular, and had been joined by the Boys' Brigade and the Girls' Life Brigade. By the 1930s, a fad for hiking spread into Britain from both Germany and the United States, youth hostels sprouted to accommodate hikers, and railroad companies took advantage of the new interest with inclusive touring packages. Immersion in rural Britain and its historical relics provided young people with an alternative, romantic, non-modern way of thinking about Britishness. Ironically, residents of rural Britain saw the influx of urban and suburban hikers by train as an unhappy sign of modernity (Trentmann 1994).

The wealthy could afford to participate in such sports as golf, cricket, and tennis, practiced at private clubs rather than on municipal greens. Many leisure activities still centered on the country house: hunting, shooting, and fishing required access to land, emphasized the ownership of land, and provided important rural employment. Such leisure activities were purposely expensive: hunting, for example, required stables, horses and feed, the care and maintenance of hounds, not to mention quite expensive clothing. The hunt balls associated with hunting parties demonstrated (or at least attempted to demonstrate) the country gentry and aristocracy's enduring leadership of rural society. For those members of the upper classes more fascinated by the trappings of modernity, disposable income purchased the costly equipment for yachting, car races, or airplane races. Although women increasingly figured among hunting parties and were spectators at some of the more notable horse-races, for the most part aristocratic leisure consisted of the outdoor activities of aristocratic men.

Some leisure activities, like gambling, were enjoyed by Britons irrespective of social class. Daily newspapers reported on horse-racing, which was popular with all audiences. Greyhound racing, imported from the United States, provided the working classes with the opportunity to watch as well as bet on races, since unlike horse racing, dog racing took place outside working hours. Football pools were the most controversial, giving rise to allegations that bookmakers engaged in profit-seeking attempts to fix matches; but it was impossible to prevent tens of thousands of working people from filling out football pool coupons weekly. Clubs, charities, and even the Irish government ran sweepstakes that attracted British bets (although interest in the Irish lottery was so strong that the British government finally forbade participation in foreign lotteries). A strong, largely nonconformist, antigambling lobby loudly protested at the immorality of gambling, but it was a subject on which there was no national consensus. As a result, money spent on legal gambling rose from 1.3 percent of individuals' total discretionary income to 5 percent in 1938 – from £63 million to £221 million (Huggins 2007b).

Interwar Britons were also united in their increased interest in recorded music, propelled by the availability of the gramophone and records – in 1930, 780,000 gramophones and almost 30 million records were produced. British audiences heard American jazz and dance music for the first time, helping to nurture what became an ongoing transatlantic musical connection between the two countries. The ability to listen to professional musicians on a whim in dance halls and on the radio downgraded the role of musical performance within the household, and the number of people who played music for their own and others' enjoyment dropped sharply.

Dance halls played jazz and dance music, and became a favorite venue for the activities of young working people, as music halls had been in previous decades. The "flapper" style emerged; women wore shorter skirts and cloche hats, left behind their whalebone corsets, and bound up their chests instead in order to achieve the desirable androgynous look. For the first time, stylish British women inherited from visiting American women the practice of wearing lipstick and rouge.

The interwar period also saw the invention and embellishment of certain twentieth-century musical traditions. The Promenade concerts – featuring light classical music and relatively low ticket prices – had been established in the late 1890s as a way of filling London's new concert venue, the Queen's Hall. Henry J. Wood became a beloved British institution; not only did he compose one of Britain's most durable patriotic medleys, "British Sea Songs" (composed to commemorate the centenary of Admiral Horatio Nelson's victory at Trafalgar), he also conducted the "Proms" from 1893 to 1944. The concerts were eventually christened the Henry Wood Promenade Concerts in his honor (Cannadine 2008). Interest in the folk music and older dance traditions of England also crystallized. In the late nineteenth century Cecil Sharp began to collect ancient folk songs and forms of Morris dancing from the few troupes that still practiced it. Before the Great War, he had begun to teach these forms to young people. By the 1930s, folk-dance classes were held weekly in London, and the English Folk Dance Society attracted large crowds at public demonstrations.

The cultural meaning of sport was changing as well. In the late nineteenth century, sports had been viewed as an essential element in the development of character for gentlemen amateurs. Eventually, sport became a well-financed form of athletic excellence confined to professionals. Different sports made the transition to professionalism at different rates, and some never quite got there at all. Cricket was still assumed to inculcate certain good personality characteristics that had made it a staple of nineteenth-century English public schools: teamwork, fair play, and sportsmanship. Many upper-class Britons also upheld the distinction between gentleman amateurs and professional players, the latter of whom were presumed to be working class. Professional players were often expected to perform ancillary tasks, including maintaining the landscaping of the cricket grounds. Amateurs – entirely of the middle and upper classes – still captained English county teams, because their presence on teams was thought to encourage civilized play. Almost all cricket pitches in England had separate entrances and changing rooms for "gentlemen" as contrasted with "players" (Williams 2006). Cricket still held a certain importance for the way in which, as a particularly British export, it culturally bound together the British Empire. Teams from Australia, New Zealand, the West Indies, and South Africa came to Britain to tour and play, and the English team traveled abroad (Tadis 2010). This indicated more than just a common appreciation for the game, since cricket in the interwar period was inextricable from its roots as an English game, symbolizing correct deportment, behavior, and loyalty to the mother country.

Another class-stratified game, rugby football, was extraordinarily popular in the 1920s. Officials heading the Rugby Football Union were eager to keep the game as it had been since the late nineteenth century: a preserve of the amateur, in which specific training was ungentlemanly, and paid coaching was banned. Rugby differed from soccer in that all players could handle the (oval-shaped) ball, although the only means of advancing the ball were by kicking it or running with it. The

Northern Rugby Football Union, which renamed itself the Rugby League in 1922, featured a rougher, more full-contact and faster version of the sport. Professional players appeared first in the industrial towns of the Northeast, where economic competitiveness and striving meritocracy were more accepted.

Soccer, referred to as "football" or "association football," was not as popular as rugby in the interwar period. It was an international game, with play centered on the North of England. Before the advent of the World Cup, championship soccer was played at the Olympics. Although Britain didn't participate in the soccer World Cup until 1950, its teams were beginning to compete in Europe and elsewhere in the 1930s and the Scotland–England match drew great interest. Association football's culture of professionalism meant that it was still a sport for working-class players and spectators.

Intellectual Currents

The interwar period saw great intellectual ferment. The Great War had undermined the family, gender roles, and the leadership position of the aristocracy; now it put pressure on the certainties of the nineteenth-century sciences and humanities. Philosophy provides a good example. Nineteenth-century British philosophers had tended to be "Idealists," arguing that interpretation influenced, and was inextricable from, human understanding of the nature of the thing perceived. Furthermore, everything in the universe had a relation to everything else, and it was impossible to understand anything without comprehending its relationship to all other objects.

In contrast with these "Idealistic" philosophers, emerging twentieth-century analytical philosophers argued that philosophy was a science. The complex world could be simplified into separate, atomistic concepts, just as scientists disaggregated the world into atoms. G.E. Moore, one of the first important twentieth-century British analytical philosophers, had no patience for metaphysical questions of the kind that the Idealist philosophers had asked. He argued that he knew that he existed, that the world existed, and that consciousness existed, all of which gave him a platform from which to support the idea that the world was strictly material. In a material world, what was best for everyone were efforts, like cultivating love and friendship, that maximized good consequences. Moore's philosophies, particularly his 1903 work *Principia Ethica*, powerfully influenced the Bloomsbury Group of writers and artists noted earlier.

Bertrand Russell, Moore's philosophical colleague at Cambridge, argued that every proposition had to be derived from "particulars," or things with which people had direct experience. Russell proposed that, just as every substance was composed of atoms, everything that could be said could be reduced, or dissected, into component "atomic facts." Each atomic fact described some attribute of a particular object, or described the relationship of two particular objects toward each other. Russell was also known for his position as part of the antiwar and later antinuclear movements, and also for winning the Nobel Prize in Literature for works such as his engagingly written *History of Western Philosophy*.

The idea of atomic facts was further refined by Russell's student Ludwig Wittgenstein. After participating in the Great War, Wittgenstein emigrated from Austria to Britain. He proposed that every statement could be broken down into elementary propositions which stood in some relation to each other. These elementary propositions were either true or untrue and could be built up into complex true or false propositions using words like "and" and "not." Propositions could then be represented in "truth tables" that gave philosophy the appearance of mathematics. Wittgenstein's theory became the cornerstone of the idea of logical positivism: that philosophy could (and should) only analyze things which were verifiable by experience.

If philosophy confined itself to the scientific study of atomic facts, then little room existed within the discipline to explore traditional concerns like ethics. British logical positivist philosopher A.J. Ayer argued that moral statements about right and wrong were simply the expression of the emotions of a given speaker, and that there was no way to evaluate or decide between moral systems. As a result, he consigned questions about religion and ultimate meaning to the realm of nonsense or mysticism. Strictly speaking, a moral statement such as "You ought not to kill innocent children" was meaningless (Jones and Fogelin 1980: 270). The enormous atrocities of the Second World War suggested later that this turn away from ethics was profoundly unhelpful, although at the time it had adherents of good faith and considerable intellectual weight.

Economics as well as philosophy underwent a sea change. Writing at the intersection of both disciplines, John Maynard Keynes was one of the most important British public intellectuals in the interwar period. In response to the Versailles conference that ended the First World War, he penned *The Economic Consequences of the Peace* (1919), which warned that if German reparations payments were set at too high a level, Germany would plunge into economic depression. In turn, this would ensure that the first democracy established in German history – the Weimar republic – was undermined at its very inception. Keynes turned out to be prescient, since the economic pressure placed on Germany by the wartime settlement resulted in hyperinflation, leading to Weimar's ultimate collapse and the attraction of many Germans to Adolf Hitler's National Socialism.

After the Great Depression of 1929 struck, Keynes proposed that an appropriate response to the crisis was government spending on jobs and other programs, since free markets (and the markets of the 1920s had been almost completely unregulated) could not be trusted to restore order. The government should pay workers, who would spend their money on goods and services, and through the multiplier effect, the impact of government spending would be even greater than its original scope. This would "prime the pump" for national recovery. Keynesian economics based on this kind of state spending became a mainstay of government policy, first in the United States and then later in Britain, from the 1930s until the late 1970s.

Political, social, and economic issues reached a wider audience in the interwar era with the advent of the Left Book Club. English publisher Victor Gollancz in 1936 began publishing a series of books intended to raise awareness about political and social issues. By 1948, a total of 257 books had been published, and 1,200 related discussion groups formed throughout the country. Members of the club paid a modest sum to receive the annual selections, which covered topics ranging from tracts on the alleviation of British poverty to oppositional histories of Italy, Nazi Germany, and the Soviet Union and support for the Spanish Civil War. The individual book clubs hired halls, produced their own newsletters, and facilitated film and lecture series, further projecting the Left Book Club's influence (Neavill 1971).

British science flourished in the interwar period, with particular dominance in the field of medicine. J.J.R. Macleod, a Scottish physiologist, studied carbohydrates and carbohydrate metabolism. Along with the Canadian researchers Frederick Banting and Charles Best, Macleod discovered that injections of insulin could provide a way of managing diabetes, which until then had been a fatal illness. British medical research also resulted in the discovery of neurons (nerve cells) and their method of operation; an understanding of the way in which muscles performed work; the discovery of trace substances necessarily for the maintenance of good health, dubbed "vitamins"; and the chemical substances used in nerve transmission. Outside the field of medical research, the Scottish meteorologist Charles Thomson Rees Wilson won the Nobel Prize for his invention of the cloud chamber, and James Chadwick won for discovering the first subatomic particle, the neutron. Sir John Cockcroft and the Irish scientist Ernest Walton gained recognition for their experiments in changing an atom of one substance into another by bombarding the atom's nucleus. Discoveries about the nature of the ionosphere led to the development of radar, which proved crucial in the defeat of the Luftwaffe during the Second World War.

Scientists in Britain were also involved in the explorations that led to the development of nuclear weapons. Refugee scientists Rudolf Peierls and Otto Frisch, working in Birmingham in 1940, determined the amount of uranium needed for an atomic bomb, but Britain lacked the resources to commit to nuclear development once the decision had been made to pursue the bomb. As a result, despite the early British lead in the theoretical development of nuclear weapons, the American government assumed the larger role in an unequal nuclear partnership. At Los Alamos, New Mexico, site of the Manhattan Project, the British delegation included many of the top theoretical physicists from Central Europe, who had fled under pressure from the Nazis (Lee 2006).

Some science was pseudoscience, as assumptions about racial, cultural, and class superiority influenced its agenda. J.B.S. Haldane and other geneticists followed the agenda of "reform eugenics." They viewed human potential as the interaction of both heredity and environment, but they still hoped to engineer better humans. Some argued for the sterilization of the "feeble minded;" others for widespread education and a meritocracy which allowed people from the working classes to rise. Interwar eugenics was linked to the development of birth control, since there was alarm that the "least fit" in British society were having more children than those of superior racial stock and social class. It was also linked to concerns about declining national greatness; aliens who might amalgamate their stock with those of the English were particularly feared (Stone 2001).

Anxieties about the dominant scientific outlook were expressed in literature. Aldous Huxley, grandson of the nineteenth-century biologist Thomas Henry Huxley, wrote *Brave New World*, a work whose title has come to serve as short-hand for everything that might go wrong through the use of scientific technology. Huxley conjured up what to us appears to be a dystopian future, in which genetic engineering using artificial wombs, happiness drugs, mass production (the residents of the Brave New World calculate the year in terms of "Our Ford") and sleep-learning combine to produce a contented and hierarchical populace. A proponent of eugenics, Huxley found the rise of mass consumer culture depressing, and doubted that democracy had a future in a world in which the vast majority of the population simply wanted to keep their heads down and be told what to do.

The talented essayist Eric Blair, writing under the pen-name George Orwell, also looked to the future with cynicism, and though a socialist, he directed some of his strongest criticisms toward fellow British socialists and left-wing movements abroad. His *Road to Wigan Pier* evoked the social conditions of the Northern poor during Britain's Great Depression. He interlaced his descriptive observations with an argument for inclusive socialism, at the same time lambasting what he saw as the limiting British socialist tendency to adopt every alternative lifestyle and ignore basic questions of social justice and decency. *Homage to Catalonia* (1938) was a tribute to the men and women then sacrificing their lives as part of the left wing in the Spanish Civil War, and is acknowledged even in Spain as one of the most accurate expressions of that conflict. Set in the form of a barnyard tale, *Animal Farm* (1945) translated recent Soviet history into a fable starring animals: pigs foment a revolution against people, and for a while there is equality; but then the pigs realize the benefits of bureaucracy, and soon some animals are "more equal than others" (Besancon 1984). After the war, he wrote his most famous novel, *1984* (1949), a chronicle of a chilling future of industrial decay, in which "Big Brother" watched every person's movements through a ubiquitous telescreen, criminal thoughts as well as actions were prosecuted, history was rewritten on a daily basis, and words were redefined under the aegis of the state. Huxley's and Orwell's works betray the ambiguity and discomfort of interwar culture, a discomfort with technology, mass political organization and individualism, that go back to the nineteenth century.

Mass Culture and Broadcasting

Rebellion against Victorian trends was not the only factor leading cultural pundits to wonder where Britain was headed. The twentieth century saw an incredible transformation in the types of media available for the transmission of culture. Because they were largely national, broadcast media provided common cultural experiences across class, could educate and entertain, and helped to break down regional cultural and dialectic barriers. This accelerated a process already underway in the print media, as the national press's circulation began to exceed that of the local press. Broadcast media also provided a wider audience with access to the news, but structured that access in ways that limited alternate viewpoints (for example, radio and television presenters were less likely to air the opinions of radicals than of members of government or the judiciary). Broadcast media encouraged the development of a consumer culture, although that produced costs as well as benefits.

The first broadcast medium of importance in Britain was radio. John Reith was appointed general manager of the privately owned British Broadcasting Company in 1922, and in 1927 it became a state-run monopoly. British radio was nationally broadcast using a system of regional relays, and it was also noncommercial, in contrast with the United States, where radio had been both local and supported through advertising from its inception. In the 1920s, possession of a radio set was still unusual. Young (and almost always male) hobbyists built crystal sets that required painstaking tuning in to get a signal at all. Many people engaged in communal listening at pubs, clubs, workplaces, or even piped into the streets through public address systems. By the 1930s, radio ownership became more prevalent, although fewer people owned their own radio sets in Northern Ireland and the North of England than in the South and the Midlands.

Lord Reith envisioned the BBC as a platform for broadcasting important occasions like sermons and royal addresses, but also hoped that the radio could be used to provide culturally uplifting entertainment, and to inculcate values of cultural appreciation at the same time. The BBC rotated the times of regular programs in order to force the listener to schedule his listening; and programs were regularly separated by periods of silence to allow the listener to reflect on what he or she had just heard. The exception to the constantly changing schedule was *Children's Hour*, a 30-minute program featuring radio "Aunties" and "Uncles" telling stories to a child audience.

Like all broadcast media, radio had the potential to elevate the importance of particular events. Almost from its inception, the BBC experimented with broadcasting sports like rugby matches and the Oxford and Cambridge University Boat Race. Producers included crowd noise to give the listener the feeling of being there, and broadcasters followed the eights in a launch equipped with an aerial, attempting to provide commentary. Regional relay stations began to broadcast their own local sports events, and national broadcasts expanded to include events as diverse as tennis at Wimbledon, motor racing, skeet (or clay) shooting, table tennis, darts, and snooker. Sports became favorite listening material for those who could not afford to attend matches in person, joining variety shows, light music, and serialized theater as the favorite programs enjoyed by listeners in the 1930s (Huggins 2007a). The BBC's weekly *Radio Times,* a guide to programming, reached a circulation of around 3 million by the end of the 1930s. In contrast, although invented in the interwar period, television was still a very limited medium, numbering its viewers as yet only in the tens of thousands.

Film was the other new mass medium of the interwar period. Most films shown in Britain originated in Hollywood, where the film industry was well developed and well financed; the British film industry accounted for only about 10 percent of the films screened in Britain in the 1920s. Audiences gravitated toward cartoons, Westerns, and romantic films starring such luminaries as Rudolf Valentino and Theda Bara. In 1927, however, Parliament passed the Cinematograph Films Act, requiring that a certain percentage of films screened originate in Britain, the percentage to increase annually thereafter. The idea behind this was not particularly economic – rather, it was felt that British culture itself would suffer without films that reflected British values. This aim was largely frustrated, however, since British filmmakers responded with cheaply and easily made "quota quickies" to make up the required percentage of domestic films, which were normally shown in conjunction with better-made American feature films. Despite the low quality of many of the films, the government's action is recognized as having nurtured the film industry, providing the opportunity for young aspiring film workers to learn the trade (Jarvie 2006).

British cinemas boomed in the 1930s as unemployed people turned to the ever changing program at their local theater for an escape. Among better-off people, too, the cinema was a popular form of entertainment. There were movie theaters for everyone: picture palaces like the Odeon for the middle classes; stripped-down "fleapit" theaters costing less than sixpence for admission for those who could not afford luxury. By 1939 there were 4,800 cinemas in Britain, up from 3,000 in 1926.

Interwar cinemagoing marked a break with the everyday, and, in its own way, was a group experience. Picture palaces featured gloved ushers holding flashlights and shepherding patrons to velvet seats; more modest showing rooms in industrial warehouses had a rowdy atmosphere and patrons could buy potato chips. Audiences sometimes had sing-alongs. Cinema could be escapist, but it could also be educational. News Cinemas provided a 90-minute, varied program of news, features, and cartoons, at a low admission price. By the later 1930s British studios had elevated three performers to stardom: Gracie Fields, George Formby, and Jessie Matthews. They had also begun to carve out a niche for themselves in the genre of the historical or imperial epic, as characters like Disraeli and Henry VIII were profiled in grand costume dramas. The age of the British Empire was waning, but the popular film *The Four Feathers* (1939) told the story of a young man rejected by his fiancé and given white feathers by his friends (a symbol of cowardice) when he refused to fight in the Sudan. He subsequently travels to the Sudan on his own and saves their skins, redeeming his own prior cowardice in the process. Such films helped to nurture a sense of nationhood and pride even in the twilight of imperial adventure.

Film sparked a more fraught cultural discussion than did radio, and the impact of American culture was not the only aspect of Hollywood that was discussed and feared. Cultural critics like F.R. Leavis talked about a cultural crisis, as high-quality leisure gave way to the lowest common elements of mass culture. The passivity of the moviegoing audience was one major objection; the nature of what was being shown was another. Between 1930 and 1933 the government took on the question of film censorship in response to concerns that children were being admitted to inappropriate films. The British Board of Film Censors, an advisory group formed in the late 1920s, took on a more active role, classifying films as either "U" (suitable for general audiences) or "A" (suitable for those over 16 years of age). By 1936, the British Film Institute was encouraging theaters to offer matinees with movies that catered especially for the child audience, with a preference for action films with happy endings and positive moral messages (Kuhn 2002).

British interwar culture and intellectual life was overlaid with economic depression and bracketed by the profound losses of the First World War and the mounting dread of an incipient Second World War. Britons nonetheless displayed vitality and innovation in the application of technology to leisure, in participation in and appreciation of new forms of entertainment and culture, and in the spread of leisure time itself. Though history now marks this as a distinctive period between two major international conflicts, it was for most Britons a time of new experiences: of radio, film, motorcycles, and American jazz music. These marked the further cultural integration of Britain – or at least the possibility of such, for easier communication and greater cultural homogeneity could produce a backlash as well as acceptance. In high and popular culture, in science, gender expectations, and the arts, the period between the wars drew on aesthetic, technological and social movements that predated the First World War and outlasted the Second.

References

Besancon, Alain (1984) Orwell in Our Time. *Survey*, 28 (1): 190–197.

Cannadine, David (2008) The "Last Night of the Proms" in Historical Perspective. *Historical Research*, 81 (212): 315–349.

Gilbert, Sandra M. (1983) Soldier's Heart: Literary Men, Literary Women, and the Great War. *Signs*, 8 (3): 422–450.

Hilliard, Christopher (2005) Modernism and the Common Writer. *Historical Journal*, 48 (3): 769–787.

Huggins, Mike (2007a) BBC Radio and Sport, 1922–1939. *Contemporary British History*, 21 (4): 491–315.

Huggins, Mike (2007b) Betting, Sport, and the British, 1918–1939. *Journal of Social History*, 41 (2): 283–306.

Jarvie, Ian (2006) Contributions to the Social and Economic History of British Cinema. *Historical Journal of Film, Radio and Television*, 28 (1): 111–120.

Jones, W.T., and Fogelin, Robert J. (1980) *A History of Western Philosophy: The Twentieth Century, to Quine and Derrida*. Fort Worth: Harcourt Brace.

Korte, Barbara, and Einhaus, Ann-Marie (2004) Short-Term Memories: The First World War in British Short Stories, 1914–1939. *Literature and History*, 18 (1): 54–66.

Kuhn, Annette (2002) Children, "Horrific" Films, and Censorship in 1930s Britain. *Historical Journal of Film, Radio, and Television*, 22 (2): 197–202.

Lee, Sabine (2006) "In No Sense Vital and Actually Not Even Important"? Reality and Perception of Britain's Contribution to the Development of Nuclear Weapons. *Contemporary British History*, 29 (2): 159–185.

Lunn, Joe (2005) Male Identity and Martial Codes of Honor: A Comparison of the War Memoirs of Robert Graves, Ernst Junger, and Kande Kamara. *Journal of Military History*, 69 (3): 713–735.

Neavill, Gordon Barrick (1971) Victor Gollancz and the Left Book Club. *Library Quarterly*, 41 (3): 197–215.

Stone, Dan (2001) Race in British Eugenics. *European History Quarterly*, 31 (3): 397–425.

Tadis, Alexis (2010) The Fictions of (English) Cricket: From Nation to Diaspora. *International Journal of the History of Sport*, 27 (4): 690–711.

Trentmann, Frank (1994) Civilization and Its Discontents: English Neo-Romanticism and the Transformation of Antimodernism in Twentieth-Century Western Culture. *Journal of Contemporary History*, 29 (4): 583–625.

Williams, Jack (2006) "The *Really* Good Professional Captain has *Never Been Seen!*" Perceptions of the Amateur/Professional Divide in County Cricket, 1900–1939. *Sport in History*, 26 (3): 429–449.

Further Reading

Carnevali, Francesca, and Strange, Julie-Marie (eds) (2007) *Twentieth-Century Britain: Economic, Cultural and Social Change*. Harlow: Longman.

Curran, James (2002) Media and the Making of British Society, c.1700–2000. *Media History*, 8 (2): 135–154.

Ford, Basil (1992) *Modern Britain: The Cambridge Cultural History*. Cambridge: Cambridge University Press.

Graves Robert, and Hodge, Alan (1963) *The Long Week-End: A Social History of Britain, 1919–1937*. New York: Norton.

Huggins, Mike (2008) Sport and the British Upper Classes, c.1500–2000: A Historiographic Overview. *Sport in History*, 28 (3): 364–388.

Ridgwell, Stephen (1996) The People's Amusement: Cinema and Cinema-Going in 1930s Britain. *Historian*, 52: 17–21.

Rosenbaum, S.P. (1981) Preface to a Literary History of the Bloomsbury Group. *New Literary History*, 12 (2): 329–344.

Suga, Yasuko (2006) Modernism, Commercialism, and Display Design in Britain. *Journal of Design History*, 19 (2): 137–153.

11

London Burning
Britain in the Second World War

It was September 1940, and the presence of German troops on the French border convinced 11-year-old Colin Ryder-Richardson's parents to send him from Wales to Canada, under the auspices of the Children's Overseas Reception Board. Ninety children boarded the ship *City of Benares*, but the Atlantic Ocean was full of German U-boats, and after four days at sea the ship was torpedoed. In his pajamas, struggling with the decision about whether his life jacket went on over or under his bathrobe, Colin was loaded into a lifeboat by the ship's nurse, in the midst of a Force 10 gale. In the freezing cold and wet, the occupants of the lifeboat began to die; but although the nurse herself appeared to be dead or dying, Colin was clinging to her hand, unable to let go. Eventually, he noted, the storm swept her away (Arthur 2004: 103). Of the 90 children on board the *City of Benares*, all but 13 died; Colin, one of the few survivors, was awarded a war medal for bravery by King George VI.

In contrast with the Great War, the Second World War came home to the British Isles in every sense of the word. The war required massive mobilization of soldiers, both in Britain and throughout its imperial possessions and dominions. But there was no "front line," since with the advent of more advanced air power and rocketry, the Luftwaffe, the German air force, could target homes and schools and churches in the South of England; and the German navy could make shipping channels into shooting galleries. Families were separated by the war once it became clear that city children would be safer in the countryside of northern England and Scotland. Successful prosecution of the war demanded a complete revamping of the workforce, bringing in both single and married women to work in war plants. Those who lived through the war often interpreted their wartime years as having changed the tone of British society. The shared sacrifice of wartime bred the expectation of a more egalitarian society after the war.

Empire, State, and Society: Britain Since 1830, First Edition. Jamie L. Bronstein and Andrew T. Harris.
© 2012 Jamie L. Bronstein and Andrew T. Harris. Published 2012 by John Wiley & Sons, Ltd.

Declaration of War

Hitler's decision to invade Poland, after having absorbed Austria and dismantled Czechoslovakia, led to a British declaration of war on September 3, 1939. In a rare radio address – rare because he suffered from a severe speech impediment – King George VI announced the decision to his people, at home and abroad, over the BBC. Britain had a responsibility, he explained, to defend a way of life lived without fear and without barbarism: this was a war about ideology. It was not an unexpected decision; fearing Hitler's intentions, Parliament had in the spring passed the Emergency Powers Act which gave the government extraordinary powers of action during wartime. The government could suspend any Act of Parliament unilaterally, imprison suspected Nazi sympathizers without trial, and impose rationing and industrial conscription. A small War Cabinet and a series of ministries dedicated to planning economic supply could make rapid decisions. The government raised taxes, set wages and prices, and subjected private industry to state power.

Oddly, the declaration of war was followed by a long period of waiting. During the first nine months of the war, later referred to as the "phoney war" because Britain felt little immediate effect, Hitler turned his attention to Norway, Belgium, the Netherlands, and France, temporarily sparing Britain the destructive force of the German war machine. Fearing possible German invasion, Britons formed the Local Defence Volunteers, later renamed the Home Guard. Although the organization at first lacked uniforms and weapons, the Home Guard eventually helped to guard Germans taken prisoner and man anti-aircraft guns, surveillance towers, and vital assets. Otherwise, however, the government neither geared up for total war nor expressed any expectations of sacrifice, calling it "business as usual."

The fall of Norway in April of 1940 sparked an acrimonious Parliamentary debate, during which members expressed their lack of confidence in Prime Minister Neville Chamberlain's wartime leadership. The government fell, and Winston Churchill was chosen to head a new national government. Churchill had many marks against him: he was widely believed to be antilabor, and to have ordered troops to fire on a group of striking miners at Tonypandy in Wales in 1910. His mismanagement of the Gallipoli campaign in the First World War also continued to taint his political reputation. He was one of the oldest men asked to serve a first term as Prime Minister, and, with bouts of depression that he referred to as "the Black Dog," he seemed temperamentally unsuited to the stressful role of wartime commander. But Churchill rose to the occasion, becoming an extraordinarily popular national leader. Although he suffered from a lisp, his skill at crafting speeches that spoke to what the British public needed to hear at key moments of the war helped win him support across the political spectrum. As he argued before Allied representatives on June 12, 1941:

> This then, my lords and gentlemen, is the message which we send forth today to all states and nations, bound or free, to all the men in all the lands who care for

freedom's cause. To our Allies and well-wishers in Europe, to our American friends
and helpers drawing ever closer in their might across the ocean, this is the message:
lift up your hearts, all will come right. Out of depths of sorrow and sacrifice will be
born again the glory of mankind. (Churchill 1941)

Churchill governed at the head of a national coalition, leading to greater wartime
political stability: he formed part of an inner War Cabinet of five, which included
two members of the Labour Party, Arthur Greenwood and the new Labour leader,
Clement Attlee.

Soon after Churchill's assumption of power, disaster struck in France. The
British and French armies retreated before German forces. Poorly led although
evenly matched numerically with the German army, Allied troops had to evacuate
their positions in western France and head to the coastline at Dunkirk for rescue.
Under strafing fire from German planes, almost 340,000 troops were fetched back
to England by every manner of boat imaginable – 850 boats and ships in all. Only
the troops were saved; guns and vehicles had to be abandoned where they stood.
On June 21, 1940, France surrendered to the Nazis, dividing that country in theory
between Vichy France, which cooperated with the Nazis, and a "Free French"
exile government headquartered in London. For practical purposes France had
surrendered.

Dunkirk should have been Britain's lowest hour, and yet many came to see it as
victory snatched from the jaws of defeat. This interpretation of Dunkirk owes much
to radio personality J.B. Priestley and his broadcast "postscripts on the news." One
of the first celebrity anchormen, Priestley was eminently listenable, with warm,
Yorkshire tones. His broadcasts helped to shape a common understanding of the
war, and drew home audiences away from the broadcasts of the Nazi propagan-
dist "Lord Haw-Haw," who broadcast in an English accent from Hamburg. (Lord
Haw-Haw was in fact the New York-born William Joyce, raised in Ireland, schooled
in England, and a member of the British Union of Fascists before leaving for
Germany at the onset of war.) Priestley celebrated Britain's Everyman in the
evacuation of Dunkirk, noting that even the pleasure steamers that brought people to vacations on the Channel Islands in better times now labored to bring
the bloodied soldiers home from France: "We've known them and laughed at
them, these fussy little steamers, all our lives. We have watched them load and
unload their crowds of holiday passengers – the gents full of high spirits and bot-
tled beer, the ladies eating pork pies, the children sticky with peppermint rock"
(Nicholas 1995). The *Gracie Fields*, the steamer that used to ply the waters between the British mainland and the Isle of Wight, had gone down at Dunkirk,
but, Priestley said, she would "go sailing proudly down the years in the epic of
Dunkirk. And our great grandchildren, when they learn how we began this war
by snatching glory out of defeat, then swept on to victory, may also learn how
the little holiday steamers made an excursion to hell and came back glorious"
(Moss 2003: 156).

Britain Alone?

After France surrendered, Germany faced no other European enemies, and Britain was now alone against Nazi Germany. This solitude was not complete, for it included the strength of 5 million colonial troops throughout the empire and the tacit support of the United States. At first the Luftwaffe conducted daytime raids on British cities. Then, once the Royal Air Force began to inflict high casualty rates on German planes, Germany shifted to sustained nighttime bombing known afterward as the Blitz. Beginning on September 7, 1940, and continuing for the next 76 nights (with the exception of a mercifully cloudy November 2), German planes attacked, blanketing London with bombs and wreaking havoc on other cities as well. In the North of England, Hull lost its shopping areas and docks. Destruction of the Liverpool suburbs forced residents to sleep on tarps in open fields. Downtown Manchester experienced just three bombing raids, but they devastated transport and public utilities. Coventry was also largely destroyed, losing both its cathedral and commercial district. A total of 60,000 British civilians died in the Blitz.

Fortunately, Britain bore the brunt of German attacks alone for only a short period. Churchill's premiership marked the inauguration of what he called a "special relationship" between Britain and the United States. The two countries were not traditional allies, despite being "divided by a common language" (a sentiment attributed in different forms to George Bernard Shaw, Oscar Wilde, and Winston Churchill). Throughout the nineteenth century, they had been enemies, clashing directly in the War of 1812, and then again over the *Alabama* claims during the Civil War. The presence in the United States of East Coast elites with transatlantic ties went some way toward forging bonds, though many Americans distrusted the motives, practice, and history of British imperialism. The failure of the United States to join the League of Nations, and economic competition in the interwar period, helped to solidify this atmosphere of mistrust. The United States remained nominally neutral for the first two years of the war, but President Franklin Delano Roosevelt clearly sympathized with Britain even as he promised American mothers to keep their sons out of foreign conflicts. Sensing an ally, Churchill begged Roosevelt for the "tools to finish the job," but Roosevelt first had to convince Americans that Britain's war was America's war too. In his radio broadcasts, he folksily reminded listeners that when your neighbor's house is on fire, you give him your garden hose, and so gradually paved the way for American public support of the war.

At first, America supported Britain with money and materiel. After German subs sank many British destroyers, the US exchanged 50 American destroyers for 99-year leases on British naval bases. A Congressional debate about this action ensued, and by March of 1941, Roosevelt had encouraged Congress to show its direct support for the war effort with the Lend-Lease Act. Under the auspices of Lend-Lease, Congress appropriated $50 billion worth of supplies, $31 billion of which went to Britain and the remainder to the Soviet Union, France, and China. In turn, Roosevelt pressed Churchill for the statement of war aims necessary for American support. In August of 1941, the two leaders met on a ship off Newfoundland to negotiate the Atlantic Charter, committing the United States and Britain to joint leadership in a postwar world dedicated to the values of peace and democracy.

After an unreservedly bleak first half of 1941 for the British, the complexion of the war changed markedly mid-year. On June 22, Germany violated the Nazi-Soviet nonaggression pact of 1939 with an invasion of Soviet territory. German troops penetrated deep into the Soviet Union and besieged both Moscow and Leningrad. The invasion, codenamed Operation Barbarossa, both diverted German resources to the east, giving Britain a relative respite in the conflict, and brought Britain one step closer to the "Grand Alliance" with the Soviet Union and United States that dominated the second half of the war. The other fateful step took place on December 7, 1941. In retribution for a United States embargo on oil, Japan wiped out most of the American Pacific Fleet in a surprise bombing raid on Pearl Harbor, and attacked British possessions in Malaya and Hong Kong. The British and the Americans declared war on Japan, making them allies in a common conflict. Then, on December 11, bound by the Tripartite Agreement of 1940, Italy and Germany declared war on the United States.

United by their determination to defeat a common enemy, the United States, Britain, and the Soviet Union worked closely together throughout the war. Churchill, Stalin, and Roosevelt (later replaced by Harry Truman after Roosevelt's death) met together over the next four years in Washington, Casablanca, Cairo, Quebec, Tehran, and Yalta to plan wartime strategy. Apprised by intelligence sources that the Germans had a program underway to develop a nuclear weapon, the British government and the United States also collaborated to research and construct their own nuclear device. Although eventually it became clear that German program was not as far along as had been feared, the joint British-American Manhattan Project culminated in development of the world's first atomic weapons before the end of the war.

The formation of the Grand Alliance was offset for Britain by Japan's conquest of Singapore, a crucial British possession. The loss of Singapore (1942) allowed Japan to threaten Australia and New Zealand unimpeded by the British navy, which had used Singapore as a major station. This dealt a symbolic and real death blow to Britain's imperial authority, since one of the props of empire had always been Britain's purported ability to protect its colonies of settlement. What the British lost in the Far East, though, they gained back in the Middle East, defeating Rommel's German army at El Alamein, and securing access to the worldwide supply of oil that lay underground. In the European theater, both the Allies and the Axis powers turned to large-scale bombings of civilian targets, with the Allies firebombing German cities, including the cultural center of Dresden; and the Germans launching V-1 and V-2 rockets over the English Channel at London.

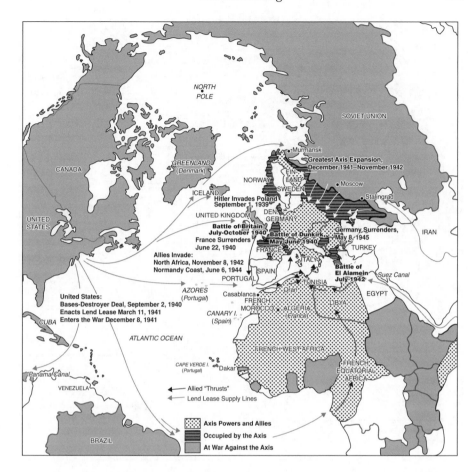

Map 11.1a Major battles of the Second World War: Europe, Africa, and the Middle East. *Source*: Based on Robert R. Palmer and Joel Colton, *A History of the Modern World since 1815* (New York: Knopf, 1984), pp. 816–817.

On June 6, 1944, the Allies conducted their long-awaited invasion of Western Europe. A successful amphibious invasion of the beaches of France was followed in fairly quick succession by the liberation of Paris in August 1944, and the German surrender on May 8, 1945. The war itself came to an end more quickly than expected after American leaders decided to use its two developed nuclear weapons on the Japanese cities of Hiroshima and Nagasaki, devastating both and forcing the capitulation of the Japanese emperor and Japan's surrender.

The Economy in Wartime

While the British economy had grown throughout the latter 1930s, rearmament also played a role in completing the nation's economic recovery. Shipbuilding resumed, and the government commissioned production of 12,000 military planes.

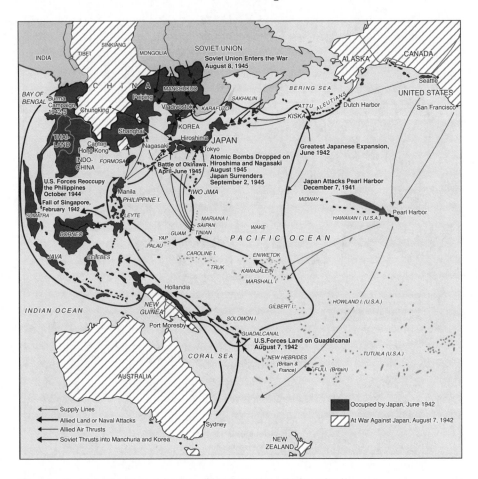

Map 11.1b Major battles of the Second World War: the Pacific theater.

When the Second World War began, unemployment actually rose because of a bad winter and the government's failure to divert labor into essential wartime industries. Eventually, however, the conscription of vast numbers of men out of the workforce offset this unemployment. The British armed forces expanded from 480,000 men in 1939 to 437,000 women and 4.7 million men by 1945.

Economic preparedness for war was only possible with centralized control of industry. The Emergency Powers (Defence) Act gave rise to a host of new ministries, including Economic Warfare, Home Security, Food, Shipping, and Supply. In 1942, the government created the Ministry of Production to facilitate economic negotiation with Britain's main creditor, the United States. Under the powers of what had become the Ministry of Labour and National Service, all men between the ages of 18 and 51 were allocated to either armed service or critical industries. Workers in these essential industries – munitions, metals, chemicals, agriculture, transportation, and infrastructure – at first endured extremely long hours, exhausting commutes, and unusual occupational hazards (such as the yellow skin or dusty lungs suffered by munitions workers). By 1942, though, the government had begun to address these issues, and war workers received wage incentives and better working conditions.

Britain also conducted total war by mobilizing the whole of the potential workforce. The government was initially slow to recruit women workers, but by 1943, 91 percent of single women between the ages of 18 and 40, and 80 percent of childless married women between those ages, were involved in some kind of national service (some women were "drafted" into factory work through a process of industrial conscription). Women occupied almost every kind of position once occupied by men: they worked in munitions factories, served as conductors in transportation, and worked in the skilled trades and in construction. They took up these jobs despite some opposition from male workers, who with legitimacy saw women's participation as a trend that could marginalize men and decrease their pay; and in fact, women were paid only 50 to 70 percent of what men had received for the same jobs.

A few women, arguing that they were performing what had been previously defined as "men's work," held demonstrations or walked off the job in pursuit of equal pay, but Parliament delayed serious consideration of the issue until many of the women employed in the war had departed from the workforce. Other women, especially those from depressed areas, were glad for the opportunity of war work, whether for extra spending money or to save for the future. As one woman from the poor mining area of Blaina in Wales noted, "I'd like to keep working after the war, in spite of all of the travelling. I'm getting used to it, and it's interesting. People are all very bright about the War. They say 'We'll be lost when it is over' though in the same breath they say 'we'd like to see it over'" (Roberts 1995). This is not to claim that the war made traditional ideas of the family obsolete; wartime uncertainty made women long for marriage and family, and the outbreak of war saw a surge in marriages as well. The subsequent increase in the divorce rate from 1 to 5 percent suggests some of these marriages were too hastily made.

The Unifying Myth of the Blitz

The Blitz came to be mythologized as the most significant force binding together Britons of different classes during the war. Contemporary political rhetoric endowed it with mythic status. Winston Churchill called for a "stiff upper lip." Britons didn't run; they bucked official disapproval to shelter in the deep tunnels of the Underground. They built corrugated metal "Anderson Shelters" in their backyards, named for Sir John Anderson, who was in charge of civil defense. When fires broke out around East London, heroic volunteer firefighters joined together to

Figure 11.1 Second World War posters exhorted Britons to grow vegetables, turn out lights, avoid talking about the war, and to keep calm and carry on. This poster targeted the mothers of thousands of children who were relocated from London and other heavily bombed areas to the British countryside to live with unfamiliar families. (National Archives. Ref. INF 13/171/3).

battle them. Even the Queen was affected by the German assault, as Buckingham Palace came under attack by German bombers, further drawing together Britons before an enemy who attacked them all.

In fact, although there was some degree of social bonding produced by the stress, there was just as much conflict, as Britons of different classes and social conditions found themselves thrown together. Before the bombing began in 1940, the government evacuated one and a half million working-class mothers and children from targeted urban areas to the countryside. Although the program of accepting evacuees was voluntary, agents of the government pressured rural dwellers to open their homes, and paid them a small monthly stipend for support of the children (although not the evacuated mothers). The evacuation program turned out to be rather haphazard, with few participants, either evacuees or hosts, getting what they were expecting. Many urban children had never seen the countryside before; many rural hosts had never seen children raised in grinding poverty, bereft of shoes, clean clothes, or toothbrushes. "If I let you and those dirty children come in they would ruin the carpet," one rural woman reportedly said to an evacuee who came to her house with her children (Beaven and Griffiths 1999).

Although urban stories dominate the historiography of the Second World War, rural dwellers had their own particular wartime experiences: of having soldiers billeted in their towns and in their homes; of having the government dictate crop choices; of seeing fields commandeered for aircraft landing strips. Activities like hop-picking and foxhunting continued, helping to draw continuities between wartime and prewar life. Rural food producers got around rationing, supplementing their diets with home-produced bacon, eggs, milk, and butter. Like urban women, rural women had some increased wartime opportunity; the Women's Garden Association drafted women to work in market gardens to replace conscripted men. Some unemployed urban men also found work as farmworkers, an opportunity for geographical mobility that they would not normally have had. The experience of the Second World War in Britain was much more diverse than a focus on London and the Blitz alone would suggest.

Nor did the war produce unified national cohesion beyond the Blitz. Munitions factories and shops saw three times as many strikes in 1944 as in 1939. The British public understood the need for food rationing, which had also been practiced during the First World War, but there were widespread allegations that grocers favored wealthier patrons in the distribution of the rationed articles: butter and margarine, meats, sugar, tea, cheese, soap, candy and chocolate. Rationing also extended to fuel: at first, the private vehicle allowance was 40 miles per week, then 75 miles per month; ultimately, cars were off-limits except for essential work. Even for items not officially rationed, consumers' choices were purposely narrowed, with clothing and furniture limited to wartime Utility designs in order to reduce waste.

The myth of wartime social cohesion during the war itself helped to discredit self-serving behavior considered insufficiently patriotic. So, for example, the "good-time girls," young women who gravitated toward some of the 2 million American GIs stationed in Britain – particularly black soldiers – met with public disapproval not simply for having sex outside of marriage or for allegedly spreading venereal disease, but also for threatening the idea that Britain was united by its whiteness (Rose 1998). Similarly, the government urged people to avoid all unnecessary travel during wartime, but between a quarter and a third of Britons seem to have managed to slip away for vacations occasionally, and even more attended sporting events.

The myth of the Blitz suggests a population used to sacrifice, but the Second World War changed popular expectations about the role government played in the provision of health and welfare. By the fall of 1940, under the supervision of Minister of Labour Ernest Bevin, the government began dictating standards for wages and hours, workplace cleanliness, safety, the provision of meals on the job, and housing and education for workers. Progressive taxation during the war helped reduce the income gap between the top earners and everyone else. The state opened inexpensive national restaurants to feed urban dwellers, and urged citizens to consume brown bread as part of their patriotic duty. Responding to Britain's perennial difficulty in feeding its populace without imports, government officials encouraged everyone to cultivate a "victory garden" on any scrap of untilled ground. The state also made available cheap clothing and furniture to fill gaps left by the redirection of private industry. The quality of medical care throughout the country improved, as bombardment put pressure on existing systems of medical delivery and encouraged the government to play a more active role. The wartime government produced a study culminating in the groundbreaking Beveridge Report (1942), which confirmed that all people had a right to a guaranteed basic income, and argued that all people should have protection against unemployment, sickness, and lack of educational opportunity: "Social insurance fully developed may provide income security; it is an attack upon Want. But Want is one only of five giants on the road of reconstruction and in some ways the easiest to attack. The others are Disease, Ignorance, Squalor and Idleness." The Beveridge Report articulated both the values and corresponding policies that later guided postwar reconstruction.

Wartime economic demands hinted at the need for a better-educated workforce. The 1944 (Butler) Education Act created a government Ministry of Education, and finally raised the school-leaving age to 15, as David Lloyd George had intended to do at the end of the First World War a quarter-century earlier. The Butler Act provided three educational streams for British youth, overseen by Local Education Authorities. Fifteen percent of schools were designated as "grammar schools," which provided an education similar to that historically enjoyed by members of the middle classes able to pay the requisite fees. Now fees were eliminated, but placement was determined by a single test, the "eleven-plus," taken at the age of 10 or 11, and children from better-off families naturally had an advantage in test preparation and early literacy. Technical schools, representing about 7 percent of schools, would train students who showed mechanical aptitude for careers in technology. But the rest of the student population, the three-quarters of children who did not score high enough on the exam, were relegated to "Secondary Modern" schools. Thus, although the 1944 Act expanded the educational system, it did so in ways that accommodated the existing division of British society by social class.

British Culture in Wartime

By the outbreak of the Second World War, the British mass media was well developed and able to carry on the necessary task of building support for the war effort. The BBC created the Forces Programme, an entertainment-based channel, initiating the idea that different radio channels might serve different preferences or demographics. The BBC also became a central method of distributing news about the war. Until the Second World War, the main vehicle for consumption of the news had been the daily newspaper. The government maintained such a tight association with newspapers that it refused to give breaking news to the BBC, forcing radio broadcasters to read bulletins from the Reuters news agency, and to hold news until the morning newspapers had had their chance to go to press. Once the war broke out, however, the BBC realized the potential utility of radio as a more effective wartime medium. In 1942 the War Reporting Unit was formed, embedding correspondents with military units for training in Britain and then dispatching them to theaters of war in Europe and the Middle East. New recording devices based on the military field telephone allowed reporters to capture the sounds of combat, and mobile transmitters mounted on trucks enabled fast news delivery. Between 10 and 15 million radio listeners listened to these broadcasts, which transformed previously unknown correspondents into national celebrities and helped Britons to understand the war effort that their home front activities were supporting (Hannon 2008).

The government also established the Council for the Encouragement of Music and the Arts (CEMA) in January 1940, to fund and encourage arts organizations that might otherwise have had trouble supporting themselves in wartime. Supported by CEMA, ballet, opera, and theater companies toured the provinces, performing in theaters and even in workplaces, and raising the morale of a beleaguered population. London's Old Vic was designated as a temporary National Theatre, and actors Laurence Olivier and Ralph Richardson were released from wartime service to become the directors of a new theater company there. Between 1940 and 1945, the Treasury grant for CEMA grew from £25,000 to £235,000, setting the stage for continued and robust government support of the arts.

Although in 1942 the wartime government asked for, and was given, the ability to suppress performances that might be too critical of the government or hinder morale, there is no evidence that this power was ever asserted (Heinrich 2010). The Ministry of Information did, however, censor radio broadcasts, warning newspapers about what they could print, and even shutting down the Communist *Daily Worker*. Books had less effective censorship (although Orwell's *Animal Farm* had its publication delayed due to fears that the thinly disguised critique of Soviet Russia would alienate Britain's ally). The social commentator and novelist J.B. Priestley, whose radio shows had been taken off the air because of his slant in favor of postwar reform, continued to communicate through his novels the message that working-class Britons deserved a much larger share of postwar resources.

The war influenced artists' output and audiences' preferences. Performances of Shakespeare's plays, and plays interpreted into films, were extremely popular during the war, since they were an integral part of the English national inheritance and had themselves been written during a period of intense international conflict. The war also spawned works based on current events. Michael Tippett – who along with the British operatic composer Benjamin Britten had a career that spanned from the 1930s into the 1970s – composed his masterwork during the war, *A Child of Our Time*. The work was drawn from life: in 1938 Jewish teenager Herschel Grynszpan assassinated a German diplomat in Paris, and the Nazis used the act as a pretext to revenge themselves against the German Jewish community in the riots of Kristallnacht. Before the war, the sculptor Henry Moore began crafting monumental reclining stone figures, particularly mothers and children. When his studio was destroyed by German bombing in 1940, he began to draw coal miners and to capture on paper the lives of the people taking shelter in the underground tunnels.

Documentary film helped both to capture the wartime experience and to forge a mythology of common endeavor and common sacrifice. The Ministry of Information in 1939 transformed the General Post Office film unit into the Crown Film Unit, which produced more than 2,000 documentary, cartoon, and instructional films during the war on all topics. Filmmakers chronicled the lives of ordinary people, instructed the public about the reasons not to talk carelessly, helped new factory workers to adjust to the realities of the wartime workplace, advised audiences about ways to avoid venereal diseases, and even explained to homeowners how to interrogate potential German spies who might show up at the door.

Humphrey Jennings was the true auteur of British wartime film. His *Listen to Britain* (1942), a snapshot of British wartime life, juxtaposed ordinary scenes against British folk songs and ambient noise, without narration. *Fires Were Started* (1943) followed brave firefighters attempting to deal with the devastating German air raids on London's East End. *A Diary for Timothy* (1945) addressed a fictional baby boy who had been born in September of 1944. The film's gentle-voiced narrator recapitulated sacrifices made during the war: by coal miners, engine drivers, farmers, soldiers, and even the baby's mother, since the baby's father had been sent as a soldier to Europe. Timothy himself embodied the hope of a better future that justified the immensity of wartime sacrifice.

War's Aftermath

Victory in the Second World War proved more satisfying than victory in the First. On both sides of the Atlantic, the public regarded this conflict as a "Good War" – not one that European powers had stumbled into haplessly, but rather, a rational response to a hostile and aggressive dictator and a corrupt regime. Despite the civilian casualties caused by German bombing raids, the casualty rate as a whole was much lower than in the previous war; only a little more than 6 percent of mobilized British troops lost their lives. The country as a whole came to terms with the reality of industrialized warfare, and was not left grappling with the loss of a generation of British youth. Finally, the fact that Britain itself had come under attack – and the cultural construction of the "myth of the Blitz" – helped define an important sense of national unity. The war proved a victory for British technology as well in its deployment of radar, computing, and nuclear physics, and for the country's ability to gear up economically to meet the demands of total war.

On the other hand, the Second World War was much more devastating for Britain's global economic, strategic, and financial position. The war irrevocably changed Britain's relationship with its empire, accelerating decolonization into the postwar period. As Angus Calder pointed out, "when Britain 'stood alone' in 1940, she stood on the shoulders of several hundred million Asians," whose cooperation had been especially central in the China-Burma-India theater of the conflict (Calder 1969: 19). The bill for this support soon came due. War also irrevocably changed the relationship between Britain and the other members of the Commonwealth. The fall of Singapore compromised any claim that the British could protect Australia and New Zealand from invasion. The war strengthened relations with Canada, which became a breadbasket for Britain and a military powerhouse, increasing its air force and navy and supplying a million men for the war effort, thereby underlining Britain's increasing reliance on colonial forces.

The war had an even more monumental impact on relations with India. Even as nationalism simmered, the Viceroy Lord Linlithgow declared war against Germany on India's behalf. When the Congress Party protested, the Viceroy promised India Dominion status at war's end. At the same time (1940), the Muslim League requested the creation of a separate state of Pakistan as a Muslim homeland, complicating Britain's commitments in the region. Winston Churchill responded to this mounting difficulty by noting that he had not "become the King's First Minister in order to preside over the liquidation of the British Empire," a strong and firm statement not wholly grounded in the reality of Britain's weakening global strength. Gandhi and the Congress Party responded with a Quit India resolution (1942), and the last major civil disobedience action under British rule. Leaders of the Quit India campaign were jailed, and protests erupted throughout the country, including 250 attacks on railroad stations, 550 on post offices, and 155 on police stations. Forty thousand British Indian troops in Singapore left their ranks to join the Indian National Army, led by former Indian National Congress president Sudhash Chandra Bose, which then offered its services to Japan. There could no longer be much pretense that what was good for Britain was good for India.

The rhetoric of the "special relationship" implied that the British and the United States were partners; but by the end of the war, the status of the United States as a political and financial superpower had made this partnership obviously unequal. In July 1944, 730 delegates representing 44 countries met at a hotel in Bretton Woods, New Hampshire to craft a postwar financial system. Institutions like the International Bank for Reconstruction and Development and the International Monetary Fund were developed to provide financial stability and prevent a major postwar depression; but the United States played the largest role in both, and the dollar rather than the pound sterling underlay the emerging financial system.

The Second World War accelerated many domestic demands for social change. Britons at home united through the common experience of food and fuel rationing, the rhetoric of common sacrifice, and eventually by improved living standards as more family members joined the workforce. This common experience moved expectations about social policy to the left during the war. The Beveridge Report (1942) called for a cradle-to-grave safety net for British citizens; the experiences of wartime made many people feel as though this was their due, and, moreover, that social reform would only be implemented by a Labour government. The war itself had been prosecuted by a National government; Winston Churchill was the most recognizable figure as Prime Minister, but Clement Attlee, the leader of the Labour Party, had been beside him as Deputy Prime Minister, and so gained credit for the way in which the war was prosecuted as well. When a general election was called for June of 1945, Winston Churchill badly misunderstood the electorate emerging from the war by criticizing Labour while refusing to cater to the new social expectations. The result was a Labour landslide – almost 48 percent of the vote to the Tories' 40 percent. The election and its outcome provided a mandate for postwar British governments to construct the "welfare state" under a new concept of the state's power and responsibilities to its citizens.

By the end of the Second World War, several cultural trajectories of the past 30 years had become clear. Even in the humanistic disciplines, science was in the ascendant, but cultural critics expressed doubts about the potential soullessness of a society narrowly focused on technology. While artists and self-consciously literary authors embraced modernism, continuing to distinguish "high culture" in a way that divided people by social class, mass culture, shared by people of most social classes, began to knit them together. Radio, and film, and to some extent music and sport, began to create a common set of cultural experiences. The apex of this trend occurred during the Second World War, when, in spite of people's very different wartime experiences, the shared narrative emphasized a shared burden.

This sense of great and unified national spirit, commemorated after and even during the war, was never again equaled in twentieth-century Britain. Many Britons carefully forgot the labor conflict of the post-1942 strikes, the uncomfortable social mixing of East End children with middle-class rural families, and the social discomfort with women in the workplace, so strong was the need to create a coherent synthesis of the war's meaning. The destruction of British cities and towns necessitated a major postwar rebuilding program, but if the myth of the Blitz was any indication, the larger meanings of British society remained intact. Over the next several decades, the certainty Britons felt at the end of the war eroded under the pressure of decolonization, economic instability, and the shift to a bipolar world in which Britain represented neither pole.

References

Arthur, Max (2004) *Forgotten Voices of World War II: A New History of World War Two in the Words of the Men and Women Who Were There.* Guilford, CT: Lyons Press.

Beaven, Brad, and Griffiths, John (1999) The Blitz, Civilian Morale, and the City: Mass-Observation and Working-Class Culture in Britain, 1940–1. *Urban History*, 86 (1): 71–88.

Calder, Angus (1969) *The People's War: Britain, 1939–1945*. New York: Pantheon.

Churchill, Winston (1941) Speech to the Allied Delegates. At http://www.ibiblio.org/pha/timeline/410612bwp.html (accessed Jan. 25, 2011).

Gilbert, Gerard (2009) Britain's Wartime Films Were More Than Just Propaganda. *Independent*, Sept. 3.

Hannon, Brian P.D. (2008) Creating the Correspondent: How the BBC Reached the Frontline in the Second World War. *Historical Journal of Film, Radio and Television*, 28 (2): 175–194.

Heinrich, Anselm (2010) Theatre in Britain during the Second World War. *New Theatre Quarterly*, 26 (2): 61–69.

Moss, Norman (2003) *19 Weeks*. New York: Houghton Mifflin.

Nicholas, Sian (1995) "Sly Demagogues" and Wartime Radio: J.B. Priestley and the BBC. *Twentieth Century British History*, 6 (3): 247–266.

Roberts, Brian (1995) A Mining Town in Wartime: The Fears for the Future. *Llafur*, 6 (1): 82–95.

Rose, Sonya O. (1998) Sex, Citizenship and the Nation in World War II Britain. *American Historical Review*, 13 (4): 1147–1176.

Further Reading

Carnevali, Francesca, and Strange, Julie-Marie (eds) (2007) *Twentieth-Century Britain: Economic, Cultural and Social Change*. Harlow: Longman.

Gilbert, Bentley B. (1971) British Social Policy and the Second World War. *Albion*, 3 (3): 103–115.

Harris, Jose (1992) War and Social History: Britain and the Home Front during the Second World War. *Contemporary European History*, 1 (1): 17–35.

Harrisson, Tom (1990) *Living Through the Blitz*. London: Penguin.

Howkins, Alun (1998) A Country at War: Mass-Observation and Rural England, 1939–1945. *Rural History*, 9 (1): 75–97.

Johnson, Paul (1994) *Twentieth-Century Britain: Economic, Social and Cultural Change*. London: Longman.

Rubinstein, William D. (2003) *Twentieth-Century Britain: A Political History*. London: Palgrave Macmillan.

Stansky, Peter (2007) *The First Day of the Blitz: September 7, 1940*. New Haven: Yale University Press.

Stansky, Peter, and Abrahams, William (1994) *London's Burning: Life, Death and Art in the Second World War*. London: Constable.

12

Winds of Change
Politics, 1945–1979

In his short story "Toba Tek Singh," the Urdu writer Sadaat Hasan Manto de-scribed the impact of the partition of British India on a group of institutionalized people with mental illness. As the country was divided into India and Pakistan, hundreds of thousands of people on each side were relocated to the other side of an arbitrary border, depending on whether they were Hindu or Muslim. The insane world outside the madhouse reflected the world within its walls; inmates did not understand how Pakistan could have been created out of what was formerly India, or why they were being sent away from their ancestral homes to live in a place they had never been to before, on the basis of ethnicity alone. The title character of the short story, Toba Tek Singh, unable to find out whether his home village has been consigned to India or Pakistan, finally makes a last stand, collapsing in the no-man's land between India and Pakistan – a no man's land for which the British were partially responsible (Manto 1955).

Since 1832, Britain had been a great naval empire, but the political story of the postwar period transformed into one of reevaluation, contraction, and change. The Second World War – and particularly the fall of Britain's naval fortress at Singapore – had illustrated how untenable worldwide military commitments were to a small island nation in an age of industrialized warfare. The war had also created a set of expectations at home – expensive expectations about what government would provide to its citizens – that could not be squared with the maintenance of a costly global empire. Britain thus found itself disengaging from its imperial role, and navigating two roles that overlapped: as a close ally of the United States, which was one of the two superpowers in a bipolar world; and later, as part of an emergent Western European economic force.

But Britain's imperial disengagement, like its imperial engagement over a century earlier, came with its own expenses. British withdrawal forced the

Empire, State, and Society: Britain Since 1830, First Edition. Jamie L. Bronstein and Andrew T. Harris.
© 2012 Jamie L. Bronstein and Andrew T. Harris. Published 2012 by John Wiley & Sons, Ltd.

creation of new borders, boundaries, and frontiers in places like India/Pakistan, Israel/Palestine, and, culturally, in Kenya and Rhodesia. This painful process often created longstanding resentment on the part of formerly colonized peoples. And, as Sadaat Hasan Manto described, it could also create death and destruction.

Three distinct periods characterized the politics of the postwar era: the initial construction of the welfare state under Labour; a long, unbroken period of Conservative dominance during a period of economic prosperity; and a more difficult period during the 1970s, when first the Conservative Party and then the Labour Party struggled with economic challenges and a lack of vision. One constant, no matter who was in power, was the steady conversion of Britain's former empire into a loosely affiliated Commonwealth of nations, punctuated by the challenge of nationalist anticolonial movements which the British sometimes met with disastrous attempts at force.

The Construction of a Welfare State

The first priority of the new Labour government was to make good on the promises of the 1942 Beveridge Report. The document had been issued by an Inter-Departmental Committee on Social Insurance and Allied Services, appointed during the war with the responsibility of investigating social ills. Having identified five ills that beset modern British society – ignorance, want, squalor, idleness and disease – the committee recommended an integrated social reform program to include national insurance and old-age pensions. The Beveridge Report became the foundation for cradle-to-grave provision. The Family Allowances Act (1945) granted parents an allowance of 5 shillings a week for each child after their first. The National Insurance Act (1946) used employer and employee contributions to provide unemployment insurance for every worker above school-leaving age (15), and payments for funerals and upon the birth of children. Those with disabilities and those who had never been employed received their benefits under the National Assistance Act (1948). This social safety net was meant to be more secure, and less stigmatizing, than the means-tested poor laws that had so appalled George Orwell during the Great Depression.

The National Health Service (1946) was a continuation of the trend toward guaranteed health care for Britons begun in 1911. While the 1911 Act had provided for compulsory national insurance for workers, funded by employers and employees as well as the state, the NHS was funded out of taxation and covered everyone. The Act establishing the NHS moved responsibility for hospitals from a patchwork of private and governmental entities to the government, and provided free and comprehensive health care to all: medical consultations, surgery, drugs, dentistry, and even eyeglasses. Doctors remained in private practice, reimbursed by the state according to the number of patients that they saw.

The social safety net was accompanied by a commitment to nationalize key sectors of the economy: the Bank of England and civil aviation (1946), the coal industry (1947), electricity, radio and telephony (1947), rail and road transportation (1948), gas, (1949) and iron and steel (1951). Attempts to nationalize the sugar industry were successfully repulsed by the major sugar producer, Tate and Lyle. Nationalization promoted several interlocked goals. It placed private owners of industry, who had the needed expertise, under the discipline of Parliament rather than the market. It allowed the government to plan production better than the private sector would ostensibly be able to do, and gave the government control over labor relationships and working conditions. Nationalization ensured that no one made an unacceptably large profit in essential services or health care, areas where items should be priced at or just slightly above cost (Tomlinson 2008).

Labour Prime Minister Clement Attlee attempted to work with trade unions, using both carrot and stick. The government reversed Conservative government policies that had restricted the work of trade unions after the General Strike of 1926 (Panitch 1977). The government also sought to negotiate industry-wide agreements to increase the mobility of labor, and sought to impose an "incomes" policy, intervening in wage negotiations with unions, in return for agreed-upon regulation of prices. Wages policies were initiated in 1948–1950, and then again between 1966 and 1968. The Trades Union Congress lobbied for taxation of profits and wealth, but the Labour Party consistently chose not to follow up on these demands.

In addition to the legislation nationalizing industries and utilities and providing for the welfare state, governments in the postwar period used legislation to regulate both the natural and the built environments. The New Towns Act (1946) provided for the construction of new towns to accommodate a growing population. The period between 1946 and 1978 saw the construction of some 28 new towns: Stevenage, Peterborough, and Milton Keynes among them. The government meant these towns to provide new businesses and self-contained living spaces for those who worked there, along the lines of the garden cities designed earlier in the century. At first, housing was configured around walkable primary schools and shopping districts, but eventually pressure on national retailers meant that large numbers of small downtown shops gave way to an automotive culture similar to that of American suburbs in the same time period (Aldridge 1996).

The Town and Country Planning Act (1947) made real the dream of a "green belt" around London – a ring of agricultural and parkland around greater London that was intended to provide a boundary to urban development, and ensure that urban dwellers had access to rural areas for recreation. The government also strove to promote forests and parks, surveying existing forests and planning for the planting of 5 million acres of new trees. Competition with farmers for available land and water resources meant that many of the government's most ambitious targets were not met (Robbins 1983: 228). The 1956 Clean Air Act – partly a response to a choking fog that hung over London and killed thousands through respiratory diseases – finally targeted the largest source of urban air pollution, the use of coal to heat homes. Homeowners received subsidies to change their fireplaces over to gas from coal, and pollution lifted (Thorsheim 2006: 182).

The Cold War

Clearly, the domestic ambitions of the postwar Labour government were large and ushered in a period of incredible change. But nationalization of industries and the provision of social welfare had to be balanced against a foreign policy agenda strongly advocated by the United States at the outset of the Cold War. Although Churchill, Stalin, and US President Franklin Roosevelt had cooperated as strange bedfellows in the wartime "Grand Alliance," as the Second World War drew to a close it was clear that Stalin's interests ran counter to those of the English-speaking nations. By 1946, in a speech delivered at Westminster College in Fulton, Missouri, Winston Churchill warned that

> from Stettin in the Baltic to Trieste in the Adriatic, an iron curtain has descended across the Continent. Behind that line lie all the capitals of the ancient states of Central and Eastern Europe. Warsaw, Berlin, Prague, Vienna, Budapest, Belgrade, Bucharest and Sofia; all these famous cities and the populations around them lie in what I must call the Soviet sphere, and all are subject, in one form or another, not only to Soviet influence but to a very high and in some cases increasing measure of control from Moscow. (Churchill 1946)

These glimmerings of a Soviet sphere of influence in the making were complicated by Britain's financial need to extricate itself from serving as the world's policeman. Britain had become involved in a civil war in Greece during the Second World War, when Greece had become an extension of the battlefield between Axis and Allied forces. Although the Greek king was eventually returned to power, by 1946–1947 a Communist insurgency had broken out. Although the British government felt a sense of responsibility for Greece, the conflict was more expensive than Britain's straitened postwar economy could bear. In response to the withdrawal of British support, the United States proclaimed the Truman Doctrine, pledging to replace Britain in the task of halting Communist expansion. Later, after the United States smarted from the "loss" of China to the Chinese Communists in 1949, the US refined this doctrine as the strategy of Containment, which became the driving force in American foreign policy through the 1960s.

The Cold War between the Soviet Union and the West became uncomfortably warm for the first time in June of 1948. Germany had been divided up into four zones at the end of the Second World War by the liberating powers; Berlin itself had been divided into an Eastern and a Western zone, although the entire city was isolated within the Soviet sphere of influence. The Soviets attempted to cut off the city of Berlin from Western influence and support, in the hopes of gaining the entire city without a fight. The siege, which lasted for 11 months, caused Britain, the United States, Australia, New Zealand, and Canada to collaborate in the Berlin Airlift, the transportation of necessary supplies by air into West Berlin around the clock for the duration. Foreign Secretary Ernest Bevin also steered Britain toward a central role in the 1949 North Atlantic Treaty Organization (NATO). NATO, a mutual defense pact, was a response to the increasing threat of Communist forces in Western Europe. It brought together Britain, the United States, Canada, Portugal, Italy, Denmark, Iceland, France, and the Benelux countries (Belgium, the Netherlands, and Luxembourg). An attack against one was considered an attack against all. In practical terms, in return for allowing the United States to station its nuclear weapons and troops in Western Europe, European countries received the benefit of American military protection.

The fact that Britain enjoyed a "special relationship" with the United States removed the pressure that Britain might otherwise have experienced to join the European Coal and Steel Community, the consortium of six countries (France, West Germany, Belgium, the Netherlands, Luxembourg, and Italy) that pooled coal and steel supplies in the first step toward what later became a common market. The Treaty of Rome (1957) created the European Economic Community, in which Britain played no part.

The "special relationship" with the United States also had an impact on Britain domestically. Partly in return for being such a staunch ally, Britain received $3.2 billion of the $14 billion in aid that the United States extended to European nations through the Marshall Plan to rebuild a devastated postwar Europe. A quid pro quo of that assistance was assurance that the participating European countries would direct their priorities appropriately – toward defense, and away from all but the most necessary social and economic reforms. American officials exerted pressure on British leaders to decrease their spending on the National Health Service, and this pressure became more insistent with the outbreak of war in Korea in 1950. Britain's participation in the Korean War increased the amount expended on defense from 7 percent (1948) to 12 percent (1952) at a time when Britain could scarcely afford it. Increased military spending put pressure on other spending. This pitted Hugh Gaitskell, Labour Chancellor of the Exchequer in 1951, against Aneurin Bevan, who had initiated the NHS. When Gaitskell attempted to rein in NHS spending by charging people half the cost of their glasses and dentures, Bevan and Harold Wilson (future Labour Prime Minister) resigned from the Cabinet in protest (Fox 2004).

The 1950s and Conservative Government

By 1951 the Labour Party, fractured and under strain, lost their Parliamentary majority to the Conservatives. Winston Churchill came back into power, having convinced the electorate through a platform called the Industrial Charter that his party planned to continue the major features of the nascent welfare state. The Conservatives remained in power for the next 14 years. They appealed to the remaining Liberal Party elements of the electorate, and exploited splits within the Labour Party over disarmament and public ownership. Winston Churchill himself was becoming a legend in his own time; in 1952, he was offered a dukedom, but declined it, and in 1953, he received the Nobel Prize in Literature. The 1953 coronation of the young Queen Elizabeth II also buoyed a kind of nostalgic nationalism that bolstered popular Conservative Party support.

Churchill's government denationalized iron and steel and the trucking industry, although the hopes for massive private investment in these areas were not realized. The government maintained many of Labour's other economic policies, along with a high rate of income taxation. R.A. Butler, who replaced Labour's Hugh Gaitskell as Chancellor of the Exchequer, preserved so many of his predecessor's Labour priorities that his approach became known as "Butskellism." The government also faced the third balance-of-payments crisis since the end of the Second World War. Although the prime interest rate rose from 2 percent to 4 percent, the economic contraction this caused was offset by an ambitious program of homebuilding under Minister of Housing Harold Macmillan (over a million new homes were built) and a reduction in income taxes meant to stimulate investment and growth.

Economic prosperity as well as policy consistency helped keep the Conservatives in government. Responding to economic growth and low interest rates – and believing in the Keynesian tenet that government could successfully prime the pump for economic growth – the Conservatives invested not only in housing stock, but also in education and social services. Although Winston Churchill's successor, Anthony Eden, had a spotty performance, his successor, Harold Macmillan, was a popular Prime Minister, whose ability to adopt a posture of seeming equality with US President Eisenhower increased his stature at home. By 1959, the Conservative Party had a 100-seat majority in the House of Commons.

The End of Empire

Struggles surrounding decolonization remained a major theme in Britain throughout the 1940s and 1950s. From the British perspective, India served as the model for decolonization, although from the Indian perspective the speed of British withdrawal left much to be desired. After Britain promised independence during the Second World War, it was up to the last Viceroy, Lord Mountbatten, to negotiate with both Jawaharlal Nehru (representing India's predominant Hindu population) and Muhammad Ali Jinnah (representing its far smaller population of Muslims). In order to retain British control over the negotiations, the handover of power happened very quickly; millions of people living on the wrong side of the arbitrary

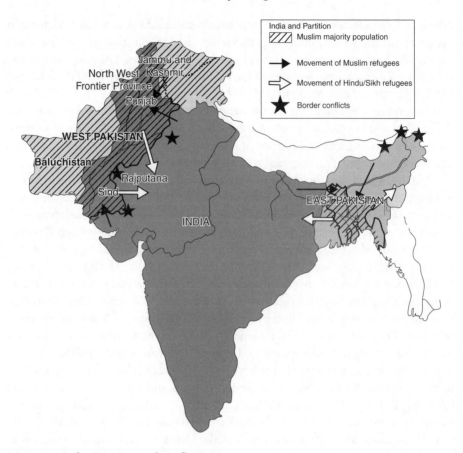

Map 12.1 India, Partition and conflict.
Source: Based on Nigel Dalziel, *The Penguin Historical Atlas of the British Empire* (London: Penguin, 2006), p. 131.

border established by Partition were forced to evacuate to the other side, at an estimated cost of 5 million lives.

In contrast with what happened in India – where the British government declared itself satisfied despite the tremendous loss of life – the end of the British mandate in Palestine was much less acceptable from the British perspective. In the wake of the Holocaust and the death of 6 million Jews at the hands of the Nazis, the Jewish communities in both the United States and Europe wanted a permanent national home for the remaining refugees. Palestine seemed like the natural location, and, as noted above, through the Balfour Declaration of 1917 the British also seemed committed to the idea. But since the First World War, violence between Arabs and Jews in Palestine had been constant, and Attlee's Labour government feared an Arab backlash if it was seen to endorse a Jewish homeland now. Jewish guerrilla fighters tried to pressure the British to support Israeli independence through acts of violence in 1946–1947, bombing the King David Hotel in Jerusalem and hanging two British soldiers. The United Nations (a supranational entity established in 1945 by the Allied powers and others) proposed a two-state solution, with both a Jewish and a Palestinian state planned; the Jews declared their independence as the State of Israel (1948), and the Palestinian lands were seized by Jordan and Egypt. Israel remained in perpetual war against the neighboring Arab states for decades afterward, and also nurtured a grievance against Britain for a perceived betrayal on the question of a Jewish homeland.

Another poorly managed decolonization process occurred in Malaya, long a crucial British possession because of its proliferation of rubber plantations, given the need for rubber tires for vehicles during the Second World War. Malaya's ethnic Chinese subjects – 2 million people out of a population of 5 million – were excluded from citizenship and faced social and economic discrimination. Many ethnic Chinese supported a Communist uprising there led by the Malayan Races Liberation Army (MRLA) beginning in 1948. MRLA strategies included targeted assassinations, including those of white plantation officials and their families.

The British government declared a state of emergency that lasted for the next 12 years, and conducted a combined counterinsurgency operation, working with the Malay states and native police officers. The operation ran into difficulties be-cause of the thickness of the jungle and the widespread support for the MRLA by the Chinese population. Eventually, the British turned to options later used in other counterinsurgency movements, including concentrating the civilian population in "strategic hamlets" and attempting to "win the hearts and minds" of the people. After 12 years, over 20,000 deaths, and the expenditure of over $3 billion, the Emergency was declared successfully concluded, and Malaya granted its independence (Ludwig 2007).

After the decolonization of India, the British saw Africa as fertile ground for a stable military base and source of manpower. Kenya was home to 67,000 Europeans (who controlled about half of the arable land), 175,000 Asians, and 6.3 million Africans. In contrast with the UK, where nationalization was rampant, Britain's elite in Kenya championed private industry. The Colonial Development Corporation, founded in 1947, had development funds available for Kenya and elsewhere in East Africa, and encouraged large corporations like Unilever, Shell Oil, and Imperial Chemical Industries to invest in Kenya. Although held back by its status as a member of the sterling area, and thus suffering for lack of access to dollars, Kenya experienced an impressive average growth rate of 3 percent between 1948 and 1960 (Tignor 1993).

At first decolonization seemed far in the future, but in 1952, rebellion broke out, led by a group calling itself the Land Freedom Army (derisively referred to as the "Mau Mau" by the British). As in Malaya, ethnic preferences led to widespread feelings of discontentment. One-fifth of the Kenyan population belonged to the Kikuyu tribe, whose land had been given to European settlers and who had borne a longstanding grievance ever since. The British responded by declaring an emergency and jailing Kenyan nationalist politicians, including Jomo Kenyatta, Kenya's most notable leader. British troops using advanced weaponry battled native Kenyan troops wielding arrows and spears. In some areas of the country, Africans were shot on sight, and British interrogators tortured prisoners for information. Tens of thousands of Africans were concentrated in "protected villages" similar to those in Malaya. The emergency lasted until 1960, and in 1963, Kenya declared its independence.

Suez and After

Violent decolonization around the world highlighted Britain's waning international strength. In part to counter this, Britain pursued a policy of nuclear deterrence in the 1950s and hoped to be a third source of global power, between the United States and the Soviet Union. Britain was forced to abandon the posture of foreign policy independence after the Suez Crisis of 1956 (Nissimi 2001). In 1955–1956, Britain and France had been negotiating about the possibility of supranational European cooperation outside of NATO. The two countries were united by the fear that the United States was shifting too much responsibility for containing the Soviet Union to Western Europe.

The nationalization of the Suez Canal by Egypt's leader, Gamal Abdel Nasser, gave Britain and France the opportunity to experiment with cooperation. France was concerned about instability in the Middle East because it menaced its already rebellious colony of Algeria. The United Kingdom feared that Middle East instability threatened Britain's primacy in the region and its access to oil. Furthermore, there was little love lost between Israel and Egypt. The three countries' leaders hatched a secret plan: Israel would attack Egypt, which actually happened on October 29 at the Sinai Peninsula; then Britain and France would invade on the pretext of restoring peace. Unfortunately for Britain and France, the United States, which had not been consulted, immediately intervened in the crisis, pressuring other European powers to help stop the war. On November 6, the United Kingdom was forced to declare a ceasefire unilaterally (Dietl 2008). Suez revealed the impossibility of a truly independent foreign policy, for even in league with two other countries, Britain could not operate against American wishes.

Anthony Eden, who had been Prime Minister during the Suez Crisis, stepped down as leader of the Conservative Party in January 1957 and was replaced by Harold Macmillan. The change in leadership helped to salve the embarrassment that the Conservative Party felt about Suez and about Eden's flawed leadership generally (Williams and Ramsden 1990: 435). Macmillan eventually restored relations with the United States, but the partnership was not an equal one. Macmillan liked to think of the British as akin to the ancient Greeks, asserting intellectual leadership over the militarily superior Romans (played in modern times by the United

Figure 12.1 British troops moving through Port Said during the 1956 Suez crisis. (© Bettmann/Corbis).

States); but the American foreign policy establishment didn't share this view of its own intellectual inferiority. The fact that the British were increasingly indebted to the United States for its nuclear deterrent made the Greeks and Romans analogy even less plausible.

Harold Macmillan and the Winds of Change

Harold Macmillan asked his staff for a policy reassessment as soon as he came into office in 1957. He saw Britain's colonies as expensive and not beneficial, and doubted the loyalty of colonial peoples. In 1960, he delivered a speech that came to be called the "Winds of Change" speech, symbolically choosing to deliver it before the South African Parliament. He acknowledged that decolonization was the most important postwar trend in British foreign policy. Decolonization was popular with those on the left, who believed that colonial peoples had a right to represent themselves democratically. But many on the right felt that the British betrayed their stewardship responsibilities to former colonies by handing over power in situations and in ways that were likely to promote instability, dictatorship, and bloodshed. Macmillan was instrumental in moving the Conservatives away from this viewpoint (Holland 1996).

The 1960s saw a raft of African declarations of independence: Nigeria (1960); Somalia (1960), formerly British Somaliland; Tanganyika (1961), which in 1964 united with Zanzibar to become Tanzania; Sierra Leone (1961); Uganda (1962); Zambia and Malawi (1964); and Gambia (1965). The decolonization process often foundered over racial questions. In 1961, South Africa withdrew its reapplication to the Commonwealth, which required that member nations officially sanction racial equality (upon becoming a republic South Africa was required to reapply for Commonwealth membership). The issue became particularly acute in Rhodesia, a haven for former British soldiers stationed in Africa. The decision by the white minority government there to declare independence in 1965 inaugurated civil war, but the British came down firmly on the side of majority rule.

The Commonwealth continued to exist in name, but its role radically changed to one of advancing democracy in, and cooperation among, Britain's former colonies. Symbolizing the shift in sovereignty, the Commonwealth secretariat's leadership rotated among the various Commonwealth countries; the Queen became a figurehead rather than a leader to whose command Commonwealth countries owed any substantive loyalty.

In addition to innovating in the field of foreign policy, the Conservatives under Macmillan changed the system of local government for London and other municipalities. The Greater London Council, created in 1963, weakened the strong local authority that had been vested in the London County Council since 1889. The new body united the traditionally left-wing stronghold of inner London boroughs with the more suburban outer London boroughs, which tended to be dominated by Conservatives. The Greater London Council covered 620 square miles and 8 million people, and was responsible for transportation planning and strategic land acquisition. It remained dominated by the Conservative Party until 1973.

After the fatigue of many years in power, the Conservative Party was finally undermined from within by a sex scandal. John Profumo, Secretary of State for War, had been having an affair with a young girl named Christine Keeler, who was herself in an affair with the Russian military attaché in London. With the news breaking a year after the Cuban missile crisis nearly escalated the Cold War into nuclear conflict, this kind of indiscretion was indefensible, and Profumo was forced to resign. At the same time, the credibility of the Labour Party had grown in opposition, after many years in which moderates and radicals within the party had savaged each other over the ongoing issue of nationalization of industries. A one-year premiership by the Scottish aristocrat Sir Alexander Douglas-Home (1963–1964) was unable to stave off what now seemed like the inevitable. Voters brought the Labour Party back into power in 1964 under the leadership of Harold Wilson.

Labour's biggest challenges were economic. The government tried various options to secure steady growth, including centrally managing the economy through the National Economic Development Council and putting restraints on wages. Finally, only devaluing the pound again – making it worth less compared with other currencies – enabled a return to prosperity before the end of the decade. With prosperity somewhat secure, the Labour government sought to reform trade unions, but the unions had so much power within the Labour Party that the government was unable to enact meaningful reform. Wages began rising rapidly in 1969 and 1970. Workers had success in striking bargains on the shop floor in various industries by leveraging against other bargaining units. If bargaining didn't work, the strike weapon was available, and was often used. During the run-up to the 1970 general election, Conservatives capitalized on the idea that unions had gotten out of control. They won handily, bringing Edward Heath into power (Rhodes 2000).

Finding Allies and Trading Partners: Britain in Search of a Role

In the 1960s, Britain "lost an empire but had not yet found a role" (in the ascerbic words of former American Secretary of State Dean Acheson). The special relationship conditioned the entire postwar period, but it seemed like an unequal friendship. The British had developed their own nuclear weapons – an atomic bomb in 1952, followed by a hydrogen bomb in 1957 – but then abandoned the idea of promoting an independent nuclear deterrent force when their planned Blue Streak program showed grave problems. Beginning in the early 1960s, the Americans stationed their Skybolt missiles on British bases, and supplemented the land-based nuclear deterrent with missiles on board Polaris submarines. When Britain pulled out of its colonial holdings in Asia in the late 1960s (everything "east of Suez"), US President Lyndon Johnson was exasperated, since the Americans were at that moment professing to hold off Communist domination in Vietnam.

Given the strain on the special relationship, the British pursued other allies. In 1959 they joined the European Free Trade Area (EFTA), a loose and hastily cobbled-together economic sphere, containing Britain, Ireland, Portugal, Denmark, Sweden, Austria and Norway. EFTA was economically unpromising, so large firms within Britain pressured Harold Macmillan to begin negotiations to join the European Economic Community (EEC). Macmillan began talks to allow Britain to join the EEC in 1961, only to see French President Charles de Gaulle veto British entry in 1963. De Gaulle issued his first veto on the grounds that the British would not agree to all of the requirements laid down for EEC member nations.

In 1967 Harold Wilson's Labour government petitioned for entry into the EEC a second time, asking for no special exemptions, but the application was vetoed again, this time stemming solely from de Gaulle's desire that France remain the most important nation in the EEC. The Commonwealth countries also were clearly waning as trading partners with Britain by this time. Britain considered other economic policy options, including forming a common market with the United States (rejected because it was clear that the US would always be the dominant trading partner). Solitary status was also considered, since the pound sterling still ranked second in the world as a reserve currency; but Britain's constant imbalance between exports and imports, and the need to keep drawing on the International Monetary Fund to keep the pound stable, showed that Britain's position was slipping. Having no other viable option, Britain attempted entry into the EEC a third and final time in 1973 and finally was allowed to join (Parr 2006).

The 1970s

As Britain prepared to enter the European Economic Community, the government had the chance to stiffen labor laws to cohere with more stringent laws elsewhere in Europe. The 1971 Industrial Relations Act passed by Edward Heath's Conservative government made collective bargaining agreements legally binding, and set up a National Industrial Relations Court to police violations. This was controversial since in many industries, informal agreements were hammered out between workers and their supervisors on the shop floor. Many workers found these informal arrangements highly functional, but the new legislation made their informality illegal.

In response to the 1971 Industrial Relations Act, the National Union of Mineworkers conducted a seven-week strike beginning in January 1972, the first national miners' strike since 1926. At issue was the pursuit of a large pay increase – between 35 and 47 percent – at a time when pay increases were supposed to be limited to 7 percent to counter inflation. A total of 280,000 members participated in the strike, blocking access to coal-fired power-plants, picketing, and participating in occasional acts of violence. Eventually the miners triumphed, but it was a short-run triumph.

In order to foster economic growth, in 1972 Heath attempted what the press called a U-turn, pursuing full employment as the government's main priority. He hoped to negotiate with trade unions to keep wages from rising too fast, but unions refused to cooperate. Slow growth worsened as a result of the oil shock of 1973. The oil-producing countries, mostly located in the Middle East, had joined together into a cartel – the Organization of the Petroleum Exporting Countries. OPEC had the power to set prices for oil, a commodity on which modern transportation completely depended. Oil was also a key input in many manufacturing processes. The result of rising oil prices and rising wages was horrendous inflation. The British government also moved to accelerate development of its own oil platforms in the North Sea.

Just as Macmillan's Conservative government presided over the creation of the Greater London Council, so Heath's Conservative government completely reorganized the ancient system of county governance to promote efficiency based on large-scale planning and regional cooperation. The Local Government Act (1972) divided nearly the entire country aside from London into a set of 39 counties (metropolitan counties for the urban areas of Greater Manchester, Merseyside, South Yorkshire, Tyne and Wear, West Yorkshire, and West Midlands, and non-metropolitan or "shire counties" for rural areas), and, within the counties, a set of 296 districts. The responsibilities traditionally accorded to local government (road engineering, waste disposal, education, libraries) were divided up between the counties and the districts. Towns too small to be districts could remain civil parishes. An Act the following year did the same for Scotland.

The Troubles

After many years of relative détente, Britain's relationship with Ireland had unraveled in what came to be called "The Troubles." Northern Ireland, although numerically dominated by Protestants, had a significant Catholic minority. Some Catholics sought to unite Northern Ireland with the Irish Free State to the south. They had good reason to feel like second-class British citizens. Unemployment was rife, particularly among the Catholics, running 20 to 30 percent. Housing was segregated, evictions were still common, and Protestant and Catholic children attended separate schools and learned different versions of their country's history. Gerrymandering had further weakened the Catholic vote. Efforts by Harold Wilson's government to inquire into and redress some of the discrimination were derailed by the development of the vigorous and loud Ulster Unionist movement, led by the Rev. Ian Paisley.

By 1968, a civil rights movement led by the Northern Ireland Civil Rights Association was building, based on methods borrowed from the civil rights movement in the United States. Rioting and bombing occurred intermittently throughout 1969, since both sides of the polarized debate had paramilitaries. The Irish Republican Army (IRA) had spun off a militant wing, the Provisional IRA, which began bombing targets in Northern Ireland. The IRA in turn was targeted by the militia raised by the Ulster Unionists, called the Ulster Volunteer Force. Harold Wilson's administration committed British troops to Ireland, solidifying the sense of Northern Ireland as an occupied territory, and the Downing Street Declaration, issued in August of 1969, reaffirmed the British government's intention to retain the six counties of Northern Ireland as part of Great Britain.

In 1971, the Royal Ulster Constabulary began Operation Demetrius, its crackdown on the IRA leadership. Many IRA leaders were arrested and mistreated or

Figure 12.2 In one of the darkest moments of Northern Ireland's "Troubles," 13 people were killed during a civil rights march in Londonderry in 1972. Here, crowds turn out for the funeral of the Bloody Sunday victims. (© Bettmann/Corbis).

detained without trial, which helped cement the sense of grievance and exclusion that Catholics felt. On January 30, 1972, "Bloody Sunday," demonstrators opposing internment without trial clashed with police in Derry, in the southern part of Northern Ireland. Police fired on the crowd, killing 30 men and one woman. In the long run, Bloody Sunday became a cause célèbre that helped unite the movement to gain independence for Northern Ireland. In the short run, it also led to massive violence, with almost 500 killings and more than 2,000 bombings occurring in 1972 alone. After Bloody Sunday, the Northern Irish parliament at Stormont was dismissed, and Northern Ireland was ruled directly from Westminster by the Secretary of State for Northern Ireland.

Parliament passed the Northern Ireland Constitution Act (1973) which provided for proportional representation of both Protestants and Catholics in a new Assembly, as well as a power-sharing executive. This attempt at joint rule was unsuccessful. The years following 1972 also saw the erection of the "Peace Line" in Belfast, a border wall 15 foot tall separating Protestant from Catholic areas. These times also saw the establishment of a grassroots organization, the Community of Peace People, which won the Nobel Peace Prize for its work to bridge the cultural divide. Even so, bombings and acts of violent retribution by both Protestants and Catholics continued unabated.

Popular Politics

Nationalism within the United Kingdom pulled more than just Northern Ireland away from Westminster. After many years of running for Parliament and losing, Gwynfor Evans, president of the Welsh Nationalist Party Plaid Cymru, finally won a seat in 1966, and by 1974 the party had three seats. Welsh nationalists emphasized the importance of retaining Welsh as a living language, and in 1967, the language was legally placed on an equal footing with English within Wales. The Scottish National Party, originally founded in the mid-1930s, picked up supporters and gained almost a third of the Scottish vote in 1974; this led to bills for devolution in Wales and Scotland in 1978. A referendum on the issue was put to voters in Wales and Scotland the following year, but neither referendum attracted enough voters for action to be taken.

Other narrowly targeted political groupings developed as well. The Campaign for Nuclear Disarmament (CND) formed in 1958 from the combination of two existing antiwar groups. CND's intellectuals included the philosopher Bertrand Russell, historian A.J.P. Taylor, and writer J.B. Priestley, along with Quakers, clergymen, and others. Together, they opposed British nuclear testing with annual marches which by the 1960s attracted tens of thousands of participants. CND encouraged the Labour Party unilaterally to forswear the use of nuclear weapons, but Labour leader Hugh Gaitskell blocked this attempt. After the Cuban missile crisis (1962) resulted in the adoption of a limited Nuclear Test Ban Treaty (1963), CND went into decline. The forerunners to Britain's Green Party, called People (1973) and the Ecology Party (1975–1976), although unimpressive at the polls, campaigned for sustainable growth and concern for the environment. The extreme right-wing National Front, which took as its platform opposition to immigration and to multilateral organizations like NATO and the United Nations, flourished briefly in some urban constituencies in 1977–1978.

The rise of the civil rights and feminist movements in the United States and the establishment of the Equal Employment Opportunity Commission there helped to encourage British women to pursue a new movement for women's liberation. Women set up battered women's shelters and rape crisis centers, advocated for child care, and sought legislation that improved women's work opportunities. The availability of birth control meant that women could now plan their families in ways that allowed them to enter the workforce more easily. In 1967, the Abortion Act decriminalized abortions, although they were only available under the National Health Service at a doctor's discretion. The Employment Protection Act of 1975 allowed women six weeks of maternity leave and compelled employers to keep jobs open for 29 weeks for women after their babies were born, although the Act was much ignored in practice (Aiston 2005).

An Equal Pay Act (1970) mandated equal pay for equal work. The main problem for equal pay in the British labor market, however, was that jobs themselves tended to be segmented by gender: women predominated in fields like nursing, teaching, and the social services sector; men predominated in science and engineering, technology, and heavier manual trades. In terms of the sheer number of women employees this job market segmentation benefited women, since more of the former kinds of jobs became available, especially in the 1970s; but the pay for these jobs was generally lower. In the private sector, businesses began to hire women at an accelerated rate compared with men – suggesting that many extremely competent women were now preparing for and seeking such jobs. The Equal Pay Act produced a 15 percent increase in women's hourly wages but it was not until the Sex Discrimination Act of 1975 that the problem of en employment "glass ceiling" was approached systematically.

Increased economic opportunities for women and better fertility control allowed postwar women to more easily support themselves as single units. With legislation liberalizing divorce, this social context increased the number of divorces in the period between 1959 and 1975. In 1949, means-tested legal aid became available for those seeking to dissolve their marriages. Legislation passed in 1964 provided the opportunity for Scottish divorcees to collect alimony for the first time. In 1971, the Divorce Reform Act removed the requirement that one of the two parties to a divorce be found at "fault." Now a married couple could divorce after two years of voluntary separation or after a minimum of one year on other grounds; and the Matrimonial Proceedings and Property Act granted women financial support that made divorce financially tenable. A similar reform followed in Scotland in 1976. Interestingly, the number of divorces peaked in the early 1980s and then leveled off, suggesting that for a long time couples had been remaining in unsatisfactory marriages because of the substantial cost of exiting such marriages (Smith 1997).

Labour, the Social Contract, and the "Winter of Discontent"

At the same time that Heath's government struggled with problems ranging across the economy, Northern Ireland, and the emergence of new demands for political and social equality, the Labour Party began to form a new consensus that it called the "Social Contract." It promised to please unions by repealing the Industrial Relations Act, nationalizing the docks, and increasing pensions. In 1974, Heath called a general election, as a plebiscite on the role of trade unions in the government. Those who thought trade unions were too powerful voted for Conservatives; but Heath's party was defeated nonetheless.

Under Harold Wilson in the mid-1970s, the Labour Party began to take bold steps toward Europe in foreign relations, and toward centralization at home. The Labour Party had traditionally criticized the EEC, calling it a union of the more prosperous nations in Europe that excluded the nascent economies of Eastern Europe, or pointing out that it was less diverse ethnically than Britain's historic

Figure 12.3 By the late 1970s, unions and employers, including government employers, were at odds, culminating in the Winter of Discontent. Here, autoworkers at British Leyland participate in a 1979 strike. (© Bettmann/Corbis).

Commonwealth. Nonetheless, the government held a referendum on the question of whether Britain should remain part of the EEC in 1975, and it stayed a member.

Wilson retired in 1976, and was replaced by James Callaghan, who had at one time or another held three of the highest posts in the land, Chancellor of the Exchequer, Home Secretary, and Foreign Secretary. On his watch, the Labour government passed health and safety legislation, and also managed to hold wages in check for three years – actually producing a wage decline across industries, something that had not been seen since 1931. But Callaghan was plagued by Britain's economic weakness. Britain had to borrow funds from the International Monetary Fund to prop up the pound; countries that borrowed from the IMF were often required to follow austerity measures like cutting the salaries of public sector workers and slashing government programs. Callaghan came under pressure not just from the IMF, on one side, but also from the trade unions, on the other. In 1978, however, the trade unions ceased to cooperate with the government, and when Callaghan's government attempted to exert cost-cutting measures against public employee unions, they responded by striking.

The "winter of discontent" of 1978–1979 saw trash pile up for weeks, since the garbage collectors were on strike. The garbage was followed by an epidemic of feasting rats. Panic buying depleted store shelves. The dead remain unburied in Liverpool, as the gravediggers employed by the local council struck. The tabloid press turned against the strikers, and Callaghan's vacationing in Guadeloupe at the moment of the crisis called his priorities into question. The poorly managed struggle shifted electoral sentiments; while 1978 polls had predicted that the Labour Party would win in a general election by 1 percent of the vote, by 1979 the Conservatives were 18 points ahead. This cleared the way for the election of someone determined to take a much harder line with the unions – Margaret Thatcher.

The period from 1945 to 1979 had pushed successive governments into accepting a redefinition of Britain's role in the world. From its position as a superpower and a member of the Grand Alliance, Britain was demoted to the status of a junior partner to the United States in a bipolar world. Late to enter the European Economic Community, Britain trailed France and Germany in leadership in Europe. Although Britain still nominally led a Commonwealth, the erratic and often violently destructive process of decolonization called into question whether the British had ever known what they were doing as an imperial power. Britain was still a powerful and important state, but now just one among the Western democracies.

The period also saw a new social consensus emerge about the proper role of the state in domestic policy. The laissez-faire economic attitudes of the nineteenth and early twentieth centuries were no longer tenable; government had a role to play in fostering business growth, regulating public utilities, and maintaining a strong private sector. Both Conservatives and Labour saw roles for the government to play in the provision of such social goods as benefits for mothers to stay home with young children; social housing; and publicly provided health care. By the late 1970s, however, pressure on oil resources and economic stagnation were causing a reconsideration of the postwar consensus about the benefits of the welfare state.

References

Aiston, Sarah (2005) A Maternal Identity? The Family Lives of British Women Graduates Pre- and Post-1945. *History of Education*, 34 (4): 407–426.

Aldridge, Meryl (1996) Only Demi-Paradise? Women in Garden Cities and New Towns. *Planning Perspectives*, 11 (1): 23–39.

Churchill, Winston (1946) "Iron Curtain Speech," Mar. 5. At http://www.fordham.edu/halsall/mod/churchill-iron.html (accessed Dec. 3, 2009).

Dietl, Ralph (2008) Suez 1956: A European Intervention? *Journal of Contemporary History*, 43: 259–278.

Fox, Daniel (2004) The Administration of the Marshall Plan and British Health Policy. *Journal of Policy History*, 16 (3): 191–211.

Holland, Robert (1996) The British Experience of Decolonization. *Itinerario*, 20 (2): 51–63.

Ludwig, III, Walter C. (2007) Managing Counterinsurgency: Lessons from Malaya. *Military Review* (May–June): 56–66.

Manto, Sadaat Hasan (1955) Toba Tek Singh. At http://wordswithoutborders.org/article/toba-tek-singh (accessed Aug. 2011).

Nissimi, Hilda (2001) Illusions of World Power in Kenya: Strategy, Decolonization and the British Base, 1946–1961. *International History Review*, 23 (4): 824–846.

Panitch, Leo (1977) Profits and Politics: Labour and the Crisis of British Capitalism. *Politics and Society*, 7 (4): 477–507.

Parr, Helen (2006) Britain, America, East of Suez, and the EEC: Finding a Role in British Foreign Policy, 1964–67. *Contemporary British History*, 20 (3): 403–421.

Rhodes, Martin (2000) Desperately Seeking a Solution: Social Democracy, Thatcherism, and the "Third Way" in British Welfare. *West European Politics*, 23 (2): 161–186.

Robbins, Keith (1983) *Eclipse of a Great Power: Britain, 1870–1975*. London: Longman.

Smith, Ian (1997) Explaining the Growth of Divorce in Great Britain. *Scottish Journal of Political Economy*, 4 (5): 519–544.

Thorsheim, Peter (2006) *Inventing Pollution: Coal, Smoke and Culture in Britain since 1800*. Athens: Ohio University Press.

Tignor, Robert L. (1993) Race, Nationality and Industrialization in Decolonizing Kenya, 1945–1963. *International Journal of African Historical Studies*, 26 (1): 31–64.

Tomlinson, Jim (2008) A Failed Experiment? Public Ownership and the Narratives of Postwar Britain. *Labour History Review*, 73 (2): 228–243.

Williams, Glyn, and Ramsden, John (1990) *Ruling Britannia: A Political History of Britain, 1688–1988*. London: Longman.

Further Reading

Carnevali, Francesca, and Strange, Julie-Marie (eds) (2007) *Twentieth-Century Britain: Economic, Cultural and Social Change*. London: Longman.

Cottrell, Robert C. (2005) *Northern Ireland and England: The Troubles*. Philadelphia: Chelsea House.

Hay, Colin (1996) Narrating Crisis: The Discursive Construction of the "Winter of Discontent." *Sociology*, 30 (2): 253–277.

Joshi, Heather, Layard, Richard, and Owen, Susan (1985) Why Are More Women Working in Britain? *Journal of Labor Economics*, 3 (1, part 2): S147–S176.

Levin, Bernard (1970) *Run It Down the Flagpole: Britain in the Sixties*. New York: Atheneum.

Rubinstein, William D. (2003) *Twentieth-Century Britain: A Political History*. London: Palgrave Macmillan.

13

Building a Welfare State
Society and the Economy, 1945–1979

On July 20, 1957, Conservative Prime Minister Harold Macmillan, known to his admirers as "Supermac," addressed loyal crowds at a rally in Bedford. With un-characteristic optimism, he noted that increased production in major industries such as steel, coal and motor cars had led to a rise in wages, export earnings and investment:

> Indeed let us be frank about it – most of our people have never had it so good . . . Go around the country, go to the industrial towns, go to the farms and you will see a state of prosperity such as we have never had in my lifetime - nor indeed in the history of this country.

Macmillan invoked the "rationing, shortages, inflation and one crisis after another" that had beset Britain immediately after the Second World War, and invoked the specter of socialism. He urged industry, government, and the public to collaborate, to moderate their demands, and to ensure Britain's prosperity by cooperating on a policy to restrict wage increases (Middleton 1957). Wartime austerity was over; fueled by pent-up demand among the working classes for access to cars, refrigerators, televisions, and washing machines, Britain's economy was undergoing what would be known as a "golden age."

Eleven years after Harold Macmillan's speech, another Conservative politician gave a notable speech. When Parliament debated the 1968 Race Relations Bill, Enoch Powell, a member of the Shadow Cabinet (opposition party leaders who "shadow" the jobs of the Cabinet in power), warned in apocalyptic terms against unrestricted immigration (*Telegraph* 2007). He predicted that immigrant minorities would never assimilate, and that in allowing such immigration the British were building a funeral pyre for their own culture. He reported that a constituent had

Empire, State, and Society: Britain Since 1830, First Edition. Jamie L. Bronstein and Andrew T. Harris.
© 2012 Jamie L. Bronstein and Andrew T. Harris. Published 2012 by John Wiley & Sons, Ltd.

told him: "In this country in fifteen or twenty years the black man will have the whip hand over the white man." Reminding his audience of the fall of the Roman Empire, he said that he felt like the Roman who had envisioned the River Tiber "running with much blood." The last metaphor earned his speech the nickname "Rivers of Blood speech," and for giving it, Enoch Powell was immediately ejected from the Conservative Shadow Cabinet. Nonetheless, the policies that he promoted were not far out of line with the platform of the Conservative Party at the time, which proposed assisted voluntary repatriation of immigrants to Britain belonging to ethnic minorities, and limitations on further immigration of their relatives. Just as sentiment in the United States had swung toward Richard Nixon, who promised "law and order" against the threatening divisions of the counterculture, so in Britain, sentiment swung toward the Conservative Party, helping that party win the 1970 election.

The divergence between Macmillan's speech and Powell's illustrates a correlation between prosperity and political tolerance. In the immediate postwar period, a moment of cross-class cooperation born of the myth of the Blitz led to the construction of a welfare state of unprecedented proportions. A baby boom, the expansion of the home market for consumer goods, and low unemployment all contributed to a sense of unlimited possibilities; jobs were so plentiful that West Indian migrants were encouraged to come to Britain and perform service jobs that others preferred not to do. By the end of the 1960s, however, doubts had begun to arise about Britain's productivity compared with that of other countries, and whether trade unions were becoming too powerful. By the 1970s the brief sense of common purpose had given way to an age of fractured social relationships and economic strife (Hillman 2008).

Economic Change and Economic Policies

The immediate period after the Second World War saw a continuation of wartime austerity. As happened during the previous war, Britain had run up an enormous debt, in the form of bonds sold to governments, rather than a direct transfer of funds. This meant that the nation owed much more to other countries than it actually had in its reserves. Because this situation destabilized the pound, it was imperative that the country retool for domestic production of goods that other countries would want to purchase. To worsen the situation further, the end of the lend-lease program with the Americans meant that any new supplies had to be paid for in cash. The Anglo-American Financial Agreement of 1946, a large line of credit ($3.75 billion) that the United States extended to Britain, resulted in a run on the pound in 1947, and a second suspension of convertibility into dollars. Eventually, the pound had to be devalued, from $4.03 to $2.80 in terms of dollars, which radically reduced British consumers' ability to purchase imported goods, but made British goods more attractive abroad.

The government responded to the monetary crisis with spending cutbacks during a year that saw one of the coldest winters on record. The state rationed bread and potatoes, which had not even been rationed during the war. A fuel shortage compounded the cold and privation; few workers were interested in entering the dank and dangerous coal pits, now that women were leaving the workforce in droves and opportunities had opened in clean and modern factories. The government failed to prioritize hiring in the coal industry; miners in the pits were less productive, due partly to the cold weather, which also interfered with the shipment of mined coal; and the National Union of Miners still sought to guard against foreign workers, even in the midst of a labor shortage. The coal shortage resulted in rolling electricity blackouts.

American aid helped Britain pull itself out of these postwar economic woes. The Americans continued to protect the British trading bloc known as the sterling area, in which the pound was used as a reserve currency; this helped to prop up the British currency from an even more precarious situation. More importantly, the US Congress funded the Marshall Plan (1948). The Marshall Plan's purpose was twofold: to help European countries repair the damage of wartime and rebuild their economies; and to create good relations with the United States that would enable these countries to keep the Soviet sphere of influence at a distance from each country's domestic politics. Britain received $3.2 billion in Marshall Plan aid from 1948 to 1951 – more than any other European country (Tomlinson 2000). All of the countries receiving Marshall Aid spent a large proportion of it on consumption items, helping to fortify and keep content a populace that had suffered through years of grueling conflict. Clement Attlee's Labour government encouraged all excess funds to be invested in productive industries to improve exports.

Massive investment in new industries – including pharmaceuticals and aircraft – soon produced full employment in Britain (Clarke 1999). Although British trade unions blocked attempts by American advisors to introduce "scientific management" as a way of increasing productivity, over the next ten years, Britain rebounded from its immediate postwar slump. Consumer rationing ended incrementally – clothing in 1949, food in 1954, and coal in 1958. Troops demobilized from a force of 2 million in 1946 to 810,000 in 1948 (still far ahead of prewar levels). Working-class women, once relegated to the somewhat humiliating relationships of domestic service, now found opportunities in retail, factories, and offices, so that by 1951, only 11 percent of women worked as domestics. In turn, middle-class women expended more of their energy personally managing their households.

Economic Golden Age

The period from the mid-1950s through the early 1970s saw continual and robust economic growth and very low unemployment (ranging from only 1 percent in the southeastern part of England to between 2 and 3 percent in the North and Scotland, and up to 6 percent in Northern Ireland). Inflation and unemployment trends normally move in opposite directions (more people at work earning more wages often mean prices become higher, as people can bid more for goods and services). But in this period, inflation remained relatively low for a long time, only beginning to accelerate seriously after 1968. The average number of hours worked fell from almost 48 per week to almost 45, but by the end of the period people commanded wages six times as high as at the beginning.

Low prices were only one component of the "economic golden age" – a sellers' market in labor was another. For the first time, working people were able to exercise substantial power over the conditions of their employment simply by voting with their feet: a job could be quit on Thursday and another job found on Monday. Rather than pursue two factory incomes, the majority of working families relied upon a male breadwinner who put in large amounts of overtime. Male manual workers worked an average of almost 48 hours a week; truck drivers worked 56 hours a week. The availability of easy credit encouraged expenditures that then needed to be paid off through overtime, meaning that workers were so incredibly fatigued when they got home from work that they could do nothing but watch television, unlike members of the middle classes, who might have a similar take-home pay but much more leisure time. The "golden age" brought many a tradeoff: widespread consumer affluence for long and monotonous work.

What was the nature of this consumer affluence? The 1950s saw many more people able to purchase durable goods for the first time. Most households could now afford to purchase such things as refrigerators, washing machines, vacuum cleaners, cars, and television sets. In 1950, there was one car for every 14 Britons; by 1965, one for every six; by 1973, one for every four. By 1973, 90 percent of homes had a television; an important consolation for women engaged in keeping house on housing estates that lacked the working-class neighborliness of nineteenth-century cities.

As in the United States, the arrival of a fully automotive society changed the transportation map of Britain. Automobile trips rose to account for three-quarters of all transportation by the mid-1970s, forcing governments to respond to road congestion with a massive infrastructure-building program. Cities acquired bypasses that took automobile traffic around their edges – the first one constructed around Preston in 1958. Bypasses helped cut down on traffic to downtowns, but also made visiting downtown businesses more difficult. The construction of bypasses also made possible the construction of Britain's system of fast, numbered, multilane motorways. By the 1970s, Britain had constructed over 1,000 miles of motorway.

A distinguishing factor of the affluence in Britain in the 1950s, in contrast with the United States, was the commitment successive governments made to ensure that prosperity was as widely shared as possible. Providing a "social minimum" – a floor below which no one would, theoretically, be allowed to fall – was a key program of the Labour Party. Redistributive taxation financed the social minimum, helping to compress social classes rather than worsen economic differences. In 1949, the top 1 percent of British earners earned 11 percent of total income, and enjoyed 6 percent of it after taxation; by 1975, those numbers had declined to 5.6 percent and 3.6 percent respectively. The top 10 percent's share of total income declined from 33 percent (27 percent after taxes) to 25 percent (22 percent after taxes). The biggest beneficiaries of the income shift seemed to be middle-class people, since those in the bottom 50 percent of income earners saw their portion of the nation's income barely increase at all (Floud and McCloskey 1994).

Good health is another aspect of affluence. The National Health Service brought existing hospitals under the aegis of the central government, and undertook for the first time that everyone – including visitors to Britain – would have access to primary health-care services, including vision and dental care, initially free at the point of service. The NHS, and developments like antibiotics and the polio vaccine, were accompanied by further improvements in public health. Infant mortality fell; life expectancy rose by three additional years for men and four years for women. A healthier populace could be a harder working populace, making economic prosperity and health mutually self-reinforcing.

The Baby Boom

Postwar affluence, good health, and the ability of more male breadwinners to support stay-at-home wives all contributed to a baby boom. The average age of first marriage in Britain (still high compared to the United States) fell throughout the period between 1951 and 1964, and people who married younger had more children. Policymakers had to scramble to plan new towns and more housing, to accommodate what they anticipated would be 6 million more Britons by 1981, and also to provide more inpatient beds for the elderly, and many more teachers for the nation's schools. Worries about "manpower" needs abounded with a large population of children to be supported by fewer workers. By the early 1970s the demographic boom ended, the nation's fertility rate declined again to the levels of the early 1950s, and there was a net outflow of migrants from Britain of 27,000 per year (O'Hara 2004). But for the decades that the boom lasted, Britons faced the social implications of many more children.

One natural focus of this new concern was education. The postwar period saw revisions to the 1944 Education Act, impelled by concerns that working-class children did not have equal educational opportunity. By the 1950s, it was clear that the eleven-plus test (a test that tracked children into predetermined educational paths at age 11) had not significantly lifted the number of working-class students gaining entrance into grammar schools. Parent involvement in education, particularly the ability of educated parents to help and supervise their children, was so important even by age 11 that many working-class children remained disadvantaged. A 1958 study also revealed that although about 10 percent of students were incorrectly assigned at age 11, it was extremely difficult to transfer from one kind of secondary school to another. The number of grammar school places also varied by geographic region, meaning that many deserving students were denied a place on the basis of where they happened to live; and depending on the area there were sometimes more grammar school places available for boys than for girls.

Seeing these inequities, Anthony Crosland, Labour Secretary of State for Education in the 1960s, spearheaded the replacement of the secondary modern/grammar school division by the comprehensive school, whose job it was to cater to all students. By 1970, one-third of students in secondary education attended comprehensive schools. This did not completely achieve the social egalitarianism that Crosland hoped for, however. Grammar schools still existed in some places, and many middle-class children who would previously have gone to grammar schools sought places at an increasing number of fee-paying independent schools (what Americans would call private schools), which came to be known for their academic focus and business networking opportunities. Technical high schools, which had been meant to catch the middle students between grammar schools and secondary moderns, quickly disappeared, to be replaced by technical colleges and polytechnics, but the end result of this shift was a very small number of students with vocational training.

A streamlining of the educational testing system accompanied the streamlining of the school system. Students successfully finishing their basic secondary education at age 15 took the CSE (Certification of Secondary Education) or took "O level" exams that pronounced them qualified in particular subjects. Able students could move on to further study that culminated in "A Level" exams (in preparation for university admission). The introduction of these exams sparked controversy about children being tracked into exam and nonexam streams, just as there had been in the original three-tiered Butler Act system. But by 1980, 80 percent of children were educated in comprehensive schools, testimony that if British secondary education had not become perfect, it had still become slightly more egalitarian.

The expansion of secondary education was accompanied by an expansion of university education, but access to postsecondary education remained much more limited than in the United States. Immediately after the Second World War, fewer than 2 percent of all students attended university. Although a third of the children of professional parents attended, less than 1 percent of children of working-class parents had the opportunity. Beginning in 1962, any student who could gain admission to university was funded by his or her Local Education Authority, so that finances were no longer the barrier they had once been. Britain's prestigious "ancient universities," including Oxford and Cambridge, had broadened their course offerings since the nineteenth century, but the admissions process for a place in one of their colleges was still so highly competitive that they were unable to meet the national demand. In the late nineteenth and early twentieth centuries the ancient universities had been joined by the "red brick" universities, in cities like Birmingham, Manchester, and Leeds. After the Second World War, increasing appreciation of Britain's need for trained scientists, engineers, and government officials led to the construction of a spate of "plate glass" universities (named after their concrete-and-glass architecture), along with the establishment of polytechnics beginning in 1969, and the launch of the innovative televised Open University. Founded in 1969 and enrolling its first students by 1971, the Open University allowed returning students, the homebound, and other nontraditional students to earn a university degree through televised lectures and correspondence courses, stretching the usual three-year period to earn a bachelor's degree to five years or more. Eventually, the Open University became the largest institution of higher learning in Britain.

As a result of this expansion, by 1968, 6 percent of 18-year-olds attended university (although only 3 percent of all students came from working-class homes) (Schwarz 2004). Although barriers to postsecondary education remained high, large numbers of working-class people during the 1960s (over 80 percent) said they aspired to university education for their children, and almost 20 percent achieved upward mobility into the middle or managerial classes over the course of their lifetimes. For members of the working classes, university education was seen as the key to escaping from the time culture of the factory. "I want him to be a geologist," one worker said, referring to a child. "In my crowd none of us want our children to work hard. We want them to be professional people. Their work is not a burden, it's a pleasure" (Rule 2001: 230).

New Roles for Men and Women

In the immediate postwar period, many women reverted to their prewar roles as consumers, wives, and mothers. The first generation of female university gradu-ates, before the war, had felt that they had to choose between career and family; but in the post-1945 period, it was much more common for career women to also choose marriage and children. Marriage and motherhood were still firmly en-trenched as social expectations, even in a time of relative sexual freedom. Daycare workers and daycare centers were increasingly available, but choices about child care were restrained by beliefs from the 1950s onward that children who were not raised primarily by their own mothers would turn out to be socially deviant juvenile delinquents (Aiston 2005).

For women who did work primarily inside the home, the process of doing housework was completely redesigned and rationalized for life without domestic servants. The norm of the Victorian era that every function of life should ide-ally have its discrete and private space also collapsed; separate dining rooms and kitchens became dining rooms and kitchens separated by a pass-through hatch, which in turn became eat-in kitchens. Social expectations were toned down to match this new informality. No longer was a home-cooked five-course meal, prepared and served by staff, the expectation for a good hostess; convenience foods like canned soups and sauces in packets now greeted the food shopper. Electric hotplates rather than servants kept food warm. Buffets replaced sit-down dinners (Lees-Maffei 2007).

A new life-course was developing for women, in which work played an intermittent role: before marriage, or before the birth of the first baby, and possibly again once children were older. By the 1960s, half of all married women were in the workforce; but their position in the workforce was part of a dual role, with continued primary responsibility for housework. Women's career paths tended not to be prioritized within a couple; women undertook "jobs" rather than "careers." This trend was enhanced by the tenacious wage differential between men and women (women in the 1960s earned on average half as much as men doing the same jobs) (Spencer 2000). Women were particularly numerous in the clerical field – a field that had been dominated by men since its inception in the early nineteenth century – and those jobs were redefined as "women's work." By 1966, a full 40 percent of girls leaving school between the ages of 15 and 18 were entering clerical work, and by 1970, a full 70 percent of clerical workers were women.

Women's combination of marriage and family with careers would not have been possible without the postwar availability of more advanced forms of birth control. Condoms, diaphragms, and by the 1960s, the contraceptive pill, allowed couples to plan smaller families and to separate sex from reproduction. While Victorian women had practiced abstinence within marriage for fear that pregnancy might ruin their long-term health, by the late 1960s, two-thirds of women surveyed professed that a good sex life was essential to happiness (Brooke 2001). Reflecting a new focus on the body, women's magazines shifted from printing articles on preparing family meals to advising their readers on personal appearance and sexual techniques. The increased emphasis on women's sexuality created a backlash in some quarters, as memoir-writers in this period longed for a simpler time of the uncomplicated nuclear family, in which a mother's only role was within the home, asexual and devoted completely to the welfare of her husband and children.

Young working-class men also forged their own culture as the breadwinner ideal became a reality for the first time in a period of full employment. Men were knit together by the common experience of wartime or national service, by factory floors still sex-segregated by task, and by workplace cultural expectations (like the practice of doubling up, covering for each other on the factory floor so that workmates could take breaks) (Francis 2007). The postwar working-class man was also often a proud member of a trade union. Unionism flourished, aided by the willingness of both Labour and Conservative governments to negotiate with trade unions, and by the prestige of politicians of the Second World War era who had had their start in the labor movement. Between 1951 and 1968, British white-collar unionization increased by 30 percent, and by 1979 44 percent of white-collar workers would be unionized. Central government agencies were completely unionized by 1974.

Race and Immigration

Just as the American prosperity in the 1950s and 1960s led to the introduction of a guest-worker program there, so British prosperity resulted in an invitation to workers from the empire to perform some of the available service jobs. Although there had been about 4,000 West Indians living and working in Britain during the Second World War, the importation of West Indian labor to Britain in the modern period began in earnest in 1948 when the ship *Empire Windrush* brought 500 young men specifically to take up jobs. West Indian migrants began to concentrate in Greater London, and to a lesser extent in cities like Liverpool where there were existing black communities dating back to the nineteenth century. Black workers were particularly targeted for jobs as bus conductors, porters, and kitchen staff – jobs that had once been integral to the native-born working class but which, with the availability of high-paying factory jobs, were now seen as beneath them. Black women were also hired as nurses, but found it harder to reach managerial positions in health care. Furthermore, many white British people viewed West Indian migrants as visitors from outside the social fabric, who should not be encouraged to marry and have children.

Figure 13.1 Jamaican immigrants who came over on the *Empire Windrush*, at Tilbury in 1948. (© Hulton-Deutsch Collection/Corbis).

Migration from the West Indies to Britain accelerated after 1952 due to immigration restrictions into the United States. Black migrants concentrated into a few neighborhoods, which became targets for racial hatred. In late August and early September of 1958, white working-class youth descended on Nottingham and the areas of Notting Hill, Shepherd's Bush, Kensal New Town, Paddington and Maida Vale in London. For three weeks, the rioters attacked people and property. The ideology of the British Empire had inculcated a strong sense that white superiority and imperial rule were key elements of "Britishness," and the influx of migrants, not just from the West Indies but from Asian areas of the former empire, helped to problematize this notion.

Many West Indian men strove to assimilate, and to embody ideas of gentlemanliness that had been engendered during the late nineteenth century. At the same time, some white Britons continued to harbor racial stereotypes of West Indian men as more sexual, or less thrifty, or less responsible toward their offspring, than white Britons. Some West Indian men saw elements of apathy or laziness within their own community, and identified it with a small and disreputable subculture that chose to "hustle" rather than to find legitimate work. Racial fears were also expressed about relationships between Jamaican men and white women – aided by definitions of masculinity within the immigrant community that might include the values of virility and sexual conquest.

Although many West Indian men started out with skills, when they migrated to Britain they could only secure unskilled jobs; only 5 percent experienced upward mobility in the first generation. West Indian men did not have the same depth of industrial training as their British counterparts; and they lacked technical credentials. These factors then became self-fulfilling, as stereotypes about the qualifications of black workers fed into a refusal to offer them more demanding jobs (Collins 2001). Stereotypes about black men were accompanied by discriminatory policing, which helped to create among black youths a feeling that they had no legal methods of protest. Through their personal experiences, combining a sense of nationality derived from the West Indies with a sense of inclusion in an imperial Britain, West Indians and their British-born children insisted that "Britishness" should have a much more cosmopolitan meaning.

The British Nationality Act of 1948 featured an inclusive notion of citizenship – those born in the Commonwealth and those born on British soil shared a common citizenship which implied freedom of movement. But over time, the idealism expressed in this legislation was subject to a race-based backlash. Ideas about race in Britain began to harden during the late 1950s and 1960s, as the rate at which Commonwealth migrants entered the United Kingdom began to accelerate. While 20,000 people entered every year in the mid-1950s, in 1961 the total number rose to 100,000. Migrants came not only from the West Indies, but from Cyprus, from Hong Kong, and particularly, from India and Pakistan. As Neville Kirk points out, black and Asian Commonwealth migrants represented a small fraction of the total population – 500,000 out of 50 million – but they had a bigger psychological significance for those who saw them as inimical to Britishness (Kirk 2008).

A series of legislative enactments followed: The 1962 Commonwealth Immigrants Act controlled the immigration of all Commonwealth passport holders except those who held UK-issued passports. Prospective immigrants now needed to apply for a work voucher, graded according to the applicant's employment prospects. This was particularly problematic when Jomo Kenyatta's Kenyan government began a program of "Africanization." Twenty-three thousand Asians, who had been transplanted to Kenya from India when it was under British rule, found their livelihoods in Kenya threatened and sought to migrate to Britain, where they held citizenship. In the middle of this migration, Parliament rushed into law the 1968 Commonwealth Immigrants Act, which denied automatic entry to those whose British passports had been issued outside the British Isles. Those with a parent or grandparent who had been born, adopted or naturalized in the United Kingdom were exempt from this new law, which, intentionally or not, tended to sort immigrants along racial lines (Samantrai 2002).

After the 1971 Immigration Act, immigrants to Britain included political refugees and the extended families of those who had already migrated to Britain. These legal immigrants entered alongside up to a million illegal migrants. The evolution of ideas about citizenship culminated in the British Nationality Act of 1981, which transformed citizenship so that even babies born in Britain were not necessarily British citizens, unless either their mother or their father was already a citizen or settled in Britain.

Restrictions on migration to the United Kingdom were counterbalanced by Acts to prohibit racial discrimination. The 1968 Race Relations Act – the legislation that had so enraged Enoch Powell – prohibited discrimination on the basis of ethnicity in the provision of housing and employment (although the government was specifically exempted from these rules). The 1976 Race Relations Act more expansively prohibited discrimination in employment or the provision of public services on the basis of "colour, race, nationality or ethnic or national origins." Whether the discrimination was direct or indirect, it was prohibited, although affirmative action to bring underrepresented groups into the workforce was not prohibited. Victimization of any person on racial grounds was prohibited, and government created the the Commission for Racial Equality to enforce the law. Despite these state initiatives, segregated housing patterns continued throughout the period to 1979, and people continued to befriend and marry others of their own ancestry or ethnic group.

What's the Matter with Britain?

By the late 1960s, the economic golden age was drawing to a close – and some economists and social commentators wondered whether it had ever existed. When compared with other countries like Germany, the United States, and Japan, Britain had a declining share of exports (from 25 percent of the world's exports in 1950 to less than 10 percent in 1975). Britain's lack of price competitiveness compared with other manufacturing nations was partly to blame, and Britain consistently lagged behind all other countries with developed manufacturing sectors between 1950 and 1979. Why did the British charge more for their products? As has been noted, Britain was slow to adopt mass-production techniques; British craftsmen, having honed their skills on the shop floor rather than in schools of technology, successfully insisted on their autonomy, which they protected by unionizing according to sets of skills rather than in large unions across industries (as was the case in the United States). British employers, who communicated with each other about the prices of inputs and outputs to a greater extent than American firms, settled for slightly lower productivity growth in exchange for industrial peace. Government policies favoring high employment led to overstaffing in many industries, but again, to greater welfare for working people in the short run. In the short run, there was a social consensus that profits were less important than people, but over time, the success of the union movement created its own backlash; ever growing proportions of the British public would complain that trade unions had too much power in government – 62 percent in 1962, 73 percent in 1970, and 81 percent in 1974 (Crewe et al. 1996).

The government also engaged in much closer regulation of the economy than was the case in the United States. In 1962, under the Conservative Party, the National Economic Development Council was created, with representation by employers, trade unions, and the government. The hope was that this organization would set targets for growth in various industries, and give businesspeople the confidence they needed to invest. Its recommendations were, however, too vague to produce much change. The government also pursued "stop-go" policies. High rates of employment and economic growth pushed up inflation and increased imports in the "go" phase of the cycle; this, in turn, left Britain with a balance-of-payments deficit, and the government would subsequently try to rein in inflation during the "stop" phase with tax increases and higher interest rates.

When the Conservatives were replaced by Labour, Prime Minister Harold Wilson criticized "stop-go" economic policies, claiming that a steadier rate of growth was needed to promote constant investment. He called for more investment in science, including more science education and the establishment of a Ministry of Technology, reaching out to a technophile middle class that respected expertise. The economic policies of the Labour government included tax increases and a rise in the prime interest rate (the Bank Rate). Under Labour's George Brown, the Department of Economic Affairs produced a National Plan for economic development (1965), along with a National Board for Prices and Incomes, which was supposed to adjudicate any wage increases above a certain level. Labour also undertook an energetic propaganda campaign aimed at all levels: government, employers, workers, and the public – to reassure them of the benefits of economic planning for productivity growth. Ultimately, however, Labour's desire for more centralized economic planning conflicted with the powers held by the Treasury, which was fond of using the "stop" weapon and continued to do so.

The Labour governments of the 1960s and 1970s moved away from the focus on equalizing fortunes that had been such a concern of the immediate postwar governments. This left intact a situation in which income disparity diminished, but the asset ownership by different groups remained very unequal. In 1960, for example, 75 percent of property was owned by the wealthiest 5 percent of the population. Government spending during the Wilson administration (1964–70) was highest in the areas of defense and education, followed closely by the National Health Service (O'Hara 2006). The expense of maintaining British forces in the Far East led the British to pull out of parts of Asia. It was a move criticized by the United States, currently engaged in war in Vietnam, but the Wilson government had little choice. What were the results of these policies? The unemployment rate was always under 3 percent, and the economic growth rate remained respectable throughout the late 1960s, fluctuating from a high of 5.5 percent in 1964 to a low of 1.9 percent in 1966. Nonetheless, this was lower than the desired growth rate of 7–8 percent per year, and so was seen as a failure in relative terms (Carnevali and Strange, 2007).

In addition to suffering from relatively low productivity, high prices, and inconsistent levels of central planning, the British consistently suffered from imbalances of trade, importing more than they exported to other countries. In order to support the pound, the British government was forced to pursue not just devaluation, but also to borrow from the International Monetary Fund (IMF), the lender of last resort for countries in financial crisis. The IMF would only let countries borrow money under certain conditions. Since the pound sterling was the second most important world currency, until 1965 the IMF did not impose many restrictions on British governments wanting to borrow. After 1965, it was much less likely to make exceptions for the British, and insisted that the government cut domestic spending and disclose the rationales behind policies (Clift and Tomlinson 2008). As a result of Britain's difficulty with reconciling government spending, foreign investment, and military readiness with relatively low exports, runs on the pound were common throughout the mid to late 1960s; in 1967 the pound was devalued to $2.40.

Finally, the British economy was vulnerable because it was already in transition from a manufacturing to a postindustrial economy. The British share of world manufacturing exports was in steady decline throughout the period between 1954 and 1975. Both consumers and manufacturers required imports, whether of finished goods or of parts of goods, and Britain supplied fewer of these things as countries like Japan innovated. British firms that did continue to manufacture failed to compete effectively. The British automotive industry declined, with Rolls-Royce branching out into the manufacture of aircraft engines; the steel industry increased output, but within the matrix of a much larger world market for steel. Most notable was the decline in the textile industry, which had by now completely fallen from its former position of global strength.

Although the switch to a postindustrial economy may seem inevitable in hindsight, in the 1960s the British government tried to discourage the transition from manufacturing to service industries. In 1966, the government levied the Selective Employment Tax, a payroll tax under which manufacturing workers were refunded more than they had paid in. In essence, SET served as a transfer payment to manufacturing workers – encouraging people to pursue factory jobs. Within a short time this was phased out, and British politicians came to accept that the switch to a postindustrial economy was inevitable, with jobs in sectors like financial services, transportation, energy generation, and hospitality and tourism employing a large segment of the workforce. The public sector also grew greatly, since burgeoning sectors of the economy, like healthcare, were almost entirely under government control.

The shift to a postindustrial economy was symbolized by the switch away from coal as the major motive power of British industry and heating. After the immediate postwar shortage of coal and miners, the National Coal Board did pursue advanced coal production techniques. Ultimately, however, there was no way for these to reverse the decline in the demand for coal. In 1960, coal generated 73.7 percent of British energy, but this decreased to 46.6 percent in 1970. The number of coal workers would also decline from 517,000 in 1963 to 281,500 in 1970. The natural resource that had helped Britain to become the first industrial nation became less important (Phillips 2006).

Along with the demise of coal came the discovery of new forms of energy, like natural gas. The National Coal Board had already begun to scale back coal production and exploration when, in 1965, gas was first discovered in the North Sea. The discovery of gas was followed only a few years later by the discovery of substantial oil deposits. Many hoped that these finds would promote something like energy independence at a time when other industrialized economies, the United States included, were in the thrall of energy-exporting countries.

Pockets of Poverty

Some areas of Britain – following the North–South prosperity divide – were left out of this transition to a postindustrial economy altogether. This was felt poignantly in 1966 at Aberfan in Wales. A 50-year-old coal tipple belonging to the Merthyr Vale Colliery became waterlogged from an underground spring, and came crashing down onto a local primary school, inundating classrooms ten feet deep with viscous and choking sludge. Five teachers and 139 primary school students, most between the ages of seven and ten, were killed. A tribunal subsequently investigated the matter, and concluded that the National Coal Board had been willfully negligent in dumping coal waste on top of known underground streams.

The postwar prosperity divide was also palpable in depressed urban areas. British cities, while less likely to go up in riots and flame than American urban centers, were no less plagued by overcrowding, something that was made worse by "urban renewal" schemes to clear former slums. In places like Glasgow and Liverpool, families who could afford to fled from the depressed inner cities to "new towns" on the edge of urban areas. Even these new towns tended to be segregated by class, with middle-class housing more spacious and sometimes available for freehold purchase, while working-class people were relegated to higher-density housing that was only available for rent (Homer 2000).

Successive governments attempted to respond to regional underdevelopment and unemployment through a great fad for regional planning, which hit its peak in the late 1960s and early 1970s. Economic planning councils were set up for each region of the country, but each competed with the others, and none had the ability to shape a fully national policy of resource allocation for economic development. Prosperity remained concentrated in London and the new towns located within hailing distance of London.

Both prosperous southern England and the neglected remainder of Britain were hearkening to new realities about the international economic picture by the beginning of the 1970s. Internationally, the international monetary system created at Bretton Woods, in which the dollar was pegged to gold at $35 an ounce, and other currencies were pegged to the dollar, collapsed in 1971. The United States, under pressure from defense-related spending (the Vietnam War) and social spending (Lyndon Johnson's Great Society programs), was forced to abandon the gold standard. For the rest of the 1970s, currencies would "float," with their value being determined by supply and demand from countries that wanted to hold the currency in their reserves. Tremendous balance-of-payments deficits resulted, reaching £5 (US) billion by 1973. The value of the pound declined to $1.60 in 1976, prompting an emergency loan to Britain from the International Monetary Fund, before settling back at $1.75 in 1977. In 1976, inflation in Britain had reached a jaw-dropping 25 percent, and wages rose between 25 and 30 percent annually to keep up. By 1979, the British economy appeared to have reached a crisis point. Given these inflationary pressures, it was very hard for trade unions to hold back demands for higher wages.

The economic golden age of the 1950s and 1960s was real, but it was short. Britons emerged on the other side with better health and more consumer comforts, but in a postindustrial economy, and given the significant barriers remaining to higher education, it was still unclear how long prosperity could continue, particularly for manual workers. Trade unions had gained membership and power – but had the pendulum now swung too far in one direction, helping to render Britain relatively unproductive compared with other countries? Women and minorities made some social progress, but there was discomfort and a longing for the time when Britain had experienced social peace, even if that peace had come at the price of inequality. By the 1970s, confidence had given way to a rhetoric of national decline, and for many people, the absurdity of the Winter of Discontent crystallized their frustrations, and led to widespread worries about whether there was anything that Britain could do to jump-start its economy or gain back some of the confidence it had enjoyed in the Victorian era.

References

Aiston, Sarah (2005) A Maternal Identity? The Family Lives of British Women Graduates Pre- and Post-1945. *History of Education*, 34 (4): 407–426.

Brooke, Stephen (2001) Gender and Working-Class Identity in Britain during the 1950s. *Journal of Social History*, 34 (4): 774–795.

Carnevali, Francesca, and Strange, Julie-Marie (eds) (2007) *Twentieth-Century Britain: Economic, Cultural and Social Change*. London: Longman.

Clarke, Ian (1999) Institutional Stability in Management Practice and Industrial Relations: The Influence of the Anglo-American Council for Productivity, 1948–1952. *Business History*, 41 (3): 64–69.

Clift, Ben, and Tomlinson, Jim (2008) Negotiating Credibility: Britain and the International Monetary Fund, 1956–1976. *Contemporary European History*, 17 (4): 545–566.

Collins, Marcus (2001) Pride and Prejudice: West Indian Men in Mid-Twentieth-Century Britain. *Journal of British Studies*, 40 (3): 391–418.

Crewe, Ivor, Fox, Anthony, and Day, Neil (1996) *The British Electorate, 1963–1992: A Compendium of Data from the British Election Studies*. Cambridge: Cambridge University Press.

Floud, Roderick, and McCloskey, Deidre N. (1994) *Economic History of Britain since 1700: 1939–1992*. Cambridge: Cambridge University Press.

Francis, Martin (2007) A Flight from Commitment? Domesticity, Adventure, and the Masculine Imaginary in Britain after the Second World War. *Gender and History*, 19 (1): 163–185.

Hillman, Nicholas (2008) A "Chorus of Execration"? Enoch Powell's "Rivers of Blood" Forty Years On. *Patterns of Prejudice*, 42 (1): 84–104.

Homer, Andrew (2000) Creating New Communities: The Role of the Neighborhood Unit in Post-war British Planning. *Contemporary British History*, 14 (1): 63–80.

Kirk, Neville (2008) Traditionalists and Progressives: Labor, Race and Immigration in Post–World War II Australia and Britain. *Austrialian Historical Studies*, 39: 53–71.

Lees-Maffei, Grace (2007) Accommodating "Mrs. Three-in-One": Homemaking, Home Entertaining, and Domestic Advice Literature in Post-war Britain. *Women's History Review*, 16 (5): 723–754.

Middleton, Drew (1957) Macmillan Wins Inflation Debate. *New York Times*, July 26, p. 2.

O'Hara, Glen (2004) "We are Faced Everywhere with a Growing Population": Demographic Change and the British State, 1955–64. *Twentieth-Century British History*, 15 (2): 243–266.

O'Hara, Glen (2006) "Dynamic, Exciting, Thrilling Change": The Wilson Government's Economic Policies, 1964–1970. *Contemporary British History*, 20 (3): 383–402.

Phillips, Jim (2006) The 1972 Miners' Strike: Popular Agency and Industrial Politics in Britain. *Contemporary British History*, 20 (2): 187–207.

Rule, John (2001) Time, Affluence and Private Leisure: The British Working Class in the 1950s and 1960s. *Labour History Review*, 66 (2): 223–242.

Samantrai, Ranu (2002) *AlterNatives: Black Feminism in the Post-Imperial Nation*. Stanford: Stanford University Press.

Schwarz, Leonard (2004) Professions, Elites and Universities in England, 1870–1970. *Historical Journal*, 47 (4): 941–962.

Spencer, Stephanie (2000) Women's Dilemmas in Postwar Britain: Career Stories for Adolescent Girls in the 1950s. *History of Education*, 29 (4): 329–342.

Telegraph (2007) Enoch Powell's "Rivers of Blood" Speech. Nov. 6. At http://www.telegraph.co.uk/comment/3643823/Enoch-Powells-Rivers-of-Blood-speech.html (accessed Sept. 2010).

Tomlinson, Jim (2000) Marshall Aid and the "Shortage Economy" in Britain in the 1940s. *Contemporary European History*, 9 (1): 137–155.

Further Reading

Ayers, Pat (2004) Work, Culture and Gender: The Making of Masculinities in Postwar Liverpool. *Labour History Review*, 69 (1): 153–167.

Broadberry, S.N., and Crafts, N.F.R. (1996) British Economic Policy and Industrial Performance in the Early Postwar Period. *Business History*, 38 (4): 65–91.

Giles, Judy (2001) Help for Housewives: Domestic Service and the Reconstruction of Domesticity in Britain, 1940–1950. *Women's History Review*, 10 (2): 299–324.

Jackson, Ben (2005) Revisionism Reconsidered: "Property-Owning Democracy" and Egalitarian Strategy in Post-war Britain. *Twentieth-Century British History*, 16 (4): 416–440.

Johnson, Paul (ed.) (1994) *Twentieth-Century Britain: Economic, Social and Cultural Change*. Harlow: Longman.

Matthews, Derek (2007) The Performance of British Manufacturing in the Post-war Long Boom. *Business History*, 49 (6): 763–779.

Millward, Robert (1994) British Industry since the Second World War. *History Today*, 44 (6): 49–54.

Rush, Anne (2007) Reshaping British History: The Historiography of West Indians in Britain in the Twentieth Century. *History Compass*, 5 (2): 463–484.

Silverstone, Rosalie (1976) Office Work for Women: A Historical Review. *Business History*, 18: 98–110.

14

Meet the Beatles
Cultural and Intellectual Developments, 1945–1979

On May 15, 1966, *Time* magazine ran a cover story on "Swinging London" that, fairly or not, embodied the cultural meaning of Britain in the 1960s, both for Americans and for the British themselves. "London is switched on," journalist Piri Halasz enthused. "Ancient elegance and new opulence are all tangled up in a dazzling blur of op and pop. The city is alive with birds (girls) and beatles, buzzing with minicars and telly stars, pulsing with half a dozen separate veins of excitement" (Halasz 1966). London was all color and style and living in the moment; the stuffiness of tradition was a thing of the past, and even Prince Charles had long hair. Decolonization was certainly taking place all throughout the former empire; Britain may have been suffering from declining productivity and a consistent trade imbalance, but the one British export that was reliably in demand was cultural production, from the fashion designers of Carnaby Street to the musicians of the first wave of the "British invasion" (as the cultural influence of British music on the US was termed).

But while many of the products and practices of Swinging London were popular, especially with young people, they were controversial among those who saw in loud music, long hair, and micro-miniskirts the potential for moral decay. Nor was the conflict between permissiveness and tradition the only cultural struggle: whether art should be supported by the state or subject to the forces of commercialization was another. Should the BBC and the Arts Council, funded by taxpayers, have the opportunity to shape tastes and promote "uplifting" programming? Or was it better to trust decisions about art and music to consumers? Although historians have often identified the 1980s as the decade in which the decision in favor of commercial forces was finally made, it is clear that the 1960s and 1970s laid much of the groundwork for that change.

Empire, State, and Society: Britain Since 1830, First Edition. Jamie L. Bronstein and Andrew T. Harris.
© 2012 Jamie L. Bronstein and Andrew T. Harris. Published 2012 by John Wiley & Sons, Ltd.

Postwar government support of culture carried with it the same mandate to uplift the downtrodden worker that had animated Matthew Arnold in the nineteenth century. With the necessity of uplift in mind, the postwar British welfare state extended financial support to the arts as well as to individuals. The government subsidized theater companies like the Royal Shakespeare Company and the National Theatre, the latter officially provided with funding by law in 1949. Successful plays could then be transferred to more commercial theaters. Ballet and opera were also heavily subsidized, the Arts Council ran its own galleries, and individual authors and poets received grants in support of their work. Despite the good intentions of people who wanted to use the Arts Council to promote greater cultural awareness, the arts flourished best in places that already had a strong and culturally committed middle class. The industrial Northeast, for example, lagged in theater construction and attendance (Vall 2010). Into this breach left by government-supported arts would step radio, television, and spectator sports, ready to absorb all leisure hours passively and at minimal cost.

The Festival of Britain

Certainly one of the most impressive government-supported arts projects in the first decade after the Second World War, the Festival of Britain of 1951 celebrated the end of wartime austerity and the hundredth anniversary of the Great Exhibition. Throughout the country, local residents wearing period costumes performed in historical dramas; Liverpool, Edinburgh, York, and other towns received special arts grants for the occasion. A festival ship containing exhibits put in at Britain's major ports. Cities held fireworks displays and regattas, outdoor puppet shows and Morris dancing. In London, the highlight of the Festival of Britain was a new concert hall, the Royal Festival Hall, built on a site of derelict warehouses and factories on the south bank of the Thames. Close by, audiences toured the temporary Dome of Discovery, and for the first time saw 3-D films. Exhibitions concentrated on the land and the people of Britain, attempting to tell a new story in which the excellences of traditional "Britishness" – commitment to democracy and craftsmanship, for example – were combined with new ideals of technological advance and meritocracy.

Such a large expenditure on enjoyment, in the midst of periodic winter electricity cuts and continued meat rationing, made some annoyed, particularly in the Tory opposition. The Festival cost £11.5 million in tax money – critiqued as an unnecessary expenditure at a time of war in Korea and cuts to the new National Health Service. But novelist and playwright J.B. Priestley dismissed such naysaying, noting, "if the time has arrived when a great national festival would bring us keen enjoyment, a renewed zest for life, a sudden lift of the spirit, and would create energy, then we must celebrate such a Festival, no matter what its demands are on precious materials and labour" (Priestley 1951). Culture could provide uplift, which was necessary to balance the demands of modern life. The Festival of Britain also symbolized the transformation from the postwar shortage economy to a more buoyant consumer economy, in which, it was hoped, tourism would be a central feature (Grant 2006).

Design

Although wartime austerity and materials shortages hampered British designers from innovating, in 1944 the government had appointed a Council of Industrial Design to collect examples of the best industrial designs for furniture and other home products. The Festival of Britain gave designers the opportunity to display "contemporary" furniture made of lightweight metal, plywood, vinyl, and plastic, and finished in bright colors. The Design Centre in London was opened in 1956 to display innovative design from Britain and elsewhere. Another set of designers called the Independent Group (1952) celebrated mass culture and the American consumer influence on design. Companies began to incorporate their own design teams and to think more about making consumer products fashionable as well as durable. One notable success was the Mini, the iconic British car of what came to be called Swinging London.

Literature and Theater

At first, postwar British literature continued interwar cultural trends. Evelyn Waugh, popular at the end of the Second World War, wrote *Brideshead Revisited* (1945) documenting upper-class life in the interwar years. Graham Greene, whose career spanned the period from the 1930s to the end of the 1970s and included secretly working for the British spy organization MI6, continued to produce thrillers about British expats in the declining empire (he referred to them as "entertainments") and novels that grappled with issues like religion and the struggle between good and evil. The Welsh poet Dylan Thomas, who had been poetically productive in the 1930s, finally emerged into wider fame with the publication of *Deaths and Entrances* in 1946. He would make over 200 recordings for broadcast on BBC radio before his untimely death in 1953.

In the 1950s, British literature and playwriting broke with the tradition of focusing on the British upper classes, either as authors or as the subjects of authorship, reflecting wider social concerns and a wider culture-consuming public. The working-class upstart Colin Wilson wrote *The Outsiders* (1956), a well-received work of philosophy and literary criticism, in the British Library, then went "home" to sleep on Hampstead Heath in a sleeping bag. John Osborne's path-breaking play

Look Back in Anger chronicled the life of the original "angry young man," a college dropout turned candy vendor living in a flat with his downwardly mobile girlfriend Alison, and his best friend, Cliff. In the play, Jimmy rages against the class system, the decline of the British Empire, women, and his own father, who had had the temerity to die when Jimmy was a child. Jimmy's abuse of those close to him is presented as an authentic, and admirable, rebellion against middle-class mores in several ways, as he ends up attracting Alison's best friend Helena by the end of the play. Other plays dealing with a similar subject matter included Shelagh Delaney's *A Taste of Honey* (1958) and Arnold Wesker's *The Kitchen* (1959).

Readers of British literature seeking to escape from working-class realism could immerse themselves in fantastic alternate realities devised by two of postwar Britain's most influential writers. C.S. Lewis, an Oxford don who wrote about Christianity, garnered a wide audience with his Chronicles of Narnia, seven children's fantasy novels beginning with *The Lion, the Witch, and the Wardrobe* (1949). Lewis's best friend, the Beowulf scholar J.R.R. Tolkien, penned a children's book called *The Hobbit*, set in a "Middle Earth" filled with elements of Old English and Norse mythology. The popularity of that book encouraged him to develop the mythology into a trilogy, *The Lord of the Rings*, in the 1950s. During the period of the counterculture, the *Lord of the Rings* trilogy's fantasy elements sparked a chord, and it has since become one of the most popular works of fiction ever written.

Postwar literature also reflected a reevaluation of the British Empire. Nevil Shute, one of England's best-selling writers of popular fiction in the immediate postwar period – his works sold over 14 million copies – had initially celebrated the empire as a potential improvement of Great Britain. By the end of his career, having moved to Australia, he was more cynical, and wrote about former colonies having to turn to their own devices. *On the Beach* (1957), published in the shadow of the Suez Crisis, is the sad chronicle of Australian survivors of a superpower-fueled nuclear holocaust, who are waiting to commit suicide or to die of radiation poisoning in one of the last inhabited areas of the globe.

The postwar period saw a revived interest in poetry, as Philip Larkin, Ted Hughes, and John Betjeman were all popular. Betjeman, who became British Poet Laureate in 1972, nostalgically evoked the familiar paraphernalia of prewar English life, and wrote in a light and humorous vein. Larkin's three postwar collections of poems were much darker. His *Aubade* (1977) captures the terror that comes with contemplating the infinity of death:

> The mind blanks at the glare. Not in remorse
> – The good not done, the love not given, time
> Torn off unused – nor wretchedly because
> An only life can take so long to climb
> Clear of its wrong beginnings, and may never;
> But at the total emptiness forever,
> The sure extinction that we travel to

> And shall be lost in always. Not to be here,
> Not to be anywhere,
> And soon; nothing more terrible, nothing more true.

More cheap paperbacks were also making their way into people's homes: the popular taste was for science fiction, romance, spy thrillers, and other kinds of genre fiction that could be quickly cranked out. But no matter what type of literature they favored, Britons had greater access to books after the 1964 Libraries and Museums Act, which mandated that large local authorities maintain an efficient and comprehensive library service, and placed lending libraries under the supervision of the Secretary of State.

The theater was also becoming more accessible – physically, if not thematically. During the 1930s, left-wing actors had formed the Theatre of Action, which combined themes of class struggle with dance and music. The idea continued into the 1950s with Joan Littlewood's Theatre Workshop in Stratford, in the East End of London, which toned down the social criticism but still staged experimental productions. The 1960s saw the rise of more experimental or "alternative" theater, including socialist theater companies sparked by the New Left; plays and other theatrical "experiences" were staged at pubs, restaurants, miners' holiday camps, and even, in one notable case, in a public swimming pool (Page 1973). The Royal Shakespeare Company reduced the cost of its tickets, touring more often, reaching out to student groups, and experimenting with versions of Shakespeare plays set in different times and settings.

Art and Music

In the visual arts, as in literature, realistic and working-class themes emerged in the 1950s. A "kitchen sink school" of artists from 1954 to 1957 (named after a kitchen sink in one of John Bratby's paintings) included mundane details of working-class life in its depictions. The artist L.S. Lowry, born at the end of the nineteenth century, had been painting scenes of the smoke-filled industrial North since the 1920s, but it was only after the Second World War that he became extremely well known. He depicted generic industrial landscapes populated by generic crowds, making his pictures simultaneously about every working-class person's childhood, and no one's. Lowry's fame coincided with continued clearing of urban slums. As the factory landscapes succumbed to new housing estates, highway construction, and other signs of progress, enthusiasm for England's "industrial heritage" increased (Waters 1999).

American modernism also influenced British artists, forcing a reappraisal of what was significant enough to sculpt or beautiful enough to paint. Henry Moore continued to create his giant rounded figures, but his reputation was eclipsed by sculptors like Anthony Caro, who welded together or collected "found materials" – basically discarded items – into abstract sculptures that didn't represent anything directly. Francis Bacon painted disturbing expressionist portraits of people on the margins of society, often with desiccated heads and screaming mouths. Lucien Freud, Sigmund Freud's grandson, painted nudes with their eyes averted from the artist, in ways that were completely unsparing of all of the eccentricities of real human bodies. His interest in fleshiness drew him to paint models like the performance artist Leigh Bowery, who didn't fit the stereotype of what most people found pleasing (Storr 1988).

By the late 1950s, the pop art craze emerged in Britain, as artists saw new vistas in modern technology and advertising. Art schools emphasized collage and abstract painting, rather than requiring students to master older, more exacting drawing and painting techniques. The National Council for Diplomas in Art and Design even recommended that teachers of fine arts were not there to teach technique, but rather to teach an attitude that could express itself in any number of ways (Brighton 1981). Thus, by the end of the 1960s, modernism had been unseated by the avant-garde. The artists Gilbert and George declared themselves themselves "living sculptures," and Richard Long arranged stone or tree bark into circles, or geometric figures on maps, and then forced himself to follow the paths he had created, as "walking sculptures." Art that was self-referential or avant-garde was not meant to be appreciated by the masses; rather, it was meant to provoke and confuse.

As with the visual arts, British classical music in the wartime and postwar period became more experimental and courted controversy. Michael Tippett's prewar *Child of Our Time* and Benjamin Britten's 1945 opera *Peter Grimes*, which concerns the fate of an English fisherman accused of having abused and murdered two of his apprentices, marked the emergence of British opera as a major force. Under its second conductor, Sir Malcolm Sargent, the Last Night of the Proms exhibited all kinds of invented traditions in its concerts, including four consecutive patriotic set-pieces in which the audience joined in with singing, noisemaking and the waving of flags, and the conductor would make a speech. The event was also televised annually, representing British culture both internally and abroad.

Film

While art and literature and classical music linked postwar Britain with the high culture of the prewar era, the mass media and youth culture appealed to audiences that were broader and more economically and socially diverse. Moviegoing remained extremely popular; on average, in 1946, each of the approximately 50 million people in Britain attended 33 films a year (McCrillis 2001). Although most films shown were made in the United States, government regulations provided that 30 percent of feature films shown had to be British made. As a result, in addition to many poorly made "B movies" intended to accompany American films, British filmmakers specialized in film adaptations of Shakespeare plays and other theatrical works.

While before the war, British studios had had difficulty carving out a niche for themselves when faced with behemoth Hollywood studios, after the war, smaller studios specialized in genre films that became popular both at home and abroad. From the end of the Second World War until 1955, the Ealing Studios produced distinctive comedies that combined dark, sarcastic comedy with slapstick. Their most notorious product, *Kind Hearts and Coronets* (1949), featured Alec Guinness playing eight different members of the same family. Another British studio, Hammer, dominated the production of horror films between the 1950s and the 1970s, producing such classics as *Dracula* (1958), *The Mummy* (1959), and *The Curse of Frankenstein*, which was followed by six sequels. Almost as soon as the Ealing Studios era ended, the James Bond era began. Sean Connery played Ian Fleming's dashing spy with a good deal of self-mockery, and his tailor-made cars and weapons and the over-the-top nature of the films' villains provided half the fun. Pinewood Studios, where most of the Bond films were produced, also created 27 *Carry On* films between the late 1950s and the late 1970s. These low-budget films recycled broad, slapstick humor filled with sexual innuendo – and featuring the same cast – transposing both to different situations (camping, the army, and jungle exploration, for example).

The postwar period also saw the growth of a more serious filmmaking culture. Building on the fascination with the Northern working-class by the school of "angry young men," British filmmakers innovated in the 1950s with the Free Cinema movement, a focus on documentary realism, often about the vagaries of working-class life. Lindsay Anderson's *O Dreamland*, for example, is an unsettling 12-minute black-and-white film that chronicles the Dreamland amusement park in Kent. Amid carnival barkers, wild animals in small cages, and weird laughing dolls, men, women and children with grim facial expressions walk around attempting to have fun (Anderson 1953). Other late 1950s and early 1960s movies dealt with controversial issues: with abortion (*Saturday Night and Sunday Morning*), with teen pregnancy and homosexuality (*A Taste of Honey*), and juvenile delinquency (*The Loneliness of the Long-Distance Runner*). All of these films shared a common sense that the class structure of Britain continued to keep individuals oppressed, no matter which government happened to be in power. These films won several British Academy Awards, but proved less popular among moviegoing audiences than horror movies and spy films (Shafer 2001).

By the mid-1960s, the culture of Swinging London began to appear on screen. Films like *To Sir with Love*, *Alfie*, and *Georgy Girl* humanized some of the choices made by young people that in that past might have been considered deviant. Some films portrayed Swinging London as empty – a cold world of high fashion, psychedelic music, and young people doing drugs and having sex without responsibility or consequences. Michelangelo Antonioni's film *Blow-Up* (1966) chronicles a dissipated young fashion photographer who thinks that he has witnessed, and captured on film, a murder in a park. His attention is drawn to this fact by a woman who stalks him, trying to get the picture back. Ultimately, when he goes back to try to find the body or any evidence of the crime, there is no body and no evidence. The film is meant to be more than just a murder mystery – calling into question the very nature of reality – but is also famous as a sixties slice-of-life.

The continuing postwar cultural and economic divide was perceptible in the emerging career of Ken Loach, who would chronicle the Northern working classes in his films over the next several decades. His debut, *Kes* (1969), follows the life of Billy Casper, a 15-year-old destined to be a school dropout who is alternately ignored and abused by his family members and seems to have nothing to care about or look forward to. Billy briefly comes to life when he finds a kestrel in the countryside, learns all about falconry, and trains the bird, before learning a fairly tragic lesson about the futility of it all.

Radio and Television

While the film industry, which was fully commercial, had begun to provide a great diversity of products, radio and television, still operating under government monopoly, were much slower to respond to the desire for variety. In 1946, the BBC launched a third radio channel, joining the Home and the Light programs that already existed. The Third Programme was intended to be an uplifting and challenging mixture of classical music, scholarly lectures, dramatic performances, poetry reading, and other kinds of high culture. It persisted until 1970, with declining audiences, as those seeking entertainment turned to television; its successor, Radio 3, adopted a classical music format.

The BBC opposed local radio, commercial radio, or the airing of much pop music. First of all, radio was supposed to be intellectually uplifting; allowing people to listen to what they *enjoyed* was like allowing children a diet of candy. Second, the BBC was hamstrung by limitations on the length of its programming day, and by agreements with union musicians that dictated how much airtime could be spent playing recorded music. But radio waves do not respect national borders. By the mid-1960s British pop music fans were able to pick up signals from Radio Luxembourg, a commercial station getting round the rules and broadcasting content from the Continent often prerecorded in London. Other "pirate radio stations" also stepped into the gap: broadcasting from ships outside the three-mile limit of Britain's territorial waters, stations like Radio Caroline and Radio London attracted millions of listeners by focusing on the pop charts. Pirate stations eventually forced the BBC to broaden its radio policy, promoting BBC Radio 1 as the BBC's own "popular music radio station" in 1967, and then introducing local radio stations by 1973.

Television programming sparked the same conflict between government-subsidized and commercial, and between uplifting the public and catering to its desires. Television was not seen as a neutral force; critics like Richard Hoggart wrote off television as part of a demeaning "mass culture" (ironically, his personal story of growing up in perceived working-class inferiority would be folded into the long-running television soap opera *Coronation Street*). Labour politicians opposed television-watching on the grounds that it transformed previously active members of society into passive receptacles for entertainment. They even argued for a television moratorium on election night, just in case Labour voters might stay home watching *Rawhide* rather than voting. Conservative politicians criticized sex and violence on television and argued that it was degrading British morality. British television was strictly regulated in its early years, and television programming ceased entirely between 6 and 7 p.m. each day so that parents could put their young children to bed (Black 2005).

Whether or not the government ought to allow commercial television was particularly controversial. A look at the United States showed the downside of a commercial funding model as networks pandered to the lowest common denominator, and shows were liberally interspersed with jingles and animated cartoon ads hawking products. On the other hand, the British television-watching public clamored for choice, and choice could not be supplied solely by the publicly funded BBC. Over some objection, the commercial station Independent Television (ITV) joined the BBC in broadcasting in Britain in 1955. Television choice was a rousing success; by 1960, 78 percent of people polled owned a television set (whereas only 24 percent owned a refrigerator) (Black 2005: 552).

In 1962, the Pilkington Committee on Broadcasting studied ITV and determined that it didn't measure up to the public service standards on which the BBC had been based – although the viewing audience preferred ITV, exposing the always possible rift between the BBC's lofty goals and those of British viewers. In 1963, the BBC received permission to start a second television channel, BBC2. Like BBC1, it was noncommercial, but it featured programs like *That Was the Week That Was*, which poked fun at the news and public figures. The presence of sex and sarcasm on television elicited a backlash campaign against such liberties led by Mary Whitehouse, who became the main public advocate for regulation of television content.

The ability to televise sports had a major influence on the way sports were played, beginning with the launch of BBC2. Individual telegenic players were catapulted into celebrity. Companies could directly sponsor sporting events, and then their banners would be featured in the televised coverage, eroding the BBC ban on commercialism. The increased funding that was available for sports teams attracted more entrepreneurs trying to make a profit from sports management. Televising events like the World Cup helped to build a sense of sports as transnational. Televising sports also affected the wider culture, making it less likely that spectators would go to games, and more likely that they would enjoy the communal aspect of spectatorship from the comfort of their living rooms, or in pubs or other group settings. Finally, television sports helped continue the tradition of a gender-segregated sporting culture; between 60 and 70 percent of television-sports audiences were male (Whannel 2009).

Youth Culture

While Britain had always had strong artistic, literary, and theatrical traditions, postwar innovations in radio, television, and fashion had a strong demographic component, as the decades in between the end of the Second World War and the 1970s witnessed the rise of youth culture. Part of this was demographic; between 1951 and 1965, the number of teenagers had risen by a million, and the number of young people over minimum school-leaving age who were still in school had doubled. These teenagers also had good incomes, since young people's wages were increasing faster than those of other groups. For the first time, observers were able to identify youth as a separate phase of life characterized by common experiences – particularly since National Service, the two-year stint in the armed forces required of all boys until 1957, did not begin until age 18. In 1969, the voting age was lowered to 18, and the following year, the age of majority was lowered from 21 to 18, acknowledgement of the power earned by this new group.

Swinging London made possible, and was made possible by, legal reforms that increased toleration for sexual practices of all kinds. The first piece of legislation in this area was the Obscene Publications Act 1959, which enabled publishers to claim that works labeled obscene should still be published on the grounds of literary merit. The book *Lady Chatterley's Lover* by D.H. Lawrence, published in Italy in 1928 but not in Britain until 1960, became a test case for hitherto unprintable words, and explicitly sexual passages. A number of witnesses testified to the book's literary merit, and its publisher, Penguin Press, was acquitted of obscenity. The book became a bestseller as their reward.

As in the United States in the 1950s, homosexuality in Britain was publicly stigmatized; cold warriors feared that the Russians would easily be able to blackmail homosexuals by threatening to expose them. The loosening sexual mores of the 1960s and the publication of American Professor Alfred Kinsey's report on human sexuality helped to bring homosexuality into public discussion, and even the Church of England called for reform of the laws regulating homosexual behavior by the early 1950s. In 1967, the Sexual Offenses Act decriminalized private sexual activity between consenting adults, although the age of consent for homosexual couples (21) was much higher than that for heterosexuals (16). Public homosexual activity, and activity with youths over 16, carried higher penalties than they had before. As in the United States, a vocal civil rights movement seeking equal rights for gay Britons followed in the early 1970s.

In theory, young people freed from the traditional responsibilities of contributing to the family income, or early marriage, could more freely take part in the new sexually permissive culture of the 1960s. The birth control pill became available after 1961, and by 1969, it was available to both married and unmarried people under the National Health Service. The idea that Britain might plunge into a morass of sexual immorality worried many, including the jurist Patrick Devlin; he felt that without enforcement of morals laws, the social fabric itself would fall apart. "For society is not something that is kept together physically; it is held by the invisible bonds of common thought. If the bonds were too far relaxed the members would drift apart. A common morality is part of the bondage. The bondage is part of society; and mankind, which needs society, must pay its price" (Devlin 1959). Devlin needn't have worried that the culture of sexual openness automatically entailed a culture of sexual promiscuity: a 1971 study revealed that one-quarter of men surveyed and two-thirds of women were virgins when they married (Carnevali and Strange 2007).

Teenagers also became consumers of products aimed solely at them: a new music industry and its records and concerts; trendy clothing; magazines; and transportation like motorcycles or the ubiquitous Vespa scooters. Teens and their subcultures were the subject of considerable societal attention about ganglike masculine behavior. "Teddy Boys" cultivated combed-back long hair and dressed in velvet jackets and pegged pants, in a nod to Edwardian culture. They were succeeded in the 1960s by dueling youth cultures, the "Mods" and the "Rockers." The Mods aped Italian style, wearing tailored suits and skinny neckties and riding Vespa scooters; the Rockers adopted jeans, leather jackets, bad attitudes, and motorcycles. Fashion designers from the United States and Paris came to London to discover the latest youth fads and design clothing and a great number of small designers and manufacturers worked in London to meet the demand. This represented an inversion of the way that fashion had been designed in the past: now it was coming up from the street rather than coming down from big design houses (Majima 2008).

The British cultural explosion also extended to music. By 1963, the Beatles were wildly popular in Britain, and soon after in America. Four young men from Liverpool, Paul McCartney, John Lennon, Ringo Starr, and George Harrison had four consecutive chart-topping single records, two similarly successful albums, and their own radio show, and were promoted as the North of England version of British popular culture. With their fresh sound, moplike haircuts, and irreverent sense of humor, they both appealed to young people and initially created less controversy than other, more patently sexual, rock and roll musicians. By 1964, the Beatles were featured on the *Ed Sullivan Show* in the United States, and had acquired an American audience of screaming girl fans to match their British audience. In 1965, they appeared in New York's Shea Stadium before an audience of 55,000 fans.

The Beatles were about merchandising as well as music. Films like *A Hard Day's Night* (1964) and *Help!* (1965) transformed the techniques of the French "New Wave" cinema of the 1960s – absurdity, bright colors, jump cuts, shaky cameras – into a fun and Anglicized product. Their third film, *Yellow Submarine* (1968), turned the Beatles into animated cartoons. The band's progress over the decade mirrored the larger progress of the transnational counterculture, from sweet to oppositional and edgy. The Beatles were irreverent – John Lennon at one point said they were "more popular than Jesus" – emerged as critics of the Vietnam War, and openly based songs on their marijuana and LSD experiences. The Beatles also integrated music with plastic art: the British artist Peter Blake designed the visually impressive cover for their *Sergeant Pepper's Lonely Hearts Club Band* album as a nostalgic collage. And the Beatles, with all their many facets, were only one group among a dominating wave of British bands: the Rolling Stones, the Who, the Yardbirds, and Led Zeppelin among them.

The 1960s also saw the beginning of significant ethnic diversity within Britain's youth culture, linked to immigration initially from Jamaica. Under the pressures of unemployment, young rural Jamaicans first moved to the capital, Kingston, where they formed their own "Rude Boy" culture. Rude Boys, or "Rudies," dressed alike, in high-cuff pants, suspenders, and boots, wore flat-top haircuts, and drank the Jamaican beer Red Stripe. They feuded over territory, engaged in some petty theft, and enjoyed music played by "masters of ceremonies" over public address systems at dance clubs. As these young men migrated to Britain, they brought their music – the so-called "first wave" of ska – and the Rude Boy culture with them (Heathcott 2003). Eventually, the violence on the dance floor propelled a slowing down of the musical beat within this genre, to become "rocksteady," at half the tempo of ska, and then, finally, the more mellow style of reggae.

In the 1970s, the Rude Boy culture spawned Punk. Punks adopted a version of Rude Boy dress, including the pressed shirts, boots and suspenders, and closely cropped hair. Marijuana and LSD, the youth drugs of choice in the 1960s and the 1970s, were replaced by the more dangerous heroin (Goodyear 2003). The Sex Pistols, the most famous British band affiliated with the punk movement, shocked audiences in 1977 with their hard-rocking and barely tonal version of the National Anthem, *God Save the Queen*. The song, which told the Queen she had no future and referred to England as a "fascist regime," hit the top of the British charts despite being banned by the BBC – or perhaps because of its prohibition. While the punk movement was predominantly white, in the wake of race riots in Britain in 1976–7, disaffected white youth also latched onto black culture, developing an interest in reggae and helping to create a second wave of ska called "Two Tone." Now, black and white Rude Boys adopted the costume and instrumentation of ska music in bands like UB40 and the Specials. Music and youth cultures formed the most adaptable edge of British identity.

Leisure and Sport

Like youth culture, sport became more commercialized in the postwar period, as spectatorship grew and athletic participation became professionalized. Britain hosted the 1948 Olympic Games, and the government used the opportunity to raise Britain's public profile even as the drive for decolonization was lowering it. King George VI presided over the opening ceremony with royal splendor, and a film of the Olympiad was made to commemorate Britain's athletic leadership. As in many other Olympic contests, British athletes did not distinguish themselves: the country came in sixth with 23 medals, only three of them gold (Beck 2005). The 1952 Helsinki Olympics were even worse, with the British taking only a single gold medal, in horse-riding. Britain's international sports standing increased in 1953 when the British expedition led by New Zealander Sir Edmund Hillary and Sherpa Tenzing Norgay conquered Everest. And in 1954 there would be one for the record books, as Roger Bannister became the first human clocked running a mile in under four minutes.

Rugby football continued its course of professionalization, accelerated by the fact that as other countries overtook Britain in the standings, Britain no longer had the primary say about the rules of the game. In addition, changing values – from an emphasis on gentlemanly norms in sport to one on commercial success – helped to make amateurism obsolete. While rugby football had been more popular between the wars, in the period of postwar austerity, association football (what Americans call soccer) became the more popular spectator sport, and one joke called it "the Labour Party at prayer." Between 1949 and 1960 football attendance was at its peak, staying above 30 million attendees every year. Although at first the salaries of British football players were extremely low compared to those offered abroad, and some of the best players decamped to teams in Italy and France, once the "maximum wage" was eliminated in 1961, players' earning power quintupled.

The country's national football team was hampered in competition by the long-standing belief that there was no intellectualizing the game: that physical prowess would beat strategy every time. In 1966, England won the World Cup, followed by wins in the European Cup in subsequent years by Glasgow Celtic and Manchester United. The wins came in the midst of a transition from football as a stadium spectator sport to one that could be watched largely on television; but these wins were a fluke, not a trend. Compared with teams in other countries, British teams failed to modernize their coaching, their training, or their stadiums. By the 1970s, football had become integrated across Europe, with some of the best English players playing on European teams, and English teams recruiting players from South America and from Europe. The 1970s also saw the rise of soccer hooliganism. Within British stadiums, fans of opposing teams had to be segregated from each other to cut down on the drunken fighting; fights then broke out in Underground stations or on special trains on the way to and from games.

Like rugby, football, and cricket, tennis underwent professionalization; but un-like the other sports, it did not happen until the postwar period. Beginning in the 1950s, allegations flew that tennis amateurs had accepted payments of various kinds, including clothing, equipment, and cash. Individual players crossed the line from amateur to professional status, and the number of tennis tournaments open to professionals proliferated. In 1968, the British led the transformation to an open tennis circuit by offering prize money at Wimbledon and allowing both amateurs and professionals to play against each other (Jeffreys 2009).

Traditional English sports like riding and hunting declined in popularity after the Second World War, in part because much land had changed hands over the previous 20 years through sales of estates. The traditions of raising and keeping birds for use in large shooting parties had also declined. The countryside was also increasingly under pressure from urban visitors, who didn't necessarily sympathize with the rural way of life. The governments of the 1960s and 1970s undertook a massive spending campaign to build leisure facilities for the public, and thereby encouraged broader public participation in sporting activities. In the decade be-ginning in 1971, government funds built over 400 indoor sports centers and more than 500 swimming pools (Gratton et al. (2003).

Intellectual Developments

Although postwar Britain had lost some of its political and economic dominance, it had gained cultural steam. And although some of the economic basis of British leadership in the world was eroded by decolonization, in academic and intellectual areas the British continued to lead. For example, Britain continued to produce most of the world's best analytic philosophers, rediscovering the field of ethics. R.M. Hare revived the idea (originally Kant's) that certain moral imperatives could be inferred from logic. For example, moral rules should be universal: anyone making the statement that someone "ought" to take a particular moral course of action should be willing to abide by those same strictures himself. In contrast, Elizabeth Anscombe took a different approach and argued that the best way to advance hu-man flourishing was to investigate virtues and vices, as scholars had done in ancient Greece. A truly virtuous person was a person in whom certain beneficial character traits were second nature. British ethicists began applying ethical theories to social questions, including in-vitro fertilization, abortion, euthanasia, and environmental protection (Kenny 2008: 245–247).

In the postwar period, British scientists became well known for their work in medical research and technology, for which they won a disproportionate number of Nobel Prizes in physiology and medicine. James Whyte Black, a Scottish physi-ologist, began work in the 1950s that would culminate in two widely used drugs – one for heart problems and one for acid reflux. John Vane won a Nobel Prize for his work with aspirin. British scientists discovered the exact nature of antibodies, and also played key roles in the development of the computed tomography (CT) scan, which for the first time enabled doctors to see cross-sections of soft tissue in live patients without cutting them open. But perhaps the best-known British Nobel laureate of this period was Francis Crick, who in 1953, with his American collaborator James D. Watson, discovered the double-helix that is DNA, the basic building block of life.

Not all British scientists found support from the wider culture. Before the Second World War, the Cambridge mathematician Alan Turing developed the idea for a computing machine, to execute any algorithm encoded on a paper tape. Turing and a number of his mathematical colleagues, including crossword-puzzle fanatics and a chess master, were recruited in 1939 to work on a code-breaking project for the British government. The Germans had invented a cryptography machine called Enigma, which could render all of their messages in code, supposedly only translatable on the other end with a similarly configured Enigma machine. Turing tackled the Enigma problem with a machine he designed called a "bombe," which simulated the actions of several Enigma devices simultaneously, using a brute force method of calculation that was much faster than doing it by hand. Cracking the Enigma code was instrumental in the Allied victory against Germany.

After the war, Turing created a blueprint for a computer that could take its instructions from software rather than hardware, and so be capable of numbers of calculations vastly greater than those carried out by his wartime machines. He speculated about the possibility of artificially intelligent computers, and devised a test – the "Turing test" – to illustrate when machines could be considered to be able to think (in short, if a computer can fool a human into thinking that the computer itself is human, then it passes the Turing test). For all this, Turing is now considered to be one of the fathers of modern computing and artificial intelligence. Yet in 1952 Turing, who was homosexual, was arrested on charges of "gross indecency" – homosexual sex was still illegal in Britain – and sentenced to estrogen treatments. Two years later, he killed himself by eating a poisoned apple.

Intellectual developments in the postwar period were not limited to the insides of university lecture halls or laboratories. The late 1950s and early 1960s saw the emergence of a "New Left." Cultural critics like Richard Hoggart, who chronicled his working-class upbringing in *The Uses of Literacy* (1957), and Raymond Williams, who wrote *Culture and Society* (1957), worried about the deterioration of British culture. Their criticism seemed borne out by the content of early television, as audiences gravitated toward quiz shows and bad soap operas. E.P. Thompson, author of *The Making of the English Working Class* (1963), showed how a member of the New Left could be "engaged." He combined his scholarly project (in Thompson's case, to document the social and cultural history of working people in early nineteenth-century Britain) with teaching adult learners through the Workers' Educational Association (WEA) and participating in the Campaign for Nuclear Disarmament.

People seeking a foundation for self-education or social change could turn not just to the Open University and to the WEA, but also to the mass-produced paperback book. Between 1958 and 1964, a large number of cheap paperbacks published in the Penguin Specials series depicted a country mired in national malaise. Many of these works advocated the integration of science and technology into the business of government; the replacement of the old ruling order by a "technocracy." In his Rede lecture "Two Cultures and the Scientific Revolution," C.P. Snow questioned the division of British society into two cultures: the practical, hopeful one embraced by scientists and engineers, and the much more humble, pessimistic one advocated by scholars in the humanities. He called for dynamism and a new sense of purpose, which could only be accomplished by integrating more science into British life (Grant 2003). For Snow, this cultural battle played out on the larger field of the Cold War: if the British and the Americans failed to disseminate technology in the developing world, the Communists would certainly do so.

The postwar period saw the birth of a new environmental awareness, although British environmentalism was more muted than its counterparts in Germany or the United States. The British left, with its emphasis on working-class living standards, saw saving natural features as less important than – and to some extent in opposition to – its primary goals (Hay and Hayward 1988). British companies also had a history of working very closely with the government through voluntary regulation, which took into account of what companies could do within economic constraints, rather than setting overall standards for environmental purity. Nonetheless, a concern for the environment potentially had a wide constituency: it could be linked with concern for the loss of rural England to development; a desire to preserve hiking paths; or a wish to revive artisanal crafts and older ways of living. The postwar ecological campaign was both political and media driven. Parliament passed Acts to prevent pollution of rivers and to remediate old mining operations (1951), regulate all water resources (1963), and control pollution generally (1974). Environmental groups also used publicity – particularly in the form of tragic photographs and heartrending stories – to promote faster action than the state could or would provide. In 1978, a Greenpeace vessel was able to stop a seal harvest in the north of Scotland by facilitating coverage of doomed baby seals (Shead 1998; Lowe 1984).

The past, present and future of the British landscape was part of a larger question of British identity. The first ten years after the close of the war saw the continuation of a general confidence about the "British national character": the Briton was slow to anger but could protect his country when provoked, and Britain itself, although diverse in its landscape and ways of life, was linked together by tradition, and by the values of conscience and calmness. Forged together by the common experience of the Second World War, Britons of all classes had provided themselves with a massive social safety net and were beginning to experience the prosperity of the postwar period. Despite industrialization and technology, authentic Britishness lay in the countryside and the small village.

After the Suez crisis, however, this quietly celebratory mood disappeared, and the idea that there was some positive, easily agreed-on content to "Britishness" or "Englishness" could not hold up. Events in foreign policy showed British priorities overshadowed by the Cold War between the Soviet Union and the United States; Britain had lost an empire and not yet found a role in the world, or even a role in a unified Europe. Its traditional preoccupations came under fire from the new youth culture, the developing counterculture, and the varied cultural concerns of immigrants. Mass culture, although it provided some glue that held people together, was criticized for its shallowness. National concerns about British decline and the nature of identity waned during the heyday of Swinging London, but would emerge again as Britain moved out of the cultural spotlight during the 1970s.

References

Anderson, Lindsay (dir.) (1953) *O Dreamland*. At http://www.youtube.com/watch? v=LLlKR1x1oWY (accessed May 28, 2010).

Beck, Peter (2005) Britain and the Cold War's "Cultural Olympics": Responding to the Political Drive of Soviet Sport, 1945–58. *Contemporary British History*, 19 (2): 169–185.

Black, Lawrence (2005) Whose Finger on the Button? British Television and the Politics of Cultural Control. *Historical Journal of Film, Radio and Television*, 25 (4): 547–575.

Brighton, Andrew (1981) "Where are the Boys of the Old Brigade?": The Post-war Decline of British Traditionalist Painting. *Oxford Art Journal*, 4 (1): 35–43.

Carnevali, Francesca, and Strange, Julie-Marie (eds) (2007) *Twentieth-Century Britain: Economic, Cultural and Social Change*. London: Longman.

Devlin, Patrick (1959) The Enforcement of Morals. *Proceedings of the British Academy*, 24: 129–151.

Goodyear, Ian (2003) Rock against Racism: Multiculturalism and Political Mobilization, 1976–1981. *Immigrants and Minorities*, 22 (1): 44–62.

Grant, Mariel (2006) "Working for the Yankee Dollar": Tourism and the Festival of Britain as Stimuli for Recovery. *Journal of British Studies*, 45 (4): 581–601.

Grant, Matthew (2003) Historians, the Penguin Specials, and the "State of the Nation" Literature, 1958–1964. *Contemporary British History*, 17 (3): 29–54.

Gratton, Chris, Shibli, Simon, and Coleman, Richard (2003) Sport and Economic Regeneration in Cities. *Urban Studies*, 42 (5–6): 985–999.

Halasz, Piri (1966) Great Britain: You Can Walk Across It on the Grass. *Time*, May 15. At http://www.time.com/time/magazine/article/0,9171,835349,00.html (accessed July 12, 2011).

Hay, P.R., and Hayward, M.G. (1988) Comparative Green Politics: Beyond the European Context? *Political Studies*, 36: 433–448.

Heathcott, Joseph (2003) Urban Spaces and Working-Class Expressions across the Black Atlantic: Tracing the Routes of Ska. *Radical History Review*, 87: 183–206.

Jeffreys, Kevin (2009) The Triumph of Professionalism in World Tennis. *International Journal of the History of Sport*, 26 (15): 2253–2289.

Kenny, Anthony (2008) *Philosophy in the Modern World*, vol. 4. Oxford: Oxford University Press.

Lammers, Donald (1977) Nevil Shute and the Decline of the "Imperial Idea" in Literature. *Journal of British Studies*, 16 (2): 121–142.

Lowe, Philip (1984) Bad News or Good News: Environmental Politics and the Mass Media. *Sociological Review*, 32 (1): 75–90.

Majima, Shinobu (2008) From Haute Couture to High Street: The Role of Shows and Fairs in Twentieth-Century Fashion. *Textile History*, 39 (1): 70–91.

McCrillis, Neal R. (2001) "Simply Try for One Hour to Behave Like Gentlemen": British Cinema during the Early Cold War, 1945–1960. *Film and History*, 31 (2): 6–12.

Page, Malcolm (1973) Experimental Theatre in London: A Guide to the "Off-West-End." *Kansas Quarterly*, 3 (2): 118–128.

Priestley, J.B. (1951) The Renewed Dream of a Merrie England. *New York Times*, July 15.

Shafer, Stephen (2001) An Overview of the Working Classes in British Feature Film from the 1960s to the 1980s: From Class Consciousness to Marginalization. *International Labor and Working-Class History*, no. 59 (Spring): 3–14.

Sheail, John (1998) "Never Again": Pollution and the Management of Watercourses in Postwar Britain. *Journal of Contemporary History*, 33 (1): 117–133.

Storr, Robert (1988) In the Flesh: Lucien Freud. *Art in America*, 76 (5): 128–137.

Vall, Natasha (2010) Bringing Art to "the Man in the Back Street": Regional and Historical Perspectives of Labour and the Evolution of Cultural Policy in Europe, 1945–1975. *Labour History Review*, 75 (1): 30–43.

Waters, Chris (1999) Representations of Everyday Life: L.S. Lowry and the Landscape of Memory in Postwar Britain. *Representations*, no. 65: 121–150.

Whannel, Gary (2009) Television and the Transformation of Sport. *Annals of the American Academy of Political and Social Science*, 625: 205–216.

Further Reading

Cannadine, David (2008) The "Last Night of the Proms" in Historical Perspective. *Historical Research*, 81 (212): 315–349.

Curran, James (2002) Media and the Making of British Society, c.1700–2000. *Media History*, 8 (2): 135–154.

Ford, Boris (1992) *Cambridge Cultural History of Britain*, vol. 9. Cambridge: Cambridge University Press.

Goldblatt, David (2006) *The Ball is Round: A Global History of Soccer*. New York: Riverhead.

Mandler, Peter (2006) *The English National Character: The History of an Idea from Edmund Burke to Tony Blair*. New Haven: Yale University Press.

Marwick, Arthur (1991) *Culture in Britain since 1945*. Oxford: Blackwell.

Murphy, Robert (2008) *Sixties British Cinema*. London: British Film Institute.

Neff, Terry (ed.) (1987) *A Quiet Revolution: British Sculpture since 1965*. New York: Thames & Hudson.

Rudin, Richard (2007) Revisiting the Pirates. *Media History*, 13 (2–3): 235–255.

Rycroft, Simon (2002) The Geographies of Swinging London. *Journal of Historical Geography*, 28 (4): 566–588.

Vogel, David (1983) Cooperative Regulation: Environmental Protection in Great Britain. *Public Interest* (Summer): 88–106.

15

From Rule Britannia to Cool Britannia

Politics, 1979–2007

Louis Mountbatten, Earl Mountbatten of Burma and cousin to Queen Elizabeth, was the last Viceroy of India at the time of the British departure. On August 28, 1979 he was taking a late morning cruise on his 28-foot fishing boat, at Mullaghmore on the Irish coast. With him were his daughter and her husband; her mother-in-law, the Dowager Lady Brabourne; two grandsons; and another teenage boy helping to crew. Suddenly the boat exploded, killing Mountbatten and two of the boys instantly (the Dowager Lady Brabourne later died of her injuries), and shattering the boat into an array of pieces no larger than a matchbook. The work was instantly recognizable as that of the Provisional IRA (Borders 1979).

In the late 1970s, the Troubles in Northern Ireland entered a new phase. The Provisional IRA had reorganized into cells, and pushed forward its political agenda through the use of terror tactics. Large numbers of IRA leaders had been arrested, and were being held in H-block of Long Kesh prison, nicknamed "The Maze." Although the IRA prisoners wanted political prisoner status – which would have conferred, among other things, the right to have visitors and to wear their own clothing rather than prison uniforms – they were, instead, treated like the rest of the prison population. Prisoner disobedience quickly accelerated to include hunger striking by October 1980.

The two separate hunger strikes received widespread publicity. One of the hunger strikers, Bobby Sands, emerged as the prisoners' leader; and so fierce was public support for the strikers that Sands was elected to Parliament while in prison. But by 1979, the context of British-Irish relations had changed, with the succession to the post of Prime Minister of a woman determined to restore Britain to its former imperial self-confidence. Margaret Thatcher's will was even more immovable than her signature sprayed hair. Despite the relatively small concessions at stake in granting political prisoner status to the H-block prisoners, Thatcher categorically

Empire, State, and Society: Britain Since 1830, First Edition. Jamie L. Bronstein and Andrew T. Harris.
© 2012 Jamie L. Bronstein and Andrew T. Harris. Published 2012 by John Wiley & Sons, Ltd.

refused to be seen negotiating with terrorists. Bobby Sands died on May 5, 1981; he was among ten strikers who became martyrs to their movement. Thatcher's response was characteristic: "Mr. Sands was a convicted criminal. He chose to take his own life. It was a choice that his organization did not allow to many of its victims" (Cottrell 2005: 101).

Margaret Thatcher's long premiership would initiate a fundamental reordering of British priorities in the last quarter of the twentieth century. Under her leadership, elements of the welfare state began to be forcefully pared back, calling into question the notion of a social minimum. This reticence about social provision would continue into the ministries of New Labour in the first decade of the twenty-first century. While the "special relationship" with the United States had languished during the 1970s, Thatcher presided over its renewal, a stance that would help to draw Britain into conflicts in which the United States was particularly interested, including the Cold War and the 1991 and 2003 wars in Iraq; sometimes to Britain's detriment, politically and financially, But this relationship also enabled Britain to leverage its position within the European Union.

Thatcherism

When Margaret Thatcher came to power in 1979 she represented a radical discontinuity with the postwar social consensus. Her priorities came to be known as "Thatcherism," because they marked such a change even from the previous priorities and strategies of her own Conservative Party. Traditionally, the Conservative Party had emphasized the importance of the countryside, and a conviction that the wealthy owed a voluntary obligation toward the poor. Thatcher supported a newer, late twentieth-century free-enterprise strain of Conservatism that shared the ideals of US President Ronald Reagan, elected in 1980. Thatcher's ideals included privatization of many of the industries that had been made public by postwar Labour; she believed that free markets were naturally more efficient than publicly controlled enterprise. In this way, she was more like a nineteenth-century Liberal than a traditional Conservative.

One of the Thatcher government's first steps was to dismiss Keynesian (demand-side) economics, and to focus instead on cutting taxes. Keynesians had argued that government spending grew the economy through a "multiplier effect" as people used government funds (grants, salaries, etc.) to buy other goods and services. Keynesian economics also held that full employment, rather than inflation, should be the government's first priority. In contrast, "free marketeers" like Thatcher argued that when taxes were too high, people had no incentive to work, and businesses had no incentive to hire. They argued that government should restore money to the wealthiest individuals, who had the ability to use their money to create jobs – and then prosperity might trickle down to everyone else. Under

Thatcher, tax rates were adjusted according to this philosophy. The top income tax rate was cut from 83 to 60 percent, and a Value Added Tax (VAT), a sales tax, made up for some of the lost revenue.

Along with cutting taxation, Thatcherites were concerned with controlling inflation. Low rates of inflation were thought to be central in promoting business investment. In both Britain under Thatcher and the United States under Ronald Reagan, this would be accomplished through "monetary policy," or control of the money supply. When the government wanted to increase the money supply, it could cut taxes or increase public-sector spending; if it wanted to constrict the money supply, it could do the opposite.

At first, this economic strategy did not work very well. Rising oil prices in 1980, combined with the generous wage agreements that had been struck in the 1970s, and a rise in the prime lending rate of the banks, produced double-digit inflation and unemployment. Manufacturing industries left Britain and relocated their plants in countries where the workforce could be paid less. Because Britain manufactured less, it had to import more, leading to a balance-of-payments deficit. The government had to prop up the pound using high interest rates, which then hampered borrowing even further by making it in effect more expensive. By 1982, only 25 percent of the electorate professed to be satisfied with Thatcher's performance. But while the Conservative government of the early 1970s had reversed course under a similar set of circumstances – which had been called the "U-turn" – Thatcher refused to countenance the idea that her economic plans might be wrong, noting, "You turn if you want to. The Lady's not for turning."

Thatcher believed that privately owned companies, regulated by the market, were more efficient than government-owned companies could ever be. Her government thus sought to reverse the nationalizations that took place after the Second World War. Industries privatized in the quest for greater efficiency included gas, electricity and water, air travel (which became British Airways), British Telecom, British Aerospace, automobile manufacturing, and finally, rail transit. Shares in some of the new enterprises were sold, tripling the number of British shareholders (and thus their belief in market mechanisms). In other cases, foreign firms successfully bid to operate what formerly had been British industries. Results were mixed. Some of the most bureaucratized public services, like British Telecom, seemed to benefit from privatization in the short run, now able to modernize infrastructure while under government regulation. But privatization also created monopolies in sectors that had once been essential public services, like home heating and communications.

Thatcherism and its embrace of free markets embodied larger changes taking place within the Conservative Party. Just as Thatcher took great pride in her humble origins as the daughter of a Grantham grocer, so many more Conservative MPs were now being elected from the ranks of the new professional middle classes, rather than from the ranks of the aristocracy and country gentry. The Conservative Party also increasingly drew its strength from the wealthier and less industrial South of England. Workers in the South saw themselves as potentially more upwardly mobile than those in the North, so that Thatcher's talk of building an "opportunity state" of house-owners and shareholders was likely to be more appealing than more funding for council houses (low-income housing for the poor) or NHS hospitals. This division between the wealthy South and the poorer North widened by the mid-1980s, because with the ebbing of British manufacturing it was mostly Northern, formerly unionized men – who had not voted Conservative to begin with – who bore the brunt of the unemployment.

The British economy during the Thatcher years had its peaks and valleys. By the mid-1980s inflation had decreased from over 20 percent to 7 percent. Deregulation of banks and building societies expanded consumer credit, and people enjoyed the ability to buy things they had never been able to afford. Imports increased, but were balanced by British exports of North Sea Oil. Worker productivity expanded. Many also appreciated Thatcher because under the 1980 Housing Act, she made it possible for them to purchase at a discount the council houses they had been renting. Homeownership grew to encompass 62 percent of the population. On the other hand, Thatcher presided over a permanent loss of 2 million relatively high-paid manufacturing jobs – jobs replaced by lower-paid service jobs as Britain's became a postindustrial economy. By 1990 Britain had sunk back into economic depression, with high interest rates, showing that Thatcher had not had a magic bullet.

While Thatcher may not have met all of her economic goals, she had more success with her ideological goals. One of these was to diminish the power of the trade unions, which she thought interfered with free markets. Two Employment Acts, one in 1980 and a second in 1982, limited picketing and sympathy strikes and made unions liable for the illegal acts of their members, and civilly liable for damages. A Trade Union Act (1984) required that a majority of union members voting in a ballot approve any given strike, and called for union leaders to stand for reelection at least every five years.

Over the course of the twentieth century the fortunes of the miners had come to reflect the fortunes of the larger union movement. The miners' failure in the lockout of 1926 had foreshadowed the hardship that many working people suffered during the Great Depression; victory in the 1972 strike had shown the immense power wielded by trade unions in that decade. But that power was short-lived, as between 1972 and 1984 the National Coal Board had modernized mining to make it much more technologically efficient. With the introduction of other sources of energy, including nuclear power, coal's preeminence had ended and the workforce in the mines had shrunk from over 450,000 in the immediate aftermath of the Second World War to 200,000 workers. By the early 1980s, economists studying the issue were predicting that technology would soon eliminate another 70,000 mining jobs (Winterton 1993).

In 1984, the National Coal Board announced the imminent closure of 20 coal pits. Workers at individual coalfields in the North went on strike. As additional participants joined in, Arthur Scargill, president of the National Union of Miners (NUM),

Figure 15.1 Margaret Thatcher's priorities included scaling back the power of Britain's trade unions. Here, miners who participated in the bitter 1984 strike protesting the closure of many coal pits optimistically display the "V" for victory sign. (© Bettmann/Corbis).

declared the combined actions a national strike, without having called a national ballot. The fact that the strike was technically illegal disadvantaged miners and their families, who could not collect either strike pay or welfare (Gier-Viskovatoff 1998). Although the Trades Union Congress (TUC) executive supported the strike, there was little support from other groups except the dockworkers – and their sympathy strike only lasted ten days.

The miners' strike was characterized by attempts to capture the popular imagination through symbolic activities like marches and mass meetings, and by violence on both sides. On June 18, 1984, near the Orgreave coking plant, thousands of picketers clashed with thousands of police, who advanced while clapping truncheons against plastic riot shields. The striking coal workers remained off the job for almost a year, but government stockpiling of coal limited their leverage, and ultimately, the workers trickled back in defeat and without a new contract. The number of miners unionized under the NUM declined to 53,000 in 1990 and 5,000 in 1997, as British Coal closed 32 of its 50 mines in 1992.

The miners' strike was followed by a failed 1986 strike of newspaper printers. In the wake of the strike, newspapers, following the example of Rupert Murdoch's *Times*, switched to computerized printing methods that made the printers' skills obsolete. Not all British trade unions lost their power as spectacularly as the miners and printers had, but other trade unions were rolled back through legislation that eliminated some of their legal immunities. Still others weakened as manufacturing – which had provided a living wage – declined, to be replaced with lower-paid, lower-skilled, service jobs.

Along with attempting to shrink the union movement in order to create efficiency in industry, Thatcherism advocated creating efficiency in local government. In a 1983 White Paper called *Streamlining Our Cities,* her government argued that getting rid of the entire top tier of local government would produce savings through the abolition of redundant jobs; eliminate conflict between levels of government; and make government more accountable to citizens. Despite public feedback that overwhelmingly opposed these steps, Metropolitan County Councils (county governments for urban areas) and the Greater London Council were eliminated, and other county governments and local councils saw their budgets slashed. Elected councilors were replaced by "joint boards" in charge of amenities like fire services and police and transportation. The people serving on these boards were not directly accountable either to the public or to the major political parties, giving the chairmen in particular wide latitude in pursuing policies. The result was a decline in public accountability and knowledge about how local government even operated (Leach and Game 1991).

The most serious objection to the reorganization came in London, where the Greater London Council had been around since the early 1960s, when it replaced the London County Council. The Greater London Council had a checkered history, including a scheme to demolish thousands of homes in order to build ring roads around London; but during the 1970s it was dominated by the Labour Party, which made it a counterweight to Thatcher's power. Beginning in 1981, the Greater London Council had taken steps that Thatcher considered particularly controversial: cutting the cost of public transportation, emphasizing nondiscriminatory policies, and declaring London a "nuclear-free zone" among them. Thatcher had taken a particular dislike to Ken Livingstone, a forceful socialist who led the GLC (Young 1001; Kosecik and Kapucu 2003). With the GLC's abolition in 1986, responsibility for London governance passed partly to London's boroughs and partly to central government in Whitehall.

"Rolling back the state" did not apply to services Thatcher saw as either crucial to national security, or integral to national morality. Section 28 of the Local Government Act 1988 specified that local authorities must not "intentionally promote homosexuality or publish material with the intention of promoting homosexuality" or "promote the teaching in any maintained school of the acceptability of homosexuality as a pretended family relationship."[1] The Official Secrets Act 1989 redefined the rules surrounding the disclosure of matters of "national security" in the press. The Interception of Communications Act (1985) gave the government wide latitude to wiretap telephones. The growth of the state under Thatcher, and the restriction of civil liberties, led to the Charter 88 movement, harking back to the People's Charter of the nineteenth century by calling for a written Constitution to guarantee the liberties of the people.

Since the Second World War, education and health had been crucial government responsibilities. While, under Thatcher, schools were not privatized as such, the competitive ideal was extended to them in several ways. Against the protests of teachers, the government imposed a national curriculum. Achievement testing of children at various grades produced "league tables" that gave parents some basis for comparison among schools. "Grant-maintained" schools also got the opportunity to opt out of local education authority supervision and determine their own plans, similar to charter schools in the United States. Also like charter schools, they were allowed to be more selective in the composition of their student body than local schools.

Judging the National Health Service to be inefficient, Thatcher's government divided the country into 200 individually managed health districts. Doctors were ordered to prescribe generic drugs if they were available, and medical services were contracted to private firms where possible. Doctors could now be paid directly by the state, and then use that money to allocate medical care to their clients. Hospitals were run by trusts rather than by local health authorities, which meant that they could be shut down if they were unable to support themselves financially. Cutbacks in funding for the NHS produced perceptible deterioration in the quality of British health care: fewer nurses, longer waiting lists for surgeries, and higher charges for prescriptions.

By the mid-1980s, Thatcherism had made the British state almost unrecognizable, having slashed public sector funding for education and infrastructure, thwarted Labour's power in the localities, privatized previously public utilities, and reduced union demands by emasculating the legal authority of unions themselves. Income support, rather than being seen as a right, was transformed into a tool to encourage people to enter into the private labor force. Most of all, Thatcherism had helped to shift the understandings on which the postwar British state operated, from an understanding which prioritized social welfare to one which embraced free markets. This approach was not without cost, and the major cost was growing income inequality. Household unemployment hovered at almost 20 percent, and the number of poor people – defined as those living on less than half the national average income – more than doubled to 10 million between 1979 and 1994, and then increased to 14 million by 1997.

Thatcher's Foreign Policy

In foreign policy as in economic policy, Thatcher harked back to the nineteenth century, using military power to assert Britain's greatness. Part of that greatness involved hitching Britain's star to one of the two superpowers, so Thatcher worked to revive the "special relationship" with the United States. In 1985 she became the first Prime Minister since Churchill to address both Houses of the US Congress, and she was rumored to be President Reagan's close advisor on foreign policy. Her support of President Reagan included allowing American aircraft to use British military bases, and supporting the deployment of American missiles in Western Europe, despite consistent opposition from antinuclear activists. Thatcher also backed Reagan when it was discovered that in defiance of Congress, his administration had authorized the sale of weapons to Iran to finance right-wing guerrillas ("Contras") in Nicaragua. The two leaders sometimes disagreed – over Britain's war in the Falkland Islands, over the United States's invasion of Grenada – but these disagreements did not disrupt the overall feeling of solidarity.

Thatcher and Reagan were committed Cold Warriors, who continued the long-standing Anglo-American policy of promoting openness in the Soviet Union. In 1985, Mikhail Gorbachev succeeded to the position of Soviet premier, and promoted a new policy of negotiation with the West and a disassembly of the Soviet state – "perestroika." By 1989 these policies, and the USSR's internal instability, culminated in the dissolution of the Soviet Union into its component republics, the destruction of the Berlin Wall separating East and West Berlin, the reunification of East and West Germany, and the emergence of Eastern European nations from the shadow of the Soviet Union.

As suggested at the beginning of the chapter, Thatcher also retained a hard line toward Ireland; but she met an equally aggressive stance from the IRA. Between 1981 and 1983, the IRA claimed responsibility for four bombings of very public areas of London. The campaign culminated in 1984 with a bombing of the Conservative Party Conference in Brighton, which failed to kill the Prime Minister but did claim the lives of five other people. Gerry Adams, who came to lead the Irish nationalist party Sinn Fein in 1983, professed that armed struggle had to be a political weapon; and the Provisional IRA continued its campaign of targeted bombings, including, in 1990, an attempt on the life of Queen Elizabeth II. Little progress was made toward a peaceful settlement.

Thatcher was more successful in the Falklands, a tiny archipelago of islands located off the coast of Argentina. An old outpost of empire, the islands housed more sheep than people, being home to about 1,200 British descendants. In 1983, trading conventional warfare for the security of the American nuclear threat, Thatcher's government called home the one British aircraft carrier in the area. This gave the dictatorial leader of Argentina, General Galtieri, the impression that Britain was giving up sovereignty over the islands. Galtieri needed a symbolic military victory at home as much as Thatcher did, and so he moved troops to seize the islands. Mortified by this invasion of British territory, Thatcher's Foreign Minister stepped down, and Britain went to war. Thatcher sent 100 ships and 10,000 troops to the South Atlantic for maneuvers that lasted ten weeks.

The Falklands war strained US–UK relations, cost Britain 254 lives, with 777 British soldiers wounded, and taxed the national budget £700 million ($1.19 billion); but as a piece of political theater it was an unqualified success. The tabloid press revived jingoism; when British torpedoes sank the Argentine warship, the *General*

Belgrano, to the tune of almost 400 lives, the *Sun* trumpeted, "GOTCHA!" Thatcher herself brooked no questions about the advisability of a war over little of importance, demanding that the press "Rejoice!" rather than prying into the issue. And the war was clearly good for her party in the next election, which she called a year early and which the Conservatives won by a landslide.

Although the Falklands War seemed to reinvigorate the spirit of the late Victorian British Empire, Thatcher also witnessed the decolonization of the empire's last remaining outposts. Rhodesia, a former British colony with a minority of white settlers in control, became an independent Zimbabwe in 1981. Whereas in Rhodesia Britain supported control by the black majority, Thatcher's government supported South Africa economically despite the segregationist policy of apartheid. Nonetheless due to the joint efforts of Frederik Willem DeKlerk and Nelson Mandela, that institution ended in 1989, paving the way for a more racially egalitarian South Africa. Finally, Thatcher also signed a treaty in 1984 promising that the port of Hong Kong would be returned to China in 1997.

Thatcher expressed British exceptionalism not only through her maverick foreign policy, but also through her attitude toward European integration. She approved of the elements of European unity that promised to uphold competition and free trade, but disapproved of those that sapped decision-making power from the individual member nations. Britain was required to contribute large amounts of money to the European Community budget, and Thatcher objected that much of this went to subsidize agriculture in other member countries. She also refused to consider joining a single European currency (Sharp 1991). In the end, however, the movement toward a united Europe transcended any single prime minister, and by the time Thatcher stepped down Britain had committed to a single European market.

Although Margaret Thatcher succeeded for an extended period on her own terms, her administration was not without missteps. The most serious among these was the poll tax or community charge. When she was elected for a third time in 1987 a centerpiece of her program was a plan to convert local taxation, which had been rates linked to the value of property, into a flat tax payable by all adults. Local governments were all entitled to spend the same amount of money linked to this tax; if they wanted to increase their budgets, they were forced to increase the poll tax. While Thatcher argued that the poll tax made local government accountable and less likely to undertake expensive projects, in an atmosphere of inflation it favored the wealthy, and hit those renting houses particularly hard, since they had never paid property taxes directly. The poll tax elicited a huge backlash; 200,000 people marched in London, riots broke out in other cities, and over 4 million people just refused to pay. Within two years the poll tax would be replaced by a Council Tax, a property tax that resembled the prior system (Clarke 1999; McConnell 1997).

Thatcher's leadership also disintegrated over the question of Britain's failure to join the Exchange Rate Mechanism (ERM) of the European Union. This would have set the British pound at a fixed rate pegged to the other European currencies.

When Thatcher, worn down by her party, agreed to join the ERM, the government was unable to maintain the value of the pound at its agreed-upon level, and British interest rates skyrocketed, leaving many people with variable-rate mortgages owing more on their mortgages than their houses were worth. Thatcher had made targeting inflation a mainstay of her policy throughout the 1980s: now inflation was again at a high level, calling into question the sacrifices people had had to make (Wickham-Jones 1991).

John Major

After a Conservative Party leadership challenge in November 1990, Thatcher stepped down and was replaced by John Major. Like Thatcher, John Major had come up from humble beginnings; unlike Thatcher, he had no magnetic personality. Nonetheless, Major gamely continued Thatcher's privatization priorities. The Citizen's Charter, issued by Major's government, impelled government bureaucracies to be accountable to their clients, listing their customer-service goals, publishing information on wait times, and compensating people who were inconvenienced. Beginning in 1994, all public services that could be contracted out to private firms were required to be.

Despite public opposition to the privatization of utilities, Major's government privatized water and electricity provision, disbanded British Coal and sold off inefficient pits. In a return to conditions at the very beginning of the railroad industry in Britain, British Rail was privatized and its component lines sold to different service providers. One company, Railtrack, remained responsible for the infrastructure of the rails and signals. In many cases, the government sold assets for less than they were worth, and in the case of Railtrack, promised to provide continued subsidies regardless of whether or not the company was profitable or efficient. Particularly in the case of British rail, privatization did not bring the efficiency miracle expected by Major's government. Trains were commonly delayed due to Railtrack's inability to keep the track in good order, and Tony Blair's later ministry saw a series of high-profile train accidents that were imputed to poorly maintained track. By 2002, Railtrack was bankrupt.

To the extent that they could be, national policies were carried out not by local governments but by "quangos": quasi-autonomous nongovernmental organizations. Quangos – like the Water Services Regulation Authority – were theoretically able to operate more commercially than governmental organizations, because they had an "arms-length" relationship to them. Realistically however, many quangos were expensive and not particularly helpful. John Major's Chancellor of the Exchequer, Norman Lamont, worked hard to lower interest rates from the high teens. But while prices declined, unemployment also grew, causing the government to have to borrow in order to spend more on unemployment payments and wage supplements for people in poorly paid essential professions.

With Major as party leader, voters reelected the Conservatives, with a small loss of seats, to a fourth consecutive Parliamentary term in 1992. Soon afterward, Major's recommendation that Britain join the ERM – made when he was Thatcher's Chancellor of the Exchequer – came back to haunt him. On September 16, 1992, a day that came to be called "Black Wednesday," the German central bank raised interest rates. The German central bank was the issuer of the Deutschmark, to which other European currencies were pegged. Major's government raised interest rates to try to maintain international interest in the British pound, but this in turn was bad for domestic businesses. John Major was eventually forced to take Britain out of the ERM, and to devalue the pound by 20 percent. Although the devaluation helped interest rates to drop and the economy to recover, the ERM experience made many skeptical about European integration.

In contrast with Margaret Thatcher, Major, who had himself left school at age 16, understood what it was like to be a member of the working class and so supported spending on education, employment, and the NHS. But this expansion was paid for through taxes (like the tax on home heating fuel) that fell more heavily on the poor. And doubts about food safety compounded the economic woes (Doig 1989). The first recognized cases of Bovine Spongiform Encephalopathy had been discovered among British cows in 1986. At first scientists had no idea how the disease was transmitted; then they identified it as having stemmed from the widespread practice, in industrial agriculture, of grinding the leftover parts of sheep and cows and putting them into livestock feed. In 1988, the government had outlawed this practice of recycling, but – without much evidence – assumed that there was no risk to humans from the presence of BSE in the food chain. Although other EU countries boycotted British beef, the government continued to claim that beef was not just safe to consume, it was healthy (Jones 2001). Agriculture Minister John Gummer even encouraged his four-year-old daughter to eat a hamburger at a televised event in 1990 to show how confident he was in the safety of the food.

By 1996, it became clear that some British meat was unsafe. A new variant of an older neurological disease, Creutzfeld-Jacob Disease, struck young Britons with a history of eating British beef, and there appeared to be a direct link between the bovine and human illnesses (thus leading to even the human disease being nicknamed "Mad cow disease"). Variant CJD quickly robbed its victims of the ability to walk, talk, think, and breathe. Only after the human–bovine link was discovered were over 3 million cattle slaughtered. More than 160 Britons died of VCJD between 1996 and 2007 (NCJDRSU 2010).

John Major's Foreign Policy

While John Major tripped over many domestic obstacles, his government made progress in Northern Ireland, cracking down on Ulster Unionist violence and holding secret talks with Sinn Fein leaders (although in 1992 two IRA bombs went off in the City of London, killing three people and causing over £750 million worth of damage). In the 1993 Downing Street Declaration, Britain and the Irish Republic agreed that only the people of Ireland had the right and the responsibility to decide their future. Two years later, this negotiation paid off in a framework document that provided for the continuation of a divided Ireland until the people of the two Irelands had decided otherwise. In 1994, the Provisional IRA laid down its arms as a goodwill gesture, and US President Bill Clinton met with Sinn Fein leader Gerry Adams, helping encourage him to lead Sinn Fein toward acceptable negotiation strategies. As always, however, any agreement was provisional; massive bombings of Manchester and the City of London in 1996 undermined the creation of trust.

Major also continued to try to maintain the "special relationship" with the United States, which had now become primarily a military alliance. British troops joined American forces in reacting to the Iraqi invasion of Kuwait during the six-week First Gulf War in 1990. Although Saddam Hussein was not successfully removed from power, in the short run the event seemed to be a victory for the British and American forces. Britain also forged significant links with Europe by signing the Maastricht Treaty (1992), which transformed the European Community into the European Union. The treaty bore the stamp of Britain's independent streak; it affirmed that EU member countries would be able to handle their own foreign, justice, and immigration policies. Britain also opted out of the Social Chapter, which bound EU countries to common policies on working conditions, health and safety, and treatment of the unemployed. Finally, Major successfully negotiated Britain's remaining apart from the new common European currency, the euro, planned for 1999. A closer physical link with the Continent came in 1994, with the completion of a tunnel under the Channel. Nicknamed the "Chunnel," it allowed a direct rail line between Britain and France. Within a 200-year period, the British government had shifted from preparing to repel a French invasion to positively welcoming one.

The Birth of New Labour

From 1979 to 1997, the Labour Party remained in the wilderness. There were able Labour leaders; in 1983 Neil Kinnock, who had been elected to Parliament from a Welsh coal-mining constituency, took the first steps toward New Labour by rebranding the Labour Party as less radical and more mainstream. His successful moves included Labour's acceptance of membership in NATO, and the announcement that Labour did not plan to renationalize industries privatized under Thatcher. The Labour Party gained Parliamentary seats on the basis of these changes in 1992, but not enough to put it in power. In 1992, Scottish lawyer John Smith replaced Kinnock as party leader, and moved the party even further toward the political center, by changing the process of voting so that trade unions had less power within the party structures.

Four conservative general election victories in a row had the Labour Party asking whether there had been a decisive shift away from the postwar social consensus that had once made its election possible. Was Labour passé as a political party? After John Smith's sudden death from a heart attack in 1994, Tony Blair's appointment as party leader finally seemed to offer the party some hope. Like Bill Clinton, who led the Democrats to victory in the United States in 1992, Blair, a young, presentable lawyer with a young family, was committed to a centrist ideology that appealed to businessmen as well as traditional Labour voters.

The Labour Party won the 1997 election in a landslide, with 419 seats and a 177-seat majority. Winning decisively in Scotland and Wales, in the North, and in major cities, it brought to power substantially more women and MPs from minority ethnic groups, along with representatives disproportionately drawn from the middle classes rather than from trade union backgrounds. Tony Blair portrayed himself as a new, more presidential kind of British leader. While under the "Westminster model" of government the Cabinet was supposed to be the central institution for gathering information and making decisions, Blair moved to a model in which he was the main node at which information was gathered, often through one-on-one meetings with his ministers. Also central to Blair's strategy as Prime Minister was the idea of the "permanent campaign," which required considering the political implications of every decision, and using public relations techniques to spin decisions in the best way possible.

Accepting the idea that the national consensus on social provision had changed, New Labour adopted some of the goals of prior Conservative governments. Rather than rapidly increasing spending, Chancellor of the Exchequer Gordon Brown locked the government into levels of spending fixed during the Major era. Blair's government continued to take the position that income support (welfare), rather than an entitlement, was meant to tide people over until they could be trained and enter the private workforce. But his government combined that determination with a higher minimum wage; in 1999 some workers' incomes increased as much as 40 percent as a result. The government also tried to root out cases of people collecting disability benefits when actually capable of working. When taxes needed to be raised, the Labour government taxed in ways that were not immediately obvious: pension funds were taxed, or people lost the tax relief they had once been able to claim for interest on their mortgages (Rhodes 2000). By the early 2000s, these strategies had paid off with high growth and low interest rates, and Gordon Brown cut taxes further, creating a 10 percent tax bracket for the lowest earners. Poor working families were also recognized by the state with an income supplement.

By now, the Treasury had a surplus, and Tony Blair was able to promise more traditional Labour reforms, like smaller class sizes in primary and secondary schools, and more NHS doctors and hospital beds. While Blair's Education Secretary, David

Blunkett, continued to emphasize a traditionalist approach to the curriculum and to support achievement tests, he also eliminated grant-maintained schools, and spent more on school building and on programs targeted to at-risk youth. Blair proposed investing large sums in the NHS to modernize facilities, but also putting more doctors on salary and limiting the number allowed in private practices. By 2005, the government planned to eliminate waiting times for surgeries, and patients would be able to coordinate all their care by calling one centralized office. But rising demand for medical procedures and increasing costs undermined these plans.

Government Reforms and Devolution

The boldest step that Blair's government took was a constitutional one. In 1999, Parliament passed the House of Lords Act, which excluded all but 92 hereditary peers from that body, and cut the total membership of the House of Lords from 1,295 to 694. Discussions then ensued about whether in the future the Lords should be appointed, elected, or some combination of the two, and what the role of the upper chamber ought to be, but in the short run, no further action was taken. With the addition of newly appointed life peers and the elimination of hereditary peers, the House of Lords took on a greater role, defeating the government 245 times between 2001 and 2005 (Flinders 2006).

A mayor and elected assembly for London had been a priority of Tony Blair's since 1994, and in 1999 the Greater London Authority Act created both. The Labour Party refused to support left-wing mayoral candidate Ken Livingstone, despite his leadership of the abolished Greater London Council, so he ran as an Independent and won two terms of office. The mayor's job was to work with and persuade the boroughs that made up greater London, rather than to command them. He was officially responsible for planning for London's projected growth (from 7.4 million people in 2001 to 8.1 million by 2016), and in charge of certain public services, including transportation, although boroughs controlled their own internal development, traffic light timings, and road construction (Pimlott and Rao 2004). As a result of what was judged a successful experiment in London, the 2000 Local Government Act introduced the possibility of elected mayors, the use of ballot initiatives and referenda, and the auditing of local accounts in other cities.

After the failed 1970s votes on devolution for Scotland and Wales, the issue of Britain's regional autonomy receded, since it certainly got no support from Margaret Thatcher. But devolution resurfaced within the Labour Party in 1992 as a priority of Labour leader John Smith. The fact that Conservatives won no seats in Scotland and Wales in the 1997 general election also opened the way for Blair's New Labour to be the strong voice in favor of devolution (Tomaney 2000). Leadership on devolution within the Labour Party was matched by agitation for devolution within Scotland itself. In 1989, a Scottish Constitutional Convention asserted the people's right to a Scottish Parliament with the power to make laws and levy taxes. Blair's government endorsed this idea, and designed a referendum on whether there should be a separate Scottish government and whether it should have the power to raise taxes. Both points of the referendum passed, and elections held in Scotland in 1999 produced a coalition government of Labour and Liberal Democrats and representation by several smaller parties. Scotland's Parliament gained responsibility for domestic issues, with powers to vary tax rates, while the British Parliament at Westminster retains responsibility for foreign affairs.

Wales was given its own opportunity to vote on a referendum about the establishment of a Welsh assembly, but the result revealed that, with about half of the eligible population voting, the proponents and opponents of the measure were almost equally divided. Despite this ambiguous result, the Labour government successfully passed the Government of Wales Act in 1998, and in 1999 elections were held for the first National Assembly for Wales. Plaid Cymru, the Welsh nationalist party, won a majority of the seats. In contrast with the Scottish assembly, the Welsh legislature has no power to vary tax rates. Nonetheless, the different regions of Britain do now, and may in the future, develop different priorities and strategies than Westminster.

New Labour's Foreign Policy

Just as the 1980s had seen the "special relationship" flourish due to the election of like-minded leaders in Britain and the United States, so too in the 1990s, though with different political ideology, the Democratic US President Bill Clinton and Tony Blair forged close ties (Marsh and Baylis 2006). Blair supported Clinton's foreign policy initiatives in Afghanistan and Iraq, and even supported Clinton during the public airing of Clinton's sexual dalliance with a White House intern. In turn, the United States joined a British-initiated United Nations effort to keep the peace in the former Yugoslavia, where Bosnian Serbs under the leadership of Slobodan Milosevic uprooted and massacred Bosnian Muslims (Vickers 2000).

When George W. Bush attained the US Presidency in January 2001, Blair continued to emphasize the closeness of the two nations. Although Blair was not a neoconservative, he and Bush both emphasized intervention in other countries' domestic policies (whether for realistic or idealistic purposes). After the terrorist attacks of September 11, 2001, the two countries collaborated to combat terrorism. George W. Bush, whose father had carried out the First Gulf War but left Saddam Hussein in power in Iraq, was determined to link the September 11 terrorist attacks and Hussein's Iraq. Bush capitalized on British intelligence apparently claiming that the Iraqis had attempted to buy yellowcake uranium from Niger. Eventually, this claim turned out to be false, but it had been useful in generating American and international support for war. Britain's entry into the Iraq War also sparked street demonstrations in London and complaints that Blair was Bush's "poodle" (Elden 2007). Once involved in the war, the British military ran short of equipment.

Less embarrassing for New Labour was the progress the government made in Ireland. Talks with Sinn Fein began in 1997, and culminated in April of 1998 with the Good Friday Agreement. The agreement proposed a government that included a 108-member Northern Ireland Assembly, with proportional representation of Catholics and Protestants. It also included institutions that would facilitate communication between Northern Ireland and the Republic of Ireland, and between Northern Ireland and the other outlying provinces of the United Kingdom. The agreement was put to a referendum, and passed by overwhelming majorities in both Northern Ireland and the Irish Republic (Tomaney 2000). In subsequent elections, the Ulster Unionist Party gained the most votes and formed a government. Larger economic changes in Europe helped to bridge the two Irelands as well; as the Republic of Ireland took off economically, for a time, Northern Ireland benefited too (Carroll 2007). The Northern Ireland Assembly instituted at Stormont as a result of the Good Friday Agreement was in place until 2002, then replaced with direct rule from Britain until finally restored again in 2007 as a result of a historic joint agreement between Sinn Fein's Gerry Adams and Ulster Unionist leader Ian Paisley (BBC 2007).

Tony Blair's ministry also saw the symbolic last act of the British Empire. On July 1, 1997, Chris Patten, the last British governor of Hong Kong, watched as the Union Jack was run down the flagpole for the last time, and Hong Kong – which had been under British control almost continuously since 1842 – was handed over to China. To the illumination of fireworks, 4,000 guests, including Prince Charles and Tony Blair, attended a state dinner. Chinese troops marched into Hong Kong, signaling the transfer of power; and the British Empire became only a memory (BBC 1997). Finally, although the Labour Party had historically opposed European integration, Blair himself proposed greater cooperation with Europe. In 1998, Britain passed the Human Rights Act, which aligned British law with the European Convention on Human Rights. Blair also pushed forward the "Lisbon agenda," with an eye toward making European Union policy more pro-business. Blair supported expansion of the EU to the countries of Eastern Europe, and also supported the idea of a deployable EU military force, separate from NATO or the United Nations. Blair's commitment to European cooperation stopped short of forming foreign policy in a European context, however, as Britain's involvement in the 2003 Iraq War demonstrated.

In 2005, the Labour Party received a majority in a general election for the third time running. By now New Labour had accomplished much of what it had set out to do: waiting lists for surgery under the NHS had declined dramatically; crime was down; and numbers of asylum-seekers had fallen significantly. But there were murmurs of discontent about the government's truthfulness on policy issues, and Labour Party members were resentful of the government's introduction of tuition fees for university students, and its support for the Iraq War (Quinn 2006). As Margaret Thatcher's popularity had waned after many years in office, so had Tony Blair's; and as Thatcher had ceded party leadership to the much less charismatic John Major, so Blair made way for his former Chancellor of the Exchequer, Gordon Brown.

The period between 1979 and 2007 saw fundamental shifts in British political ideology, as the two reigning political parties grew toward each other. Margaret Thatcher polarized the electorate with privatizations that undid some of the welfare state constructed after the Second World War; but her party never completely rejected the idea that the government should commit to the provision of public education, public health care, and some degree of welfare. In response to the Conservatives' rightward shift, New Labour also moved right, abandoning the rhetoric of socialism, committing itself to productivity and economic growth, and trying (albeit unsuccessfully in some cases) to restrain its spending. Both major parties embraced the idea that although Britain was – for good or for ill – destined to be part of a united Europe, Britain also needed the United States, becoming its partner in global interventionism. As the second decade of the twenty-first century began it was unclear whether this political convergence marked an unprecedented political Era of Good Feelings, or the start of another cycle.

Note

1   Local Government Act 1988, ch. 9, at http://www.opsi.gov.uk/acts/acts1988/ukpga_ 19880009_en_5 (accessed Dec. 23, 2009).

References

BBC (1997) Hong Kong Handed Over to Chinese Control. July 1. At http://news.bbc .co.uk/onthisday/hi/dates/stories/july/1/newsid_2656000/2656973.stm (accessed May 25, 2010).

BBC (2007) NI Deal Struck in Historic Talks," BBC News, Mar. 26. At http://news.bbc. co.uk/2/hi/uk_news/northern_ireland/6494599.stm (accessed Dec. 23, 2009).

Borders, William (1979) Irish Police Search Coast for Clues to Blast that Killed Mountbatten; Threat of Vigilante Action. *New York Times*, Aug. 29, A1.

Carroll, James (2007) How the Irish Found Peace. *New York Times*, May 21.

Clarke, Peter (1999) The Rise and Fall of Thatcherism. *Historical Research*, 72 (177): 301–322.

Cottrell, Robert (2005) *Northern Ireland and England: The Troubles*. Philadelphia: Chelsea House.

Doig, Alan (1989 The Resignation of Edwina Currie: A Word Too Far. *Parliamentary Affairs*, 42 (3): 317–329.

Elden, Stuart (2007) Blair, Neo-Conservatism and the War on Territorial Integrity. *International Politics*, 44: 37–57.

Flinders, Matthew (2006) Volcanic Politics: Executive-Legislative Relations in Britain, 1997–2005. *Australian Journal of Political Science*, 41 (3): 385–406.

Gier-Viskovatoff, Jacklyn (1998) Women of the British Coalfields on Strike in 1926 and 1984: Documenting Lives Using Oral History and Photography. *Frontiers: A Journal of Women Studies*, 19 (2): 199–230.

Jones, Kevin E. (2001) BSE, Risk and the Communication of Uncertainty: A Review of Lord Phillips' Report from the BSE Inquiry (UK). *Canadian Journal of Sociology*, 26 (4): 655–665.

Kosecik, Muhammet, and Kapucu, Naim (2003) Conservative Reform of Metropolitan Counties: Abolition of the GLC and MCCs in Retrospect. *Contemporary British History*, 17 (3): 71–94.

Leach, Steve, and Game, Chris (1991) English Metropolitan Government since Abolition: An Evaluation of the Abolition of the English Metropolitan County Councils. *Public Administration*, 69 (Summer): 141–170.

Marsh, Steve, and Baylis, John (2006) The Anglo-American "Special Relationship": The Lazarus of International Relations. *Diplomacy and Statecraft*, 17: 173–211.

McConnell, Allan (1997) The Recurring Crisis of Local Taxation in Postwar Britain. *Contemporary British History*, 11 (3): 39–62.

NCJDRSU (2010) Website of the National Creutzfeldt-Jakob Disease Research and Surveillance Unit. At http://www.cjd.ed.ac.uk/ (accessed May 19, 2010).

Pimlott, Ben, and Rao, Nirmala (2004) Metropolitan Miasma: Blurred Accountabilities in the Governance of London. *London Journal*, 29 (2): 33–45.

Quinn, Thomas (2006) Choosing the Least-Worst Government: The British General Election of 2005. *West European Politics*, 29 (1): 169–78.

Rhodes, Martin (2000) Desperately Seeking a Solution: Social Democracy, Thatcherism and the "Third Way" in British Welfare. *West European Politics*, 23 (2): 161–186.

Sharp, Paul (1991) Thatcher's Wholly British Foreign Policy. *Orbis*, 35 (3): 395–410.

Tomaney, John (2000) End of the Empire State? New Labour and Devolution in the United Kingdom. *International Journal of Urban and Regional Research*, 24 (3): 675–688.

Vickers, Rhiannon (2000) Blair's Kosovo Campaign, Political Communications, the Battle for Public Opinion and Foreign Policy. *Civil Wars*, 3 (1): 55–70.

Wickham-Jones, Mark (1991) What Went Wrong? The Fall of Mrs Thatcher. *Contemporary Record*, 5 (2): 321–340.

Winterton, Jonathan (1993) The 1984–85 Miners' Strike and Technological Change. *British Journal for the History of Science*, 26 (1): 5–14.

Young, Ken (2001) Local Government, 1920–1986: Ideal and Reality. *London Journal*, 26 (1): 57–65.

Further Reading

Green, E.H.H. (1999) Thatcherism: An Historical Perspective. *Transactions of the Royal Historical Society*, 9: 17–42.

Payne, Anthony (2006) Blair, Brown and the Gleneagles Agenda: Making Poverty History, or Confronting the Global Politics of Unequal Development? *International Affairs*, 82 (5): 917–935.

Pugh, Martin (1999) *State and Society: A Social and Political History of Britain, 1870–1997.* London: Oxford University Press.

Reitan, E.A. (2003) *The Thatcher Revolution: Margaret Thatcher, John Major, Tony Blair, and the Transformation of Modern Britain, 1979–2001.* Lanham: Rowman & Littlefield.

Rubinstein, William D. (2003) *Twentieth-Century Britain: A Political History.* New York: Palgrave Macmillan.

Whiteley, Paul, Seyd, Patrick, Richardson, Jeremy, and Bissell, Paul (1994) Thatcherism and the Conservative Party. *Political Studies*, 42: 185–203.

16

Whither Britain?

Society and Culture since 1979

During the morning rush hour on July 7, 2005, simultaneous bombings of Underground trains and a London bus killed 52 people and wounded hundreds of others. Public transportation halted as commuters and tourists alike grappled with the enormity of the attacks and waited to hear whether more would follow. By the afternoon, workers in business attire walked miles to their homes through the eerie quiet of a stunned capital city. Television stations broadcast scenes of fright and carnage taken by passengers' cell-phone cameras. To everyone's mounting horror, the perpetrators were British citizens.

What unites the citizens of a country? In some countries, ethnic nationalism is prominent: the people who live within its borders are assumed to share a common ancestry and a common language. The concept of "Britishness" had long incorporated an idea of ethnic nationalism that cast nonwhites as de facto outsiders. But as the 2005 bombing showed, breaking down ethnic nationalism was insufficient with nothing to take its place. Civic nationalism had to be encouraged, based on a common attachment to civic engagement, the idea of a collective society, and a shared commitment to tolerant values.

Many centrifugal forces beset Britain in the modern period: Britain now contained people of many races, ethnic backgrounds and religions; forces of regional self-determination had led to the emergence of relative autonomy in Scotland, Ireland, and Wales; and deindustrialization had exacerbated regional differences in prosperity. In an age of commercialization few cultural forces bound Britons together.

Empire, State, and Society: Britain Since 1830, First Edition. Jamie L. Bronstein and Andrew T. Harris.
© 2012 Jamie L. Bronstein and Andrew T. Harris. Published 2012 by John Wiley & Sons, Ltd.

Figure 16.1 Coordinated Tube and bus terror attacks on July 7, 2005 ushered in a new era of national security concern. (© Peter Macdiarmid/epa/Corbis).

The Enterprise Culture

Once the workshop of the world, by the 1980s Britain had become its desktop instead. In 1979, 32 percent of the workforce was in manufacturing, and by 1997 this had fallen to 18 percent. Rather than attempting to hold back the transition from an industrial economy to a service economy, Margaret Thatcher encouraged what she called an "enterprise culture." The government subsidized the growth of small business, and lowered the cost, taxation and complication for new firms to enter the market. As workers were made redundant, their coworkers were forced to increase productivity by working longer hours or taking on additional tasks. Why were people willing to do this? One answer may be that workers believed it was in their best interest to foster business growth. The decline in the number of members of trade unions – from 13.3 million in 1979 to fewer than 10 million in 1990, was matched by the growth in the number of people owning stocks, either as individuals or through pension funds.

Did the enterprise culture bring prosperity? Per capita real disposable income rose almost 30 percent during Thatcher's decade in the premiership; but this says little about the way in which income was actually distributed (Stelzer 1992). In fact the rich became richer: between 1979 and 1988, the top 20 percent of income earners increased their share of income earned from 37 to 44 percent. The poor also became poorer: the bottom 20 percent of earners decreased their share from

9.5 percent to 6.9 percent of income. The number of people living below the poverty line nearly doubled, from 6 million in 1979 to 11.7 million in 1986 (Buchanan 1988). Thatcher's government reallocated money for social programs, targeting its funds toward the poorest members of society. But the increase was not enough to offset the impact of unemployment. By the late 1980s, an estimated 250,000 people were homeless in Britain, and 5 million households were below the poverty line.

Thatcherite policies created two nations: the rich and the poor, but also the North and the South. Poverty in Thatcher's Britain was concentrated in the North, coincidentally in areas of predominantly Labour political support. Ninety-four percent of job losses were in the North, whereas the South benefited from opportunities in banking and the defense industries. And Britons were well aware of this division, at least in its economic sense; in 1988 a national poll revealed that 73 percent of Britons polled thought of Britain as divided between "haves" and "have-nots."

The economic and social divisions promoted by Thatcher's policies were underlined by a new narrative about the causes of poverty. In the immediate aftermath of the Second World War, the shared rhetoric of sacrifice helped justify the provision of cradle-to-grave support. This generosity had now eroded. Like President Ronald Reagan across the Atlantic, who alleged that generations of "welfare queens" exploited unemployment payments to avoid working, Margaret Thatcher believed that the "social minimum" had spawned a generation of lazy people. During her tenure as Prime Minister, Thatcher outlined her sense of values, which she deemed "Victorian" in nature: "We were taught to work jolly hard; we were taught to prove ourselves; we were taught self-reliance; we were taught to live within our income" (quoted in Chase-Levenson 2007). Thatcher's supporters argued for scaling back the welfare state on the grounds that its government programs overstepped their bounds and had become focused on imposing social equality rather than about aiding the truly deprived. To impose social equality was to remove the spur to hard work that produced ambitious people and a thriving economy.

Free Markets in Culture

A corollary of Thatcherism was the creation of free markets, including free markets in culture. Beginning in 1983, the Conservative government cut subsidies for the previously uncontroversial Arts Council, and urged national theater, dance, and other cultural groups to develop alternate sources of funding and become more efficient. In 1983, a second commercial television station, Channel 4, joined the existing stations, BBC1, BBC2, and ITV. The relative prestige of British television, in contrast with its commercial American equivalent, allowed serious directors and actors to collaborate on multipart historical dramas that became instant classics, but less highbrow fare also found an enthusiastic international television audience.

Cable television had existed since the 1950s, providing broadcast channels in areas with a weak signal, but cable reached only a small number of houses. Beginning in 1984, cable companies began to offer British customers as many television channels as they liked, along with other broadband services. A competitor to cable, Sky Television, owned by the Australian publishing magnate Rupert Murdoch, began direct satellite broadcasting to British households in 1989. In 1990, Sky TV merged with a floundering satellite television startup, British Satellite Broadcasting, to form the company BSkyB. By the late 1990s, the merged company was broadcasting hundreds of channels in digital format to the British Isles from European satellites, and so ended the age of carefully monitored British television programming once direct state support declined.

Thatcher's government cut back on subsidies to the film industry, eliminating the 25 percent levy on film receipts that had been plowed back into British film studios, and privatizing the National Film Finance Corporation, which earlier had been a direct source of grants to filmmakers. Even so, there were bright spots; television's Channel 4 helped underwrite film production, the moviegoing audience steadily increased, and a few films received great critical acclaim. *Chariots of Fire* won Best Picture at the American Academy Awards in 1982. Other well-received British films included *The Killing Fields*, which chronicled the terror of Pol Pot's Cambodia, and *A Passage to India*, directed by David Lean and based on E.M. Forster's novel of the same name. Ismail Merchant and James Ivory collaborated on a number of lushly filmed period dramas in the 1980s and 1990s, including *A Room with a View* and *Howards End*, also based on E.M. Forster novels.

Socially conscious directors like Mike Leigh, Ken Loach, and Stephen Frears used individual lives as microcosms of the dark side of Thatcherism. Unemployed, politically disempowered men found their community and family standing in decline. Immigrants had to reconcile their ethnic traditions with the values of Thatcherite Britain. Stephen Frears's *My Beautiful Laundrette* (1985), based on a screenplay by Hanif Kureishi, tells the story of a discontented young man of Pakistani ancestry, Omar, who takes the opportunity to rise in society in Thatcherite style by taking over and improving his uncle's failing launderette. The fact that Omar is gay and the lover of a white supremacist adds to the film's sense of cultural dislocation.

The free market in culture also extended to participatory sports. Throughout the late nineteenth and early twentieth centuries cities and counties built public baths, municipal bowling greens, and parks to provide leisure experiences to those who could not afford to pay for them, under the theory that leisure should unite citizens across class. This assumption died out during the Thatcher years. Municipal facilities were taken over by private clubs, driving out casual users. John Major adopted as his government's sports program the promotion of elite sport, using funds from the National Lottery. In a mirroring of the quest for economic efficiency, sports that failed to pay off in Olympic medals, and participatory sports at the nonelite level, were no longer a national priority (Green 2007).

Even the election of a Labour government in 1997 did not change this; the government funneled money to those sports and athletes that had the best chance of showcasing Britain on an international stage. Sport was now seen not as a net drain on resources, but rather as a potential seed for economic development, particularly in cities that had lost their major manufacturing base to deindustrialization. In this mode Birmingham (1992) and Manchester (1996, 2000) both bid unsuccessfully on the Olympic Games. In 2002, Manchester hosted the Commonwealth Games, benefiting from the Blair government's decision to invest about £670 million in the construction of new athletic facilities and infrastructure there. Although the gains in employment from the Commonwealth Games did not meet expectations, the general confidence in the power of large sporting events to attract tourists and international attention led to government backing for London's successful bid for the 2012 Olympics (Gratton et al. 2005).

The transition from ill-funded amateur play to professional league play continued during the modern period. England's national rugby team fully embraced the trend, hiring first a trained coach, and then a series of technical assistant coaches to manage certain aspects of the game. As a result, the international profile of England's team finally began to improve by the early 1990s, allowing them to win several important championships (Collins 2010). Rugby continued to be most popular in Wales and in the North of England.

Association football's popularity also continued. Although racism could be evident among fans, British-born black players began to break into the professional game, comprising 15 percent of professional players by 1990. The 1980s saw a proliferation of homemade fan magazines for individual British football teams, eventually numbering in the hundreds; and then supporters' associations for individual teams. The introduction of televised football matches via satellite, the addition of corporate logos to players' jerseys, and the foundation of the Premier League changed the game of football by transforming football players into major celebrities. The linkage of celebrity and sport elevated the salaries paid to football players in other leagues as well (Bale 1986).

While the nature of play was improving, the hooliganism that had sprung up in the late 1960s and 1970s around football matches worsened in the 1980s, as groups of drunken fans planned trips to spread mayhem. In May 1985 at Heysel in Brussels, 39 people were killed and 300 injured when a wall collapsed in the stadium and crushed Juventus fans as they tried to escape Liverpool supporters. British teams were banned from European matches for five years. Nor was Heysel the only football tragedy. At a 1985 Bradford City game, a conflagration at the stadium spread so fast in the antiquated stands that it killed 56 people. But it took the Hillsborough disaster of 1989 to propel the government into changing its laissez-faire stance toward football. At a game between Liverpool and Nottingham Forest, a poorly designed stadium, too many fans packed into a turnstile area, and incompetent crowd control by police resulted in 96 dead and 400 injured.

After the Hillsborough disaster, a government-initiated investigation recommended reconstruction of dilapidated stadiums, the installation of closed-circuit television, and crackdowns on troublesome crowd members. Football clubs also made the conscious decision to gentrify the sport, adding seating for the first time, increasing ticket prices, and giving members of official football associations priority in ticket sales. Audience numbers increased, seemingly responding to the better standard of play available in the Premier and Championship Leagues; but the demographic of football also changed. Increasingly, it was a spectator sport for the professional classes rather than a symbol of working-class solidarity.

Literature and Theater

British authors embraced the opportunities of a mass reading public. Comic writers like David Lodge, Sue Townsend, and Helen Fielding produced mass entertainment rather than great literature for the ages. Douglas Adams's *Hitchhiker's Guide to the Galaxy* series parodied contemporary British life and bureaucracy through the prism of a zany space adventure. Jeffrey Archer parlayed his early career as a Member of Parliament into a career writing bestselling potboilers (and then subsequently went to prison for perjury, in an interesting case of life imitating art). Perhaps the best-known late-century author, J.K. Rowling, creator of Harry Potter in all of his manifestations, began her writing career as a poor single mother living with state support in a Glasgow suburb.

Some authors attempted to use literary talent to examine the cultural meanings of modern Britain, exploring themes of disaffection, race, immigration, and identity. Julian Barnes captured the dark side of growing up in England in *Metroland*, and David Mitchell hit similar notes in his mordant *Black Swan Green*. After he insulted Mohammad and spoofed the Iranian cleric Ayatollah Khomeini in his 1988 magical realist book *The Satanic Verses,* Salman Rushdie was the object of Khomeini's fatwa, or official death threat. Hanif Kureishi poked fun at the marketing of Indian religion to the British in *The Buddha of Suburbia*. Zadie Smith, the child of a white father and a Jamaican immigrant mother, wrote a beautiful novel about the experience, *White Teeth* (2000). The experiences of Bangladeshi immigrants to London were captured in books by Monica Ali. The books written by these authors – and in some cases the authors' own lives – illustrated the conflict between a society that had long defined itself in certain ways – as white, as Protestant, as committed to certain values – and a growing multiculturalism.

The National Theatre, which moved into its own building on the South Bank of the Thames in the 1970s, enabled talented playwrights to produce challenging works that helped Britain maintain cultural leadership. The theater staged bold and creative new plays by Harold Pinter, David Hare, Tom Stoppard, and Alan Bennett, among others. Plays staged at the National Theatre often moved to commercial theaters in the West End, as with Stoppard's *Arcadia* (1993), sometimes transferring to Broadway stages in New York; or were made into films, as with Bennett's *The Madness of George III* and *The History Boys*, which thereby achieved an even greater audience.

West End theater producers emulated the rest of the entrepreneurial culture by staging long-running, often musical extravaganzas frequented by tourists, such as *Les Miserables*, *Phantom of the Opera*, and *Cats*. Off West End and provincial theater also continued to flourish and to be daring in ways that West End productions could not or would not dare to be. Plays like *Shopping and F**king*, *Blasted*, and *Normal* explored the worlds of prostitution, war crimes, and serial murder respectively, and featured horrific acts of violence, either onstage or suggested to the audience. The success of these plays showed the willingness of theater audiences to step outside of their comfort zones (Urban 2004).

Art and Design

In 1982, Margaret Thatcher's government held a seminar for the Design Council, as the Council of Industrial Design had been renamed in 1972. As a result the Design Council began to emphasize "Design for Profit"; the government's attitude toward design mirrored its attitude toward the rest of the arts: what consumers wanted, rather than what government wanted them to want, should drive design and art. While in the 1980s British design languished, by the 1990s the British fashion world was being internationally celebrated for the work of innovators like Alexander McQueen, who won British Designer of the Year four times and opened boutiques in three countries.

The flashiness of 1990s British fashion, and its integral connection to the free market, extended to the plastic arts as well. Initially patronized by the advertising executive Charles Saatchi and displaying his work in the Saatchi gallery, Damien Hirst's offerings over the years have included a shark preserved in formaldehyde (*The Physical Impossibility of Death in the Mind of Someone Living*), a mother cow and calf cut into sections and displayed in separate glass cabinets, a jewel-encrusted platinum model of a human skull, and a real rotting cow's head being eaten by maggots, also in a glass box. Another member of the movement calling itself the Young British Artists, Gillian Wearing, became well known for a collection of photographs in which she stopped passers-by on the street, asked them to write anything they liked on a piece of paper, and then took pictures of them with their signs. Conceptual art of this type sparked a fierce discussion about the nature of art, and also drew much public attention, as was intended.

Music

Even Proms concerts were commodified in the modern period, and by the 1990s were televised for an international audience of millions (Cannadine 2008). British popular music performers at the end of the twentieth century still filled stadiums, even if they did not regain the dominant international position held at the end of the 1960s and in the early 1970s. The band U2 played the arena circuit to huge crowds around the world, and lead singer Bono parlayed celebrity into becoming a spokesman for poverty relief in Africa. Elton John, whose career took off in the early 1970s, reworked the song "Candle in the Wind" in 1997 to commemorate the death in a car accident of Princess Diana, ex-wife of Prince Charles. Musical talent often was less important than the marketing of a musical concept, confirmed by the success of the artificially contrived band, the Spice Girls.

But unlike much other late twentieth-century culture, music could also be diverse and participatory. Electronic music production enabled DJs to mix their own sounds and stage raves, unlicensed all-night dance parties, often in abandoned buildings or warehouses (Hesmondhalgh 1998). Migrants from the Punjab region of South Asia produced upbeat mixes based on Indian folk music called Bhangra. The Bhangra circuit started with amateur wedding bands, and then graduated to recording artists who combined folk tunes with drum machines and synthesizers (Banerji 1988). Hip-hop culture came to Britain from the United States in the early 1980s. Black British teenagers, who appreciated the way in which it reflected their struggles (with unemployment, with the police, and with widespread social biases), and disaffected white teenagers (who saw it as a culture ripe for personal expression), bought records and traded mix-tapes, listened to pirate radio stations, and took part in the "break-dancing" craze. Hip-hop blended with already present British musical forms to produce hybrids like "Fast Talking," a form of reggae-inspired rap, and Sound System, in which DJs improvised raps over existing backing tracks (Wood 2009).

Education

Proponents of freer markets in culture pointed to the potential profits made from commercialization and the increased diversity in products available with a larger market. In other areas, however, the free market diminished choice. Under Thatcher, the basis of higher-education funding changed, from grants made directly to institutions to targeted grants to nurture the kinds of courses and research (largely in science and engineering) thought to be vital to Britain's economic future. In an attempt to impose on higher education the same kinds of efficiencies that could be experienced in business, faculty tenure was eliminated, and faculty members now had to measure their research productivity in order to keep their jobs. Expectations changed for students as well in terms of who bore the costs of public higher education. Emulating the United States, Thatcher replaced some student grants with repayable student loans. By 1997, students whose families the government judged could afford to pay were required to make a monetary contribution of £1,000 per annum to their higher education expenses, although it was possible to receive a long-term student loan. Charging tuition in this way was a sharp departure from the practice of British public higher education, and while the amount remained small compared to American public universities, it reflected a significant shift in the assumptions underlying the public nature of educational opportunity.

While the funding processes for higher education changed radically, other trends continued, including a growth in the number of institutions for higher education, and a growth in the overall student population. In the early 1990s, the state eliminated the divide between universities and polytechnics, and more than 40 polytechnics were renamed universities. By 2003, there were almost 100 universities in the United Kingdom. Participation in higher education increased from 13 percent of eligible young people in 1980 to 34 percent in 1999, and women students eclipsed men, whereas they had previously been underrepresented, which also tracked American higher education. Higher education opportunities were still highly stratified by social class, however; the participation of children of parents classified as unskilled remained well below 5 percent. Average class sizes more than doubled as the number of students increased, while public funding of higher education declined. University faculty remained poorly paid, both compared to other professionals in Britain and compared with university faculty in other countries.

Crime

Crime continued to increase during the Thatcher years, and had been increasing steadily since the end of the Second World War. Racial tensions were central to crime in the modern era, and underlay Britain's attempt to grapple with race as a society. The British National Front, a fascist political party, began outreach among young people, and a skinhead musical subculture that had existed in Britain's cities since the late 1960s developed a more racist and political strain as the economic crisis of the late 1970s deepened. In 1981, race riots erupted in Brixton, a South London neighborhood with a large West Indian community, and in other diverse neighborhoods in other large cities. In response to a government investigation of the riots, the Scarman Report concluded that deep-seated distrust of the police and government had developed when urban residents were consistently deprived of opportunities for education and economic development. A second round of serious rioting in 1985 led to a Conservative drive for "law and order;" the amendment of laws to provide longer prison sentences, offer compensation to crime victims, and afford police more latitude in riot-control tactics.

The 1980s in particular saw a series of moral panics about crime, sparked by particular cases but fanned by the news cycle: child abuse, child murder, pedophilia, and satanic crime all had their moments of intense focus. In fact, the moral panics were unfounded in rational terms, for the vast majority of indictable offenses remained property crimes, with murder and rape still rare (Matthews 1995). But moral panics gave rise to a sense of distrust of the police and the law in general; more young people were arrested, but this increase was more than offset by the public failure to report many crimes. The 1981 British Crime Survey indicated that there were "three times as many thefts, twelve times as much vandalism, three times as many sexual offenses, nine times as many robberies, and twice as many burglaries as the official statistics reported" (Bailey 1988).

Immigration and Race

Unlike the United States, Great Britain never built its national story on the notion of being a "melting pot" or even a "salad bowl" of different ethnicities and cultures. The British Empire brought together people of many nations, religions and colors, but the flow of ideas and people was meant to be outward, from the metropole (Britain) to the periphery (everywhere else). The idea of "Britishness" only applied to those who lived in the United Kingdom, with "Englishness" as a central concept (thus, even the widespread migration of Irish workers to England in the 1800s had been seen as an alien and threatening wave). During the later years of the twentieth century, after decolonization, Britain grappled with the resulting questions about race and about immigration, particularly by those seeking asylum from repressive governments. Thatcher's endorsement of restrictions on immigration resonated with a large proportion of the public, and in 1981 a British Nationality Act limited migration to Britain, removed the Right of Abode for certain residents of the British Commonwealth countries, and removed the right of automatic British citizenship for those born in the United Kingdom to non-British parents.

Britain was not a color-blind society. A certain amount of sanguineness about race was brought up short in 1996, when Stephen Lawrence, an 18-year-old black man, was brutally murdered while waiting for a bus near his South London home. The police investigation that followed was insufficient. The white youths held to be responsible were tried and acquitted, although at least one of the accused bragged to the press about his involvement in the crime. A government inquiry concluded that institutionalized racism hampered the crime fighting powers of the London police.

But the issue of race did not simply divide between black and white. Muslim communities were concentrated in a few cities, particularly London, Birmingham, and Bradford, where they had chain-migrated in search of manufacturing jobs during the period of open immigration from the Commonwealth before 1962. Contrasted with other Asian migrants to Britain, Muslims from places like Pakistan and Bangladesh had lower levels of education, were less likely to be employed, and were much less likely to allow women to work outside the home. Fewer Muslims owned their own homes, and the homes they did own were more likely to be overcrowded and substandard in their construction. Finally, Muslims were politically underrepresented at all levels, from local councils to the Houses of Parliament and the European Parliament.

Particularly after the 2001 attacks on the Pentagon and the World Trade Center buildings in New York, which sparked international discussion about whether Islam was compatible with democracy, British Muslims feared being seen as disloyal to state and society, and faced vigilante violence grounded in that perception. In the spring and summer of 2002 violent disputes broke out between Muslim Pakistani communities and white nationalist groups and the police. In 2003, after a study spearheaded by the British Home Office, the government concluded that Asian and white communities did not interact with each other sufficiently, and that the answer lay in more outreach to Asian immigrant communities. After the July 7 attacks in London in 2005, the idea that more outreach was going to solve problems by itself came into disrepute, and harder solutions came to hand.

Giving up on the goal of assimilation, Tony Blair's government turned to a points system to identify immigrants who had the most to offer and who appeared to pose the least risk. Only those who were economically productive and gained citizenship could now bring their relatives. Citizenship itself became a multistep process, with a revocable "provisional citizenship" granted to those who proved that they had learned English and could pass a test about life in the UK. The government prioritized the migration of low-waged workers from inside the EU (McGhee 2009).

Sexual Mores

Worries about crime and about the assimilation of immigrant communities were accompanied by concerns about whether British society had some widely shared notion of morality. In the late 1950s, the British jurist Patrick Devlin, in considering whether homosexuality ought to be criminalized, had asserted that societies disintegrated without a common morality. The last quarter of the nineteenth century in Britain saw at least two competing sexual cultures. In some quarters the reaction against sexual liberalization in the 1960s and 1970s continued, fed by the conservatism of the "Moral Majority" in the United States. As in the United States, the appearance of AIDS in the midst of a conservative political moment led to ostracism of homosexuals and the decision not to allocate public funds for AIDS prevention. Arguing that a decline in public morals would lead to a decline in national greatness, the Thatcher government had initiated legislation with moral purpose, restricting graphic advertisements, requiring stores that sold sexual materials to be licensed, closing theaters that showed pornographic films, and banning positive depictions of homosexuality in government statements and in schools.

When it came to personal practices, though, Britons insisted on their individual liberties. Adult websites on the internet became widely popular. The total value of the British pornography industry was estimated at £1 billion, one-twentieth of the value of the industry worldwide (Barnes and Goodchild 2006). The state lowered the age of homosexual consent in 1994 from 21 years of age to 18, and then – due to pressure from the European Court of Human Rights – it was lowered again, to 16 years of age in 2000. The idea of personal liberty also extended to reproductive freedom. The abortion rate continued at about 160,000 procedures annually; an estimated 20 percent of women bearing children had had a previous pregnancy terminated (Alment 1985).

Religion

The Church of England would not be the glue holding Britain together. By the first decade of the twenty-first century, only 3 percent of the adult population attended Church of England services on a regular basis, although many more were nominally Christian, a phenomenon sociologists termed "belief without belonging" (Shaw 2009). Anglican bishops still sat in the House of Lords and were still chosen (from a short list) by the Prime Minister, but they were more likely to be left-leaning than right-wing in their politics, in contrast with politically active clerics in the United States.

The conflict between Catholicism and Protestantism that had riven Britain and its component parts over the previous two centuries had cooled somewhat. In Ireland, Catholic and Protestant politicians worked together in a coalition government. Tony Blair raised few hackles when he professed his own beliefs – sending his children to Catholic private school, declaring that he was a proponent of Christian socialism, and eventually converting to Catholicism himself (Chandler 1997; Stelzer 1996).

Other religious groups had a more difficult time. Britain continued to be home to a small community of Jews. While many had arrived in the late nineteenth-century migration as manual workers, by the late twentieth century third- and fourth-generation Jews had largely climbed into the ranks of the middle classes. While the first generations of Jews in Britain had strongly supported the Liberals and then Labour, by the time of the Thatcher administration many in the Jewish community were supporting the Conservatives, on the grounds that they were more likely to be friendly to Israel. This was especially true among the most Orthodox Jews, whose friendship networks were organized around their coreligionists. Support for Israel led to further dissension within the Jewish community and within Britain at large. Beginning in 2002, higher education unions in Britain began proposing an academic boycott of Israel, asserting that Israeli treatment of Palestinians mirrored South African apartheid. In response, some Jewish groups accused the academics of anti-Semitism (Kotler-Berkowitz 2001).

Britain's approximately 1.8 million Muslims, half of whom were British-born, experienced the most difficulty in reconciling their religious practices with the wider culture. Although many Christian and Jewish religious schools were state supported, by 2007 this was true for only 7 of over 100 Muslim religious schools. Muslims were also one of the last groups to be protected from discrimination in employment – and then, only because Britain had to subscribe to civil rights guarantees put in place for all European Union countries. Despite these limited protections, Muslims had difficulty establishing a foothold for certain cultural practices, including single-sex religious schools, prayer at work, and observation of the fast of Ramadan.

New Labour and "Cool Britannia"

When Tony Blair came to power in 1997, part of his political goal was to put in place a new, unifying narrative for Britain – to reinvigorate Britain by "rebranding" it. He used the power of government and private media to draw attention to the fact that Britain had a new and vigorous art scene, that British music was once again popular, that British restaurants served some of the most innovative food in Europe, and that London had become one of the most cosmopolitan cities on the planet. *Time* magazine had already dubbed London the "coolest city in the world," and the notion of "Cool Britannia" was born.

Part of Blair's rebranding centered on the celebration of the year 2000. The idea for a celebration of the millennium distantly echoed the 1951 Festival of Britain. But while the Festival of Britain focused on arts and theater and musical presentations all across the country, the Millennium celebrations centered on a year-long installation of a single large dome, to be built in Greenwich at the end of a new line for the London Underground. Delays hampered construction of the Underground line, and when the Millennium Dome itself was finally completed it was a disappointment, both in terms of the subject matter it focused on, and the number of people who chose to attend. More successful as a tourist attraction was the London Eye, a 443-foot-tall Ferris wheel erected on the south bank of the

Thames in 1999. Tourists boarded 25-person observation pods for a slow half-hour circular trip and a panoramic view for miles. In the first ten years of its existence, it attracted more than 30 million visitors.

Another aspect of Blair's rebranding effort involved an attempt to remake the British people: using both persuasion and dissuasion to increase social responsibility and so decrease state expenditures necessary by decreasing the need for services. The government counseled citizens to avoid obesity and teenage pregnancy, and in Blair's third term, instituted a ban on smoking inside all public places and workplaces. Much publicity was given to initiatives to change the behavior of habitual offenders: young people, and even entire families, who committed petty crimes, used drugs, or disturbed their neighborhoods were identified as antisocial, and were subject to behavior orders, curfews, and a plethora of neighborhood surveillance cameras. Schools and parents were encouraged to collaborate on bringing slow learners up to speed (Perri 6 et al. 2010).

In the later twentieth century, the British monarchy, in the person of Queen Elizabeth II, continued to have an almost completely ceremonial role – more important as a tourist attraction than to the daily lives of most people. Over the course of the Thatcher, Major, and Blair ministries, funding for the royal family was vastly trimmed back. The marriage of heir to the throne Prince Charles to the photogenic Lady Diana Spencer excited monarchists on both sides of the Atlantic in 1981, as did the birth of princes William and Harry. Nonetheless, in a signal that every institution has to bow to modernity, the marriage ended in divorce, and Charles eventually married his long-time mistress, Camilla Parker-Bowles. Princess Diana's untimely death in a car crash in France in 1997 plunged the nation into mourning. Prince Charles fell out of favor as heir to the throne, and in the first decade of the new century royal-watchers focused on princes William and Harry.

While "Cool Britannia" fizzled after the turn of the millennium, Britain continued to demonstrate leadership in some areas, particularly technology. The first "test-tube baby," Louise Brown, was born in Greater Manchester in 1978; the doctors who treated her mother for infertility, and ended up spawning an entire industry for assisted fertility, received the Nobel Prize in Medicine in 2010. Martin John Evans first cultivated embryonic stem cells from mice in 1981, and pioneered technologies of genetic targeting. Along with his colleagues, he perfected a way of making a "knockout mouse," with specific genes turned off, that could serve as a test subject for targeted therapies. Evans and his collaborators received the Nobel Prize in Medicine in 2007. Britain also attempted to exert international leadership on climate change and green technology, although its relationship with the United States did not give it enough leverage to demand cooperation with these initiatives.

Britain experienced vast transformations between 1830 and 2007. The nation that accumulated and then shed a worldwide empire had by the late twentieth century ceded some of its sovereignty to Europe, and some, through foreign policy partnership, to the United States. Britain had loosened political control over its constituent regions through devolution of decision-making in Scotland and Wales, thereby reversing centuries of accumulated centralization of state power. Britain built up the first manufacturing economy, served as the center of the sterling area and the financier of infrastructure around the globe, and then dismantled the first industrial economy and transformed into a postindustrial society. The aristocracy, which had monopolized the political structure for hundreds of years, declined in importance, replaced in political and cultural leadership by the middle class. Working people had transformed from a completely unrepresented group to a group with representation but little power, to targets of social concern, and finally to ostensibly equal citizens under the welfare state. How to define the working class after industrial society and after the shift away from the welfare state under Thatcher remains an open question.

Geopolitically, Britain began the period as an unmatched superpower presiding over a long period of internal peace. The nation was damaged and financially overdrawn by two world wars and the Great Depression, and struggled to define itself within Europe and through its relationship with the United States. National identity shifted too: from Anglo-Saxon, Protestant, and anti-French, to a multi-ethnic, multireligious, highly diverse society without the clarity provided by a common vision or a common enemy. What government could do or should do for its citizens shifted: from the Liberalism of John Stuart Mill to the cradle-to-grave provision of the welfare state, and then, curiously, to the Thatcherite look backwards to laissez-faire Victorian liberalism. It remains an appealing country and an intriguing history to explore because it has imprinted the world so richly with its language, its cultural norms, its institutions, and its follies. That it is now diminished in financial and military strength from its Victorian heights does not mitigate the realization that its struggles over values, rights, empire, governance, class, and ethnicity are the struggles of the Western world, and these struggles define the challenges of our time.

References

Alment, Anthony (1985) Warnock: The Next Stage. *Contemporary Review*, 246 (1433): 300–303.

Bailey, Victor (1988) Crime in the 20th Century. *History Today*, 38 (5): 42–48.

Bale, John (1986) Sport and National Identity: A Geographic View. *British Journal of Sports History*, 3 (1): 18–41.

Banerji, Sabita (1988) Ghazals to Bhangra in Great Britain. *Popular Music*, 7: 201–213.

Buchanan, Keith (1988) Planned Ruination: Thatcher's Britain. *Monthly Review*, 39 (9): 1–10.

Barnes, Anthony, and Goodchild, Sophie (2006) Porn UK. *Independent*, May 28. At http://www.independent.co.uk/news/uk/this-britain/porn-uk-480084.html (accessed Dec. 9, 2010).

Cannadine, David (2008) The "Last Night of the Proms" in Historical Perspective. *Historical Research*, 81 (212): 315–349.

Chandler, Andrew (1997) Faith in the Nation? The Church of England in the 20th Century. *History Today*, 47: 9–15.

Chase-Levenson, Michael (2007) Our Favorite Ghosts: Why Are We Still So Obsessed with the Victorians? *Slate*, Mar. 22. At http://www.slate.com/id/2162372/ (accessed Dec. 7, 2010).

Collins, Tony (2010) Amateurism and the Rise of Managerialism: The Case of Rugby Union, 1871–1995. *Sport in History*, 30 (1): 104–120.

Gratton, Chris, Shibli, Simon, and Coleman, Richard (2005) Sport and Economic Regeneration in Cities. *Urban Studies*, 42 (5–6): 985–999.

Green, Mick (2007) Olympic Glory or Grassroots Development? Sport Policy Priorities in Australia, Canada, and the United Kingdom, 1960–2006. *International Journal of the History of Sport*, 24 (7): 921–953.

Hesmondhalgh, David (1998) The British Dance Music Industry: A Case Study of Independent Cultural Production. *British Journal of Sociology*, 49 (2): 234–251.

Kotler-Berkowitz, Laurence A. (2001) Ethnicity and Politics: Cohesion, Division, and British Jews. *Political Studies*, 49: 648–669.

Matthews, Roger (1995) Crime in England and Wales. *Annals of the American Academy*, 539: 169–182

McGhee, Derek (2009) The Paths to Citizenship: A Critical Examination of Immigration Police in Britain since 2001. *Patterns of Prejudice*, 43 (1): 41–64.

Perri 6, Fletcher-Morgan, Charlotte, and Leyland, Kate (2010) Making People More Responsible: The Blair Government's Program for Changing Citizens' Behavior. *Political Studies*, 58: 427–449.

Shaw, Jane (2009) Anglican History in the 21st Century: Remembering All the Baptized. *Anglican and Episcopal History*, 78 (4): 353–363.

Stelzer, Irwin (1992) What Thatcher Wrought. *Public Interest*, no. 102 (Spring): 18–51.

Stelzer, Irwin (1996) Christian Socialism in Britain. *Public Interest*, 124: 3–11.

Urban, Ken (2004) Towards a Theory of Cruel Britannica: Coolness, Cruelty, and the "Nineties." *New Theatre Quarterly*, 20 (4): 354–372.

Wood, Andy "Original London Style": London Posse and the Birth of British Hip Hop. *Atlantic Studies*, 6 (2): 179–190.

Further Reading

Anwar, Muhammad (2008) Muslims in Western States: The British Experience and the Way Forward. *Journal of Muslim Minority Affairs*, 28 (1): 125–137.

Buford, Bill (1992) *Among the Thugs*. New York: Norton.

Goldblatt, David (2006) *The Ball Is Round: A Global History of Soccer*. New York: Riverhead.

Greek, Cecil E. (1992) Antipornography Campaigns: Saving the Family in America and England. *International Journal of Politics, Culture, and Society*, 5 (4): 601–616.

Greenaway, David, and Haynes, Michelle (2003) Higher Education in the UK: The Role of Fees and Loans. *Economic Journal*, 113 (485): F150–166.

Himmelfarb, Gertrude (1991) *Poverty and Compassion: The Moral Imagination of the Late Victorians*. New York: Vintage.

McKibbin, Ross (2002) Class, Politics, Money: British Sport since the First World War. *Twentieth Century British History*, 13 (2): 191–200.

Reitan, Earl (2003) *The Thatcher Revolution: Margaret Thatcher, John Major, Tony Blair and the Transformation of Britain, 1979–2001*. London: Rowman & Littlefield.

Appendix

Reigns and Ministries since 1830

Monarch	Prime Minister	Party
King William IV (Jun 26, 1830– Jun 20, 1837)	Arthur Wellesley, Duke of Wellington (Jan 22, 1828– Nov 22, 1830)	Tory
	Charles Grey, Earl Grey (Nov 22, 1830– Jul 16, 1834)	Whig
	William Lamb, Viscount Melbourne (Jul 16, 1834– Nov 17, 1834)	Whig
	Arthur Wellesley, Duke of Wellington (Nov 17, 1834– Dec 10, 1834)	Tory
	Sir Robert Peel (Dec 10, 1834– Apr 18, 1835)	Tory
Queen Victoria (Jun 20, 1837– Jan 22, 1901)	William Lamb, Viscount Melbourne (18 Apr 1835–30 Aug 1841)	Whig
	Sir Robert Peel (Aug 30, 1841– Jun 30, 1846)	Conservative
	Lord John Russell (Jun 30, 1846– Feb 23, 1852)	Liberal
	Edward Geoffrey Stanley, Earl of Derby (Feb 23, 1852– Dec 19, 1852)	Conservative
	George Hamilton-Gordon, Earl of Aberdeen (Dec 19, 1852– Feb 6, 1855)	Conservative
	Henry John Temple, Viscount Palmerston (Feb 6, 1855– Feb 20, 1858	Liberal
	Edward Geoffrey Stanley, Earl of Derby (Feb 20, 1858–Jun 12, 1859)	Conservative

Empire, State, and Society: Britain Since 1830, First Edition. Jamie L. Bronstein and Andrew T. Harris.
© 2012 Jamie L. Bronstein and Andrew T. Harris. Published 2012 by John Wiley & Sons, Ltd.

Monarch	Prime Minister	Party
	Henry John Temple, Viscount Palmerston (Jun 12, 1859–Oct 18, 1865)	Liberal
	John Russell, Earl Russell (Oct 29, 1865–Jun 28, 1866)	Liberal
	Edward Geoffrey Stanley, Earl of Derby (Jun 28, 1866–Feb 27, 1868)	Conservative
	Benjamin Disraeli (Feb 27, 1868–Dec 3, 1868)	Conservative
	William Ewart Gladstone (Dec 3, 1868–Feb 20, 1874)	Liberal
	Benjamin Disraeli (Feb 20, 1874–Apr 23, 1880)	Conservative
	William Ewart Gladstone (Apr 23, 1880–Jun 23, 1885)	Liberal
	Robert Arthur Talbot Gascoyne-Cecil, Marquess of Salisbury (Jun 23, 1885–Feb 1, 1886)	Conservative
	William Ewart Gladstone (Feb 1, 1886–Jul 25, 1886)	Liberal
	Robert Arthur Talbot Gascoyne-Cecil, Marquess of Salisbury (Jul 25, 1886–Aug 15, 1892)	Conservative
	William Ewart Gladstone (Aug 15, 1892–Mar 5, 1894)	Liberal
	Archibald Primrose, Earl of Rosebery (Mar 5, 1894–Jun 25, 1895)	Liberal
King Edward VII (Jan 22, 1901–May 6, 1910)	Robert Arthur Talbot Gascoyne-Cecil, Marquess of Salisbury (Jun 25, 1895–Jul 12, 1902)	Conservative
	Arthur James Balfour (Jul 12, 1902–Dec 5, 1905)	Conservative
	Sir Henry Campbell-Bannerman (Dec 5, 1905–Apr 8, 1908)	Liberal
King George V (May 6, 1910–Jan 20, 1936)	Herbert Asquith (Apr 8, 1908–Dec 7, 1916)	Liberal, then National Coalition
	David Lloyd-George (Dec 7, 1916–Oct 23, 1922)	National Coalition
	Andrew Bonar Law (Oct 23, 1922–May 22, 1923)	Conservative

Monarch	Prime Minister	Party
	Stanley Baldwin (May 22, 1923–Jan 22, 1924)	Conservative
	Ramsay MacDonald (Jan 22, 1924–Nov 4, 1924)	Labour
	Stanley Baldwin (Nov 4, 1924–Jun 5, 1929)	Conservative
	Ramsay MacDonald (Jun 5, 1929–Jun 7, 1935)	Labour
King Edward VIII (Jan 20, 1936–Dec 11, 1936, abdicated)	Stanley Baldwin (Jun 7, 1935–May 28, 1937)	Conservative
King George VI (Dec 11, 1936–Feb 6, 1952)	Neville Chamberlain (May 28, 1937–May 10, 1940)	Conservative/National Coalition government
	Winston Churchill (May 10, 1940–Jul 26, 1945)	Conservative/National Coalition government
	Clement Attlee (Jul 26, 1945–Oct 26, 1951)	Labour
Queen Elizabeth II (Feb 6, 1952–)	Winston Churchill (designated Sir Winston Churchill in 1953) (Oct 26, 1951–Apr 6, 1955)	Conservative
	Sir Anthony Eden (Apr 6, 1955–Jan 10, 1957)	Conservative
	Harold Macmillan (Jan 10, 1957–Oct 19, 1963	Conservative
	Sir Alec Douglas-Home (Oct 19, 1963–Oct 16, 1964)	Conservative
	Harold Wilson (Oct 16, 1964–Jun 19, 1970)	Labour
	Edward Heath (Jun 19, 1970–Mar 4, 1974)	Conservative
	Harold Wilson (Mar 4, 1974–Apr 5, 1976)	Labour
	James Callaghan (Apr 5, 1976–May 4, 1979)	Labour
	Margaret Thatcher (May 4, 1979–Nov 28, 1990)	Conservative
	John Major (Nov 28, 1990–May 2, 1997)	Conservative
	Tony Blair (May 2, 1997–Jun 27, 2007)	Labour
	Gordon Brown (Jun 27, 2007–May 11, 2010)	Labour
	David Cameron (May 11, 2010–)	Conservative

Bibliography

Aiston, Sarah (2005) A Maternal Identity? The Family Lives of British Women Graduates Pre- and Post-1945. *History of Education*, 34 (4): 407–426.

Aldridge, Meryl (1996) Only Demi-Paradise? Women in Garden Cities and New Towns. *Planning Perspectives*, 11 (1): 23–39.

Alment, Anthony (1985) Warnock: The Next Stage. *Contemporary Review*, 246 (1433): 300–303.

Anderson, Lindsay (dir.) (1953) *O Dreamland*. At http://www.youtube.com/watch?v=LLlKR1x1oWY (accessed May 28, 2010).

Anwar, Muhammad (2008) Muslims in Western States: The British Experience and the Way Forward. *Journal of Muslim Minority Affairs*, 28 (1): 125–137.

Arthur, Max (2004) *Forgotten Voices of World War II: A New History of World War Two in the Words of the Men and Women Who Were There*. Guilford, CT: Lyons Press.

Atkins, Frederick (1890) *Moral Muscle and How to Use It*. Chicago: Fleming Revell.

August, Andrew (2007) The *British Working Class, 1832–1940*. Harlow: Pearson Longman.

Ayers, Pat (2004) Work, Culture and Gender: The Making of Masculinities in Postwar Liverpool. *Labour History Review*, 69 (1): 153–167.

Bailey, Victor (1988) Crime in the 20th Century. *History Today*, 38 (5): 42–48.

Baldwin, Jerome (2010) Canadian Capture of Vimy Ridge. *Military Heritage*, 11 (4): 26–33.

Baldwin, Stanley (1924) What England Means to Me. At http://whatenglandmeanstome.co.uk/?page_id=121 (accessed Dec. 15, 2010).

Bale, John (1986) Sport and National Identity: A Geographic View. *British Journal of Sports History*, 3 (1): 18–41.

Banerji, Sabita (1988) Ghazals to Bhangra in Great Britain. *Popular Music*, 7: 201–213.

Bannister, Robert (1979) *Social Darwinism: Science and Myth in Anglo-American Social Thought*. Philadelphia: Temple University Press.

Barnes, Anthony, and Goodchild, Sophie (2006) Porn UK. *Independent*, May 28. At http://www.independent.co.uk/news/uk/this-britain/porn-uk-480084.html (accessed Dec. 9, 2010).

Empire, State, and Society: Britain Since 1830, First Edition. Jamie L. Bronstein and Andrew T. Harris.
© 2012 Jamie L. Bronstein and Andrew T. Harris. Published 2012 by John Wiley & Sons, Ltd.

BBC (1997) Hong Kong Handed Over to Chinese Control. July 1. At http://news.bbc.co.uk/onthisday/hi/dates/stories/july/1/newsid_2656000/2656973.stm (accessed May 25, 2010).

BBC (2007) "NI Deal Struck in Historic Talks, "BBC News, Mar. 26. At http://news.bbc.co.uk/2/hi/uk_news/northern_ireland/6494599.stm (accessed Dec. 23, 2009).

Beaven, Brad, and Griffiths, John (1999) The Blitz, Civilian Morale, and the City: Mass-Observation and Working-Class Culture in Britain, 1940–1. *Urban History*, 86 (1): 71–88.

Beck, Peter (2005) Britain and the Cold War's "Cultural Olympics": Responding to the Political Drive of Soviet Sport, 1945–58. *Contemporary British History*, 19 (2): 169–185.

Beckett, Ian (1985) Aspects of a Nation in Arms: Britain's Volunteer Training Corps in the Great War. *Revue Internationale d'Histoire Militaire*, 63 (11): 27–39.

Beltran, Concha (2005) Natural Resources, Electrification, and Economic Growth from the End of the Nineteenth Century until World War II. *Revista de Historia Economica*, 23 (1): 46–79.

Bentley, Michael (2001) *Lord Salisbury's World: Conservative Environments in Late-Victorian Britain*. Cambridge: Cambridge University Press.

Besancon, Alain (1984) Orwell in Our Time. *Survey*, 28 (1): 190–197.

Biagini, Eugenio (2000) *Gladstone*. New York: St Martin's Press.

Black, Jeremy, and McRaild, Donald (2002) *Nineteenth-Century Britain*. London: Palgrave Macmillan.

Black, Lawrence (2005) Whose Finger on the Button? British Television and the Politics of Cultural Control. *Historical Journal of Film, Radio and Television*, 25 (4): 547–575.

Borders, William (1979) Irish Police Search Coast for Clues to Blast that Killed Mountbatten; Threat of Vigilante Action. *New York Times*, Aug. 29, A1.

Boyer, George K. (2004) Living Standards, 1860–1939. In Roderick Floud and Paul Johnson (eds), *The Cambridge Economic History of Modern Britain*, vol. 2. Cambridge: Cambridge University Press.

Boyer, George, and Hatton, Timothy (1994) Did Joseph Arch Raise Agricultural Wages? Rural Trade Unions and the Labour Market in Late Nineteenth-Century England. *Economic History Review*, 47 (2): 310–334.

Briggs, Asa (1959) *Chartist Studies*. London: Macmillan.

Briggs, Asa (1965) *The Making of Modern England, 1784–1867: The Age of Improvement*. New York: Harper & Row.

Brighton, Andrew (1981) " Where are the Boys of the Old Brigade?": The Post-war Decline of British Traditionalist Painting. *Oxford Art Journal*, 4 (1): 35–43.

Brittain, Vera (1978) *Testament of Youth*. New York: Penguin.

Brittain, Vera, *et al.* (1998) *Letters from a Lost Generation – First World War Letters of Vera Brittain and Four Friends: Roland Leighton, Edward Brittain, Victor Richardson, Geoffrey Thurlow*, ed. Alan Bishop and Mark Bostridge. London: Little, Brown. Extract at http://www.guardian.co.uk/world/2008/nov/14/first-world-war-vera-brittain (accessed Nov. 8, 2010).

Broadberry, S.N., and Crafts, N.F.R. (1996) British Economic Policy and Industrial Performance in the Early Postwar Period. *Business History*, 38 (4): 65–91.

Brooke, Stephen (2001) Gender and Working-Class Identity in Britain during the 1950s. *Journal of Social History*, 34 (4): 774–795.

Buchanan, Keith (1988) Planned Ruination: Thatcher's Britain. *Monthly Review*, 39 (9): 1–10.

Buford, Bill (1992) *Among the Thugs*. New York: Norton.

Butler, Samuel (1917) *The Way of All Flesh*. New York: E.P. Dutton.

Calder, Angus (1969) *The People's War: Britain, 1939–1945*. New York: Pantheon.

Cannadine, David (1999) *The Decline and Fall of the British Aristocracy*. New York: Vintage.

Cannadine, David (2001) *Ornamentalism: How the British Saw Their Empire*. Oxford: Oxford University Press.

Cannadine, David (2008) The "Last Night of the Proms" in Historical Perspective. *Historical Research*, 81 (212): 315–349.

Carey, John (ed.) (1987) *Eyewitness to History*. New York: Avon.

Carnevali, Francesca, and Strange, Julie-Marie (eds) (2007) *Twentieth-Century Britain: Economic, Cultural and Social Change*. Harlow: Longman.

Carroll, James (2007) *How the Irish Found Peace*. New York Times, May 21.

Chandler, Andrew (1997) Faith in the Nation? The Church of England in the 20th Century. *History Today*, 47: 9–15.

Chase, Malcolm (2007) *Chartism: A New History*. Manchester: Manchester University Press.

Chase-Levenson, Michael (2007) Our Favorite Ghosts: Why Are We Still So Obsessed with the Victorians? *Slate*, Mar. 22. At http://www.slate.com/id/2162372/ (accessed Dec. 7, 2010).

Churchill, Winston (1941) Speech to the Allied Delegates. At http://www.ibiblio.org/pha/timeline/410612bwp.html (accessed Jan. 25, 2011).

Churchill, Winston (1946) "Iron Curtain Speech," Mar. 5. At http://www.fordham.edu/halsall/mod/churchill-iron.html (accessed Dec. 3, 2009).

Clarke, Ian (1999) Institutional Stability in Management Practice and Industrial Relations: The Influence of the Anglo-American Council for Productivity, 1948–1952. *Business History*, 41 (3): 64–69.

Clarke, Peter (1999) The Rise and Fall of Thatcherism. *Historical Research*, 72 (177): 301–322.

Clausen, Christopher (2001) The Great Queen Died. American Scholar, 70 (Winter): 41–49.

Clift, Ben, and Tomlinson, Jim (2008) Negotiating Credibility: Britain and the International Monetary Fund, 1956–1976. *Contemporary European History*, 17 (4): 545–566.

Coetzee, Franz (1992) English Nationalism and the First World War. *History of European Ideas*, 15 (1–3): 363–367.

Colley, Linda (1992) *Britons: Forging the Nation 1707–1837*. New Haven: Yale University Press.

Collins, Marcus (2001) Pride and Prejudice: West Indian Men in Mid-Twentieth-Century Britain. *Journal of British Studies*, 40 (3): 391–418.

Collins, Tony (2010) Amateurism and the Rise of Managerialism: The Case of Rugby Union, 1871–1995. *Sport in History*, 30 (1): 104–120.

Cottrell, Robert (2005) *Northern Ireland and England: The Troubles*. Philadelphia: Chelsea House.

Crangle, John V. (1981) English Nationalism and British Imperialism in the Age of Gladstone and Disraeli, 1968–1880. *Quarterly Review of Historical Studies*, 21 (4): 4–12.

Crewe, Ivor, Fox, Anthony, and Day, Neil (1996) *The British Electorate, 1963–1992: A Compendium of Data from the British Election Studies*. Cambridge: Cambridge University Press.

Crowe, Hilary (2007) Profitable Ploughing of the Uplands? The Food Production Campaign in the First World War. *Agricultural History Review*, 55 (2): 205–228.

Curran, James (2002) Media and the Making of British Society, c.1700–2000. *Media History*, 8 (2): 135–154.

Dangerfield, George (2011) *The Strange Death of Liberal England: 1910–1914*. Piscataway: Transaction. First published 1935.

Davidoff, Leonore, and Hall, Catherine (1987) *Family Fortunes: Men and Women of the English Middle Class, 1780–1850*. Chicago: University of Chicago Press.

Davis, James Richard Ainsworth (1907) *Thomas H. Huxley*. London: E.P. Dutton.

DeGroot, Gerard (1999) A Lost Generation? The Impact of the First World War. *Modern History Review*, 11 (1): 18–21.

Devlin, Patrick (1959) The Enforcement of Morals. *Proceedings of the British Academy*, 24: 129–151.

Dietl, Ralph (2008) Suez 1956: A European Intervention? *Journal of Contemporary History*, 43: 259–278.

Doig, Alan (1989 The Resignation of Edwina Currie: A Word Too Far. *Parliamentary Affairs*, 42 (3): 317–329.

Douglas, Roy (1970) Voluntary Enlistment in the First World War and the Work of the Parliamentary Recruiting Committee. *Journal of Modern History*, 42 (4): 564–585.

Eastwood, David (1994) *Governing Rural England: Tradition and Transformation in Local Government, 1780–1840*. Oxford: Oxford University Press.

Eichengreen, Barry (1987) Unemployment in Interwar Britain: Dole or Doldrums? *Oxford Economic Papers*, n.s., 39 (4): 597–623.

Elden, Stuart (2007) Blair, Neo-Conservatism and the War on Territorial Integrity. *International Politics*, 44: 37–57.

Engels, Friedrich (1969) *The Condition of the Working Class in England in 1844*. London: Panther Books. Originally published 1845. At http://www.marxists.org/archive/marx/works/1845/condition-working-class/ch04.htm (accessed Dec. 18, 2007).

Evans, Eric J. (1983) *The Forging of the Modern State: Early Industrial Britain, 1783–1870*. London: Longman.

Fee, Elizabeth (1979) Nineteenth-Century Craniometry: The Study of the Female Skull. *Bulletin of the History of Medicine*, 53 (3): 415–433.

Fisher, Tim (2005) Fatherhood and the British Fathercraft Movement, 1919–1939. *Gender and History*, 17 (2): 441–462.

Flanders, Judith (2004) *Inside the Victorian Home*. New York: Norton.

Fletcher, Anthony (2009) Between the Lines. *History Today*, 59 (11): 45–51.

Flinders, Matthew (2006) Volcanic Politics: Executive-Legislative Relations in Britain, 1997–2005. *Australian Journal of Political Science*, 41 (3): 385–406.

Floud, Roderick, and Johnson, Paul (eds) (2004) *The Cambridge Economic History of Modern Britain*, vol. 2. Cambridge: Cambridge University Press.

Floud, Roderick, and McCloskey, Deidre N. (ed.) (1994) *Economic History of Britain since 1700: 1939–1992*. Cambridge: Cambridge University Press.

Ford, Boris (1992) *Modern Britain: The Cambridge Cultural History*. Cambridge: Cambridge University Press.

Fox, Daniel (2004) The Administration of the Marshall Plan and British Health Policy. *Journal of Policy History*, 16 (3): 191–211.

Francis, Martin (2007) A Flight from Commitment? Domesticity, Adventure, and the Masculine Imaginary in Britain after the Second World War. *Gender and History*, 19 (1): 163–185.

Fussell, Paul (2000) *The Great War and Modern Memory*. Oxford: Oxford University Press.

Garside, W.R. (1985) The Failure of the "Radical Alternative": Public Works, Deficit Finance and British Interwar Unemployment. *Journal of European Economic History*, 14 (3): 537–555.

Garside, W.R. (1987) Public Works and Mass Unemployment: Britain's Response in a European Perspective, 1919–1939. *Archiv für Sozialgeschichte*, 27.

Gash, Norman (1971) *Politics in the Age of Peel*. New York: Norton.

Gaskell, Elizabeth (1998) *Mary Barton*. Oxford: Oxford University Press.

Gier-Viskovatoff, Jacklyn (1998) Women of the British Coalfields on Strike in 1926 and 1984: Documenting Lives Using Oral History and Photography. *Frontiers: A Journal of Women Studies*, 19 (2): 199–230.

Gilbert, Bentley B. (1971) British Social Policy and the Second World War. *Albion*, 3 (3): 103–115.

Gilbert, Gerard (2009) Britain's Wartime Films Were More Than Just Propaganda. *Independent*, Sept. 3.

Gilbert, Sandra M. (1983) Soldier's Heart: Literary Men, Literary Women, and the Great War. *Signs*, 8 (3): 422–450.

Giles, Judy (2001) Help for Housewives: Domestic Service and the Reconstruction of Domesticity in Britain, 1940–1950. *Women's History Review*, 10 (2): 299–324.

Gleadle, Kathryn (2005) Charlotte Elizabeth Tonna and the Mobilization of Tory Women in Early Victorian England. *Historical Journal*, 50 (1): 97–117.

Goldblatt, David (2006) *The Ball is Round: A Global History of Soccer*. New York: Riverhead.

Goodyear, Ian (2003) Rock against Racism: Multiculturalism and Political Mobilization, 1976–1981. *Immigrants and Minorities*, 22 (1): 44–62.

Grant, Mariel (2006) "Working for the Yankee Dollar": Tourism and the Festival of Britain as Stimuli for Recovery. *Journal of British Studies*, 45 (4): 581–601.

Grant, Matthew (2003) Historians, the Penguin Specials, and the "State of the Nation" Literature, 1958–1964. *Contemporary British History*, 17 (3): 29–54.

Gratton, Chris, Shibli, Simon, and Coleman, Richard (2003) Sport and Economic Regeneration in Cities. *Urban Studies*, 42 (5–6): 985–999.

Graves Robert, and Hodge, Alan (1963) *The Long Week-End: A Social History of Britain, 1919–1937*. New York: Norton.

Greek, Cecil E. (1992) Antipornography Campaigns: Saving the Family in America and England. *International Journal of Politics, Culture, and Society*, 5 (4): 601–616.

Green, E.H.H. (1999) Thatcherism: An Historical Perspective. *Transactions of the Royal Historical Society*, 9: 17–42.

Green, Mick (2007) Olympic Glory or Grassroots Development? Sport Policy Priorities in Australia, Canada, and the United Kingdom, 1960–2006. *International Journal of the History of Sport*, 24 (7): 921–953.

Greenaway, David, and Haynes, Michelle (2003) Higher Education in the UK: The Role of Fees and Loans. *Economic Journal*, 113 (485): F150–166.

Greg, W.R. (1875) On Life at High Pressure. In *Proceedings of the Royal Institution*, vol. 7. London: William Clowes.

Hake, Alfred Egmont (1914) The Death of General Gordon at Khartoum, 1885. In Eva March Tappan (ed.), *The World's Story: A History of the World in Story, Song and Art*, vol. 3: *Egypt, Africa, and Arabia* (Boston: Houghton Mifflin, 1914). At http://www.fordham.edu/halsall/islam/1885khartoum1.html (accessed Dec. 15, 2008).

Halasz, Piri (1966) Great Britain: You Can Walk Across It on the Grass. *Time*, May 15. At http://www.time.com/time/magazine/article/0,9171,835349,00.html (accessed July 12, 2011).

Hall, Catherine (1992) *White, Male and Middle Class: Explorations in Feminism and History*. Cambridge: Polity.

Hammond, Michael (2006) *The Big Show: British Cinema Culture in the Great War, 1914–1918*. Exeter: University of Exeter Press.

Hannon, Brian P.D. (2008) Creating the Correspondent: How the BBC Reached the Frontline in the Second World War. *Historical Journal of Film, Radio and Television*, 28 (2): 175–194.

Hardy, Dennis (1992) Utopian Communities in Britain in the Early Twentieth Century: The Example of New Town. *Communal Societies*, 12 (1): 90–112.

Harling, Philip, and Mandler, Peter (1993) From "Fiscal-Military" State to Laissez-Faire State, 1760–1850. *Journal of British Studies*, 32 (Jan.): 44–70.

Harris, Jose (1992) War and Social History: Britain and the Home Front during the Second World War. *Contemporary European History*, 1 (1): 17–35.

Harrisson, Tom (1990) *Living Through the Blitz*. London: Penguin.

Harvey, A.D. (1999) London's Boroughs. *History Today*, 49 (7): 15–17.

Hatton, T.J., and Bailey, R.E. (1988) Female Labour Force Participation in Interwar Britain. *Oxford Economic Papers*, n.s., 40 (4): 695–715.

Hay, Colin (1996) Narrating Crisis: The Discursive Construction of the "Winter of Discontent." *Sociology*, 30 (2): 253–277.

Hay, Douglas, and Rogers, Nicholas (1997) *Eighteenth-Century English Society*. Oxford: Oxford University Press.

Hay, P.R., and Hayward, M.G. (1988) Comparative Green Politics: Beyond the European Context? *Political Studies*, 36: 433–448.

Heathcott, Joseph (2003) Urban Spaces and Working-Class Expressions across the Black Atlantic: Tracing the Routes of Ska. *Radical History Review*, 87: 183–206.

Heinrich, Anselm (2010) Theatre in Britain during the Second World War. *New Theatre Quarterly*, 26 (2): 61–69.

Hesmondhalgh, David (1998) The British Dance Music Industry: A Case Study of Independent Cultural Production. *British Journal of Sociology*, 49 (2): 234–251.

Hiley, Nicholas (1998) Ploughboys and Soldiers: The Folk Song and the Gramophone in the British Expeditionary Force, 1914–1918. *Media History*, 4 (1): 61–76.

Hilliard, Christopher (2005) Modernism and the Common Writer. *Historical Journal*, 48 (3): 769–787.

Hillman, Nicholas (2008) A "Chorus of Execration"? Enoch Powell's "Rivers of Blood" Forty Years On. *Patterns of Prejudice*, 42 (1): 84–104.

Himmelfarb, Gertrude (1991) *Poverty and Compassion: The Moral Imagination of the Late Victorians*. New York: Vintage.

Hobsbawm, Eric (1968) *Industry and Empire: The Birth of the Industrial Revolution*. New York: New Press.

Holland, Michael (2004) Swing Revisited: The Swing Project. *Family and Community History*, 7 (1): 87–100.

Holland, Robert (1996) The British Experience of Decolonization. *Itinerario*, 20 (2): 51–63.

Homer, Andrew (2000) Creating New Communities: The Role of the Neighborhood Unit in Post-war British Planning. *Contemporary British History*, 14 (1): 63–80.

Houghton, Walter (1957) *The Victorian Frame of Mind*. New Haven: Yale University Press.

Howkins, Alun (1998) A Country at War: Mass-Observation and Rural England, 1939–1945. *Rural History*, 9 (1): 75–97.

Hucker, Jacqueline (2009) Battle and Burial: Capturing the Cultural Meaning of Canada's National Memorial on Vimy Ridge. *Public Historian*, 31 (1): 89–100.

Huggins, Mike (2007) BBC Radio and Sport, 1922–1939. *Contemporary British History*, 21 (4): 491–315.

Huggins, Mike (2007) Betting, Sport, and the British, 1918–1939. *Journal of Social History*, 41 (2): 283–306.

Huggins, Mike (2008) Sport and the British Upper Classes, c.1500–2000: A Historiographic Overview. *Sport in History*, 28 (3): 364–388.

Hunt, E.H., and Pam, S.J. (2002) Responding to Agricultural Depression, 1873–1896: Managerial Success, Entrepreneurial Failure? *Agricultural History Review*, 50 (2): 225–252.

Hunt, Karen (2010) The Politics of Food and Women's Neighborhood Activism in First World War Britain. *International Labour and Working-Class History*, 77: 8–26.

Hynes, Samuel (1968) *The Edwardian Turn of Mind*. Princeton: Princeton University Press.

Ingram, Rev. George S. (1863) *Bishop Colenso Answered by His Own Concessions and Omissions*. London: William Freeman.

Jackson, Ben (2005) Revisionism Reconsidered: "Property-Owning Democracy" and Egalitarian Strategy in Post-war Britain. *Twentieth-Century British History*, 16 (4): 416–440.

Jarvie, Ian (2006) Contributions to the Social and Economic History of British Cinema. *Historical Journal of Film, Radio and Television*, 28 (1): 111–120.

Jay, Elisabeth (1986) *Faith and Doubt in Victorian Britain*. Atlantic Highlands: Macmillan.

Jeffreys, Kevin (2009) The Triumph of Professionalism in World Tennis. *International Journal of the History of Sport*, 26 (15): 2253–2289.

Jenkins, T. (1996) *Disraeli and Victorian Conservatism*. New York: St Martin's Press.

Jenkins, T. (2005) Lord Salisbury and the Unionist Ascendancy, 1886–1902: Understudied and Undervalued, Does Lord Salisbury Not Deserve Better? *Modern History Review*, 16 (3): 13–18.

Jeremy, Paul (1977) Life on Circular 703: The Crisis of Destitution in the South Wales Coalfield during the Lockout of 1926. *Llafur: The Journal of the Society for the Study of Welsh Labour History*, 2 (2): 65–75.

Johnson, Paul (ed.) (1994) *Twentieth-Century Britain: Economic, Social and Cultural Change*. London: Longman.

Johnson, Paul (1996) Economic Development and Industrial Dynamism in Victorian London. *London Journal*, 21 (1): 27–37.

Johnson, Paul, and Nicholas, Stephen (1992) Male and Female Living Standards in England and Wales, 1812–1857: Evidence from Criminal Height Records, *Economic History Review*, 48 (3): 470–481.

Joll, James, and Martel, Gordon (2006) *The Origins of the First World War*. London: Longman.

Jones, Edgar (2006) The Psychology of Killing: The Combat Experience of British Soldiers during the First World War. *Journal of Contemporary History*, 41 (2): 229–246.

Jones, Kevin E. (2001) BSE, Risk and the Communication of Uncertainty: A Review of Lord Phillips' Report from the BSE Inquiry (UK). *Canadian Journal of Sociology*, 26 (4): 655–665.

Jones, W.T., and Fogelin, Robert J. (1980) *A History of Western Philosophy: The Twentieth Century, to Quine and Derrida*. Fort Worth: Harcourt Brace.

Joshi, Heather, Layard, Richard, and Owen, Susan (1985) Why Are More Women Working in Britain? *Journal of Labor Economics*, 3 (1, part 2): S147–S176.

Joyce, Patrick (1993) *Visions of the People: Industrial England and the Question of Class, c.1848–1914*. Cambridge: Cambridge University Press.

Kazamias, Andreas M. (1966) Spencer and the Welfare State. *History of Education Quarterly*, 6 (2): 73–95.

Kenny, Anthony (2008) *Philosophy in the Modern World*, vol. 4. Oxford: Oxford University Press.

Kern, Stephen (2003) *The Culture of Time and Space*. Cambridge: Harvard University Press.

Kingsley Kent, Susan (1987) *Sex and Suffrage in Britain, 1860–1914*. Princeton: Princeton University Press.

Kirk, Neville (2008) Traditionalists and Progressives: Labor, Race and Immigration in Post–World War II Australia and Britain. *Austrialian Historical Studies*, 39: 53–71.

Korte, Barbara, and Einhaus, Ann-Marie (2004) Short-Term Memories: The First World War in British Short Stories, 1914–1939. *Literature and History*, 18 (1): 54–66.

Kosecik, Muhammet, and Kapucu, Naim (2003) Conservative Reform of Metropolitan Counties: Abolition of the GLC and MCCs in Retrospect. *Contemporary British History*, 17 (3): 71–94.

Kotler-Berkowitz, Laurence A. (2001) Ethnicity and Politics: Cohesion, Division, and British Jews. *Political Studies*, 49: 648–669.

Koven, Seth (2004) *Slumming: Sexual and Social Politics in Victorian London*. Princeton: Princeton University Press.

Kuhn, Annette (2002) Children, "Horrific" Films, and Censorship in 1930s Britain. *Historical Journal of Film, Radio, and Television*, 22 (2): 197–202.

Lammers, Donald (1977) Nevil Shute and the Decline of the "Imperial Idea" in Literature. *Journal of British Studies*, 16 (2): 121–142.

Leach, Steve, and Game, Chris (1991) English Metropolitan Government since Abolition: An Evaluation of the Abolition of the English Metropolitan County Councils. *Public Administration*, 69 (Summer): 141–170.

Lee, Sabine (2006) "In No Sense Vital and Actually Not Even Important"? Reality and Perception of Britain's Contribution to the Development of Nuclear Weapons. *Contemporary British History*, 29 (2): 159–185.

Lees-Maffei, Grace (2007) Accommodating "Mrs. Three-in-One": Homemaking, Home Entertaining, and Domestic Advice Literature in Post-war Britain. *Women's History Review*, 16 (5): 723–754.

Levin, Bernard (1970) *Run It Down the Flagpole: Britain in the Sixties*. New York: Atheneum.

Levine, Philippa (2007) *The British Empire: Sunrise to Sunset*. Harlow: Pearson Longman.

Liddington, Jill, and Norris, Jill (1978) *"One Hand Tied Behind Us": The Rise of the Women's Suffrage Movement*. London: Virago.

Lightman, Bernard (ed.) (1997) *Victorian Science in Context*. Chicago: University of Chicago Press.

Lloyd-Jones, Roger, and Lewis, Myrddin J. (1994) Personal Capitalism and British Industrial Decline: The Personally Managed Firm and Business Strategy in Sheffield, 1880–1920. *Business History Review*, 68 (3): 364–411.

Lowe, Philip (1984) Bad News or Good News: Environmental Politics and the Mass Media. *Sociological Review*, 32 (1): 75–90.

Lubenow, W.C. (1986) Irish Home Rule and the Social Basis of the Great Separation in the Liberal Party in 1886. *Historical Journal*, 28 (1): 125–141.

Ludwig, III, Walter C. (2007) Managing Counterinsurgency: Lessons from Malaya. *Military Review* (May–June): 56–66.

Lunn, Joe (2005) Male Identity and Martial Codes of Honor: A Comparison of the War Memoirs of Robert Graves, Ernst Junger, and Kande Kamara. *Journal of Military History*, 69 (3): 713–735.

Majima, Shinobu (2008) From Haute Couture to High Street: The Role of Shows and Fairs in Twentieth-Century Fashion. *Textile History*, 39 (1): 70–91.

Mandler, Peter (1990) *Aristocratic Government in an Age of Reform: Whigs and Liberals, 1930–1852*. Oxford: Oxford University Press.

Mandler, Peter (2006) *The English National Character: The History of an Idea from Edmund Burke to Tony Blair*. New Haven: Yale University Press.

Manto, Sadaat Hasan (1955) Toba Tek Singh. At http://wordswithoutborders. org/article/toba-tek-singh (accessed Aug. 2011).

Marsh, Steve, and Baylis, John (2006) The Anglo-American "Special Relationship": The Lazarus of International Relations. *Diplomacy and Statecraft*, 17:173–211.

Marshall, S.L.A. (1964) *World War I*. Boston: Houghton Mifflin.

Martin, Ross (1980) *TUC: The Growth of a Pressure Group, 1868–1976*. Oxford: Clarendon Press.

Marwick, Arthur (1991) *Culture in Britain since 1945*. Oxford: Blackwell.

Matthews, Derek (2007) The Performance of British Manufacturing in the Post-war Long Boom. *Business History*, 49 (6): 763–779.

Matthews, Roger (1995) Crime in England and Wales. *Annals of the American Academy*, 539: 169–182.

Mayhew, Henry (2009) *London Labour and the London Poor*, vol. 1. London: Cosimo Press. First published 1861.

McCalman, Janet (1971) The Impact of the First World War on Female Employment in England. *Labour History*, 21: 36–47.

McConnell, Allan (1997) The Recurring Crisis of Local Taxation in Postwar Britain. *Contemporary British History*, 11 (3): 39–62.

McCrillis, Neal R. (2001) "Simply Try for One Hour to Behave Like Gentlemen": British Cinema during the Early Cold War, 1945–1960. *Film and History*, 31 (2): 6–12.

McDermott, James (2010) Conscience and the Military Service Tribunals during the First World War: Experiences in Northamptonshire. *War in History*, 17 (1): 60–85.

McGhee, Derek (2009) The Paths to Citizenship: A Critical Examination of Immigration Police in Britain since 2001. *Patterns of Prejudice*, 43 (1): 41–64.

McKibbin, Ross (2002) Class, Politics, Money: British Sport since the First World War. *Twentieth Century British History*, 13 (2): 191–200.

Mechanics' Magazine (1855) Polluted State of the Thames. Vol. 63 (July 7).

Middleton, Drew (1957) *Macmillan Wins Inflation Debate*. New York Times, July 26, p. 2.

Millward, Robert (1994) British Industry since the Second World War. *History Today*, 44 (6): 49–54.

Morris, R.J. (2005) *Men, Women, and Property in England, 1780–1870*. Cambridge: Cambridge University Press.

Moss, Norman (2003) *19 Weeks*. New York: Houghton Mifflin.

Mowat, Charles Loch (1968) *Britain between the Wars*. Cambridge: Cambridge: University Press.

Mullay, A.J. (2003) Off the Rails: The Scottish General Strike, 1926. *History Scotland* (Nov.–Dec.): 28–36.

Murphy, Derrick (2001) Joseph Chamberlain: Radical and Imperialist. *Modern History Review*, 12 (3): 27–30.

Murphy, Robert (2008) *Sixties British Cinema*. London: British Film Institute.

Murray, Bruce K. (1980) *The People's Budget, 1909–1910: Lloyd George and Liberal Politics*. Oxford: Clarendon Press.

NCJDRSU (2010) Website of the National Creutzfeldt-Jakob Disease Research and Surveillance Unit. At http://www.cjd.ed.ac.uk/ (accessed May 19, 2010).

Neavill, Gordon Barrick (1971) Victor Gollancz and the Left Book Club. *Library Quarterly*, 41 (3): 197–215.

Neff, Terry (ed.) (1987) *A Quiet Revolution: British Sculpture since 1965*. New York: Thames & Hudson.

New York Times (1885) Gordon's Diary. July 12.

Newsome, David (1997) *The Victorian World Picture Perceptions and Introspections in an Age of Change*. New Brunswick: Rutgers University Press.

Nicholas, Sian (1995) "Sly Demagogues" and Wartime Radio: J.B. Priestley and the BBC. *Twentieth Century British History*, 6 (3): 247–266.

Nissimi, Hilda (2001) Illusions of World Power in Kenya: Strategy, Decolonization and the British Base, 1946–1961. *International History Review*, 23 (4): 824–846.

Norgate, Paul (1989) Wilfred Owen and the Soldier Poets. *Review of English Studies*, 40 (160): 516–530.

Norris, Jacob (2008) Repression and Rebellion: Britain's Response to the Arab Revolt in Palestine of 1936–1939. *Journal of Imperial and Commonwealth History*, 36 (1): 25–45.

O'Hara, Glen (2004) " We are Faced Everywhere with a Growing Population": Demographic Change and the British State, 1955–64. *Twentieth-Century British History*, 15 (2): 243–266.

O'Hara, Glen (2006) " Dynamic, Exciting, Thrilling Change": The Wilson Government's Economic Policies, 1964–1970. *Contemporary British History*, 20 (3): 383–402.

Packenham, Thomas (1992) *The Scramble for Africa: White Man's Conquest of the Dark Continent from 1876 to 1912*. New York: Avon.

Page, Malcolm (1973) Experimental Theatre in London: A Guide to the "Off-West-End." *Kansas Quarterly*, 3 (2): 118–128.

Panitch, Leo (1977) Profits and Politics: Labour and the Crisis of British Capitalism. *Politics and Society*, 7 (4): 477–507.

Parr, Helen (2006) Britain, America, East of Suez, and the EEC: Finding a Role in British Foreign Policy, 1964–67. *Contemporary British History*, 20 (3): 403–421.

Parry, Jonathan (1993) *The Rise and Fall of Liberal Government in Victorian Britain*. New Haven: Yale University Press.

Parsons, Gerald (ed.) (1988) *Religion in Victorian Britain, vol. 1: Traditions*. New York: St Martin's Press.

Payne, Anthony (2006) Blair, Brown and the Gleneagles Agenda: Making Poverty History, or Confronting the Global Politics of Unequal Development? International Affairs, 82 (5): 917–935.

Pedersen, Susan (1990) Gender, Welfare, and Citizenship in Britain during the Great War. *American Historical Review*, 95 (4): 983–1006.

Pennell, Catriona (2009) British Society and the First World War. *War in History*, 16 (4): 506–518.

Perri 6, Fletcher-Morgan, Charlotte, and Leyland, Kate (2010) Making People More Responsible: The Blair Government's Program for Changing Citizens' Behavior. *Political Studies*, 58: 427–449.

Perry, P.J. (1972) Where Was the "Great Agricultural Depression"? A Geography of Agricultural Bankruptcy in Late Victorian England and Wales. *Agricultural History Review*, 20 (1): 30–45.

Phillips, Jim (2006) The 1972 Miners' Strike: Popular Agency and Industrial Politics in Britain. *Contemporary British History*, 20 (2): 187–207.

Pimlott, Ben, and Rao, Nirmala (2004) Metropolitan Miasma: Blurred Accountabilities in the Governance of London. *London Journal*, 29 (2): 33–45.

Plowden, Alison (1974) *The Case of Eliza Armstrong: A Child of 13 Bought for £5*. Extract at http://www.attackingthedevil.co.uk/pmg/tribute/armstrong/bailey/sentence.php (accessed Aug. 2011).

Porter, Andrew (ed.) (1999) *The Oxford History of the British Empire, vol. 3: The Nineteenth Century*. Oxford: Oxford University Press.

Porter, Bernard (2004) *The Lion's Share: A Short History of British Imperialism, 1850–2004*. Harlow: Pearson Longman.

Porter, Roy (1990) *English Society in the Eighteenth Century*. London: Penguin.

Price, Richard (1999) *British Society, 1680–1880: Dynamism, Containment and Change*. Cambridge: Cambridge University Press.

Priestley, J.B. (1951) The Renewed Dream of a Merrie England. *New York Times*, July 15.

Pugh, Martin (1999) *State and Society: A Social and Political History of Britain*. London: Oxford University Press.

Pugh, Martin (2006) The General Strike. *History Today*, 56 (5): 40–47.

Quinn, Thomas (2006) Choosing the Least-Worst Government: The British General Election of 2005. *West European Politics*, 29 (1): 169–78.

Rappaport, Erika (2001) *Shopping for Pleasure: Women in the Making of London's West End*. Princeton: Princeton University Press.

Reay, Barry (1996) *Microhistories: Demography, Society and Culture in Rural England, 1800–1930*. Cambridge: Cambridge University Press.

Reitan, E.A. (2003) *The Thatcher Revolution: Margaret Thatcher, John Major, Tony Blair, and the Transformation of Modern Britain, 1979–2001*. Lanham: Rowman & Littlefield.

Rhodes, Martin (2000) Desperately Seeking a Solution: Social Democracy, Thatcherism and the "Third Way" in British Welfare. *West European Politics,* 23 (2): 161–186.

Ridgwell, Stephen (1996) The People's Amusement: Cinema and Cinema-Going in 1930s Britain. Historian, 52: 17–21.

Robbins, Keith (1983) *The Eclipse of a Great Power: Modern Britain, 1870–1975.* London: Longman.

Roberts, Brian (1995) A Mining Town in Wartime: The Fears for the Future. *Llafur,* 6 (1): 82–95.

Rose, Sonya (1992) *Limited Livelihoods: Gender and Class in Nineteenth-Century England.* Berkeley: University of California Press.

Rose, Sonya O. (1998) Sex, Citizenship and the Nation in World War II Britain. *American Historical Review,* 13 (4): 1147–1176.

Rosenbaum, S.P. (1981) Preface to a Literary History of the Bloomsbury Group. *New Literary History,* 12 (2): 329–344.

Royle, Edward (1974) *Victorian Infidels: The Origins of the British Secularist Movement, 1791–1866.* Manchester: University of Manchester Press.

Rubinstein, William D. (2003) *Twentieth-Century Britain: A Political History.* New York: Palgrave Macmillan.

Rudin, Richard (2007) Revisiting the Pirates. *Media History,* 13 (2–3): 235–255.

Rule, John (2001) Time, Affluence and Private Leisure: The British Working Class in the 1950s and 1960s. *Labour History Review,* 66 (2): 223–242.

Rush, Anne (2007) Reshaping British History: The Historiography of West Indians in Britain in the Twentieth Century. *History Compass,* 5 (2): 463–484.

Rycroft, Simon (2002) The Geographies of Swinging London. *Journal of Historical Geography,* 28 (4): 566–588.

Saler, Michael (1998) Making It New: Visual Modernism and the "Myth of the North" in Interwar England. *Journal of British Studies,* 37 (8): 419–440.

Samantrai, Ranu (2002) *AlterNatives: Black Feminism in the Post-Imperial Nation.* Stanford: Stanford University Press.

SarDesai, S.R. (2008) *India: The Definitive History.* Boulder: Westview.

Schwarz, Leonard (2004) Professions, Elites and Universities in England, 1870–1970. *Historical Journal,* 47 (4): 941–962.

Scott, Peter (2000) Women, Other "Fresh" Workers, and the New Manufacturing Workforce of Interwar Britain. *International Review of Social History,* 45: 449–474.

Scott, Peter (2007) Consumption, Consumer Credit and the Diffusion of Consumer Durables. In Francesca Carnevali and Julie-Marie Strange (eds), *Twentieth-Century Britain: Economic, Cultural and Social Change.* Harlow: Pearson Longman.

Seaman, Owen (1914) Pro Patria. In *Songs and Sonnets for England in Wartime.* London: John Lane.

Shafer, Stephen (2001) An Overview of the Working Classes in British Feature Film from the 1960s to the 1980s: From Class Consciousness to Marginalization. *International Labor and Working-Class History,* no. 59 (Spring): 3–14.

Sharp, Paul (1991) Thatcher's Wholly British Foreign Policy. *Orbis,* 35 (3): 395–410.

Shaw, Jane (2009) Anglican History in the 21st Century: Remembering All the Baptized. *Anglican and Episcopal History,* 78 (4): 353–363.

Sheail, John (1998) "Never Again": Pollution and the Management of Watercourses in Postwar Britain. *Journal of Contemporary History,* 33 (1): 117–133.

Sheridan, Dorothy (1984) Mass Observing the British. *History Today,* 34 (4): 42–46.

Silverstone, Rosalie (1976) Office Work for Women: A Historical Review. *Business History,* 18: 98–110.

Smith, Ian (1997) Explaining the Growth of Divorce in Great Britain. *Scottish Journal of Political Economy,* 4 (5): 519–544.

Spencer, Stephanie (2000) Women's Dilemmas in Postwar Britain: Career Stories for Adolescent Girls in the 1950s. *History of Education,* 29 (4): 329–342.

Sretzer, Simon, and Mooney, Graham (1998) Urbanization, Mortality and the Standard-of-Living Debate: New Estimates of the Expectation of Life at Birth in Nineteenth-Century British Cities. *Economic History Review,* 51: 84–112.

Stansky, Peter (1997) *On or About December 1910: Early Bloomsbury and its Intimate World.* Cambridge: Harvard University Press.

Stansky, Peter (2007) *The First Day of the Blitz: September 7, 1940.* New Haven: Yale University Press.

Stansky, Peter, and Abrahams, William (1994) *London's Burning: Life, Death and Art in the Second World War.* London: Constable.

Stead, W.T. (1885) The Maiden Tribute of Modern Babylon. *Pall Mall Gazette,* July 6. At http://www.attackingthedevil.co.uk/pmg/tribute/mt1.php (accessed Aug. 2011).

Stedman Jones, Gareth (1983) *Languages of Class: Studies in English Working-Class History, 1832–1982.* New York: Cambridge University Press.

Stelzer, Irwin (1992) What Thatcher Wrought. *Public Interest,* no. 102 (Spring): 18–51.

Stelzer, Irwin (1996) Christian Socialism in Britain. *Public Interest,* 124: 3–11.

Stone, Dan (2001) Race in British Eugenics. *European History Quarterly,* 31 (3): 397–425.

Storr, Robert (1988) In the Flesh: Lucien Freud. *Art in America,* 76 (5): 128–137.

Strachey, Lytton (1918) *Eminent Victorians.* New York: Putnam's. At http://www.bartleby.com/br/189.html (accessed Dec. 15, 2008).

Suga, Yasuko (2006) Modernism, Commercialism, and Display Design in Britain. *Journal of Design History,* 19 (2): 137–153.

Summers, Judith (1989) *Soho: A History of London's Most Colourful Neighborhood.* London: Bloomsbury. Extract at http://www.ph.ucla.edu/epi/snow/broadstreetpump.html (accessed June 29, 2011).

Tabili, Laura (1994) *We Ask for British Justice: Workers and Racial Difference in Late Imperial Britain.* New York: Cornell University Press.

Tadis, Alexis (2010) The Fictions of (English) Cricket: From Nation to Diaspora. *International Journal of the History of Sport,* 27 (4): 690–711.

Telegraph (2007) Enoch Powell's "Rivers of Blood" Speech. Nov. 6. At http://www.telegraph.co.uk/comment/3643823/Enoch-Powells-Rivers-of-Blood-speech.html (accessed Sept. 2010).

Thane, P.M. (1990) The "Menace" of an Aging Population. *Continuity and Change,* 5 (2): 283–305.

Thirsk, Joan (ed.) (2000) *Cambridge Agricultural History of England,* vol. 7. Cambridge: Cambridge University Press.

Thompson, Andrew (2005) *The Empire Strikes Back? The Impact of Imperialism on Britain from the Mid-Nineteenth Century.* New York: Longman.

Thompson, Dorothy (1984) *The Chartists: Popular Politics in the Industrial Revolution.* New York: Pantheon.

Thompson, Edward (1963) *The Making of the English Working Class.* New York: Vintage.

Thompson, F.M.L. (1988) *The Rise of Respectable Society: A Social History of Victorian Britain.* Cambridge: Harvard University Press.

Thompson, F.M.L. (ed.) (1990) *The Cambridge Social History of Britain.* Cambridge: Cambridge University Press.

Thorsheim, Peter (2006) *Inventing Pollution: Coal, Smoke and Culture in Britain since 1800.* Athens: Ohio University Press.

Tignor, Robert L. (1993) Race, Nationality and Industrialization in Decolonizing Kenya, 1945–1963. *International Journal of African Historical Studies,* 26 (1): 31–64.

Todd, Selina (2006) Flappers and Factory Lads: Youth and Youth Culture in Interwar Britain. *History Compass,* 46: 715–730.

Tomaney, John (2000) End of the Empire State? New Labour and Devolution in the United Kingdom. *International Journal of Urban and Regional Research,* 24 (3): 675–688.

Tomlinson, Jim (2000) Marshall Aid and the "Shortage Economy" in Britain in the 1940s. *Contemporary European History,* 9 (1): 137–155.

Tomlinson, Jim (2008) A Failed Experiment? Public Ownership and the Narratives of Postwar Britain. *Labour History Review,* 73 (2): 228–243.

Toynbee, Arnold (1961) *The Industrial Revolution.* Boston: Beacon Press. First published as *Lectures on the Industrial Revolution in England,* 1884.

Trentmann, Frank (1994) Civilization and Its Discontents: English Neo-Romanticism and the Transformation of Antimodernism in Twentieth-Century Western Culture. *Journal of Contemporary History,* 29 (4): 583–625.

Urban, Ken (2004) Towards a Theory of Cruel Britannica: Coolness, Cruelty, and the "Nineties." *New Theatre Quarterly,* 20 (4): 354–372.

Vall, Natasha (2010) Bringing Art to "the Man in the Back Street": Regional and Historical Perspectives of Labour and the Evolution of Cultural Policy in Europe, 1945–1975. *Labour History Review,* 75 (1): 30–43.

Vickers, Rhiannon (2000) Blair's Kosovo Campaign, Political Communications, the Battle for Public Opinion and Foreign Policy. *Civil Wars,* 3 (1): 55–70.

Vogel, David (1983) Cooperative Regulation: Environmental Protection in Great Britain. *Public Interest* (Summer): 88–106.

Wahrman, Dror (1995) *Imagining the Middle Class: The Political Representation of Class in Britain, c.1780–1840.* Cambridge: Cambridge University Press.

Walkowitz, Judith (1992) *City of Dreadful Delight: Narratives of Sexual Danger in Late-Victorian London.* Chicago: University of Chicago Press.

Wallace, Alfred Russel (1890) Human Selection. *Fortnightly Review,* n.s., 48 (Sept.): 325–336. At http://digitalcommons.wku.edu/dlps_fac_arw/5/ (accessed Mar. 14, 2011).

Waters, Chris (1999) Representations of Everyday Life: L.S. Lowry and the Landscape of Memory in Postwar Britain. *Representations,* no. 65: 121–150.

Watson, Janet (2007) *Fighting Different Wars: Experience, Memory, and the First World War in Britain.* Cambridge: Cambridge University Press.

Watts, Duncan (1993) Juggler Joe: Radical and Unionist. *Modern History Review,* 5 (1): 20–23.

Whannel, Gary (2009) Television and the Transformation of Sport. *Annals of the American Academy of Political and Social Science,* 625: 205–216.

Whitehead, J.W.R., and Carr, Christine M.H. (1999) England's Interwar Suburban Landscapes: Myth and Reality. *Journal of Historical Geography*, 25 (4): 483–501.

Whiteley, Paul, Seyd, Patrick, Richardson, Jeremy, and Bissell, Paul (1994) Thatcherism and the Conservative Party. *Political Studies*, 42: 185–203.

Wickham-Jones, Mark (1991) What Went Wrong? The Fall of Mrs. Thatcher. *Contemporary Record*, 5 (2): 321–340.

Wiener, Martin (1981) *English Culture and the Decline of the Industrial Spirit 1850–1980*. Cambridge: Cambridge University Press.

Wiener, Martin J. (1990) *Reconstructing the Criminal: Culture, Law, and Policy in England, 1830–1914*. Cambridge: Cambridge University Press.

Williams, Glyn, and Ramsden, John (1990) *Ruling Britannia: A Political History of Britain, 1688–1988*. London: Longman.

Williams, Jack (2006) " The *Really* Good Professional Captain has *Never Been Seen!*" Perceptions of the Amateur/Professional Divide in County Cricket, 1900–1939. *Sport in History*, 26 (3): 429–449.

Williamson, Jeffrey G. (1981) Urban Disamenities, Dark Satanic Mills, and the British Standard of Living Debate. *Journal of Economic History*, 41 (1): 75–83.

Winkler, Jonathan (2009) Information Warfare in World War I. *Journal of Military History*, 73 (3): 845–867.

Winter, Alison (1997) The Construction of Orthodoxies and Heterodoxies in the Early Victorian Life Sciences. In Bernard Lightman (ed.), *Victorian Science in Context*. Chicago: University of Chicago Press.

Winter, Jay (2002) Migration, War and Empire: The British Case. *Annales de Démographie Historique*, 1: 143–160.

Winterton, Jonathan (1993) The 1984–85 Miners' Strike and Technological Change. *British Journal for the History of Science*, 26 (1): 5–14.

Wood, Andy " Original London Style": London Posse and the Birth of British Hip Hop. *Atlantic Studies*, 6 (2): 179–190.

Young, Ken (2001) Local Government, 1920–1986: Ideal and Reality. *London Journal*, 26 (1): 57–65.

Index

Note: page references in *italics* indicate illustrations.

Empire, State, and Society: Britain Since 1830, First Edition. Jamie L. Bronstein and Andrew T. Harris.
© 2012 Jamie L. Bronstein and Andrew T. Harris. Published 2012 by John Wiley & Sons, Ltd.